TRUTH AND TRANSITIONAL JUSTICE

With a unique perspective on the encounter between transitional justice and Islamic law, this book analyses the relocation of transitional justice truth seeking from the international paradigm to the legal systems of Muslim-majority settings.

The Arab uprisings and new and old conflicts in the Middle East, North Africa and other contexts where Islam is a prominent religion have sparked an interest in localising transitional justice in the legal systems of Muslim-majority societies. Taking into consideration the inherently pluralistic socio-legal realities of these communities, this project explores the synergies and tensions between international law and Islamic law in furthering the truth-seeking component of transitional justice. As such, it responds to the pressing need to understand how the norms and discourse of shari'ah can inspire and support initiatives to uncover truth about past (and ongoing) abuse in order to ensure accountability for widespread human rights violations perpetrated during conflict and authoritarianism.

This book will be a useful reference for scholars, practitioners and policymakers wanting to better understand the normative underpinnings of (potential) transitional truth-seeking initiatives in the legal systems of Muslim-majority societies. At the same time, it proposes a more critical and creative way of thinking about the challenges and opportunities of localising transitional justice in contexts where Islamic law principles and ideas carry different meanings.

Volume 86 in the series Studies in International Law

Studies in International Law
Recent titles in this series

Intertemporal Linguistics in International Law: Beyond Contemporaneous and Evolutionary Treaty Interpretation
Julian Wyatt

The Responsibility to Protect and the Failures of the United Nations Security Council
P M Butchard

The Role of Multilateral Environmental Agreements: A Reconciliatory Approach to Environmental Protection in Armed Conflict
Britta Sjostedt

Prosecutorial Discretion at the International Criminal Court
Anni Pues

Judicial Deference in International Adjudication: A Comparative Analysis
Johannes Hendrik Fahner

Human Rights Commitments of Islamic States: Sharia, Treaties and Consensus
Paul McDonough

Intervention in Civil Wars: Effectiveness, Legitimacy, and Human Rights
Chiara Redaelli

General Principles as a Source of International Law: Art 38(1)(c) of the Statute of the International Court of Justice
Imogen Saunders

The Law of Humanity Project: A Story of International Law Reform and State-making
Ukri Soirila

Extraterritoriality and Climate Change Jurisdiction: Exploring EU Climate Protection under International Law
Natalie L Dobson

International Law and the War with Islamic State: Challenges for Jus ad Bellum and Jus in Bello
Saeed Bagheri

Private Actors as Participants in International Law: A Critical Analysis of Membership under the Law of the Sea
Armando Rocha

Truth and Transitional Justice: Localising the International Legal Framework in Muslim Majority Legal Systems
Alice Panepinto

For a complete list of titles in this series, see
www.bloomsburyprofessional.com/uk/series/studies-in-international-law

Truth and Transitional Justice

Localising the International Legal Framework in Muslim Majority Legal Systems

Alice Panepinto

•HART•
OXFORD • LONDON • NEW YORK • NEW DELHI • SYDNEY

HART PUBLISHING

Bloomsbury Publishing Plc

Kemp House, Chawley Park, Cumnor Hill, Oxford, OX2 9PH, UK

1385 Broadway, New York, NY 10018, USA

29 Earlsfort Terrace, Dublin 2, Ireland

First published in Great Britain 2022

A catalogue record for this book is available from the British Library.

A catalogue record for this book is available from the Library of Congress.

ISBN: HB: 978-1-50992-126-3
ePDF: 978-1-50992-128-7
ePub: 978-1-50992-127-0

Typeset by Compuscript Ltd, Shannon
Printed and bound in Great Britain

To Olympia

Acknowledgements

ACKNOWLEDGING THE MANY people who enabled me to complete this book would require its own volume. This project develops my doctoral thesis completed at Durham University: as it took me longer to write the book than it did to finish my PhD, I benefitted from the academic influence, mentoring and friendship of many fine scholars in other institutions too, including at Warwick University and at Queen's University Belfast. I am especially indebted to Aoife O'Donoghue, James Sweeney and Michael Bohlander for supervising my PhD, and examiners Javaid Rehman and Johnny Doak for engaging thoroughly with it. I am grateful to Ustinov College for providing me with a generous scholarship, and Theresa McKinven's support. The questions addressed in the book were inspired by my studies at SOAS; their evolution was informed by working outside academia in the Middle East. Special thanks to the numerous colleagues who reviewed work in progress: firstly, Kevin Hearty for reading the full draft and Shaheen Sardar Ali for offering feedback on the draft book proposal; Brendan C Browne, Alessandro Corda, Ciara Hackett, Amanda Kramer, Louise Mallinder, Anne-Marie McAlinden in Belfast, and many more for reviewing sections along the way; and Nicola Pratt for providing her expert view on the research ethics component. The fresh research would not have been possible without the assistance of Dr Hadi, Rawan, Judge Adel Maged, Etaf and others, and, most importantly, the distinguished scholars of Islamic law that gave up their time to respond to my questionnaire. Eduardo Monteiro Burkle's exemplary research assistance ensured the manuscript was eventually submitted. All errors and omissions naturally remain my own.

Friends in academia, human rights circles and other walks of life have been a constant source of strength and laughter along the way, despite being scattered all over the world: all my colleague-friends in Belfast and Jerusalem, as well as Kai, Enrica, Beatrice, Ntina, Rumy, Jane, Emma, Chiara, Raffy, Almedina, Anna, Beth, and many more.

Asking questions about how different world views meet has been a feature of my entire life, as the child of two cultures, whose primary representatives (my parents) all too often disagreed. My family has enabled my academic journey, in particular my mother Kate, the archetypal 'reviewer 2' who still enjoys reading my work with a red pen. My aunt Tess and sister Lydia complete my trinity. My father Pino taught me to read the room and stand up for myself: a valuable skill in academia. Now, with Cesare and Olympia, life is about little things that give big ideas more meaning and make me see the world in Technicolor.

Table of Contents

Introduction

RECENT POLITICAL TURMOIL as well as historic and ongoing conflicts and authoritarianism across the Arab region and elsewhere in Muslim-majority contexts have ushered in the language, concepts and tools of transitional justice (TJ), truth seeking and accountability for mass violence.[1] The TJ literature straddling law and sister disciplines offers rich insights and critiques on how these ideas and practices have travelled and might adapt to the Middle East and North Africa (MENA) and other Muslim-majority settings.[2] This book adds to that growing body of work to reflect more pointedly on the role, possibilities and limitations of Islamic law in supporting the truth-seeking element of TJ as framed in international law. Taken as a whole, the project explores possible answers to two interlinked questions: (1) How can the truth-seeking element of the international legal framework for TJ be embedded in Muslim-majority societies? (2) To what extent does Islamic law and jurisprudence support the notion of the right to truth about past violence, as emerging in international law?

To be clear from the outset on what I intend by 'Muslim-majority societies' or 'settings' or 'contexts' (used interchangeably in this book): I am referring to contexts where the faith, identity or heritage of the majority of individuals making up the collective is Islam (Sunni or Shia) or informed significantly by Islam either directly or indirectly. This denotation is not synonymous with 'Muslim' states specifically, or member states of the Organisation of Islamic

[1] On the convergence and tensions of combining research on postconflict and TJ, see inter alia K Fisher 'Defining a Relationship between Transitional Justice and Jus Post Bellum: A Call and an Opportunity for Post-conflict Justice' (2020) 16(3) *Journal of International Political Theory* 287.

[2] See, for instance, MC Bassiouni, *Shari'a and Islamic Criminal Justice in Time of War and Peace* (Cambridge, Cambridge University Press, 2014); KJ Fisher and R Stewart (eds), *Transitional justice and the Arab Spring* (Abingdon, Routledge, 2015); CL Sriram (ed), *Transitional Justice in the Middle East and North Africa* (Oxford, Oxford University Press, 2016); N Aboueldahab, *Transitional Justice and the Prosecution of Political Leaders in the Arab Region: A Comparative Study of Egypt, Libya, Tunisia and Yemen* (Oxford and Portland, OR, Hart/Bloomsbury, 2017); N Sultany, *Law and Revolution: Legitimacy and Constitutionalism after the Arab Spring* (Oxford, Oxford University Press, 2017); C Zoli, MC Bassiouni and H Khan, 'Justice in Post-conflict Settings: Islamic Law and Muslim Communities as Stakeholders in Transition' (2017) 33(85) *Utrecht Journal of International and European Law* 38; HO Yusuf, 'Transitional Justice in the Middle East and North Africa – Taking Account of Islam' (2017) 14(1) *Muslim World Journal of Human Rights* 145; and in relation to specific states, eg R Abou-El-Fadl, 'Beyond Conventional Transitional Justice: Egypt's 2011 Revolution and the Absence of Political Will' (2012) 6(2) *International Journal of Transitional Justice* 318; and others.

Cooperation (OIC).[3] The discussion in this book includes secular states with a majority Muslim population, eg Turkey; Muslim-majority non-state armed groups, eg *daesh* (I use the Arabic intentionally[4]); larger Muslim-majority communities as part of a diverse population, eg Nigeria or Albania; and smaller Muslim-majority communities as part of a diverse population, eg in the United Kingdom or the United States. For the purposes of this book, no 'Muslim-majority society' is or can be imagined as ideally 'Muslim', regardless of the views (and stereotypes) of Muslim-identifying people and communities or non-Muslim-identifying people and communities.

Fatima Mernissi's analysis of 'two distinct dimensions' of the Muslim world offers a helpful conceptual starting point to make sense of the complex, and sometimes contradictory, invocation of religious identity and tradition: on the one hand, 'what people actually do, the decisions they make, the aspirations they secretly entertain or display', and on the other hand, 'the discourses they develop about themselves' used 'to articulate their political claims'.[5] The invocation of tradition, falling within the second dimension described by Mernissi, can be understood 'as a psychological need to maintain a minimal sense of identity in a confusing and shifting reality'.[6] As such, whenever Islamic law and the *shari'ah* are invoked, observers should be mindful of the layered and intertwined normative, social, political, psychological (and more) functions these utterances, which, *pace* the black-letter lawyers among us, cannot be taken out of context or at face value.

There is no 'common model of an essential Muslim society': the variety of social and political forms can be understood 'only in terms of the normal practice of social and political analysis, like any other range of societies', as Sami Zubaida (and many others) state quite factually.[7] It goes without saying that like all social groups, 'Muslim-majority societies' are complex communities, where the presence of Islam operates alongside the rest of the rich human experience of gender, race, dis/ability, orientation, class, political affiliation, economic situation, internal powers and colonial legacies, and more.[8] The ways in which these

[3] OIC membership is often adopted as a benchmark to identify communities where Islamic law is relevant, see eg P McDonough, *Human Rights Commitments of Islamic States* (Oxford, Hart, 2020).

[4] For a brief explanation: FG Marei, 'Islamic State (Daesh)' in JK Zartman (ed), *Conflict in the Modern Middle East: An Encyclopaedia of Civil War, Revolutions and Regime Change* (Santa Barbara, ABC-CLIO, 2020).

[5] F Mernissi, *Beyond the Veil: Male–Female Dynamics in Modern Muslim Society* (Bloomington, Indiana University Press, 1987) viii.

[6] ibid.

[7] S Zubaida, 'Is There a Muslim Society? Ernest Gellner's Sociology of Islam' (1995) 24(2) *International Journal of Human Resource Management* 151.

[8] The literature in this area is vast; as a sample, the growing scholarship on 'sexual and gender diversity' eg V Hamzić, *Sexual and Gender Diversity in the Muslim World: History, Law and Vernacular Knowledge* (London, IB Tauris, 2016), and M Rahman, 'Queer as Intersectionality: Theorizing Gay Muslim Identities' (2010) 44(5) *Sociology* 944.

are studied matter.[9] It must be made absolutely clear that no 'Muslim-majority society' is like another, and there is a richness and variety of the lived experiences (and views of) of Islam as a faith and culture (and *shari'ah* as a normative system of beliefs) at individual and collective level, and I urge readers to bear this in mind throughout the book. As such, I use the phrase 'Muslim-majority society' as a placeholder concept in this book, and readers should be wary of reading too much into it and mindful that it can become deeply problematic if essentialised or rarefied.[10] In adopting this phrase, however, this project runs into a paradox of its own making: the risk, of course, is that it falls unwittingly into the same trap that it seeks to avoid.

Just as the notion of *shari'ah* operates contextually within the social structures and power dynamics expected of any given society, the concept of TJ and its normative underpinnings cannot be understood in the abstract. In academic writing, the term 'transitional justice' is invoked in two main ways: as an umbrella term for the 'full range of processes and mechanisms' that make up TJ, but also to describe the more theoretical 'modified notion of justice inherent in these policies'.[11] The latter understanding lends itself to a more theoretically situated analysis, focusing on the distinctiveness of TJ as a concept rather than on its mechanisms.[12] The former, instead, essentially uses the language and refers to the initiatives now identified and advocated by the UN, as a main promoter of TJ.[13] Through the UN's work a particular understanding of TJ tools and practices has consolidated as the international standard of the field, grounded in international law,[14] human rights[15] and international criminal law.[16] This has acquired normative value and cemented the primacy of international law – despite the fact that upon closer scrutiny, there is no clear, coherent and discrete

[9] S Siddiqui, 'Good Scholarship/Bad Scholarship: Consequences of the Heuristic of Intersectional Islamic Studies' (2020) 88(1) *Journal of the American Academy of Religion* 142.

[10] For the fundamental admonishments, see the classic E Said, *Orientalism* (New York, Pantheon Books, 1978).

[11] Summarised in JA Sweeney, *The European Court of Human Rights in the Post-Cold War Era: Universality in Transition* (Abingdon, Routledge, 2013) 22. For an example of TJ as an umbrella term, L Oette, 'Law Reform in Times of Peace Processes and Transitional Justice: The Sudanese Dimension' in L Oette (ed), *Criminal Law Reform and Transitional Justice: Human Rights Perspectives for Sudan* (Farnham, Ashgate, 2013) 18.

[12] RG Teitel, *Transitional Justice* (New York, Oxford University Press, 2000).

[13] L Grover, 'Transitional Justice, International Law and the United Nations' (2019) 88 *Nordic Journal of International Law* 359. See in particular UN, *The Rule of Law and Transitional Justice in Conflict and Post-conflict Societies: Report of the Secretary-General* S/2004/616 (23 August 2004), and UN, *Guidance Note of the Secretary General: UN Approach to Transitional Justice* (March 2010).

[14] Grover (n 13).

[15] P Arthur, 'How Transitions Reshaped Human Rights: A Conceptual History of Transitional Justice' (2009) 31 *Human Rights Quarterly* 321.

[16] LE Fletcher, 'International Criminal Law and the Subordination of Emancipation: The Question of Legal Hierarchy in Transitional Justice' in KJ Heller et al (eds), *The Oxford Handbook of International Criminal Law* (Oxford, Oxford University Press, 2020).

international normative framework of TJ.[17] In fact, the normative framework of TJ appears to be a composite, fluid medley of international, regional and domestic law, coexisting with a range of local norms, which include unofficial, cultural and religious elements understood in social and political contexts – and a modicum of romanticisation around each of those sources.[18] Christine Bell convincingly describes the international normative framework supporting TJ as a 'mess' – a position adopted throughout this book.[19]

Within this normative context the notion of transitional truth seeking, shaping collective memories and acknowledging competing narratives about past harm feature as central components of TJ premised (primarily) on human rights.[20] Knowing the truth about events and responsibilities related to gross human rights violations and details of the abuse itself is 'seen as an important precondition for transitional justice goals'.[21] It carries an individualised purpose for victims, survivors and their immediate loved ones, as well as for society at large.[22] But the enthusiasm and value placed on truth seeking in times of transition has been questioned, given that 'the truth neither is nor does all that we expect of it' and is not 'monolithic, objective or verifiable as we would like it to be'.[23] Given the truth's 'inevitably political and contested character' it should be 'approached and pursued as a dynamic, long-term process, embracing – rather than resisting – its limitations and tensions'.[24] At times truth seeking is knowingly avoided or deferred.[25] And despite its ambiguities and

[17] See generally L McGregor, 'International Law as a Tiered Process? Transitional Justice at the Local, National and International Level' in K McEvoy and L McGregor (eds), *Transitional Justice from Below: Grassroots Activism and the Struggle for Change. Human Rights Law in Perspective* (Oxford, Hart, 2008).

[18] See eg P McAuliffe, 'Romanticization versus Integration: Indigenous Justice in Rule of Law Reconstruction and Transitional Justice Discourse' (2013) 5 *Goettingen Journal of International Law* 41; and A Kochanski, 'The "Local Turn" in Transitional Justice: Curb the Enthusiasm' (2020) 22(1) *International Studies Review* 2.

[19] C Bell, 'The "New Law" of Transitional Justice' in K Ambos et al (eds), *Building a Future on Peace and Justice: Studies on Transitional Justice, Peace and Development* (Berlin, Springer-Verlag, 2009).

[20] Teitel (n 12) 88 ff.

[21] M Klinkner and H Davis, *The Right to the Truth in International Law: Victims' Rights in Human Rights and International Criminal Law* (Abingdon, Routledge, 2020) 13.

[22] See eg J Doak, 'The Therapeutic Dimension of Transitional Justice: Emotional Repair and Victim Satisfaction in International Trials and Truth Commissions' (2011) 11(2) *International Criminal Law Review* 263; and O Bakiner, 'Truth Commission Impact: An Assessment of How Commissions Influence Politics and Society' (2014) 8(1) *International Journal of Transitional Justice* 6.

[23] E Daly, 'Truth Skepticism: An Inquiry into the Value of Truth in Times of Transition' (2008) 2 *International Journal of Transitional Justice* 23, 23. See also D Mendeloff, 'Truth-seeking, Truth-telling, and Postconflict Peacebuilding: Curb the Enthusiasm?' (2004) 6 *International Studies Review* 355 outlining critiques.

[24] G Girelli, *Understanding Transitional Justice: A Struggle for Peace, Reconciliation, and Rebuilding* (London, Palgrave Macmillan, 2017) 43–44.

[25] See I Kovras, *Truth Recovery and Transitional Justice: Deferring Human Rights Issues* (London, Routledge, 2014).

uncertainty around its normative status, truth seeking remains a core feature of TJ. The question that guides part of this project is whether, and to what extent, truth seeking is supported by a wider range of legal sources, and in particular Islamic law.

Building on these considerations, this book addresses some fundamental questions about how the truth-seeking element of the international legal framework of TJ can be localised in Muslim-majority societies, and to what extent Islamic law and jurisprudence can support the notion of the right to truth about past violence, as emerging in international law. The findings problematise the starting questions further: what aspects of the two legal spheres discussed can and should be compared, and why, and who decides? How does the invocation of religion conceal other power struggles? And what do the differences as to the role and uses of Islamic law ideas within Muslim-majority contexts reveal as part of the process? This research project does not seek definitive, clear-cut answers for scholars, or a simple set of ready-made recommendations for policymakers and civil society groups participating in transitional truth seeking initiatives in Muslim-majority societies. Instead, this book more modestly asks the questions, joins some dots and tries to sketch a more comprehensive and problematised picture of the complexity of this endeavour, paving the way for other more detailed studies of country-specific scenarios as well as more in-depth doctrinal analysis in law and related disciplines.

The findings of this project indicate that despite different manifestations and justifications that underpin the truth-seeking aims and the right to truth as emerging in the international legal framework, on the one hand, and the traditions and practices of Islamic law, on the other, there is broad convergence in the substantive aims. That tentative meeting requires further study both doctrinally and practically to understand better how the international legal framework guiding transitional truth seeking and *shari'ah* may jointly galvanise the efforts of victims and societies to find out the truth about past abuse, hold perpetrators to account and shape collective memories about legacies of violence. This project offers a stepping stone in that direction, motivated by the emerging norm in international human rights law that victims and societies everywhere deserve to know the truth about harm suffered individually and collectively if they so wish, even when the state itself is implicated or complacent.

The book builds on the TJ literature concerned with the influence of cultural, social and political contexts (including the ambiguous role of international actors)[26] to explore the meeting between local conceptions and expressions of

[26] eg R Shaw and L Waldorf (eds), *Localizing Transitional Justice: Interventions and Priorities After Mass Violence* (Stanford, CA, Stanford University Press, 2010); L Viaene and E Brems, 'Transitional Justice and Cultural Contexts: Learning From the Universality Debate' (2010) 28(2) *Netherlands Quarterly of Human Rights* 199; M Mutua (2015) 'What Is the Future of Transitional Justice?' 9(3) *International Journal of Transitional Justice* 1; M Schotsmans, 'The Role of Tradition in Transitional Justice' in M Schotsmans, E Brems and G Corradi (eds), *International Actors and*

justice (including tradition and religion) and the emerging international law framework for TJ truth seeking. To resist neocolonial interference and abstract normative ideals imposed from above, it has long been recognised that TJ should be 'home-grown' and emerging 'out of local context and adapted by the people themselves to the specific conditions of their country'.[27] Moreover, even religion as a 'major "carrier" of ethics of reconciliation' can help shape TJ, including for truth-seeking aims.[28] This supports the claim that in some Muslim-majority contexts, for some people, invoking Islamic values and jurisprudence may boost the legitimacy and sustainability of TJ processes.[29] That being said, vernacular justice is not a panacea and must be approached mindfully: firstly, 'the stretching of local justice to deal with unfamiliar crimes (for example, genocide) and extraordinary situations (for example, civil wars)' can be challenging (if not outright artificial), and secondly, there may be tensions between local justice and international human rights law standards.[30] These ambiguities must be reckoned with as an integral part of the analysis of how the local and global normative dimensions supporting TJ truth seeking meet.

In Muslim-majority societies emerging from mass violence (and often still subjected to it), the potential role of Islamic law cannot be overlooked, but neither can it be overstated. Despite the suggestion that Islamic principles in TJ may ensure greater local legitimacy in truth-seeking initiatives, drawing on religious principles and relying on the support of religious actors in the localisation process is deeply political and often problematic.[31] Nevertheless, in recent years scholars have started to develop an interest in the role of Islam in relation to TJ processes in the aftermath of both conflict and authoritarianism. With regard to post-conflict, an emerging position is that '*shari'a* is not only compatible with contemporary approaches to post-conflict justice modalities, widely used in the international community, but also *appropriate* for use in Muslim societies'.[32] As Corri Zoli, Cherif Bassiouni and Hamid Khan have argued,

Traditional Justice in Sub-Saharan Africa (Cambridge, Intersentia, 2015); L Waldorf, 'Local Transitional Justice: Customary Law, Healing Rituals, and Everyday Justice' in O Simić, *An Introduction to Transitional Justice* (Abingdon, Routledge, 2017).

[27] Yusuf (n 2) 152, also discussing AA An-Na'im, 'Editorial Note: From the Neocolonial "Transitional" to Indigenous Formations of Justice' (2013) 7(2) *International Journal of Transitional Justice* 197, 197.

[28] ibid 160. See also D Philpott, 'What Religion Brings to the Politics of Transitional Justice' (2007) 61(1) *Journal of International Affairs* 93.

[29] See on peacebuilding and Islam, JK Zartman, 'Development and Peace Through Traditional, Cultural, Islamic Mediation' (2020) 15(2) *Journal of Peacebuilding & Development* 164, with reference also to Afghanistan, Iraq, Somalia and Sudan.

[30] Waldorf (n 26) 165.

[31] E Kazemi, 'Transitional Justice in Tunisia: When Religion Meets State' (2019) 13 *International Journal of Transitional Justice* 590. More broadly on religious actors in TJ, see I Cismas, 'Reflections on the Presence and Absence of Religious Actors in Transitional Justice Processes: On Legitimacy and Accountability' in R Duthie and P Seils (eds), *Justice Mosaics: How Context Shapes Transitional Justice in Fractured Societies* (New York, ICTJ, 2017).

[32] Zoli, Bassiouni and Khan (n 2) 52, and also Bassiouni (n 2).

'grounding contemporary post-conflict processes in classical and contemporary Islamic legal doctrine makes it more accessible to Muslim societies seeking historically meaningful legal mechanisms to deal with the aftermath of conflict'. Addressing the legacies of conflict is an obligation under Islamic law in order to uphold the interdependent principles of peace, accountability, truth, justice and forgiveness.[33] This is based on the 'legal theoretical approaches of *maqasid al-shari'a*, the higher goals and values of Islamic law which must be implemented into legislation and jurisprudence, and *siyasa al-shari'a*, the government policy associated with preserving *shari'a* values and norms'.[34] As such, post-conflict TJ processes may benefit from the additional contextualisation and grounding in Islamic law – but this is not necessarily straightforward or divorced from complex political realities.

Islamic law may also play a part in transitions from authoritarian regimes, in addition to post-conflict scenarios. Hakeem O. Yusuf considers the advantages of taking account of Islamic values and practices in processes of TJ in MENA where Islam, as a holistic system of beliefs, carries some influence.[35] Engaging with Islam would benefit the sustainability and legitimacy of TJ in the aftermath of both conflict and authoritarianism. Focusing on legitimacy, Yusuf presents a case for the inclusion of religious values and worldviews of the people and society for whom the TJ process is being developed.[36] While vigilance is due with regard to possible tensions between some traditional values and contemporary international human rights standards, and the pitfalls that come with artificially stretching concepts to fit certain aims and narratives, the potential of religion as a legitimising driver of justice in transition merits further attention.[37] This book unpacks this proposition and offers a doctrinal and practical analysis to ground the localisation of TJ truth seeking from the international legal framework to the legal systems of Muslim-majority societies.

Despite the overall compatibility between the general aims of the Islamic justice system and contemporary understandings of post-conflict and post-authoritarianism justice in international law, 'often neither Muslim governments nor other actors apply the *shari'a* or contemporary international law to conflict and post-conflict justice situations'.[38] In practice, the uses of (secular) criminal law in Muslim-majority societies emerging from recent histories of violence depart substantially from the ambitious justice aims sought by Islamic law as well as the international legal framework for truth seeking. Recent prosecutions

[33] Zoli, Bassiouni and Khan (n 2) 52–53.

[34] ibid.

[35] Yusuf (n 2).

[36] ibid 150–51, discussing B Oomen, 'Justice Mechanisms and the Question of Legitimacy: The Example of Rwanda's Multi-layered Justice Mechanisms' in K Ambos et al (eds), *Building a Future on Peace and Justice: Studies on Transitional Justice, Peace and Development* (Berlin, Springer-Verlag, 2009) 184.

[37] See further Cismas (n 31).

[38] Zoli, Bassiouni and Khan (n 2) 55.

of political leaders in the Arab region (as an example of Muslim-majority settings) have failed to address legacies of past harm adequately, as illustrated in Noha Aboueldahab's work. In Egypt, Libya, Tunisia and Yemen, the transitions did not constitute a shift 'from violent, non-liberal rule to peaceful, liberal-democratic rule', challenging the predominant understanding that transitions occur in a liberalising context.[39] These 'chaotic transitions' have resulted in highly 'politicised and limited transitional justice' designed to 'advance narrow interests' and 'inhibit systemic reform'.[40] Moreover, there is an evident lack of consensus around the aims – including the truth seeking aims – of transitions after the Arab uprisings: this impacts negatively on the prospects of shared initiatives to shed light on the past.[41]

The spiralling towards civil conflict and authoritarian resurgence – and thus new layers of violence – across MENA (and in other Muslim-majority societies reckoning with violent legacies) has not fostered accountability for widespread past harm.[42] The questionable democratic outcomes of these transitions exacerbate the constraints of truth-seeking efforts, as successor (and old) elites implicated in past and present serious violence tend to protect themselves from scrutiny. All of these factors converge in constraining the possibilities of meaningful truth seeking either through prosecutions or extrajudicial mechanisms. Challenges to accountability in those settings (like in others) also result from the contradictory agendas of international and domestic actors with regards to criminal accountability or immunity, the limited scope of investigations excluding most violations and alleged perpetrators, and weak and politicised judiciaries.[43] And while prosecutions (despite their failures) have been the leading TJ mechanism in the region,[44] the potential nuance of Islamic law, and the possibility of including victims and survivors more centrally in the process in light of human rights requirements, are generally overlooked. Instead, the top-down, highly politicised approach to accountability has been driven by narrow prosecutorial aims, which are ill-suited to complex transitions,[45] and have done little to uncover the truth about past violence.

[39] Aboueldahab (n 2) 2. On paradigmatic transitions, see T Carothers, 'The End of the Transition Paradigm' (2002) 13(1) *Journal of Democracy* 5.

[40] MW Hanna, 'Egypt and the Struggle for Accountability and Justice' in KJ Fisher and R Stewart (eds), *Transitional justice and the Arab Spring* (London, Routledge, 2014) 172 discussing Egypt specifically.

[41] KJ Fisher and R Stewart, 'After the Arab Spring: A New Wave of Transitional Justice?' in KJ Fisher and R Stewart (eds), *Transitional Justice and the Arab Spring* (London, Routledge, 2014).

[42] Discussed in S Lacroix and JP Filiu (eds), *Revisiting the Arab Uprisings: The Politics of a Revolutionary Moment* (Oxford, Oxford University Press, 2018) 1–2. See also H Van der Merwe, 'Transitions in the Middle East and North Africa: New Trajectories and Challenges for Transitional Justice?' in KJ Fisher and R Stewart (eds), *Transitional Justice and the Arab Spring* (London, Routledge, 2014).

[43] Aboueldahab (n 2) 2–4.

[44] ibid 8.

[45] ibid 126–27.

Looking beyond criminal culpability for past harm in the context of TJ, and uncoupling truth seeking from prosecutions, might offer greater chances of success in enabling victims and societies to see their right to truth realised. The rich and varied literature on truth seeking in relation to transitions attests to this – although closer scrutiny of past experiences reveals that any truth-seeking effort (including truth commissions) is partial, ambiguous and vulnerable to the political climate of its context.[46] Nonetheless, the emerging right to truth in international law provides a normative foundation for victims and societies to demand effective and impartial investigations by authorities and challenge partial or imprecise findings through legal and extralegal channels (such as investigative journalism, the work of civil society and the arts), moving beyond the oversimplified dichotomies of truth versus justice, or truth versus reconciliation. In principle, the right to truth after widespread past harm includes both individual and collective dimensions, and is uncoupled from criminal investigations: any mechanism (existing within a given legal system or created anew) capable of investigating the past – with or without a retributive aim – can contribute to uncovering the truth about violent legacies shrouded in convenient silence.[47] Framing the right to truth in the language of human rights emancipates this concept from the strictures of criminal law, and consequently enables more flexible solutions without compromising international law standards. The concept and possibilities of the right to truth in relation to TJ in Muslim-majority societies, however, is underexplored in the literature. This book addresses this gap by investigating how truth seeking set out in the international legal framework of TJ can be localised in Muslim-majority contexts, and, relatedly, how Islamic law supports the notion of a right to truth – and can thus contribute to its consolidation in international law.

METHODOLOGY

The two core research questions that guide this project – How can the truth-seeking element of the international legal framework for TJ be localised in Muslim-majority societies? To what extent does Islamic law and jurisprudence support the notion of the right to truth about past violence, as emerging in international law? – have been approached doctrinally and critically from a law-in-context standpoint. In order to do so, this book adopts and builds on the comparative law methods proposed by Rodolfo Sacco,[48] in which the distinction

[46] See discussion in ch 3 of this book.

[47] See discussion in ch 4. For a detailed analysis of the evolution of the right to truth in international law, see A Panepinto, 'The Right to the Truth in International Law: The Significance of Strasbourg's Contributions' (2017) 37(4) *Legal Studies* 739; JA Sweeney 'The Elusive Right to Truth in Transitional Human Rights Jurisprudence' (2018) 67(2) *ICLQ* 353; Klinkner and Davis (n 21).

[48] R Sacco, 'Legal Formants: A Dynamic Approach to Comparative Law' (Instalment I of II) and (Instalment II of II) (1991) 39 *American Journal of Comparative Law* 1 and 343.

(and hierarchy) between positive or recognisable 'law' and other forms and expressions of norms is collapsed (discussed in greater detail in Chapter 2). This methodological lens offers greater precision in identifying the legal formants within a given legal system and analysing convergences and tensions between different norms within pluralistic legal systems.[49] It allows interdisciplinary perspectives to be embedded more seamlessly, because comparative methods are premised on the reality that official positive law is only part of the intricate tapestry of a legal system. Furthermore, it enables a joint discussion of canon and critique of norms as operating within their socially and culturally informed reality – and a way to see normative influences which tend to be invisible to the naked legal eye. The versatile toolkit of this comparative approach is concerned holistically with the 'law' and 'that which is normative', offering an agile method through which the research questions are tackled, as well as a theoretical framework upon which this entire book rests.

The heart of the analysis is the juxtaposition of the norms guiding the truth-seeking element of the international legal framework of TJ and the normative principles underpinning Islamic law and jurisprudence, as a direct and indirect factor of the legal cultures of Muslim-majority societies, which converge on broadly equivalent aims despite wildly different premises. Both legal spheres comprise law and 'that which is normative' that cannot be disentangled from the complex environment in which it emerges and operates, contests and is contested, and adapts or becomes irrelevant. Human actions, agency, disempowerment and apathy determine the fate of individual norms, legal systems and 'legalised' projects. This is true of the norms guiding the truth-seeking element of the international legal framework of TJ: the divergence of truth-seeking experiences in societies facing legacies of past violence, and pursuing (or not) justice for victims and accountability for perpetrators attests to the infinite challenges and opportunities of this sort of endeavour, despite international law constituting in principle a uniform reference for all (as discussed in Chapters 1, 3 and 4). Likewise, the normative principles underpinning Islamic law and jurisprudence may be broadly defined in principle (despite variations between schools of law), but the ways in which they are interpreted and applied is potentially infinite, resulting in significant differences in the presence and uses of *shari'ah* between Muslim-majority societies, reflecting historic, political, social and cultural factors unique to each setting (as discussed in Chapters 5 and 6). Comparative law methods, jointly with other interdisciplinary tools, allow for a closer and more sophisticated scrutiny of both legal spaces that go beyond abstract notions of truth seeking/ TJ/international law, and Islamic law and jurisprudence/*shari'ah*/'the Islamic legal tradition'. The normativity of these concepts operates beyond the confines of positive official law and is far from

[49] SE Merry, 'Legal Pluralism' (1988) 22 *Law & Society Review* 869.

neatly presented and recognisable (fitting the famous claim by Christine Bell that the law of TJ is a 'mess'[50]). The overall comparability of these normative impulsions, deriving from two fundamentally different projects, is an unresolved issue. This book sheds light on the opportunities and challenges of comparing the two systems as they overlap in the specific aim of truth seeking after mass violence.

This book requires readers to take a leap of faith if they have been trained and socialised to think about the law as a higher-order ideal. This is a sentiment shared by many – but not all – lawyers and non-lawyers alike. Yet for norms guiding the truth-seeking element of the international legal framework of TJ and the normative principles underpinning Islamic law and jurisprudence, the sanctity of law – espoused in different guises by positivists and naturalists – rests on shaky foundations. There is a subtext of raw emotion in claiming that the law requires this, or prohibits that, or that the law's intention is something or other. Law is exquisitely human, but dressed up in respectable garb by invoking procedures, higher aims of justice, divinity or other authoritative sources of legitimacy.[51] Despite its rarefied characteristics[52] – true or imagined – law is a human by-product of society that assumes meaning depending on context. This book asks readers to relinquish our collective cultural deference to black-letter law and consider 'that which is normative' (whether official or unofficial) more critically. Comparative law methods – and in particular Rodolfo Sacco's notion of legal formants – adopted in this project help demystify and reconceptualise both spheres of law considered to allow for their closer analysis, critique and juxtaposition.[53] In this project, the tools of comparative law are intended to be used in a more critical manner, with a postcolonial agenda.[54] This is because assuming the bounty of the international framework of TJ ignores the continuities between colonial pasts and postcolonial presents, thus perpetuating structural injustices through tools and discourses of TJ.[55]

Mindful of the theoretical and methodological caveats of comparative law (discussed in more detail in Chapter 2), this project is informed by the aims of comparative international law, which offers a richer understanding of

[50] Bell (n 19).

[51] See the discussion around law as mask in W Weyrauch, 'Law as Mask-Legal Ritual and Relevance' (1978) 66(4) *California Law Review* 699.

[52] For some reflections on aura of infallibility and authority that surrounds law (and medicine), see K Calavita, *Invitation to Law and Society: An Introduction to the Study of Real Law* (Chicago, IL, University of Chicago Press, 2016) 8–9.

[53] Sacco (n 48).

[54] J Schacherreiter, 'Postcolonial Theory and Comparative Law: On the Methodological and Epistemological Benefits to Comparative Law through Postcolonial Theory' (2016) 49(3) *Verfassung und Recht in Übersee/Law and Politics in Africa, Asia and Latin America* 291.

[55] HO Yusuf, 'Colonialism and the Dilemmas of Transitional Justice in Nigeria' (2018) 12(2) *International Journal of Transitional Justice* 257.

international law through the tools of cognate disciplines.[56] Indeed, the inherent pluralisms of the international framework of TJ and of Islamic law lend themselves to being investigated through contextual, sociolegal approaches. Conceptualising and invoking the international framework of TJ and Islamic law is an expression of legal culture – but as David Nelken famously noted, legal culture 'is both hard to pin down and, at the same time, difficult to escape'.[57] This project, therefore, strives to equalise, and question, the theoretical normative value of both the international framework of TJ and of Islamic law, without seeking a fixed hierarchy, or clear demarcation, between the two. As such, it seeks to unsettle the more frequent research and policy questions around whether and to what extent Islamic law can accommodate international law, or theologically driven questions as to whether international law is compatible with Islamic law.

This study is predominantly desk-based and draws on a wide variety of primary and secondary sources mostly in English (or English translation) to unpack and problematise the localisation of the international framework of TJ in Muslim-majority contexts. Chapter 2, in particular, explains the theoretical underpinnings and the methodological approaches this project adopts in answering the research questions in light of the material surveyed. In addition to consulting written work emerging from a variety of disciplines in law and other subjects (taken in context), this research is complemented by three responses received to a questionnaire designed to elicit the views of established Islamic law scholars on the right to truth in *shari'ah*. A total of six potential interviewees were identified and approached in 2020 through the author's networks in the Middle East, with the help of local research assistants. These participants were sampled purposively,[58] based on the researcher's need to obtain 'official' and 'authoritative' information on how the right to truth is, and can be, conceptualised in Islamic law. The choice of interviewees was made according to their certified knowledge of Islamic law and recognition, within their respective communities, as authoritative repositories and interpreters of Islamic law. The questionnaire was also submitted to the office of the Grand Imam of Al Azhar in Egypt, but after a year of constructive written exchanges mediated through a local research assistant, I did not receive a written answer from that important seat of Islamic learning (if received, that data will be used for follow-on research).

The principal aim of the questionnaire was to elucidate the Islamic support for the right to truth and the aims of truth seeking after serious violence, as

[56] A Roberts et al, 'Comparative International Law: Framing the Field' (2015) 109 *American Journal of International Law* 467.

[57] D Nelken, 'Disclosing/Invoking Legal Culture: An Introduction' (1995) 4 *Social & Legal Studies* 435.

[58] On sampling, see inter alia OC Robinson, 'Sampling in Interview-based Qualitative Research: A Theoretical and Practical Guide' (2014) 11(1) *Qualitative Research in Psychology* 25.

understood by contemporary Islamic law scholars with classical religious and legal training in *shari'ah* and intimate knowledge of the Quran, the hadith and the core texts of classical Islamic jurisprudence. In light of the two research questions that guide this project, the interviews sought to test the two intertwined propositions that the truth-seeking element of the international legal framework for TJ can be localised in the legal systems of Muslim-majority societies, and that Islamic law and jurisprudence support the notion of the right to truth about past violence, as emerging in international law. The decision to conduct qualitative interviews through questionnaires and not orally was intended to allow scholars sufficient time to reflect on the questions, consult relevant Islamic law sources and formulate more in-depth comprehensive written answers,[59] integrated in Chapter 6. Written, signed answers to the questionnaire were provided by a prominent Shia Seyyed, a scholar of *mujtahid* rank (as explained in chapter 5), and by a very senior secular jurist affiliated to a centre of Sunni study; oral answers transmitted electronically were also provided by an Islamic law *sheikh* who teaches within the Hanafi school of jurisprudence and is also affiliated to the most prominent learning centre of the Sunni tradition. All three interviewees are native Arabic speakers and their answers to the questionnaire were translated into English for this project. As one respondent requested anonymity, in light of the small number of interviewees the researcher decided to present excerpts in a way that does not reveal any of the participants' identities.[60]

The findings reveal that there is an overall convergence between the international and Islamic value placed on truth seeking, and the related right to truth. The interviews offer detailed references to Quranic provisions, hadith and traditions of the Prophet's companions (including Ali, Mohammed's successor in the Shia tradition) that relate directly or indirectly to the notions and lexicon of TJ truth seeking and the right to truth. These findings reaffirm the broad compatibility between the international law framework underpinning transitional truth seeking and the *shari'ah*. Despite the contemporary political implications of some of the questions posed, the questionnaire steered away from asking whether specific countries should pursue justice for the victims and accountability for perpetrators of serious abuse because *shari'ah* commands it, as well as international law. While this was undoubtedly at the forefront of some interviewees' minds, with specific reference to their countries of origin or residence, it was important for the questions to remain focused on the doctrinal aspects of

[59] On the peculiarities of interviewing through emails, see inter alia N James and H Busher, 'Internet Interviewing', in JF Gubrium et al (eds), *The Sage Handbook of Interview Research: The Complexity of the Craft* (London, Sage, 2012); and C Hewson, 'Qualitative Approaches in Internet-Mediated Research: Opportunities, Issues, Possibilities' in P Leavy (ed), *The Oxford Handbook of Qualitative Research*, 2nd edn (Oxford, Oxford University Press, 2020).

[60] On the need to think holistically about how data is presented to ensure confidentiality, see eg. K Kaiser, 'Protecting Confidentiality' in JF Gubrium et al (eds), *The Sage Handbook of Interview Research: The Complexity of the Craft* (London, Sage, 2012).

Islamic law to fill an important gap in the knowledge available on this topic, as well as to ensure the safety of everyone involved in line with ethical considerations. Any country-specific conclusions inferred from these findings are not the direct intention of this book, although it is hoped that further research building on these general points might offer doctrinal and practical support in ensuring that victims and societies as a whole reckon with the past and perpetrators of abuse are held to account in some way (not necessarily through criminal law, as discussed).

STRUCTURE OF THE BOOK

The six chapters that make up this book address different aspects of the two core research questions that guide the project: How can the truth-seeking element of the international legal framework for TJ be localised in Muslim-majority societies? To what extent does Islamic law and jurisprudence support the notion of the right to truth about past violence, as emerging in international law? Taken together, the chapters build the argument gradually and outline the scope for convergence of the two legal spheres in relation to truth seeking and the right to truth. To do so, they unpick some of the assumptions about the international legal framework for TJ, the truth-seeking element and the emerging right to truth as well as Islamic law and jurisprudence through the comparative law approach articulated in Chapter 2. The partial results of this project are presented throughout, with the overall findings restated in the conclusions.

Chapter 1 considers the legal framework underpinning TJ truth seeking and argues that international law and local informal/unofficial sources are more closely intertwined than generally assumed. As a pluralistic space, TJ can and should engage with contextual and bottom-up normative influences, which include religious norms and the role of religious actors, to complement international humanitarian law, human rights and criminal law. The balance between global and local norms reflects the specificities of each setting, but also political manipulations, new and old structural inequalities and forms of violence – of which we should remain vigilant. Transitional truth seeking must be understood in this context: adopting both international and local normative justifications for uncovering truths about widespread violence helps garner wider support and legitimacy, but the impact of social and political realities of each scenario cannot be overlooked in the pursuit of truth.

Chapter 2 adopts the analytical lens of legal pluralism to identify and interpret the norms that underpin the international framework for TJ and any given local setting – including Muslim-majority societies. It explains how comparative law, and in particular Sacco's theory of legal formants,[61] is a useful tool

[61] Sacco (n 48).

to capture and understand these complexities and the localisation of the international framework of TJ. With regards to localising TJ truth seeking from international law to Muslim-majority legal systems, comparative law helps reveal how public international law (PIL) and Islamic law (as a formant of the legal systems of Muslim-majority societies embarking on transitional truth seeking) cross-fertilise, thus strengthening the normative framework both in its abstract global dimension and in its local applications.

Chapter 3 investigates truth seeking through the notion of legal truth as a central, yet contested, element of TJ that contributes to the formation of collective memories. After reviewing key aspects of truth seeking in TJ and the notion of the legal truth, this chapter analyses how legal truths emerge as a product of legal/legalised mechanisms, including trials and truth commissions. The construction and limits of legal truth, and the influence of context and key stakeholders, mean that it remains inherently open to challenge and revisitation. In particular, the legalised procedures and normative function of formalised truth seeking gives these processes ritual and performative characteristics that call for a deeper critical evaluation of the legal truth and its normative underpinnings. This chapter, therefore, argues that the notion of legal truth encapsulates the possibilities and limitations of the 'truth' in relation to TJ.

Building on these considerations, Chapter 4 turns to the concept of a right to truth as increasingly utilised in different settings to empower victims and societies to find out about past abuses linked to conflict or authoritarianism. It demonstrates that despite uncertainties around its contours and formal status in international law, the right to truth is emerging as an actionable right for victims and societies to discover responsibilities for past harm. The first part explores the empirical emergence of the right to truth in different forums, including the Inter-American Commission on Human Rights, the European Convention on Human Rights and UN systems. Taken comparatively, these developments are more than the sum of their parts and indicate a growing awareness and recognition of the potential of the right to truth in holding perpetrators to account and delivering justice to victims and societies more broadly. The second part of this chapter considers the significance of these cumulative reiterations of the right to truth across different forums, drawing on Austin's notion of performative utterances.[62] It argues that despite the fact that it is premature to qualify the right to truth as customary international law or a general principle, its repeated enunciation and different uses must be appreciated as evidence of an emerging norm in international law. Its further consolidation and acceptance depend on the uses and understandings of the right to truth in other legal systems, as will be discussed in relation to Islamic law in the final chapter.

Chapter 5 adopts the comparative-law lens presented in Chapter 2 to address the normative force of Islamic law in the legal systems of Muslim-majority

[62] JL Austin, *How to Do Things with Words* (Oxford, Oxford University Press, 1962).

societies through an analysis of its sources and methods, the centrality of human endeavours throughout time, and the general convergence of the *shari'ah* and the international legal framework underpinning the truth-seeking element of TJ. This enables a frank and constructive examination of Islamic norms in their social context, without the risk of entering theology or the fiction of 'unseeing' the role of religion (or overstating it). The discussion of two core elements of Islamic law and jurisprudence, the *maqasid as-shariah* and *maslaha*, which underpin its holistic understanding of substantive justice, provide a strong foundation for truth seeking in Muslim-majority societies today. This sets the scene for the final chapter, which explores in more detail how the right to truth and truth-seeking can be conceptualised and pursued through Islamic law.

Finally, Chapter 6 builds on the preceding discussion to illustrate how the right to truth (as conceptualised in the international legal framework of TJ) may be situated in the legal systems of Muslim-majority societies informed by Islamic law and jurisprudence. Despite the absence of a clearly defined notion of the right to truth in Islamic law, the high justice aims of the *shari'ah* offer clear doctrinal support for the victim and their family's right to know the truth about violence suffered, and the authorities' corresponding duty to investigate for the benefit of society as a whole, even when the state itself is implicated. This leads to two key conclusions: first, there are no Islamic justifications that prevent truth seeking for harm arising from conflict or authoritarianism, given that the *shari'ah* espouses a broad notion of justice with an emphasis on victim satisfaction. Second, the possibilities offered by Islamic legal thinking on this topic can help build the international consensus around the right to truth and consolidate its development in international law.

This book demonstrates that there is a strong basis in Islamic law, traditions and practices to embed the notion of transitional truth seeking and the right to truth in the legal systems of Muslim-majority societies influenced directly or indirectly by *shari'ah* principles. These findings offer further evidence to empower victims and societies in demanding accountability for those responsible for serious harm during conflict and authoritarianism; in light of the emerging right to truth in international law and equivalent principles emanating from the *shari'ah*, knowledge of past harm can be pursued through both legal/legalised and non-judicial tools in line with both normative systems. As such, it is absolutely clear that gaps in accountability, including the practice of shielding state officials and other powerful groups and individuals from investigation for past abuse, is not tolerated in Islamic law. When the truth about past harm is obfuscated, the justifications are primarily political. The findings presented in this book offer a more incisive and inclusive argument in support of the right to know the truth about serious violence through the joint action of international law standards and Islamic law principles.

1

Transitional Justice between International Law and Local Norms

I. INTRODUCTION

IDENTIFYING THE NORMATIVE underpinnings of transitional truth seeking and TJ as a whole is not a straightforward task for lawyers and non-lawyers alike. Different TJ experiences, each emanating from a unique context and striving towards specific aims, seem to be based on a mixture of different levels of norms including international, domestic and local. In considering how the truth-seeking element of the international legal framework for TJ can be embedded in Muslim-majority societies, and the extent to which Islamic law supports the notion of the right to truth, the current international legal framework of TJ must nevertheless be defined somehow before proceeding to an analysis of equivalent *shari'ah*-based norms. Since the notion of a normative framework of TJ based (primarily) on international standards appears something of a placeholder concept, with the multiple normative sources that underpin the law of TJ being far from a coherent whole operating in full harmony, unpacking what is meant by the international legal framework of TJ requires careful consideration to avoid oversimplification or projecting a romanticised notion of what the law actually is. For this reason, it is important to problematise and politicise the law of TJ, which is necessarily a blend of different official and unofficial norms depending on context, championed by contextual actors with specific agendas. Once the international normative underpinnings of TJ are seen not only as law in the 'black-letter' sense, but also as the evolving product and meeting of specific social, cultural and political contexts, they lose their abstract primacy. One important consequence of this is to allow the influence and role of local, informal, unofficial, culturally specific and religious norms to be recognised and considered much more candidly.

The uncertainty about the contours of the legal framework for TJ at the domestic and international level is not per se a bad thing: it reflects the fact that each TJ experience is unique, and blends international, domestic and local norms, practices and ideas. In fact, the 'mess' of TJ, a viewpoint convincingly described by Christine Bell and adopted throughout this work, is not in conflict with the degree of flexibility required to respond to each scenario.[1] Moreover, it also enables additional normative forces, including unofficial norms and religious principles, to permeate and contribute to the process more seamlessly. As such, TJ experiences, both in theory and in practice, display features of legal pluralism, as discussed in more detail in Chapter 2. The interaction between different normative sources can help shed light on the distinctive conception of law and legality after mass violence and during periods of radical political change.[2] For the UN, the standard goals of TJ – accountability, justice and reconciliation – may be achieved through a variety of 'judicial and non-judicial processes and mechanisms, including prosecution initiatives, facilitating initiatives in respect of the right to truth, delivering reparations, institutional reform and national consultations'.[3] Against this backdrop, the truth-seeking element of TJ may be supported by a range of normative sources, which may include both international law as well as local understandings of justice. In Muslim-majority contexts, the normative force of Islamic law and jurisprudence may therefore offer an additional basis for attempts to uncover the truth about past harm.

This chapter provides a background to the content which follows by analysing the normative framework of TJ as a relatively fluid combination of international, domestic and local unofficial norms juxtaposed and applied differently, by various actors, according to specific contexts. It problematises the way in which the law of TJ is understood as a static and rarefied notion, suggesting instead that the normative pull of the framework derives from those who promote TJ internationally and locally, and is thus deeply political. The first section unpacks the notion of a global normative framework of TJ to reveal a synthesis of different legal regimes, soft law and normative practices of key actors (notably the UN) and specific donors[4] that find contextual applications in times of legal turmoil. The second part investigates the main areas of international law that underpin TJ, namely international humanitarian law (IHL), international human rights law (IHRL) and international criminal law (ICL). The third part considers how the indeterminacy and gaps of the normative framework of TJ premised on international law might be complemented by local understandings of justice. It analyses the opportunities and challenges of the turn to the local, including

[1] C Bell, 'The "New Law" of Transitional Justice' in K Ambos, J Large and M Wierda (eds), *Building a Future on Peace and Justice: Studies on Transitional Justice, Peace and Development* (Berlin, Springer-Verlag, 2009).

[2] See in general R Teitel, *Transitional Justice* (New York, Oxford University Press, 2000).

[3] See United Nations, *The Rule of Law and Transitional Justice in Conflict and Post-conflict Societies: Report of the Secretary-General* S/2004/616 (23 August 2004) 8, available at www.un.org/ruleoflaw/files/2004%20report.pdf and United Nations, *Guidance Note of the Secretary General: UN Approach to Transitional Justice* (March 2010) 2, available at https://www.un.org/ruleoflaw/files/TJ_Guidance_Note_March_2010FINAL.pdf.

[4] I Muvingi, 'Donor-Driven Transitional Justice and Peacebuilding' (2016) 11(1) *Journal of Peacebuilding & Development* 10.

reflection on the role of religious norms and its proponents. This discussion will set the scene for the subsequent chapter, which addresses in more detail the inescapable legal pluralism within the normative framework of TJ, and the usefulness of comparative law as a way for lawyers to import interdisciplinary tools to analyse the various layers and typologies of official and unofficial law that guide TJ in each context.

II. PROBLEMATISING THE NORMATIVE FRAMEWORK OF TRANSITIONAL JUSTICE

Transitional truth seeking, the focus of this investigation, rests largely on the somewhat indeterminate normative framework of transitional justice. In order to identify synergies and tensions between the truth-seeking element premised on the international legal framework of TJ, on one hand, and the conceptualisation of truth seeking in Islamic law and jurisprudence, on the other, we must pinpoint the defining characteristics of the two normative systems under analysis. Starting from the former, a major hurdle is the indeterminacy of the law of TJ, which nonetheless also offers the opportunity to rethink the dynamic pluralistic nature of the law of TJ and its permeability to norms outside the narrow confines of international law (discussed throughout the book). This section unpacks the notion of a global normative framework of TJ premised on international law, its synthesis of different legal regimes, soft law and normative practices of key actors (notably the UN) that operate contextually in times of legal turmoil.

The normative framework of TJ is a composite, fluid medley of international, regional and domestic law, coexisting with a range of local norms, including unofficial, cultural and religious elements understood in social and political contexts, as well as a hint of romanticisation around each of those sources.[5] The current law which guides TJ combines elements of human rights law, humanitarian law, ICL and ordinary criminal law, 'but cannot be justified in terms of any one of these regimes on their own'; instead, it can be better explained by the 'soft law standards that are emerging with reference to transitional justice, and in the practice of states and international organisations'.[6] The ways in which the normative framework of TJ is imagined varies greatly depending on who identifies the rules and their sources and for what purpose. In particular, the focus on the rule of law 'prompts the question of "which concept of the rule of law?" – and in particular whether a formal (procedural) or substantive (value-based)

[5] See eg P McAuliffe, 'Romanticization versus Integration: Indigenous Justice in Rule of Law Reconstruction and Transitional Justice Discourse' (2013) 5 *Goettingen Journal of International Law* 41; and A Kochanski, 'The "Local Turn" in Transitional Justice: Curb the Enthusiasm' (2020) 22(1) *International Studies Review* 2.

[6] Bell (n 1).

emphasis is to be preferred'.[7] A procedural emphasis would presume a technical and largely depoliticised experience, while a substantive understanding raises further questions about the values that drive and influence the process.[8] The multiple, sometimes contradictory, aims of TJ, and its various uses in a variety of postauthoritarian and postconflict scenarios, further problematise the exercise of identifying the law of TJ. Given it 'aims to maintain some degree of order, while simultaneously advancing political transformation', the ways in which the 'dominant frameworks' are used, and old and new law invoked, is somewhat contradictory and unpredictable.[9]

The normative framework of TJ, both in specific contexts as well as in general discourse, reflects the meetings, synergies, compromises and tensions between a range of official and unofficial laws (and normative values) at international/global, domestic and local levels. Over time, and through selective juxtapositions of TJ experiences from different parts of the world, a certain narrative around the evolution of TJ has crystallised influencing 'scholarly debate and policy choices' and consequently the global discourse of TJ.[10] All of this has influenced the way the normative framework is understood. Moreover, as Rosemary Nagy explains, the designation of TJ as 'a "global" project rather than an international one' captures these three layers, as well as the broader context of globalisation in which they operate.[11] The international legal framework of TJ, therefore, is only part of the law of TJ: not all the normative standards and practices associated with the field emanate from public international law (PIL) instruments.

Different actors might champion the primacy of certain norms over others: for instance, the UN promotes international law as the golden standard of transitional justice.[12] The role of international law in TJ, particularly for the legalisation and judicialisation of the field, cannot be underestimated.[13] Nonetheless, the relationship between international law and TJ is complex and contested for numerous reasons.[14] Moreover, at times local actors appropriate

[7] C Bell, C Campbell and F Ní Aoláin, 'Transitional Justice: (Re)conceptualising the Field' (2007) 3(2) *International Journal of Law in Context* 81, 83.

[8] ibid.

[9] BA Leebaw, 'The Irreconcilable Goals of Transitional Justice' (2008) 30(1) *Human Rights Quarterly* 95, 98.

[10] M Zunino, *Justice Framed: A Genealogy of Transitional Justice* (Cambridge, Cambridge University Press, 2019).

[11] R Nagy, 'Transitional Justice as Global Project: Critical Reflections' (2008) 29(2) *Third World Quarterly* 275, 276.

[12] L Grover, 'Transitional Justice, International Law and the United Nations' (2019) 88 *Nordic Journal of International Law* 359.

[13] See E De Groof and M Wiebusch, 'The Future(s) of Transitional Governance and International Law' in E De Groof and M Wiebusch (eds), *International Law and Transitional Governance: Critical Perspectives* (New York, Routledge, 2020).

[14] See eg C Turner 'Delivering Lasting Peace, Democracy and Human Rights in Times of Transition: The Role of International Law' (2008) 2 *International Journal of Transitional Justice* 126;

global norms, which take on new meanings;[15] and powerful political figures can claim aspects of the law underpinning transitional justice for 'less noble' aims.[16] Local actors might also champion alternative legal foundations for TJ, which adds to the complexities.[17] As such, who drives TJ matters in determining which norms are invoked within the suite of options available. This leads to a fluidity in what the normative framework of TJ might look like in different contexts, but also according to different actors.

Indeterminacy is a feature of the law of TJ at global, domestic, local levels, where depending on their relevance to the specific context, both official and unofficial norms operate. In other words, the law (and its manifestations as rule of law and justice) as a concept is itself deeply problematic in transitions. Ruti Teitel's landmark *Transitional Justice* book articulates this ambiguity well:

> In periods of radical political change, the law is unsettled, and the rule of law is not well explained as a source of ideal norms in the abstract. Within the context of transitional jurisprudence, the rule of law can be better understood as a normative value scheme that is historically and political contingent and elaborated in response to past political repression often perpetuated under the law.[18]

Thus, contextual 'normative value schemes' become reference points for specific TJ experiences as well as for TJ more generally as a discourse.[19] Nevertheless, when the (global) normative framework of TJ is invoked, it emerges primarily as a placeholder concept unless specifically grounded in the material realities of a given context – and then it becomes more specific to that time and place. In fact, the promise of a neat code of TJ, however much desired, is too good to be true. This lack of a defined, discrete, universal code of TJ makes the task of pinpointing what constitutes the international law of transitional justice a frustrating endeavour for black-letter lawyers seeking (and seeking to offer) clarity, especially through the instruments of ICL.[20] At the same time, radical sceptics

L McGregor, 'International Law as a Tiered Process: Transitional Justice at the Local, National and International Level' in K McEvoy and L McGregor (eds), *Transitional Justice From Below: Grassroots Activism and the Struggle for Change* (Oxford, Hart, 2008).

[15] Discussed, for example, in A Beresford and D Wand, 'Understanding Bricolage in Norm Development: South Africa, the International Criminal Court, and the Contested Politics of Transitional Justice' (2020) 46(4) *Review of International Studies* 534.

[16] H van der Merwe and MB Lykes, 'Idealists, Opportunists and Activists: Who Drives Transitional Justice?' (2018) 12 *International Journal of Transitional Justice* 381, 383.

[17] For an overview of the complexities of the local turn in TJ, see inter alia DN Sharp, 'Transitional Justice and "Local" Justice' in C Lawther, L Moffett and D Jacobs (eds), *Research Handbook on Transitional Justice* (Cheltenham, Edward Elgar, 2017).

[18] Teitel (n 2) 7, and elsewhere.

[19] On TJ as a discourse, see Zunino (n 10); C Bell, C Campbell and F Ní Aoláin, 'Justice Discourses in Transition' (2004) 13(3) *Social & Legal Studies* 305; Leebaw (n 9); P Arthur, 'How "Transitions" Reshaped Human Rights: A Conceptual History of Transitional Justice' (2009) 31(2) *Human Rights Quarterly* 321; C Bell, 'Transitional Justice, Interdisciplinarity and the State of the "Field" or "Non-field"' (2009) 3(1) *International Journal of Transitional Justice* 5.

[20] See eg K Ambos, 'The Legal Framework of Transitional Justice: A Systematic Study with a Special Focus on the Role of the ICC' in K Ambos et al (eds), *Building a Future on Peace and Justice:*

of the law's (idealised) role in the field lament excessive legalism.[21] But TJ does not have a clear body of law to call its own. Therefore, the discontent is likely operating at two levels: it is partly directed towards specific uses of specific laws for particular contexts, as well as towards the habitual invocations of the *idea* of the law's primacy in structuring TJ, which risks obfuscating the context, problems and politics of law.

An example of how the seemingly neutral and sanitised language of law is problematic is found in Rosemary Nagy's important cautioning against the 'narrowing and depoliticization of transitional justice', which has become a global project through the 'body of customary international law and normative standards'.[22] Similarly, Dustin Sharp has explained how in 'both liberal and illiberal contexts, the law and legalism associated with transitional justice may serve to obfuscate the very real power dynamics and contested political choices at the heart of any set of transitional justice mechanisms'.[23] The critique, of course, is fundamentally correct, despite the absence of a distinctive 'body' of law underpinning all TJ experiences. And in fact, as Zinaida Miller outlines in relation to the duty to prosecute in international law notably promoted in Diane Orentlicher's work, there has been a shift over time that has led to a radical rethinking of the stability of the international legal underpinnings from a 'stable certainty' to 'embedded ambivalence' informed by non-legal factors.[24] As such, it is possible to be critical of the (actual or perceived) legal dominance in TJ, and at the same time rethink its static universalising claims, despite the fact that the legal framework itself remains somewhat incoherent. The myth of an abstract and rarefied notion of law as distinct from other disciplines has long been overcome in sociolegal studies and related disciplines.[25] Similarly, in the field of TJ it would be absurd to consider law as detached from its social, political and economic contexts, as much as it would be misleading to reduce law to official, positive, written law.

Studies on Transitional Justice, Peace and Development (Berlin, Springer-Verlag, 2009). For a more critical assessment of international criminal law's role in dealing with past atrocity, see MA Drumbl, *Atrocity, Punishment, and International Law* (Cambridge, Cambridge University Press, 2007).

[21] See eg K McEvoy, 'Beyond Legalism: Towards a Thicker Understanding of Transitional Justice' (2007) 34(4) *Journal of Law & Society* 411.

[22] Nagy (n 11) 275–76.

[23] DN Sharp, 'Emancipating Transitional Justice from the Bonds of the Paradigmatic Transition' (2015) 9 *International Journal of Transitional Justice* 150, 156.

[24] Z Miller, 'Embedded Ambivalence: Ungoverning Global Justice' (2020) 11(3) *Transnational Legal Theory* 353, 372, analysing the shift between DF Orentlicher, 'Settling Accounts: The Duty to Prosecute Human Rights Violations of a Prior Regime' (1991) 100(4) *Yale Law Journal* 2537, and DF Orentlicher, '"Settling Accounts" Revisited: Reconciling Global Norms with Local Agency' (2007) 1(1) *International Journal of Transitional Justice* 10.

[25] JN Shklar, *Legalism: Law, Morals, and Political Trials* (Cambridge, Harvard University Press, 1964) 2–4. More broadly, N Lacey, 'Normative Reconstruction in Socio-legal Theory' (1996) 5 *Social & Legal Studies* 131; DN Schiff, *Socio-legal Theory: Social Structure and Law* (1976) 39(3) *MLR* 287.

There is a further consideration to make in relation to the placeholder concept of the global normative framework of TJ, which pertains to the universalising fantasies of international law that neutralises normative diversity and glosses over power dynamics.[26] As Astrid Jamar cautions in her survey of TJ dissemination, international law 'sustains unequal structures and maintains the growing North–South divide', whereby IHRL is associated with histories of 'colonial conquest and Western domination in Africa' (and elsewhere).[27] This racialised hierarchy of norms,[28] whereby international law standards reign supreme, 'continues to project a vision of the world where the North is portrayed as an international saviour and the Global South depicted as home to broken societies'.[29] This has emerged as a feature of 'the transitional justice literature [that] is defined by a Western, legalistic approach to justice, which affects the field's ability to account for indigenous and customary mechanisms of justice that do not espouse this legalistic lens'.[30]

A. A Merger of Legal Regimes, Soft Law and Normative Practices

The collage of norms, practices and principles underpinning TJ requires a step back from black-letter law thinking. In her explanation of the new law of TJ, Christine Bell describes a 'set of normative expectations', a dynamic process that merges different legal regimes – domestic criminal law, IHL, IHRL, ICL – often brokered by UN interventions.[31] A feature of the legal framework of TJ is the compromise between 'the simultaneous need for amnesty and for accountability'.[32] Bell articulates this new law of TJ as comprising four main elements: (1) a prohibition of blanket amnesties for serious international crimes; (2) the requirement of some amnesty 'to facilitate the release, demilitarization and demobilization of conflict-related prisoners and detainees'; (3) the 'normative commitment to accountability' married to the 'goal of sustaining

[26] These are amply discussed in the rich and evolving TWAIL scholarship, eg S Pahuja, *Decolonising International Law: Development, Economic Growth and the Politics of Universality* (Cambridge, Cambridge University Press, 2011); B de Sousa Santos, *If God Were a Human Rights Activist* (Stanford, Stanford University Press, 2015); M Mutua, *Human Rights Standards: Hegemony, Law, and Politics* (Albany, NY, SUNY Press, 2016); B Rajagopal, 'Counter-hegemonic International Law: Rethinking Human Rights and Development as a Third World Strategy' (2006) 27(5) *Third World Quarterly* 767.

[27] A Jamar, 'The Crusade of Transitional Justice Tracing the Journeys of Hegemonic Claims in Violence and Democracy' in *Violence and Democracy* (British Academy, 2019) 53.

[28] M Koskenniemi, 'Race, Hierarchy and International Law: Lorimer's Legal Science' (2016) 27(2) *European Journal of International Law* 415.

[29] Jamar (n 27) 59.

[30] S Vielle, 'Transitional Justice: A Colonizing Field' (2012) 4 *Amsterdam Law Forum* 58. See also the effect of donor-driven TJ in Muvingi (n 4).

[31] C Bell, *On the Law of Peace: Peace Agreements and the Lex Pacificatoria* (Oxford, Oxford University Press, 2008) 239–50.

[32] ibid 258.

the ceasefire and developing the constitutional commitments' – which can be done through quasi-legal mechanisms for accountability which do not involve prosecutions (eg truth commissions), and through a 'bifurcated approach' to hold the most serious offenders criminally accountable but provide 'forms of amnesty for those further down the chain of responsibility'; and (4) the use of international criminal justice to reverse any compromises on criminal accountability in some circumstances.[33] In addition to specific provisions set out in IHL, IHRL and ICL, there is a degree of compromise and choice involved in identifying the extent to which these norms apply to a given context, and under what conditions. This can be 'progressive and justice-promoting' but also 'exceptional and manipulated'.[34] As such, there is a malleability in the legal underpinnings of TJ, which makes the identification of its law a complicated affair.

To illustrate the 'growing awareness of fragmentation of the field of transitional justice' Fionnuala Ní Aoláin refers to the 'plethora of "soft law" norms emerging from a range of international and regional actors, and the implications for accountability and legal traction'.[35] These rules offer 'various degrees of legal traction, from binding treaty norms to soft law guidance to states'.[36] But 'the proliferation of norms also creates a fragmented universe of normative standards, most of which are non-binding'.[37] As the role of the UN in transitional justice has consolidated, so too have the legal standards it champions, which are mostly set out in soft law instruments.[38] As an example of this, Lena Grover indicates that the 'ICTJ relies on the UN's soft law instruments as forming "part of the legal basis for the field"'.[39]

Looking for the law of TJ is also driven by how various actors within and outside transitional societies employ the language and tools of transition. For lawyers as well as non-lawyers, the notion and tools of TJ have become a panacea for addressing the legacy of grave and widespread abuses after authoritarianism and conflict.[40] The scholarship has been slow in engaging in non-liberal transitions, possibly because TJ is understood as something 'inherently good'.[41]

[33] ibid 240.

[34] ibid 255–56.

[35] F Ní Aoláin, 'After Things Fall Apart: Challenges for Transitional Justice Futures' (2017) 11(1) *Human Rights and International Legal Discourse* 23.

[36] ibid.

[37] ibid.

[38] Grover (n 12) 368 and 375.

[39] ibid 368.

[40] On TJ and post-authoritarianism/democratisation, see inter alia: N Kritz (ed), *Transitional Justice: How Emerging Democracies Reckon with Former Regimes*, vol I (Washington, DC, United States Institute of Peace Press, 1995); L Huyse 'Justice after Transition: On the Choices Successor Elites Make in Dealing with the Past' (1995) 20(1) *Law & Social Inquiry* 51; with reference to postconflict/peacebuilding, see inter alia: W Lambourne, 'Transitional Justice and Peacebuilding after Mass Violence' (2009) 3(1) *International Journal of Transitional Justice* 28; CL Sriram, 'Justice as Peace? Liberal Peacebuilding and Strategies of Transitional Justice' (2007) 21(4) *Global Society* 579.

[41] TO Hansen, 'Transitional Justice: Toward a Differentiated Theory' (2011) 13 *Oregon Review of International Law* 1, 15.

One of the core preoccupations of TJ is how it might 'justly pursue societal transformation'.[42] Even the former UN Special Rapporteur on the promotion of truth, justice, reparation and guarantees of non-recurrence ('UN Special Rapporteur'), whose mandate focuses on TJ issues, has described it as 'a universal policy tool' that many think should 'resolve an apparently endless number of problems'.[43] This somewhat romantic vision has seen TJ evolve from its original, exceptional applications in the context of postauthoritarianism,[44] to its use in postconflict scenarios,[45] and even in ongoing conflict and dictatorships,[46] as well as settled democracies.[47] Gradually, the notion and tools of TJ have found a place on the international peace and security agenda at the UN Security Council,[48] and the UN as a whole continues to play a significant (yet debatable) role in its global diffusion and local implementations.[49] The shift from exceptionalism to normalisation has played a role in the blurring of transitional and non-transitional contexts in which TJ is invoked, typified in the mandate of the International Criminal Court (ICC).[50] All of these developments have influenced the normative framework of TJ.

[42] C Murphy, *The Conceptual Foundations of Transitional Justice* (New York, Cambridge University Press, 2017) 160.

[43] P de Greiff, 'Some Thoughts on the Development and Present State of Transitional Justice', (2011) 5(2) *Journal for Human Rights/Zeitschrift für Menschenrechte* 98.

[44] ibid 110. See also 'second-phase' transitional justice in R Teitel, 'Human Rights in Transition: Transitional Justice Genealogy' (2003) 16 *Harvard Human Rights Journal* 69.

[45] See on this, inter alia P van Zyl, 'Promoting Transitional Justice in Post-conflict Societies' in A Bryden and H Hänggi (eds), *Security and Governance in Post-conflict Peacebuilding* (Geneva, Centre for the Democratic Control of Armed Forces, 2005); E Mobekk, 'Transitional Justice in Post-conflict Societies – Approaches to Reconciliation' in AH Ebnother and PH Fluri (eds), *After Intervention: Public Security Management in Post Conflict Societies – From Intervention to Sustainable Local Ownership* (Vienna, Bureau for Security Policy at the Austrian Ministry of Defence, 2005); R Mani, *Beyond Retribution: Seeking Justice in the Shadows of War* (Cambridge, Polity/Blackwell, 2002). But also note the limitations of the overlap between transitional justice and jus post bellum: see eg. KJ Fisher, 'Defining a Relationship Between Transitional Justice and Jus Post Bellum: A Call and an Opportunity for Post-conflict Justice' (2020) 16(3) *Journal of International Political Theory* 287.

[46] On this point, see inter alia: P Engstrom, 'Transitional Justice and Ongoing Conflict' in CL Sriram et al (eds), *Transitional Justice and Peacebuilding on the Ground: Victims and Ex-combatants* (London, Routledge, 2012); LJ Laplante and K Theidon, 'Transitional Justice in Times of Conflict: Colombia's Ley de Justicia y Paz' (2006) 28 *Michigan Journal of International Law* 49.

[47] On the uses of transitional justice in settled democracies, see inter alia AÁ Berastegi, 'Transitional Justice in Settled Democracies: Northern Ireland and the Basque Country in Comparative Perspective' (2017) 10(3) *Critical Studies on Terrorism* 542; S Winter, *Transitional Justice in Established Democracies* (London, Palgrave Macmillan, 2014).

[48] UN Secretary-General Ban Ki-moon, Security Council, 18 October 2013, Remarks at Security Council open debate on Women, Rule of Law and Transitional Justice in Conflict-affected Situations, available at www.un.org/sg/en/content/sg/statement/2013-10-18/secretary-generals-remarks-security-council-open-debate-women-rule.

[49] See Grover (n 12).

[50] LE Gissel, 'Contemporary Transitional Justice: Normalising a Politics of Exception' (2017) 31(3) *Global Society* 353, 357.

B. The Normativity of How Transitional Justice is Understood

The discourse of TJ shapes the way its legal underpinnings are understood.[51] The normative framework of TJ is intimately linked to how certain definitions are used authoritatively in the field by academics and practitioners, including those working in and for international organisations. For Ruti Teitel, whose writing is amply cited across the literature, 'Transitional justice can be defined as the conception of justice associated with periods of political change, characterized by legal responses to confront the wrongdoings of repressive predecessor regimes' – assuming a liberalising process of change in which law plays a pivotal role in dealing with the past.[52] Christine Bell sees 'Transitional justice as the attempt to deal with past violence in societies undergoing or attempting some form of political transition' – but her view does not explicitly foreground law, nor necessarily assume a liberalising shift.[53] Among civil society organisations, the International Center for Transitional Justice defines TJ as referring 'to the ways countries emerging from periods of conflict and repression address large-scale or systematic human rights violations so numerous and so serious that the normal justice system will not be able to provide an adequate response'.[54]

Among many definitions of TJ, the one proposed in 2004 by former Secretary-General Kofi Annan has cemented the UN's understanding of the concept, its uses, and the UN's own role in promoting TJ worldwide.[55] It has also acquired significant normative connotations in the field.

> The notion of 'transitional justice' discussed in the present report comprises the full range of processes and mechanisms associated with a society's attempts to come to terms with a legacy of large-scale past abuses, in order to ensure accountability, serve justice and achieve reconciliation. These may include both judicial and non-judicial mechanisms, with differing levels of international involvement (or none at all) and individual prosecutions, reparations, truth-seeking, institutional reform, vetting and dismissals, or a combination thereof.[56]

Together with Ban Ki Moon's 2010 *Guidance Note on Transitional Justice*,[57] the UN's understanding of TJ has become increasingly dominant through its projection of authority in the field, and 'seeking to constrain the conduct

[51] See Zunino (n 10) in general on the evolution and problems of the current discourse of TJ.

[52] Teitel (n 44) 69.

[53] Bell (n 19) 7.

[54] International Center for Transitional Justice, 'Transitional Justice' at www.ictj.org/about/transitional-justice.

[55] Grover (n 12) 375. On the UN and transitional justice, see also A Davidian and E Kenney, 'The United Nations and Transitional Justice' in C Lawther, L Moffett and D Jacobs (eds), *Research Handbook on Transitional Justice* (Cheltenham, Edward Elgar, 2017).

[56] UN, *The Rule of Law and Transitional Justice in Conflict and Post-conflict Societies* (n 3).

[57] UN, *Guidance Note of the Secretary General: UN Approach to Transitional Justice* (n 3).

of states'.[58] Leena Grover offers an important critical evaluation of the significance of the UN and its partners' management of TJ and assertion of the 'hegemony of international law in the field of transitional justice'.[59] In light of the structure and agency of key actors of TJ,[60] the UN is uniquely placed to promote TJ globally and locally. While its definitions of TJ will be adopted as a starting point for the discussion in this book, it is vital not to lose sight of the limits of the UN's approach and its championing of international law as the golden standard, given the range of more articulate ways of thinking about TJ that have emerged in the literature over the past two decades.[61]

A range of scholars such as Vasuki Nesiah,[62] Dustin Sharp[63] and Catherine Turner[64] articulate the composite and evolving critiques to the dominant (and paradigmatic) perceptions of TJ that affect the ways in which its laws are conceptualised. In light of the critiques, the 'increasingly hegemonic role' of international criminal justice in transitional justice should be approached carefully, given the narrow retributive focus of that strand of international law as opposed to the more holistic human rights approach – which embraces different forms of accountability.[65] As such, the international legal framework of TJ should be considered in the round, in its political, social and cultural context; in that light, the UN is part of the dominant cultural context in the field.[66] It is worth also noting, as Kieran McEvoy sums up, that 'the more a field becomes legally institutionalized, the greater its respectability as a field of study and practice for lawyers but also for international institutions, politicians and policy makers – part of what Pierre Bourdieu terms the magnetic almost mysterious

[58] Grover (n 12) 375.

[59] ibid 377.

[60] E Skaar and E Wiebelhaus-Brahm, 'The Drivers of Transitional Justice' (2013) 31 *Nordic Journal of Human Rights* 127.

[61] Including McEvoy (n 21) 426, lamenting 'the tendency of international lawyers to eulogize the glory and majesty of international law being "brought to" previously war-torn regions [which] often appears oblivious to the strong evidence of a disconnect between such imperious aims and their perception in the communities affected by such violence'.

[62] V Nesiah, 'Theories of Transitional Justice: Cashing in the Blue Chips' in A Orford and F Hoffman (eds), *Oxford Handbook of the Theory of International Law* (Oxford, Oxford University Press, 2016).

[63] DN Sharp, 'What Would Satisfy Us? Taking Stock of Critical Approaches to Transitional Justice' (2019) 13(3) *International Journal of Transitional Justice* 580, and Sharp (n 23).

[64] C Turner, *Violence, Law and the Impossibility of Transitional Justice* (London, Routledge, 2016); C Turner, 'Transitional Justice and Critique' in C Lawther, L Moffett and D Jacobs (eds), *Research Handbook on Transitional Justice* (Cheltenham, Edward Elgar, 2017).

[65] LE Fletcher, 'International Criminal Law and the Subordination of Emancipation: The Question of Legal Hierarchy in Transitional Justice' in KJ Heller et al (eds), *The Oxford Handbook of International Criminal Law* (Oxford, Oxford University Press, 2020). Contrast this analysis with calls for a greater role for ICL, as in Ambos (n 20).

[66] See eg M Mazower, *No Enchanted Palace: The End of Empire and the Ideological Origins of the United Nations* (Princeton, NJ and Oxford, Princeton University Press, 2010); J Klabbers, 'Two Concepts of International Organization' (2005) 2(2) *International Organizations Law Review* 277.

pull of law'.[67] Despite the shortcomings of the institutional approach, the homogenising language and normative framework of TJ promoted by the UN is useful inasmuch as it communicates a general understanding of TJ and its toolkit as rooted in international law.

It is clear that the tools of international law are not the only lens through which to approach the normative framework of TJ. In the literature, the term 'transitional justice' is used in two main ways: as an umbrella term for the 'full range of processes and mechanisms' that make up TJ, essentially reflecting the list of measures indicated by the UN, and also as a term to describe the more theoretical 'modified notion of justice inherent in these policies'.[68] The latter understanding allows for a broader, theoretically situated analysis, focusing on the distinctiveness of TJ as a concept rather than a fixation on the legal foundations of TJ. Teitel sees paradigmatic TJ as a 'self-conscious construction' of the 'conception of justice associated with periods of political change'.[69] This suggests that the very notion of justice – what it is, how it operates, and what it seeks to do – in times of political transition can be (or is) modified, regardless of whether the specific mechanisms adopted are ordinary or extraordinary (this point will be revisited in the discussion that follows). Thus politics – but also social, cultural, religious and other factors – and law cross-fertilise: contexts shape norms applicable to transitions,[70] and at the same time the law (and the choice of law) affects political transformations.[71] In this context, the law oscillates between 'adherence to established convention and radical transformation'.[72] As such, TJ blends – not always smoothly – elements of legal continuity, change and rupture. The ways in which TJ is understood globally, as championed by international organisations but also as informed by academic writing and critique contributes to its normative underpinnings.

C. Transitional Justice as Legal Turmoil

The turmoil of transition, and even of failed transitions, acts as a stressor on law, exposing its malleability and vulnerability to contextual factors. As noted

[67] K McEvoy, 'Travel, Dilemmas and Nonrecurrence: Observations on the "Respectabilisation" of Transitional Justice' (2018) 12(2) *International Journal of Transitional Justice* 185, citing P Bourdieu, 'The Force of Law: Toward a Sociology of the Juridical Field' (1987) 38 *Hastings Law Journal* 805.

[68] Summarised in JA Sweeney, *The European Court of Human Rights in the Post-Cold War Era: Universality in Transition* (London, Routledge, 2013), 22. For an example of transitional justice as an umbrella term, L Oette, 'Law Reform in Times of Peace Processes and Transitional Justice: The Sudanese Dimension' in L Oette (ed), *Criminal Law Reform and Transitional Justice: Human Rights Perspectives for Sudan* (Farnham, Ashgate, 2013) 18.

[69] Teitel, *Transitional Justice* (n 2) 3; and R Teitel, 'Editorial Note – Transitional Justice Globalized' (2008) 2(1) *International Journal of Transitional Justice* 1.

[70] ibid.

[71] R Teitel, 'Transitional Justice: post war legacies' (2005-2006) 27 *Cardozo L Rev 1615*, 1616 ff.

[72] Teitel (n 2) 215.

by former UN Special Rapporteur Pablo de Greiff (writing in his academic capacity), 'in the wake of massive abuses, some of the "ordinary" expectations concerning what justice requires will not be satisfied'.[73] The elasticity of the international legal framework established after World War II, developed, promoted and adopted by the UN, offers an example of how derogations to the 'ordinary' expectations of justice in extraordinary times relate to the principle of legality, a cornerstone of international criminal justice (an area of international law which is often a factor in transitions – see discussion below).[74] When existing legal tools are ill-equipped for dealing with the nature and scope of unprecedented past abuse, TJ may upset the delicate balance between legality and morality. Given that often TJ occurs during times of rupture, some kind of extraordinary justice might emerge.[75] But exceptionalism is a double-edged sword: as it evolves, the law of TJ may be understood as 'creative, progressive and justice-promoting' as well as 'exceptional and manipulated'.[76] Moreover, over time instances of legal exceptionalism have been absorbed by the ordinary legal system and normalised.[77]

An oft-cited example of the process of disruption and normalisation is provided in the proceedings of the post-World War II International Military Tribunal (IMT) at Nuremberg.[78] In particular, the sources of international law invoked to support the notion of crimes against humanity were ambiguous, and

[73] P de Greiff, 'Theorizing Transitional Justice', in J Elster, R Nagy and M Williams (eds) *Transitional Justice: Nomos LI* (New York and London, NYU Press, 2012) 31, 58.

[74] This principle is crystallised in numerous international law instruments, inter alia: ICL: Arts 22(1), 23, 24 Rome Statute of the International Criminal Court (1998); IHRL: Art 11 Universal Declaration of Human Rights (1948), Art 15(1) International Covenant on Civil and Political Rights (1966), Art 7(1) European Convention for the Protection of Human Rights and Fundamental Freedoms (1950), Art 7(2) African Charter on Human and Peoples' Rights (1981); IHL: Art 67 IV Geneva Convention (1949), Art 75(4)(c) Additional Protocol I to the Geneva Conventions (1977). The principle of legality also constitutes a customary rule under IHL, identified by the ICRC as customary law (Customary IHL Rule 101) applicable to international and non-international armed conflicts and recognised in most national laws and military manuals, available at www.icrc.org/customary-ihl/eng/docs/v1_rul_rule101.

[75] DN Sharp, *Re-thinking Transitional Justice for the 21st Century* (Cambridge, Cambridge University Press, 2018) 6.

[76] See notably Bell (n 31) 255–56.

[77] Gissel (n 50).

[78] See BM Leyh, 'Nuremberg's Legacy within Transitional Justice: Prosecutions Are Here to Stay' (2016) 15 *Washington University Global Studies Law Review* 559. More generally, see KC Priemel and A Stiller (eds), *Reassessing the Nuremberg Military Tribunals: Transitional Justice, Trial Narratives, and Historiography* (New York, Berghahn Books, 2012); H Kelsen, 'Will the Judgment in the Nuremberg Trial Constitute a Precedent in International Law' (1947) 1 *International Law Quarterly* 153; Q Wright, 'The Law of the Nuremberg Trial' (1947) 41 *American Journal of International Law* 38; GA Finch, 'The Nuremberg Trial and International Law' (1947) 41 *American Journal of International Law* 20. Years later, C Tomuschat, 'International Criminal Prosecution: The Precedent of Nuremberg Confirmed' (1994) 5(2–3) *Criminal Law Forum* 237. For general readings on the International Military Tribunal at Nuremberg, see inter alia E Davidson, *The Trials of the Germans: An Account of the Twenty-two Defendants Before the International Military Tribunal at Nuremberg* (Columbia, MO and London, University of Missouri Press, 1966).

the IMT did not 'try seriously to demonstrate that such acts had been punishable under international law in the past'.[79] That decision was hotly debated at the time and in later years, illustrating the tension between law and morality: even the sternest contemporary critics of the influence of morality over law, including positivist Kelsen (despite his apprehensions[80]), conceded that 'to punish those who were morally responsible for the international crime of the Second World War may certainly be considered more important than to comply with the rather relative rule against ex post facto laws, open to so many exceptions'.[81] The disruption to the ordinary expectations of justice at Nuremberg paved the way for subsequent directions of international law, including clearer formulations of the categories of war crimes and crimes against humanity, as endorsed by the UN International Law Commission.[82] Gradually that exceptionalism became normalised through the entrenchment of the 'Nuremberg model' and the establishment of a permanent ICC, establishing the principle of individual criminal responsibility in international law (as opposed to the responsibility of the state as a whole which guides IHL).[83] Similar tensions have been identified in domestic courts dealing with international crimes, as illustrated in the Eichmann trial: Hannah Arendt concluded that the 'unsatisfactory condition of international law' meant that 'the realm of legality offered no alternative to kidnapping', and ultimately justice is the only 'end of the law'.[84] Whenever law is disrupted by extraordinary events and then reabsorbed by the legal system, the normative framework of TJ demonstrates its plasticity.

The considerations of morality – and related exceptions to formalism and positivism – over legal continuity remain contested. Derogations to core international legal principles, including the principle of legality, reflect natural evolutions of law even in times of non-transition.[85] What might appear to be 'new' law might not be so novel: Posner and Vermeule identify four categories

[79] W Schabas, 'Synergy or Fragmentation? International Criminal Law and the European Convention on Human Rights' (2011) 9(3) *Journal of International Criminal Justice* 609, 613ff.

[80] See M García-Salmones Rovira, 'Not Just Pure Theory: Hans Kelsen (1881–1973) and International Criminal Law' in F Mégret and I Tallgren (eds), *The Dawn of a Discipline: International Criminal Justice and its Early Exponents* (Cambridge, Cambridge University Press, 2020).

[81] Kelsen (n 78) 165.

[82] See, notably: UN International Law Commission, Nuremberg Principles, published in *Report of the International Law Commission Covering its Second Session, 5 June–29 July 1950*, Document A/1316, 11-14.

[83] Teitel (n 44) 89–90. However, the linearity from the IMT and the ICC is much more complex and contested. See eg C Schwöbel-Patel, 'The Core Crimes of International Criminal Law' in KJ Heller et al (eds), *The Oxford Handbook of International Criminal Law* (Oxford, Oxford University Press, 2020) 779: 'that which had made Nuremberg an "aberration", namely individual criminal responsibility, had quite extraordinarily become part of the accepted legal and public discourse'.

[84] H Arendt, *Eichmann in Jerusalem* (New York, Penguin, 1963) Epilogue.

[85] E Posner and A Vermeule, 'Transitional Justice as Ordinary Justice' (2004) 117 *Harvard Law Review* 761.

of law used in TJ: (1) new law, applied retroactively; (2) old law, which was never enforced; (3) old law, which was not enforced against the perpetrators from the old regime; and (4) international law.[86] The last three types find their justification in pre-existing sources, and do not raise special rule-of-law concerns. As to new law applied retroactively, the rule-of-law dilemma can be circumvented through various techniques, which place retroactive law within an existing legal framework, for instance, by appealing to higher pre-existing law (eg constitutional law, international law, *jus cogens* or (unenforced) norms of the previous regime), or through interpretative statutes that give new meaning to old laws, and modified statutes of limitations.[87] Given the international legal order today looks very different from what it was in 1945, not least because of the proliferation of international human rights instruments and the establishment of the ICC, and the prominent role of the UN, any new law responding to novel experiences of human suffering is likely to find some grounding in the global normative framework. This chimes with the notion of steady-state TJ proposed by Teitel, whereby 'transitional justice moves from the exception to the norm to become a paradigm of the rule of law'; the establishment of a permanent ICC attests to this (despite the exceptionalism of the ICC itself and its very limited scope[88]).[89]

Against this backdrop, De Greiff's assertion that 'transitional justice is neither in itself a distinctive form of justice nor a mere compromise, but rather a principled application of justice in distinct circumstances' offers a pragmatic resolution of the extraordinary/ordinary justice debate.[90] Transitional truth seeking and the emerging right to truth, as discussed in Chapters 3 and 4, are situated within this frame. The 'ordinariness' of the international law now underpinning TJ does not just flow from the fact that, in principle, (some) perpetrators are more likely to be held accountable before permanent institutions. Victims, their families, survivors and indeed society at large are also claiming the right to truth about past abuses through 'ordinary' human rights mechanisms that were conceived for non-transitional contexts, as will be discussed in Chapter 4. The emerging right to truth in international law is another interesting example of a norm attaching to exceptional circumstances – torture, forced disappearance, unlawful killing during conflict and authoritarianism – that is gradually gaining momentum to deal with serious state violence in non-transitional states as well.

The steady consolidation of TJ championed by the UN and the normalisation of previously exceptional international law instruments, however, has not

[86] ibid 762–67.
[87] ibid 791–95.
[88] See inter alia J Reynolds and S Xavier, '"The Dark Corners of the World": TWAIL and International Criminal Justice' (2016) 14(4) *Journal of International Criminal Justice* 959.
[89] Teitel (n 44) 89–90.
[90] De Greiff (n 73) 59.

resulted in a clear and coherent global law of TJ, nor has it delivered on its (UN-stated) aims of accountability, justice and reconciliation. Over time the UN has developed a strong position on accountability, evidenced in the 2012 Secretary-General's proclamation that 'in the new age of accountability', the ICC and the UN Security Council can work together to deliver justice and peace.[91] Nevertheless, despite the aims and mandates of the UN Security Council and the ICC, the international legal framework has been woefully inadequate in ensuring accountability for the worst abuses that accompany attacks on international peace and security. In recent years impunity for horrors inflicted across the world has been on the rise. Decrying the humanitarian situation in Syria, Yemen, Myanmar and Nigeria (incidentally, Muslim-majority contexts or situations in which violence is inflicted upon, or by, Muslim groups), David Miliband outlined the risks of the 'age of impunity' to a business audience in Davos in January 2020.[92] The 'retreat from the rule of law' that underpins the age of impunity is characterised by governments stepping back from 'global problems, or creating and compounding them'; to fill that void, businesses and NGOs must step up to find solutions.[93] It is against this backdrop that the primacy of states, and inter-state organisations, such as the UN, wanes in the pursuit of international peace and security, including the championing of TJ and its aims. Relatedly, the role and relevance of international law, which is the law that governs the relations between states, is called into question. Non-state actors, such as the businesses and NGOs indicated by Miliband, become more important on the international stage, including in the quest for accountability – including within the TJ frame.[94] Accordingly, non-state law could have a larger role to play in complementing some of the inadequacies of the international legal framework. As the following sections (and the next chapter) reveal, international law and local law – including unofficial and religious norms – already coexist in the global legal order that underpins transitional justice. As such, the inherent indeterminacy of international law and the force of local norms – and their possible interconnectedness – is an aspect that merits further analysis. The next part reviews the classic international law underpinnings of TJ.

[91] UN Secretary General, Press Release 17 October 2012, SG/SM/14589-SC/10794-L/3200, available at www.un.org/press/en/2012/sgsm14589.doc.htm.

[92] D Miliband, Welcome to the Age of Impunity: Speech by International Rescue Committee President and CEO David Miliband, World Economic Forum, 24 January 2020, available at www.rescue.org/press-release/welcome-age-impunity-david-milibands-world-economic-forum-speech.

[93] ibid.

[94] See eg JR Quinn, 'The Impact of State Abdication on Transitional Justice: When Non-state Actors and Other States Fill the Post-transition Gap' (2021) 9(2) *Peacebuilding* 114; D Backer, 'Civil Society and Transitional Justice: Possibilities, Patterns and Prospects (2003) 2(3) *Journal of Human Rights* 297. On the inclusion of non-state armed groups specifically, see A Bellal, 'Non-state Armed Groups in Transitional Justice Processes Adapting to New Realities of Conflict' in R Duthie and P Seils (eds), *Justice Mosaics: How Context Shapes Transitional Justice in Fractured Societies* (New York, ICTJ, 2017).

III. THE FORMAL SOURCES OF TRANSITIONAL JUSTICE: INTERNATIONAL LAW

The previous section explained how the normative framework of TJ is now formally premised on international law and championed and normalised by the UN. This part considers the main areas of international law that underpin TJ, before moving on to the role of unofficial local norms in the final section. While black-letter international law elements provide important reference points for the evolving framework of TJ, their value must nevertheless be situated in context and in relation to local norms (including unofficial law).

A. International Humanitarian Law

IHL governs various forms of armed conflict, and as such it does not automatically apply to all transitional contexts if their classification falls short of 'conflict'.[95] When approaching a situation in which TJ may develop, it is vital to ascertain whether this area of international law is applicable, and if so, which parts of it depending on the type of conflict. The indeterminacy around which norms apply to a given transitional setting exemplifies the absence of a clear, coherent and universal international law of TJ. Nevertheless, the relevance of IHL to TJ is clear in those settings where the threshold of conflict is met, and indeed there are arguments in favour of a more expansive reach of IHL (and specifically the Geneva Conventions) to ensure the highest degree of protection.[96] In these contexts, the rules of IHL may therefore be an important part of the international normative framework of TJ underpinning transitional truth seeking.

The bulk of IHL provisions apply to international armed conflicts, while a subset of norms (notably, common Article 3 of the 1949 Geneva Conventions and Additional Protocol II) are applicable to non-international armed conflict.[97] International armed conflicts encompass wars between states, military occupations and 'conflicts between government forces and national liberation movements', which include 'fighting against colonial domination and alien occupation and against racist regimes in the exercise of [the] right to self-determination'.[98] The category of non-international armed conflicts

[95] There is a rich literature on the classification of conflict in IHL; see inter alia E Wilmshurst (ed), *International Law and the Classification of Conflicts* (Oxford, Oxford University Press, 2012).

[96] S D'Cunha, 'The Notion of External NIACs: Reconsidering the Intensity Threshold in Light of Contemporary Armed Conflicts' in Terry D Gill and others (eds), *Yearbook of International Humanitarian Law 2017*, vol 20 (Berlin, TMC Asser Press 2019).

[97] E Crawford and A Pert, *International Humanitarian Law*, 2nd edn (Cambridge, Cambridge University Press, 2020) 54ff.

[98] ibid, citing Art 1(4) of Protocol Additional to the Geneva Conventions of 12 August 1949, and relating to the Protection of Victims of International Armed Conflicts (Protocol I), 8 June 1977.

(NIACs) includes civil war but excludes 'internal disturbances such as riots or sporadic violence'.[99] International courts have clarified the distinction between international armed conflict and NIACs: in *Tadić*, the International Criminal Tribunal for the former Yugoslavia (ICTY) stated the existence of the former 'whenever there is a resort to armed force between States', and of the latter 'whenever there is … protracted armed violence between governmental authorities and organized armed groups or between such groups within a State'.[100] For a conflict to be classed as a NIAC, there are 'two "threshold" requirements: organization of the non-state party(ies) to the conflict and intensity of the violence between the parties'.[101] As the literature cited in this section indicates, the rules around classification leave ambiguities and ample space for discretion, and as such, are vulnerable to politicisation.[102]

The relationship between IHL and TJ emerges in two key moments: first, it establishes a framework of reference for the conduct of hostilities, to which warring parties should adhere and might be held to account after its end; second, it sets out obligations to 'suppress all violations of IHL and to search for and prosecute those who have committed grave breaches of IHL in international armed conflicts'.[103] There are other important provisions that relate to transitions, such as obligations around truth recovery (discussed in Chapter 4). Article 32 of the Additional Protocol I to the Geneva Conventions refers to the 'right of families to know the fate of their relatives', both with respect to the remains of the deceased (Article 34) and for missing persons (Article 33).[104] Moreover, the provision set out in Article 6(5) of Additional Protocol II relating to NIACs calls upon the 'authorities in power' to 'grant the broadest possible amnesty to persons who have participated in the armed conflict, or those deprived of their liberty for reasons related to the armed conflict, whether they are interned or detained'.[105] Elizabeth Salmón also identifies a connection between the parties' conduct during conflict and 'the chances of achieving peace and reconciliation while restoring the rule of law once the hostilities have ended'.[106] As such, IHL provisions can influence all

[99] ibid.

[100] ICTY, *Prosecutor v Tadić*, Appeals Chamber Decision, 2 October 1995, Case No IT-94-1-AR72 (*Tadić* 1995), para 70, discussed inter alia in J Henckaerts, 'History and Sources' in B Saul and D Akande (eds), *The Oxford Guide to International Humanitarian Law* (Oxford, Oxford University Press, 2020) 23.

[101] ibid, discussed inter alia in D'Cunha (n 96).

[102] Discussed inter alia in Y Shereshevsky, 'Politics by Other Means: The Battle over the Classification of Asymmetrical Conflicts' (2016) 49 *Vanderbilt Journal of Transnational Law* 455.

[103] E Salmón, 'Reflections on International Humanitarian Law and Transitional Justice: Lessons to be Learnt from the Latin American Experience' (2006) 88(862) *International Review of the Red Cross* 327, 328ff.

[104] Protocol Additional to the Geneva Conventions of 12 August 1949, and relating to the Protection of Victims of International Armed Conflicts (Protocol I) (adopted 8 June 1977) 1125 UNTS 3.

[105] Protocol Additional to the Geneva Conventions of 12 August 1949, and relating to the Protection of Victims of Non-international Armed Conflicts (Protocol II) (adopted on 8 June 1977) 1125 UNTS 609.

[106] Salmón (n 103) 328.

three UN-identified aims of TJ: accountability, justice and reconciliation. As summed up by Teitel, this area of law governs many aspects of conflict, and as such, it provides a 'normative framework and language for thinking about successor justice' and 'regime wrongdoing'.[107]

Although the application of IHL may be limited to situations of armed conflict, it also overlaps with IHRL, which provides a normative continuum in war and peace.[108] Revising the *lex specialis* principle, both the International Court of Justice (ICJ) and the UN Committee on Economic, Social and Cultural Rights have restated that both bodies of law are applicable in conflict.[109] This means that even when IHL applies to TJ situations, it does not eclipse IHRL. Given the TJ preoccupation with responding to violations after hostilities end and supporting (at least in principle) justice for victims, applying IHL as opposed to only IHRL in situations of NIAC is useful to expand accountability to actors beyond official forces. In (traditional) IHRL, only states carry obligations; under IHL, there are 'obligations on all parties to an armed conflict, including non-governmental armed groups', making authorities and non-state actors accountable for violations.[110] Extending responsibility to non-state actors expands the possibilities of accountability for victims of certain IHL violations carried out by armed groups too, which are often present in situations that require transitional justice interventions.[111] Despite the lack of

[107] Teitel (n 2) 35; citing T Meron, *War Crimes Law Comes of Age: Essays* (Oxford, Clarendon Press, 1998).

[108] There is a rich literature on the relationship between IHL and IHRL, including AE Cassimatis, 'International Humanitarian Law, International Human Rights Law, and Fragmentation of International Law' (2007) 56 *ICLQ* 623; C Droege, 'The Interplay between International Humanitarian Law and International Human Rights Law in Situations of Armed Conflict' (2007) 40 *Israel Law Review* 310; O Ben-Naftali (ed), *International Humanitarian Law and International Human Rights Law* (Oxford, Oxford University Press, 2011); Y Shany, 'Co-application and Harmonization of IHL and IHRL: Are Rumours about the Death of Lex Specialis Premature?' in R Kolb, G Gaggioli and P Kilibarda (eds), *Research Handbook on Human Rights and Humanitarian Law: Further Reflections and Perspectives* (Cheltenham, Edward Elgar, 2020). Also, *Legality of the Threat or Use of Nuclear Weapons, Advisory Opinion* [8 July 1996] ICJ Rep 226, 25; for commentary, see inter alia, D Stephens, 'Human Rights and Armed Conflict – The Advisory Opinion of the International Court of Justice in the Nuclear Weapons Case' (2001) 4 *Yale Human Rights & Development Law Journal* 1.

[109] This has been widely discussed in the context of the Israeli occupation of Palestine, for example, by O Ben-Naftali and K Michaeli, 'We Must Not Make a Scarecrow of the Law: A Legal Analysis of the Israeli Policy of Targeted Killings' (2003–04) 36 *Cornell International Law Journal* 233, 275; discussing Concluding Observations of the Committee on Economic, Social and Cultural Rights: Israel, 31 August, 2001, UN Doc E/C.12/1/Add. 69 (31 August 2001) 11 and *Legality of the Threat or Use of Nuclear Weapons, Advisory Opinion* (n 108) 240.

[110] The International Committee of the Red Cross (ICRC), *Report: Strengthening Legal Protection for Victims of Armed Conflicts*, Geneva, October 2011, 5. See also H Jöbstl, 'Bridging the Accountability Gap: Armed Non-state Actors and the Investigation and Prosecution of War Crimes' (2020) 18(3) *J of Int'l Crim Justice* 567.

[111] On non-state actors and IHL in relation to transitional justice, see inter alia I Nuzov, 'Post-conflict Justice: Extending International Criminal Responsibility to Non-state Entities' in E Heffes, MD Kotlik and MJ Ventura (eds), *International Humanitarian Law and Non-state Actors* (Berlin, Springer and Asser Press 2020).

a 'general mechanism that would allow victims to assert their rights under IHL',[112] it might be useful to frame the gravity of certain types of violence addressed in TJ under IHL as well as IHRL. In principle, harm amounting to IHL violations could be addressed through regional IHRL mechanisms (where they exist). Gross human right violations and breaches of IHL have been considered jointly to include within the category of victims those who 'individually or collectively suffered harm' and 'immediate family, dependents of the direct victim and persons who have suffered harm in intervening to assist victims in distress or to prevent victimisation'.[113] For the purpose of TJ, therefore, a careful consideration of not only whether but also how IHL and IHRL interact in a specific context could offer greater opportunities to explore the most effective and legally sound way to pursue accountability for past harm (and, relatedly, justice and reconciliation, as contained in the above-mentioned UN definition).

In addition to the relationship between IHL and IHRL, the acceleration of ICL and the establishment of the ICC (discussed in the first section of this chapter) has influenced how certain IHL violations are accounted for. War crimes, crimes against humanity, genocide and aggression fall expressly within the scope of the Rome Statute, subsuming part of the remit of IHL under ICL.[114] Therefore, specific grave violations of IHL would, *ratione materiae*, fall within the jurisdiction of the ICC. Prior to the establishment of the ICC, the ICTY also linked IHL and international criminal justice, for example, in its notable decision to consider the 'private' crime of rape as a war crime, the most serious IHL violation.[115] The case of *Kunarac* (among others) suggests that ICL can be a vehicle for the implementation and the development of IHL in relation to TJ. In reality, in the absence of an IHL tribunal, the ICC may be the only forum where justice is seen to be done for victims of grave IHL breaches committed by states as well as non-state actors. Nonetheless, there is some unease at how ICL and IHL interact.[116] Bartels identifies, in particular, the tension between

[112] L Zegveld, 'Remedies for Victims of Violations of International Humanitarian law' (2003) 85(851) *International Review of the Red Cross* 497, 500.

[113] Principle 8 of the 2006 Basic Principles and Guidelines on the Right to a Remedy and Reparation for Victims of Gross Violations of International Human Rights Law and Serious Violations of International Humanitarian Law, discussed in J Doak, *Victims' Rights, Human Rights and Criminal Justice* (Oxford, Hart, 2008) 23; MC Bassiouni, 'International Recognition of Victims' Rights' (2006) 6(2) *Human Rights Law Review* 203.

[114] On this, see inter alia: A Cassese, 'On the Current Trends Towards Criminal Prosecution and Punishment of Breaches of International Humanitarian Law' (1998) 9(1) *European Journal of International Law* 2.

[115] See, notably, *Prosecutor v Kunarac, Kovac and Vukovic*, Case No IT-96-23T, Judgment 22 February 2001, discussed in R Dixon, 'Rape as a Crime in International Humanitarian Law: Where to From Here?' (2002) 13(3) *European Journal of International Law* 697.

[116] R Bartels, 'A Fine Line Between Protection and Humanisation: The Interplay Between the Scope of Application of International Humanitarian Law and Jurisdiction over Alleged War Crimes Under International Criminal Law' in TD Gill et al (eds), *Yearbook of International Humanitarian Law*, vol 20, *2017* (Berlin, TMC Asser Press, 2019).

the protection focus of IHL and the presumption of innocence and principle of legality of ICL, and how that may affect prospects of accountability ex post.[117] Moreover, he notes that the invocation of IHL might even justify the killing of alleged fighters and the infliction of collateral damage.[118] As such, there may be unintended consequences that need to be taken into account when identifying the relevant international law elements of the normative framework of TJ to pursue accountability for past harm. This, in turn, feeds into the argument that a clear, coherent and universal international law of TJ remains a fiction.

A further point to raise is that there may also be some symbolic value in privileging an IHL reading over an ICL reading of violations in the context of transitions. To further the goals of TJ more effectively in both international and non-international armed conflicts, Ilya Nuzov argues that trials through IHL rules could be 'beyond the individual-based model of criminal responsibility to encompass the criminal responsibility' of non-state entities.[119] This might be particularly useful in demanding accountability for atrocities from armed groups in their entirety, based on a more holistic understanding of their aims, practices and structure – including chain-of-command considerations.

In addition to the difficulties of justiciability and the ambiguous relationships with IHRL and ICL, the uses of IHL to 'incorporate a full account of successor justice' is challenging in itself.[120] After conflict, 'the obligation to comply with the rules of IHL requiring perpetrators of violations to be punished' may hinder the TJ, for instance, by ruling out certain amnesties or limiting some reconciliation initiatives.[121] However, unlike political crimes and minor common crimes, grave breaches of IHL, including war crimes and torture, in principle cannot be amnestied.[122] The duty to prosecute certain IHL violations sits uncomfortably with the fact that in practice amnesties might be used 'as a bargaining chip in peace processes'.[123] There is, however, a 'forceful legal argument for a flexible approach' at least in relation to NIACs,[124] based on the possibility of amnesty contained in Article 6(5) of the Additional Protocol II of the Geneva Conventions.[125] More generally, as noted by Louise Mallinder, it would not be

[117] ibid 65.
[118] ibid.
[119] Nuzov (n 111) 233.
[120] Teitel (n 2) 35.
[121] Salmón (n 103) 337.
[122] ibid 337ff.
[123] Ambos (n 20) 54.
[124] ibid 65–66.
[125] Protocol Additional to the Geneva Conventions of 12 August 1949, and relating to the Protection of Victims of Non-International Armed Conflicts (Protocol II), 8 June 1977, 1125 UNTS 609, Art 6(5): 'At the end of hostilities, the authorities in power shall endeavour to grant the broadest possible amnesty to persons who have participated in the armed conflict, or those deprived of their liberty for reasons related to the armed conflict, whether they are interned or detained.' See also J Pictet et al, *Commentary on the Additional Protocols of 8 June 1977 to the Geneva Conventions of 12 August 1949* (Geneva, Martinus Nijhoff, 1987) para 4618 explains the purpose of this provision 'to encourage gestures of reconciliation which can contribute to reestablishing normal relations in the life of a nation which has been divided'.

realistic for a state to prosecute every perpetrator, and 'selective prosecutions' exist alongside 'mechanisms to ensure the rights of the victims'.[126] This is reflected in current international practice which 'focuses on prosecuting those who are deemed "most responsible" for instigating and ordering atrocities'.[127] Moreover, truth commissions have also considered the 'punitive or sanctioning aspects of IHL' following armed conflict.[128] This illustrates possible tensions between IHL and certain aspects of TJ. Nevertheless, such tensions are also apparent with other elements of the (somewhat fragmented) international legal framework of TJ, as the following sections on ICL and IHRL illustrate.

B. International Criminal Law

Prosecutions, or at the very least calls to prosecute, at domestic and international level constitute a common feature of many TJ experiences, often coexisting alongside other accountability mechanisms (such as truth commissions). Within the tripartite aims of TJ set out by the UN – accountability, justice and reconciliation – criminal trials can be the most incisive, but also the bluntest, tool. While the focus of the discussion here is not domestic criminal justice,[129] a few general considerations are worth making as they may inform how ICL relates to TJ. Tensions between the competing aims of reconciliation and accountability have been widely discussed in the context of the 'truth v justice' debates.[130] Successor trials, in particular, carry the risks of 'show trials, unbefitting a democracy' and concealing 'manifestations of victor's justice'.[131] There may be further differences between trials in liberalising transitions and in non-liberalising transitions. With reference to the Muslim-majority Arab region (in particular, Egypt, Yemen, Tunisia and Libya) Noha Aboueldahab aptly identifies some of the key problems with prosecutions that occur during non-liberalising, complex transitions.[132] These include the limited scope of the investigations and prosecutions, with 'an emphasis on corruption and economic crimes ... as a means

[126] L Mallinder, 'Can Amnesties and International Justice be Reconciled?' (2007) 1(2) *International Journal of Transitional Justice* 208, 214.

[127] K McEvoy and L Mallinder, 'Amnesties in Transition: Punishment, Restoration, and the Governance of Mercy' (2012) 39(3) *Journal of Law and Society* 410, 416–17.

[128] Salmón (n 103) 350–53, recalling TRCs in Chile, El Salvador, Guatemala and Peru.

[129] On domestic trials, see inter alia L Laplante, 'Outlawing Amnesty: The Return of Criminal Justice in Transitional. Justice Schemes' (2009) 49 *Virginia Journal of International Law* 915.

[130] See, on this tension in general: N Roht-Arriaza and J Mariezcurrena (eds), *Transitional Justice in the Twenty-First Century: Beyond Truth versus Justice* (Cambridge, Cambridge University Press, 2006).

[131] N Kritz, 'The Dilemmas of Transitional Justice' in NJ Kritz (ed), *Transitional Justice: How Emerging Democracies Reckon with Former Regimes*, vol II (Washington, DC, United States Institute of Peace Press, 1995).

[132] N Aboueldahab, *Transitional Justice and the Prosecution of Political Leaders in the Arab Region: A Comparative Study of Egypt, Libya, Tunisia and Yemen* (Oxford, Hart, 2017).

to scapegoat certain high-level individuals to deflect attention from the lack of accountability for a more comprehensive set of human rights violations and their perpetrators'; weak and politicised judiciaries; the contradictory roles of domestic and international actors involved; and the focus on 'crimes committed during the transition, as opposed to crimes during the decades of repressive rule prior to the political transitions'.[133] This evidences the risks of using trials to shield certain chapters of history, bolster renewed illiberal regimes and other intended or unintended consequences that sit uneasily with the aims of TJ. Indeed, Aboueldahab argues that prosecutions in the Arab region challenge the notion of criminal trials as a 'liberalising ritual' theorised by Ruti Teitel.[134] Just as domestic trials may occur in liberalising and non-liberalising contexts, international criminal justice may occur in either.

Moving on to the role of international criminal justice as a component of the normative framework of 'steady-state' TJ, it can be argued that the ICC carries the potential to become a key player.[135] Some have called for a more proactive leadership of that court.[136] Given that international criminal justice as a field 'has developed at the intersection of interstate diplomacy, criminal justice and human rights advocacy', it remains powerful in TJ.[137] According to Teitel's genealogy, the Nuremberg trials at the end of World War II catalysed 'the first phase of transitional justice'.[138] At the same time ICL and IHRL were also developing.[139] As ICL separates state and individual accountability, it is able to provide new opportunities to deal with past abuse.[140] Over time, however, it has become apparent that the role of ICL and of the ICC, in particular, has been modest and more ambivalent.[141] The mandate of the ICC does not necessarily

[133] ibid 2–6.

[134] ibid 9, citing Teitel (n 2) 30.

[135] Teitel (n 44) 90. See also Ambos (n 20); and P Sullo, 'The ICC as a Transitional Justice Actor: New Space for Victims?' [2017] No 1 *Diritti umani e diritto internazionale* 239; J Gallen, 'The International Criminal Court: In the Interests of Transitional Justice?' in C Lawther, L Moffett and D Jacobs (eds), *Research Handbook on Transitional Justice* (Cheltenham, Edward Elgar, 2017).

[136] Inter alia, D Hafner and E King, 'Beyond Traditional Notions of Transitional Justice: How Trials, Truth Commissions, and Other Tools for Accountability Can and Should Work Together' (2007) 30 *British Columbia International & Comparative Law Review* 91; R Lipscomb, 'Restructuring the ICC Framework to Advance Transitional Justice: A Search for a Permanent Solution in Sudan' (2006) 106 *Columbia Law Review* 182; Ambos (n 20) 52ff.

[137] P Dixon and C Tenove, 'International Criminal Justice as a Transnational Field: Rules, Authority and Victims' (2013) 7 *International Journal of Transitional Justice* 393, 411ff.

[138] Teitel (n 44) 70ff.

[139] WA Schabas, 'Synergy or Fragmentation? International Criminal Law and the European Convention on Human Rights' (2011) 9 *Journal of International Criminal Justice* 609.

[140] Teitel (n 44) 73.

[141] See inter alia, OC Okafor and U Ngwaba, 'The International Criminal Court as a "Transitional Justice" Mechanism in Africa: Some Critical Reflections' (2015) 9(1) *International Journal of Transitional Justice* 90; A Branch, 'Dominic Ongwen on Trial: The ICC's African Dilemmas' (2017) 11(1) *International Journal of Transitional Justice* 30; L Moffett, 'Elaborating Justice for Victims at the International Criminal Court: Beyond Rhetoric and The Hague' (2015) 13 *Journal of International Criminal Justice* 281.

exclude other TJ measures, such as truth commissions.[142] Naomi Roht-Arriaza identifies two main approaches to understanding the temporal relationship between TJ and ICL: other TJ mechanisms can act as a precursor to ICL, filling in gaps or providing alternatives to prosecutions, for example, through reparations or truth commissions; or the two may run parallel to each other, as ICL seeks primarily to 'enforce the law' regardless of the circumstances, whereas other TJ tools can be more flexible.[143] As such, as a component of the international normative framework of TJ, and through the ICC, ICL has become normative in TJ, as well as offering a mechanism to be used – or not – in specific transitions.

However, as an institution and in its vulnerability to powerful states, the ICC is not without controversy.[144] Procedurally, UN Security Council (UNSC) referrals to the ICC through UN Charter Chapter VII resolutions highlight the political risks of tying ICL, grave human rights abuses and international peace and security mandates to a forum where five permanent members dominate executive decisions.[145] This has occurred in Darfur (Sudan) and Libya.[146] Likewise, other routes to activate the ICC's jurisdiction – state referrals and *proprio motu* initiatives by the Prosecutor – although based on a state's formal acceptance of jurisdiction, may result from local and global power dynamics (especially in fragile states) which a global criminal court has the responsibility to navigate carefully. As such, even the court's deterrence potential may be compromised.[147]

[142] D Đukić, 'Transitional Justice and the International Criminal Court – In "The Interests of Justice"?' (2007) 89(867) *International Review of the Red Cross* 691.

[143] N Roht-Arriaza, 'Editorial Note' (2013) 7 *International Journal of Transitional Justice* 383, 389–90.

[144] For example: K Mills, 'Bashir Is Dividing Us: Africa and the International Criminal Court' (2012) 34(2) *Human Rights Quarterly* 404; C Gegout, 'The International Criminal Court: Limits, Potential and Conditions for the Promotion of Justice and Peace' (2013) 34(5) *Third World Quarterly* 800; JA Goldston, 'More Candour about Criteria: The Exercise of Discretion by the Prosecutor of the International Criminal Court' (2010) 8(2) *Journal of International Criminal Justice* 383.

[145] Joint reading of Art 13(b) Rome Statute of the International Criminal Court (1998) A/CONF.183/9 and Charter of the United Nations, (1945), Chapter VII 'Action with Respect to Threats to the Peace, Breaches of the Peace, and Acts of Aggression'. On the interactions between the ICC and UNSC, see inter alia: D Akande, 'The Legal Nature of Security Council Referrals to the ICC and its Impact on Al Bashir's Immunities' (2009) 7(2) *Journal of International Criminal Justice* 333; L Condorelli and A Ciampi 'Comments on the Security Council Referral of the Situation in Darfur to the ICC' (2005) 3(3) *Journal of International Criminal Justice* 590; D Akande, 'The Effect of Security Council Resolutions and Domestic Proceedings on State Obligations to Cooperate with the ICC' (2012) 10(2) *Journal of International Criminal Justice* 299; C Stahn, 'Libya, the International Criminal Court and Complementarity: A Test for "Shared Responsibility"' (2012) 10(2) *Journal of International Criminal Justice* 325; M Neuner, 'The Security Council and the ICC: Assessing the First Ten Years of Coexistence' (2012) 18 *New England Journal International & Comparative Law* 283; R Aloisi, 'A Tale of Two Institutions: The United Nations Security Council and the International Criminal Court' in DL Rothe, J Meernik, and T Ingadóttir (eds), *The Realities of International Criminal Justice* (Leiden, Brill Nijhoff, 2013).

[146] Darfur: UNSC Res 1593 (31 March 2005) UN Doc S/RES/1593; Libya: UNSC Res 1970 (26 February 2011) UN Doc S/RES/1970.

[147] K Cronin-Furman, 'Managing Expectations: International Criminal Trials and the Prospects for Deterrence of Mass Atrocity' (2013) 7 *International Journal of Transitional Justice* 434.

Far from being the 'go-to' global court, the ICC's role in TJ processes is potentially as thorny as other mechanisms, and should be approached with a healthy degree of caution alongside all other potential avenues.[148] In some contexts, its narrow focus may do more harm than good for victims, or limit their participation altogether.[149] Nonetheless, the laws of ICL (including the ICC) still constitute an important part of the international normative framework of TJ that underpins transitional truth seeking. And while, once again, the ambiguities of this area of international law's contribution to TJ offer further evidence of the indeterminacy of the legal framework based on which transitional truth seeking occurs, this should not detract from the potential usefulness of ICL in certain contexts.

C. International Human Rights Law

The connections between TJ and IHRL are widely acknowledged, and even the UN promotes TJ through its human rights agenda (discussed below).[150] In the context of transitions, the purpose of IHRL is to hold states accountable for violations; on the other hand, accountability in IHL and ICL extends, respectively, to a range of parties to conflicts and all individuals responsible for international crimes (as outlined earlier). Unlike IHL, IHRL applies in both times of war and peace, and as such is relevant to a much wider range of possible TJ situations. Similarly, compared to ICL, IHRL applies to, and beyond, the four specific crimes listed in the Rome Statute. As such, human rights constitute the most far-reaching element of the international legal framework of TJ. For Frédéric Mégret and Raphael Vagliano there are two main contributions of IHRL to TJ: 'First, human rights law is broadly facilitative and empowering of transitional justice processes', and 'Second, in addition to catalysing transitional justice initiatives through imposing positive obligations on states, IHRL provides distinct limits on what measures can be taken in the name of transitional justice.'[151]

[148] See inter alia D Bosco, *Rough Justice: The International Criminal Court in a World of Power Politics* (Oxford, Oxford University Press, 2013); H Köchler, 'Justice and Realpolitik: The Predicament of the International Criminal Court' (2017) 16(1) *Chinese Journal of International Law* 1.

[149] See eg G Simpson, 'One Among Many: The ICC as a Tool of Justice During Transition' in N Waddell and P Clark (eds), *Courting Conflict? Justice, Peace and the ICC in Africa* (Royal African Society, 2008) 77, available at www.files.ethz.ch/isn/56434/2008-03_ICC%20in%20Africa.pdf; M Pena and G Carayon, 'Is the ICC Making the Most of Victim Participation? (2013) 7(3) *International Journal of Transitional Justice* 518.

[150] Academic commentary on the relationship between TJ and IHRL is significant. See inter alia Arthur (n 19).

[151] F Mégret and R Vagliano, 'Transitional Justice and Human Rights' in C Lawther, L Moffett and D Jacobs (eds.), *Research Handbook on Transitional Justice* (Cheltenham, Edward Elgar, 2017) 95.

Institutionally, the UN championing of TJ is premised on its human rights agenda, and has contributed to promoting this aspect of its normative underpinnings.[152] The Office of the High Commissioner for Human Rights (OHCHR) coordinates TJ matters in relation to human rights.[153] The Human Rights Council has specifically requested the OHCHR 'to continue to enhance its leading role, including with regard to conceptual and analytical work regarding transitional justice, and to assist States to design, establish and implement *transitional justice mechanisms from a human rights perspective*'.[154] The (former) High Commissioner for Human Rights[155] has stated that the UN deals with TJ in close connection with IHRL practice.[156] The (former) Secretary-General followed this approach in the 2010 *Guidance Note on Transitional Justice*.[157] Human rights norms and standards set out by the UN, and its human rights work, guide the international conception of TJ justice.

The academic literature has also contributed to establishing the links between TJ and human rights. As long ago as 1995 the *Transitional Justice* trilogy edited by Neil Kritz made frequent references to human rights, bearing witness to their centrality in the field.[158] Much has been said about how the two cross-fertilise and how IHRL may contribute (or not) to certain transitional aims.[159] Yet, there can also be tensions between the political goals of TJ and human rights law.[160] For example, in dealing with transitions from authoritarianism or conflict, the European Court of Human Rights (ECtHR) has upheld human rights standards set out in the ECHR and case law, instead of allowing derogations motivated by

[152] Grover (n 12) 375.

[153] See A/61/636-S/2006/980 and HRC Res 9/10 of 24/9/2008 in General Assembly, Human Rights Council, *Annual Report of the United Nations High Commissioner for Human Rights and Reports of the Office of the High Commissioner and the Secretary-General, Analytical Study on Human Rights and Transitional Justice* (6 August 2009) (A/HRC/12/18).

[154] HRC Res 9/10 (emphasis added).

[155] L Arbour, 'Economic and Social Justice for Societies in Transition' (2007–08) 40 *New York University Journal of International Law & Policy* 1.

[156] Dialogue with Member States on rule of law at the international level organised by the Rule of Law Unit: 'UN Approach to Transitional Justice' (address by Navanethem Pillay, UN High Commissioner for Human Rights), 23 December 2009, available at www.un.org/ruleoflaw/blog/keyword/dialogue-with-member-states/.

[157] United Nations, *Guidance Note of the Secretary General: UN Approach to Transitional Justice* (n 3).

[158] See generally throughout NJ Kritz (ed), *Transitional Justice: How Emerging Democracies Reckon with Former Regimes*, vols I–III (Washington, DC, United States Institute of Peace Press, 1995).

[159] Inter alia, Arthur (n 19) 358; TD Olsen, LA Payne and AG Reiter 'The Justice Balance: When Transitional Justice Improves Human Rights and Democracy' (2010) 32(4) *Human Rights Quarterly* 980; H Kim and K Sikkink, 'Explaining the Deterrence Effect of Human Rights Prosecutions for Transitional Countries' (2010) 54(4) *International Studies Quarterly* 939; ONT Thoms, J Ron, and R Paris 'State-level Effects of Transitional Justice: What Do We Know?' (2010) 4(3) *International Journal of Transitional Justice* 329; TD Olsen et al 'When Truth Commissions Improve Human Rights' (2010) 4(3) *International Journal of Transitional Justice* 457. In relation to Latin America, see Teitel (n 44) 81.

[160] Sweeney (n 68) 25–27.

exceptional circumstances.[161] Thus, how TJ is embedded in human rights norms should also be considered carefully in light of the context and aims of each transition. It is also important to be mindful of the limits of IHRL even outside the scope of transitions. The presumption of the global bounty of human rights is debatable,[162] as is the usefulness of IHRL instruments.[163] Some have discussed the limitations of human rights in resolving conflict.[164] Others suggest that promoting human rights can be 'bad politics' if it legitimises repressive states or facilitates the harm it seeks to prevent.[165] Some have gone further, describing the notion of human rights as 'fraudulent'.[166] Moreover, how its instruments are rooted in colonial legacies is well known.[167] Despite the range of critiques, human rights offer an important general legal foundation that can be adapted in light of the specificities of each context; moreover, unlike IHL and ICL, IHRL applies to everyone, everywhere, in times of war and peace, and as such can offer a more universal normative framework for TJ.

In addition to offering further normative foundations for accountability for the range of atrocities regulated by IHL and ICL discussed above, human rights provide a broader temporal reach during transitions.[168] Human rights norms apply during conflict and authoritarianism, and the transition itself, as well as after the violence ends and before it started. This allows for a consideration of root causes of conflict,[169] despite the problems associated with the expansion of TJ into questions of development and transformative justice.[170]

[161] ibid 28ff.

[162] On the critique of human rights, inter alia, see also S Marks (2011) 'Human Rights and Root Causes' 74(1) *MLR* 57; M Ignatieff, *Human Rights as Politics and Idolatry* (Princeton, NJ, Princeton University Press, 2001); C Douzinas, *Human Rights and Empire: The Political Philosophy of Cosmopolitanism* (London, Routledge, 2007); AA An-Na'im (ed), *Human Rights in Cross-cultural Perspectives: A Quest for Consensus* (Philadelphia, University of Pennsylvania Press, 1995).

[163] OA Hathaway, 'Do Human Rights Treaties Make a Difference?' (2002) *Yale Law Journal* 1935.

[164] R Manikkalingam, 'Promoting Peace and Protecting Rights: How Are Human Rights Good and Bad for Resolving Conflict?' (2008) 5(1) *Essex Human Rights Review* 1.

[165] D Kennedy 'International Human Rights Movement: Part of the Problem?' (2002) 15 *Harvard Human Rights Journal* 101, 123ff.

[166] JO Nelson, 'Against Human Rights' (1990) 65 *Philosophy* 341.

[167] See the vast TWAIL scholarship on this, eg M Mutua, 'Savages, Victims, and Saviors: The Metaphor of Human Rights' (2001) 42 *Harvard International Law Journal* 201.

[168] On time and transitional justice more generally, see N Mueller-Hirth and S Rios Oyola (eds), *Time and Temporality in Transitional and Post-conflict Societies* (Abingdon, Routledge, 2018); TO Hansen, 'The Time and Space of Transitional Justice' in C Lawther, L Moffett and D Jacobs (eds), *Research Handbook on Transitional Justice* (Cheltenham, Edward Elgar, 2017).

[169] On this see, inter alia: LJ Laplante, 'Transitional Justice and Peace Building: Diagnosing and Addressing the Socioeconomic Roots of Violence Through a Human Rights Framework' (2008) 2(3) *International Journal of Transitional Justice* 331.

[170] See arguments in P McAuliffe, *Transformative Transitional Justice and the Malleability of Post-conflict States* (Cheltenham, Edward Elgar, 2017), and earlier, R Mani, 'Dilemmas of Expanding Transitional Justice, or Forging the Nexus Between Transitional Justice and Development' (2008) 2(3) *International Journal of Transitional Justice* 253; P Gready and S Robins, 'From Transitional to Transformative Justice: A New Agenda for Practice' (2014) 8(3) *International Journal of Transitional Justice* 339; L Waldorf, 'Anticipating the Past: Transitional Justice and Socio-economic Wrongs' (2012) 21(2) *Social & Legal Studies* 171.

The 2010 *UN Guidance Note* calls for TJ to take into account 'the root causes of the conflict and the related violations of all rights, including civil, political, economic, social and cultural rights'.[171] Former UN High Commissioner for Human Rights, Louise Arbour, has made a strong case for the inclusion of economic, social and cultural rights (ESCR) as an integral part of TJ.[172] The holistic interpretation of TJ that Arbour borrows from Alexander Boraine, one of the founders of the International Center for Transitional Justice (ICTJ), 'offers a deeper, richer and broader vision of justice' that includes victims, perpetrators and society at large.[173]

Similar points are made in the literature.[174] Reflecting the expanding reach of the field, this approach situates TJ within broader questions of sustainable peace[175] and development,[176] attempting to put an end not only to political and armed violence but also to socioeconomic inequalities.[177] Integrating ESCR in TJ may help address violations that affect entire communities, including famine,[178] lack of healthcare,[179] settler-colonial harms inflicted on indigenous peoples[180] and unequal land distribution.[181] Denial of food, healthcare and structural social marginalisation all fall within the scope of 'subsistence harms', proposed by Diana Sankey as a novel category of 'interrelated mental, physical

[171] *UN Approach to Transitional Justice* (March 2010) 3.

[172] Arbour (n 155) 20.

[173] ibid, 2, quoting A Boraine, 'Transitional Justice: A Holistic Interpretation' (2006) 60 *Journal of International Affairs* 17, 18.

[174] eg S Szoke-Burke, 'Not Only Context: Why Transitional Justice Programs Can No Longer Ignore Violations of Economic and Social Rights' (2015) 50 *Texas International Law Journal* 465; DN Sharp, 'Addressing Economic Violence in Times of Transition: Towards a Positive-Peace Paradigm for Transitional Justice' (2011) 35 *Fordham Internationl Law Journal* 780.

[175] Inter alia, Sriram (n 40); Laplante (n 169).

[176] On the theme of transitional justice and development, see inter alia, P de Greiff and R Duthie (eds), *Transitional Justice and Development: Making Connections* (Social Science Research Council and International Center for Transitional Justice, 2009); Mani (n 170); R Duthie, 'Toward a Development-Sensitive Approach to Transitional Justice' (2008) 2(3) *International Journal of Transitional Justice* 292; C Huggins, 'Linking Broad Constellations of Ideas: Transitional Justice, Land Tenure Reform, and Development' in P de Greiff and R Duthie (eds), *Transitional Justice and Development: Making Connections* (Social Science Research Council and International Center for Transitional Justice, 2009) 332. For an overview of economic questions and TJ, see inter alia, Z Miller, 'Effects of Invisibility: In Search of the "Economic" in Transitional Justice' (2008) 2 *International Journal of Transitional Justice* 266.

[177] H Franzki and MC Olarte, 'Understanding the Political Economy of Transitional Justice: A Critical Theory Perspective' in S Buckley-Zistel, T Koloma Beck, C Braun and F Mieth (ed), *Transitional justice theories* (London, Routledge, 2013) 217–18.

[178] eg R C DeFalco, 'Accounting for Famine at the Extraordinary Chambers in the Courts of Cambodia: The Crimes against Humanity of Extermination, Inhumane Acts and Persecution' (2011) 5 *International Journal of Transitional Justice* 142.

[179] B Harris et al, 'Bringing Justice to Unacceptable Health Care Services? Street-Level Reflections from Urban South Africa' (2014) 8 *International Journal of Transitional Justice* 141, 160.

[180] For example in Australia, see inter alia J Balint, J Evans and N McMillan, 'Rethinking Transitional Justice, Redressing Indigenous Harm: A New Conceptual Approach' (2014) 8 *International Journal of Transitional Justice* 194.

[181] C Huggins, *Linking Broad Constellations of Ideas: Transitional Justice, Land Tenure Reform, and Development* (ICTJ Research Brief, July 2009).

and social elements' of the minimal 'conditions necessary for people to survive and live' which require recognition in TJ.[182] This approach acknowledges the material needs of victims/survivors, which can be more pressing than the realisation of civil and political rights as part of TJ.

Despite these commendable intentions, however, TJ alone is unable to respond to ESCR considerations fully; moreover, extending its reach to embed ESCR aims may be impractical,[183] and much like for civil and political rights, mostly aspirational.[184] In addition, while addressing socioeconomic rights as part of TJ could help prevent conflict recurrence, its mechanisms might fall into the trap of reproducing past inequalities through a mix of neoliberalism, colonialism, postcolonialism and globalisation.[185] Linking TJ initiatives to important, radical long-term development aims carries a double warning: firstly, the promise of security and material well-being is unlikely to be honoured by TJ mechanisms alone; secondly, focusing excessively on long-term social and economic justice aims may cause additional grievances and further exacerbate social tensions.

Gradually, a more ESCR-sensitive approach to TJ has emerged.[186] Thematically, and in relation to specific TJ experiences, the right to property is a core issue now addressed in the literature.[187] In relation to international (criminal) case law with significant human rights ramifications, such as the ICTY case of *Kupreskic*, Arbour recalls that the 'comprehensive destruction of homes and property may constitute the crime against humanity of persecution when committed with the requisite intent'.[188] This echoes IHL provisions, and in particular the Geneva Conventions in which 'intentionally using starvation of civilians as a method of warfare by depriving them of objects indispensable to their survival, including wilfully impeding relief supplies, is also recognised as an international crime'.[189] Seeking the restitution of property after conflict or

[182] D Sankey, 'Towards Recognition of Subsistence Harms: Reassessing Approaches to Socioeconomic Forms of Violence in Transitional Justice' (2014) 8 *International Journal of Transitional Justice* 121, 126.

[183] Waldorf (n 170).

[184] E Schmid and A Nolan, '"Do No Harm"? Exploring the Scope of Economic and Social Rights in Transitional Justice' (2014) 8 *International Journal of Transitional Justice* 362.

[185] I Muvingi, 'Sitting on Powder Kegs: Socioeconomic Rights in Transitional Societies' (2009) 3 *International Journal of Transitional Justice* 163, 167, 178.

[186] See eg DN Sharp (ed), *Justice and Economic Violence in Transition* (New York, Springer 2014); Gready and Robins (n 170) 345ff.

[187] eg B Atuahene, 'Property and Transitional Justice' (2010) 58 *UCLA Law Review Discourse* 65; B Atuahene, 'The Importance of Conversation in Transitional Justice: A Study of Land Restitution in South Africa' (2014) 39(4) *Law & Social Inquiry* 902; C Kamau, 'Transitional Justice as a Path to Distributive Justice: A Jurisprudential and Legal Case for Land Restitution in Kenya' (2016) 1 *Strathmore Law Review* 25.

[188] Arbour (n 155) 15. The case is *Kupreskic*, Case No IT-95-16-T, Trial Judgment, 14 January 2000.

[189] ibid, 15. See Protocols Additional to the Geneva Conventions 1949, and Relating to the Protection of Victims of International Armed Conflict (Protocol I) Art 54 para 1, 1977; and Rome Statute of the ICC Art 8 para 2(b) (xxv).

authoritarianism, however, is not straightforward. An example of this is found in the context of decommunisation in Europe: the ECtHR has favoured stability of property relations and the prospective rule of law rather than granting restitutions to original owners.[190] The Court found that 'long-extinguished' property rights could not be revived' and thus property restitution was not due after the fall of communism.[191] All of this suggests that while property rights are an apparently tangible area of ESCR in relation to TJ, their use does not always redress past harm in a tangible way. Nonetheless, as will be discussed in Chapter 3, human rights cases on property restitution after transitions might perform an important archival function, contributing to the 'legal truth' of widespread past harm with long-term material consequences.

A further area to consider in relation to ESCR and TJ is the role that economic crimes, including corruption, played in the violence.[192] TJ initiatives might uncover links between commercial loans and gross human rights violations, raising questions of corporate accountability[193] and corporate complicity.[194] International donors and international financial institutions (IFIs) may contribute to the propping up of abusive governments – as was the case with Mubarak's regime in Egypt.[195] Juan Pablo Bohoslavsky argues that 'lenders providing financial assistance to authoritarian regimes should be held responsible for complicity if they knew or should have known that they would facilitate human rights abuses', recalling that IFIs are 'under [an] obligation not to violate or become complicit in the violation of general rules of human rights law' as well as *jus cogens*.[196] An ESCR-sensitive approach to TJ may also consider what to do with massive sovereign debt incurred by former authoritarian regimes to support a system of human rights violations.[197] Accountability for these

[190] T Allen, 'Restitution and Transitional Justice in the European Court of Human Rights' (2006–07) 13 *Columbia Journal of European Law* 1.

[191] P Macklem, 'Rybná 9, Praha 1: Restitution and Memory in International Human Rights Law' (2005) 16 *European Journal of International Law* 1 citing the case of *Gratzinger*.

[192] R Carranza, 'Plunder and Pain: Should Transitional Justice Engage with Corruption and Economic Crimes?' (2008) 2 *International Journal of Transitional Justice* 310.

[193] S Michalowski (ed), *Corporate Accountability in the Context of Transitional Justice* (London, Routledge, 2013); and S Michalowski, 'No Complicity Liability for Funding Gross Human Rights Violations?' (2012) 30 *Berkeley Journal of International Law* 451, 517ff.

[194] JP Bohoslavsky and V Opgenhaffen, 'The Past and Present of Corporate Complicity: Financing the Argentinean Dictatorship' (2010) 23 *Harvard Human Rights J* 157; and JP Bohoslavsky and M Rulli, 'Corporate Complicity and Finance as a 'Killing Agent': The Relevance of the Chilean Case' (2010) 8 *Journal of International Criminal Justice* 829. On the role of big business in the Latin American dictatorships, see V Basualdo, H Berghoff, M Bucheli (eds), *Big Business and Dictatorships in Latin America: A Transnational History of Profits and Repression* (Cham, Springer International, 2021).

[195] R Abou-El-Fadl, 'Beyond Conventional Transitional Justice: Egypt's 2011 Revolution and the Absence of Political Will' (2012) 6 *International Journal of Transitional Justice* 318.

[196] JP Bohoslavsky, 'Tracking Down the Missing Financial Link in Transitional Justice' (2012) 1 *International Human Rights Law Review* 54, 78.

[197] S Michalowski and JP Bohoslavsky, 'Ius Cogens, Transitional Justice and Other Trends of the Debate on Odious Debts: A Response to the World Bank Discussion Paper on Odious Debts'

violations is an important aspect of TJ inasmuch as it casts a wider gaze over the context of abuse and its international enablers; nonetheless, the possibilities of human rights are limited.[198] As such, designers of TJ initiatives in each context would do well to creatively explore other ways of revealing how international donors and financial institutions might have enabled violence during conflict and authoritarianism that exacerbated harm inflicted locally.

Embedding TJ in the civil and political dimension of human rights (CPR) is no less complex. While violations of CPR during conflict and under authoritarianism are rife, and encompass a wide range of harm, ranging from gender-based violence, forced disappearances, torture, extrajudicial killings and official policies of targeting and discrimination, existing TJ tools prove to be ineffective in delivering the tripartite aims of accountability, justice and reconciliation. Given the criminal nature of many of these specific violations of CPR, prosecutions may seem the most attractive mechanism, although, as discussed earlier, there are serious conceptual and practical flaws to this approach. To avoid the pitfalls of criminal law, human rights norms in support of investigations (even non-criminal) can help achieve better results in line with the aims of accountability, justice and reconciliation. Specifically, and as discussed in detail in Chapter 4, the emerging right to truth can assist individual victims and survivors, as well as societies at large, in reckoning with legacies of past abuse beyond criminal accountability in the light of each context.

Ensuring that TJ initiatives rest upon solid international law foundations – and in particular human rights – has numerous advantages, of which two stand out for their potential to afford greater local relevance. Firstly, human rights, at least theoretically, provide a framework for inclusivity and non-discrimination in dealing with the past and building a better future based on basic freedoms and access to resources. Adopting a human rights focus in TJ may also help mitigate the detrimental effects of power structures or exalting certain narratives over others,[199] as well as limiting the (continued) marginalisation of large parts of society, including women and girls,[200] and also LGBT+ people.[201] Secondly, a human rights approach to TJ may also draw on local solutions to ensure TJ

(2009–10) 48 *Columbia Journal of Transnational Law* 59, 92ff. On transitional justice and odious debt, see also DC Gray, 'Devilry, Complicity and Greed: Transitional Justice and Odious Debt' (2007) 70 *Law and Contemporary Problems* 137.

[198] C Rose, 'The Limitations of a Human Rights Approach to Corruption' (2016) 65 *ICLQ* 405.

[199] Leebaw (n 9) 118.

[200] See eg C Bell and C O'Rourke, 'Does Feminism Need a Theory of Transitional Justice? An Introductory Essay' (2007) 1(1) *International Journal of Transitional Justice* 23; F Ní Aoláin, 'Women, Security, and the Patriarchy of Internationalized Transitional Justice' (2009) 31(4) *Human Rights Quarterly* 1055; B Hamber, 'Masculinity and Transitional Justice: An Exploratory Essay' (2007) 1(3) *International Journal of Transitional Justice* 375; F Ní Aoláin, 'Advancing Feminist Positioning in the Field of Transitional Justice' (2012) 6(2) *International Journal of Transitional Justice* 205; S Buckley-Zistel and R Stanley (eds), *Gender in Transitional Justice* (London, Palgrave, 2014).

[201] P Bueno-Hansen, 'The Emerging LGBTI Rights Challenge to Transitional Justice in Latin America' (2018) 12(1) *International Journal of Transitional Justice* 126.

reflects the context, including relevant informal and customary norms. Indeed, understanding the challenges and opportunities of culturally responsive TJ is key to designing (participatory) processes that suit the needs of a beneficiary community.[202] Awareness of informal normative sources (such as traditional or religious norms) is, arguably, crucial for developing human-rights-oriented TJ mechanisms that resonate with the victims' visions of justice, which may in turn increase their involvement in transitional processes. These themes will be explored in Chapters 5 and 6, with particular reference to how *shari'ah* relates to TJ, and its truth-seeking aims, in Muslim-majority settings. The final section of this chapter will consider how the indeterminacy and gaps in the normative framework of TJ premised on international law (described above) can be complemented by local understandings of justice.

IV. THE LOCAL NORMATIVE SOURCES OF TRANSITIONAL JUSTICE

Having reviewed the international legal provisions that underpin the normative framework of TJ, this section reflects on how informal local norms might inform specific contexts. The lack of a clear, static, universal law of TJ is useful because it allows for the recognition of 'multiple legal and quasi-legal orders', including international law and other forms of law, which might all possess a degree of 'legal validity' in a given community.[203] Following Bell's helpful adoption of Brian Tamanaha's definition of law as 'whatever people identify and treat through their social practices as "law"', the legal framework of TJ is understood through the lens of legal pluralism (discussed in more detail in Chapter 2).[204] Therefore, the juxtaposition between norms and principles of different specialised regimes in international law and formal and informal, official and unofficial, written and unwritten local norms operates within the complex power dynamics, interpretative efforts and the work (activism as well as inaction) of key social and political actors. Moreover, TJ operates in specific social, political and cultural contexts: Lieselotte Viaene and Eva Brems consider 'cultural challenges' as 'part of a critical evaluation' of the field, attested by a growing interest in 'bottom-up, interdisciplinary, empirical and concrete approaches'.[205] TJ initiatives that combine different types of formal as well as unofficial law (including informal, customary or religious normative principles) may help contextualise global

[202] L Viaene and E Brems, 'Transitional Justice and Cultural Contexts: Learning from the Universality Debate' (2010) 28(2) *NQHR* 199.

[203] Bell (n 31) 295–96.

[204] ibid, discussing BZ Tamanaha, 'A Non-essentialist Version of Legal Pluralism' (2000) 27 *Journal of Law and Society* 296, 319.

[205] Viaene and Brems (n 202) 211.

norms in local language and offer grassroots legitimacy[206] – but such initiatives also carry a set of challenges, as discussed throughout this book.[207]

A. The Shift to Local Transitional Justice: Opportunities and Challenges

Despite the dominance of international law in the legal framework for TJ, local, unofficial norms and practices play a crucial role in determining the bottom-up credibility and viability of TJ initiatives. In principle, the broad compatibility between the international legal framework of TJ and local norms is sanctioned in the UN report *The Rule of Law and Transitional Justice in Conflict and Post-conflict Situations*, which states that international law can be accommodated by all legal systems and traditions.[208] International law could offer 'a notion of best practice', to 'encourage people to comply through processes that include democratic dialogue on how international standards are best implemented in any one context'.[209] Moreover, the normative uncertainties of TJ offer the 'potential for genuine transformation of the international balance of powers' promulgated by international law.[210] But international law should not become a 'strait jacket' upon states or on local communities wanting to think creatively about TJ.[211] Some TJ experiences combine different layers of law at international, domestic and local levels. A high-profile example is offered in Rwanda, where the International Criminal Tribunal for Rwanda (ICTR), domestic trials and local *gacaca* courts coexisted and addressed different groups of alleged perpetrators.[212] The *gacaca* embodied a (reinterpreted) form of

[206] J Ramji-Nogales, 'Designing Bespoke Transitional Justice: A Pluralist Process Approach' (2010) 32(1) *Michigan Journal of International Law* 1.

[207] See eg P McAuliffe (n 5).

[208] United Nations, *The Rule of Law and Transitional Justice in Conflict and Post-conflict Societies* (n 3) 5.

[209] Bell (n 1) 124.

[210] MC Okello, 'Afterward: Elevating Transitional Local Justice or Crystallizing Global Governance?' in R Shaw and L Waldorf (eds), *Localizing Transitional Justice: Interventions and Priorities after Mass Violence* (Stanford, CA, Stanford University Press, 2010) 275.

[211] Turner (n 14) 149.

[212] For background on the ICTR, see inter alia: P Akhavan 'The International Criminal Tribunal for Rwanda: The Politics and Pragmatics of Punishment' (1996) *American Journal of International Law* 501; W Schabas, *The UN International Criminal Tribunals: The Former Yugoslavia, Rwanda and Sierra Leone* (Cambridge, Cambridge University Press, 2006); at national level: MH Morris, 'The Trials of Concurrent Jurisdiction: The Case of Rwanda' (1996) 7 *Duke Journal of Comparative & International Law* 349; and on the *gacaca*, P Clark, *The Gacaca Courts, Post-genocide Justice and Reconciliation in Rwanda: Justice Without Lawyers* (Cambridge, Cambridge University Press, 2010); A des Forges and T Longman, 'Legal Responses to Genocide in Rwanda' in E Stover and HM Weinstein (eds), *My Neighbor, My Enemy: Justice and Community in the Aftermath of Mass Atrocity* (Cambridge, Cambridge University Press, 2004); P Sullo, *Beyond Genocide: Transitional Justice and Gacaca Courts in Rwanda. The Search for Truth Justice and Reconciliation* (The Hague, Springer-Asser Press, 2018); S Thomson and R Nagy, 'Law, Power and Justice: What Legalism Fails to Address in the Functioning of Rwanda's Gacaca Courts' (2011) 5(1) *International Journal of Transitional Justice* 11.

community justice for lower-level perpetrators who still lived in the communities they had harmed and were 'based on indigenous models of local justice', involving, according to some estimates, up to one million individuals.[213]

Some note that 'North Atlantic' global conceptions of human rights, hierarchies of needs and procedural mechanisms to redress past violations may reject 'indigenous or "traditional" practices' presumed to be 'inconsistent with "universal" human rights norms'.[214] This tension lies at the heart of the localisation process. Acknowledging this, and reaffirming the priority given to the local level, the African Union's Transitional Justice Policy 2019 (AUTJP) includes multiple references to the importance of local ownership, 'to ensure that TJ processes are aligned to local needs and aspirations, enhance a common understanding of a shared vision, and maximize public support and ownership'.[215] This carries both a domestic, state-driven dimension as well as a local grassroots level. A significant role is afforded to traditional forms of local justice: 'alongside the formal system of national and/or special or hybrid courts, African traditional justice systems should be adapted for dealing with appropriate crimes at the community level'.[216] These systems are described as 'traditional adjudicative processes such as clan or customary courts and community-based dialogue', which may include 'acknowledgement of responsibility and the suffering of victims', 'showing remorse', 'asking for forgiveness', 'paying for compensation or making reparation' and 'reconciliation'.[217] The normative framework for justice and accountability in this report explicitly includes cultural and religious legal sources.[218] Taken as a whole, this document offers an important example of the possible integration of local, non-state norms alongside domestic and international law.

Moreover, the importance of eschewing a one-size-fits-all approach and instead engaging the local and indigenous dimensions of TJ has long been acknowledged in the literature as well.[219] In fact, an exclusive focus on formal written law and strict legalism has been viewed as offering only a partial picture

[213] W Schabas, 'Genocide Trials and Gacaca Courts' (2005) 3(4) *Journal of International Criminal Justice* 879.

[214] AA An-Na'im, 'Editorial Note: From the Neocolonial "Transitional" to Indigenous Formations of Justice' (2013) 7 *International Journal of Transitional Justice* 197.

[215] African Union, Transitional Justice Policy (2019), para 28, available at au.int/sites/default/files/documents/36541-doc-au_tj_policy_eng_web.pdf.

[216] ibid para 80.

[217] ibid para 18, and 56–59.

[218] ibid 81.

[219] eg L Waldorf, 'Mass Justice for Mass Atrocity: Rethinking Local Justice as Transitional Justice' (2006) 79(1) *Temple Law Review* 1; McEvoy and McGregor (n 14); R Shaw and L Waldorf (eds), *Localizing Transitional Justice: Interventions and Priorities after Mass Violence* (Stanford, CA, Stanford University Press, 2010); Viaene and Brems (n 202); L Waldorf, 'Local Transitional Justice – Customary Law, Healing Rituals, and Everyday Justice' in O Simić (ed), *An Introduction to Transitional Justice* (London, Routledge, 2017).

of the myriad rules regulating TJ in any given setting.[220] As the next chapter will explore in greater detail, however, turning to local norms, including unofficial and unwritten sources, requires mindfulness. Numerous challenges emerge from applications of local justice, as summed up by Lars Waldorf.[221] Firstly, by focusing on groups rather than individuals, local justice conceptions may eclipse individual justice to pursue collective benefits, favouring powerful actors to the detriment of marginalised groups.[222] An example of this is violence within a single group, such as gender-based violence (GBV) and violence against women and girls used as an internal mechanism of social control, as well as sexual violence as a weapon of war between groups (a war crime).[223] Given the frequent relegation of women to the periphery of traditional understandings of justice, certain gendered harms may be trivialised.[224] Secondly, in the quest for compromise and community harmony, local justice initiatives may tolerate some types of harm as minor in the bigger picture, such as minority rights of politically and socially marginalised groups.[225] Thirdly, certain aims of local justice may skew the focus of TJ in the direction of material rather than towards moral responsibility, ignoring root causes of conflict and power distribution.

There is a growing body of literature that unpacks the range of challenges ensuing from turning to local dimensions of justice, adding depth and nuance to how TJ localisation might be understood and implemented.[226] A more holistic problematisation of the turn to the local is outlined by Adam Kochanski: first, the framing of local TJ processes as judicial 'mask[s] the power dynamics at play between different categories of actors … that have the potential to distort these processes'; second, there are many 'assumptions about the purported benefits of localising TJ, without problematizing the extent' of their local legitimacy for all sectors of society, and more tangibly their effectiveness 'in promoting reconciliation and justice'.[227] Kochanski also interrogates what is meant by 'local

[220] On the limitations of legalism in TJ, see K McEvoy, 'Beyond Legalism' (n 21).

[221] This list draws on Waldorf, 'Mass Justice for Mass Atrocity' (n 219) 9ff, discussing J Stevens, *Traditional and Informal Justice Systems in Africa, South Asia and the Caribbean* (London, Penal Reform International, 1999) 5–7, 13.

[222] Ibid.

[223] On girl child soldiers and GBV within fighting groups, see K Fisher, *Transitional Justice for Child Soldiers: Accountability and Social Reconstruction in Post-Conflict Contexts* (London, Palgrave Macmillan, 2013), 170.

[224] See broadly, E Porter, 'Gendered Narratives: Stories and Silences in Transitional Justice' (2016) 17(1) *Human Rights Review* 35; J Lemaitre and KB Sandvik, 'Beyond Sexual Violence in Transitional Justice: Political Insecurity as a Gendered Harm' (2014) 22(3) *Feminist Legal Studies* 243.

[225] On the general topic of minority rights and transitional justice, see C Chapman, *Transitional Justice and the Rights of Minorities and Indigenous Peoples*, Research Brief (New York, ICTJ, 2009).

[226] eg Sharp (n 17); McAuliffe (n 5); and Kochanski (n 5); M Schotsmans, 'The Role of Tradition in Transitional Justice' in M Schotsmans, E Brems and G Corradi (eds), *International Actors and Traditional Justice in Sub-Saharan Africa* (Cambridge, Intersentia, 2015).

[227] Kochanski (n 5) 27.

transitional justice process', often an ambiguous all-encompassing term used in different ways, and proposes a helpful working definition:

> (1) a locally *based* practice that is (2) informal, participatory, and holistic in nature and that (3) seeks to address a legacy of human rights violations in the wake of a mass atrocity. Such initiatives bring together various societal actors in an open-ended process that aims to achieve justice, reconciliation, and memory. They often, but not always, tap into traditional symbols and rituals, can be introduced from above or from below, and typically have national and international linkages.[228]

Local TJ, therefore, is distinct from a domestic, state-based initiatives, but inherits some of its problems. Just as state-led TJ carries significant political connotations and risks,[229] the community focus of local and traditional forms of justice may strengthen abusive power structures. Viaene and Brems caution against 'incorrect simplistic notions of culture or tradition' and government attempts 'to cover up their shortcomings in dealing with the past' through cultural arguments.[230] Waldorf also warns against romanticising local justice 'by downplaying its coercive aspects and its function in asserting (or reasserting) social control'.[231] Drawing on Hobsbawm and Ranger's seminal work on *The Invention of Tradition*, 'what passes for harmonious, indigenous custom are more often than not "invented traditions" designed to promote social control and political ideologies'; as such, demystifying local justice facilitates an honest appraisal of its role in TJ.[232] Similarly, Kochanski identifies 'a "romanticized" conception of grassroots methods and an overemphasis on their legality, rather than on the *politics* driving their use'.[233] This, he continues, has 'predisposed scholars to discuss a version of local justice they *want* to see work' overlooking 'local–national power asymmetries and veiled political agendas'.[234] This book attempts to engage with this crucial point, as will be discussed in subsequent chapters regarding the deployment of Islamic law in relation to transitional truth seeking. In all social contexts there is potential for abuse by powerful actors: picking, choosing and promoting which suite of international, domestic and local norms should ground a particular TJ process – including norms governed by religion – is an exquisitely political matter.

[228] ibid 28–29.

[229] See, for example, this interesting study of Brazil: N Schneider and G Iecker de Almeida, 'The Brazilian National Truth Commission (2012–2014) as a State-Commissioned History' in B Bevernage and N Wouters (eds), *The Palgrave Handbook of State-sponsored History After 1945* (London, Palgrave Macmillan, 2018) 638.

[230] Viaene and Brems (n 202) 220.

[231] Waldorf, 'Mass Justice for Mass Atrocity' (n 219) 10.

[232] ibid 6, citing E Hobsbawm and T Ranger (eds), *The Invention of Tradition* (Cambridge, Cambridge University Press, 1983). On the *gacaca*, see eg Clark (n 212) 47ff.

[233] Kochanski (n 5) 36.

[234] ibid.

B. Religious Norms, Actors and Transitional Justice

Efforts to embed TJ in local contexts can import a range of additional normative elements, including religion.[235] When there are strong individual and collective religious sentiments in society, religious norms and actors may resonate in TJ initiatives, alongside formal domestic law, international law and other informal local norms. Even under a liberal human rights paradigm, paying attention to religion is desirable because its exclusion or restriction 'would not only be illiberal but would stifle a valuable source of healing traumatized societies'.[236] The encounter between religion and TJ emerges through two intertwined elements, namely the normativity of religious principles, and the role and authority of religious actors (as discussed in Chapter 5 in relation to Islamic law and jurisprudence). Religious principles may influence the design and development of TJ initiatives in various ways, including directly through positive (state) law that embodies religious norms, or through widely accepted unofficial norms, as well as indirectly through psychological and social factors (discussed below). Religious actors play a role in interpreting those principles, and furthering or hindering TJ initiatives.[237] Drawing on John Brewer's theorisation of the complicated relationship between religion and TJ, two main approaches emerge: one incidental (neutral), which can be either passive/coincidental or an active process capable of both positive and negative effects; and the other programmatic, which champions the positive contribution of religion to TJ.[238] Of course, in light of the discussion in the previous section, the latter is also open to misappropriation for political ends. The discussion that follows proceeds on the potential basis for both approaches.

Broad constructive synergies have been identified between the aims of TJ and religious principles. Daniel Philpott argues that the concept of 'justice' is highly valued in the Abrahamic faiths, and is reflected in the 'purposes, character and actions of God'.[239] Furthermore, the notion of 'reconciliation' and the 'restoration of a broken relationship' feature prominently in both TJ and religion; notably, forgiveness, 'the most distinctive, innovative and controversial practice' offered by religion engages the 'amnesty v accountability' debate in TJ.[240]

[235] J Brewer, D Mitchell and G Leavey, 'Northern Ireland: Religion and Transitional Justice' (2016) 14 *Conflict Studies Quarterly* 74.

[236] D Philpott, 'What Religion Brings to the Politics of Transitional Justice' (2007) 61(1) *Journal of International Affairs* 93, 95, 100; and also D Philpott, 'Religion, Reconciliation, and Transitional Justice: The State of the Field', Social Science Research Paper Working Paper (2007).

[237] See I Cismas, 'Reflections on the Presence and Absence of Religious Actors in Transitional Justice Processes: On Legitimacy and Accountability' in R Duthie and P Seils (eds), *Justice Mosaics: How Context Shapes Transitional Justice in Fractured Societies* (New York, ICTJ, 2017).

[238] Brewer et al (n 235).

[239] Philpott, 'What Religion Brings to the Politics of Transitional Justice' (n 236) 106.

[240] ibid 97ff.

A high-profile, yet contested, example of the encounter between religious principles and TJ is the invocation of a certain Christian understanding of forgiveness in the South African experience, championed by Archbishop Tutu.[241] But religion can also be employed to hinder transitions more explicitly, as a potential palliative against revolution and reform.[242] For instance, in the context of the uses of Islam by Middle Eastern leaders,[243] Sonia L. Alianak has contrasted the post-Arab Spring uprising survival of the rulers in Morocco and Jordan, who have invoked religion (and their status as purported descendants of the prophet Mohammed) to bolster their authority, with the fallen secular leaders of Tunisia and Egypt. This illustrates that invoking religion strategically for political ends in the context of transition – or frustrated transitions – can influence the fragile and uncertain process of change and accountability for past harm.

In a similar vein, the encounter between religious principles and international law that underpins TJ initiatives offers an additional space of enquiry and critique. Mashood Baderin has noted that 'religion has never been completely exiled from international law', as both address 'fundamental issues about ordering society', 'ethical and normative regimes' and are susceptible to being 'politicised and manipulated by elites'.[244] This interface has been described as a 'double-edged sword', capable of both positive and negative uses.[245] Religion can have a tolerant 'universalising influence', which marginalises regressive 'religious extremism based on an alleged dualism between good and evil'.[246] However, this form of 'humane internationalism' inspired by religion has been criticised as echoing the project of the 'gentle civilisers' of the mid-nineteenth century and theories of Christian-driven PIL.[247] Given that international law is 'about

[241] Discussed inter alia in Philpott, 'What Religion Brings to the Politics of Transitional Justice' (n 236); and C Murphy, 'Religion & Transitional Justice' (2020) 149(3) *Daedalus: Journal of the American Academy of Arts & Sciences* 185. Contrast inter alia, R Saunders, 'Questionable Associations: The Role of Forgiveness in Transitional Justice' (2011) 5(1) *International Journal of Transitional Justice* 119.

[242] SL Alianak, *The Transition Towards Revolution and Reform: The Arab Spring Realised?* (Edinburgh, Edinburgh University Press 2014).

[243] SL Alianak, *Middle Eastern Leaders and Islam: A Precarious Equilibrium* (New York, Peter Lang, 2007).

[244] M Baderin, 'Religion and International Law: Friends or Foes?' (2009) 5 *European Human Rights Law Review* 637, 638ff, citing SD Jamar, 'Religion and International Law' (2001) 16 *Journal of Law and Religion* 609.

[245] ibid 649 discussing C Evans, 'The Double-Edged Sword: Religious Influences on International Humanitarian Law' (2005) 6 *Melbourne Journal of International Law* 1.

[246] R Falk, 'Religion and Global Governance: Harmony or Clash' (2002) 19 *International Journal of World Peace* 2, also cited verbatim in Baderin (n 244) 649.

[247] N Berman, 'The Sacred Conspiracy: Religion, Nationalism, and the Crisis of Internationalism' (2011) *Leiden Journal of International Law* 1, 42, citing M Koskenniemi, *The Gentle Civiliser of Nations* (Cambridge, Cambridge University Press, 2004). On this topic, see also how Christianity (and Catholicism in particular) has been fundamental to the creation of PIL: JB Scott, *The Catholic Conception of International Law: Francisco de Vitoria, Founder of the Modern Law of Nations, Francisco Suárez, Founder of the Modern Philosophy of Law in General and in Particular of the Law of Nations: A Critical Examination and a Justified Appreciation* (Washington, DC, Georgetown University Press, 1934).

how people negotiate power, justice, and pragmatic self-interest, at home and abroad',[248] religious law may contribute to justifying or contesting power structures. Indeed, much like other norms, religious laws are interpreted and enforced by living individuals and institutions in specific political contexts.[249] Thus, while 'religion can play a positive and important normative role in international law', its contribution needs to be critically assessed for its potential to empower or disempower individuals and groups.[250]

In addition to the meeting between religious norms and TJ and international law, there is a further dimension of the encounter, which can be incidental, programmatic, or both. In certain contexts, society affords religion a formal and informal normative function on the basis of the majority's religious sentiment. At an emotional level, 'religious psychology' and 'behavioural conditioning' by parents and peer-groups affects ways of thinking about law and justice, including TJ.[251] Psychological and sociological analyses of emotions suggest that independently of positive law, spontaneous behaviour guided by individuals' legal intuitions, which Leon Petrazycki calls 'legal impulsions', can give rise to so-called 'intuitive unofficial law'.[252] Intuitive unofficial law complements positive official law (ie domestic law enforced in state courts), positive unofficial law (described by Adam Podgorecki as 'a mediator or unofficial agency resolving a conflict with reference to positive law or normative facts') and intuitive official law (for example, the *ratio decidendi* of a court judgment based on equity).[253] Consequently, even in formally secular contexts, religious principles may still emerge in the form of 'legal impulsions' that affect the TJ process (this concepts chimes with Rodolfo Sacco's 'cryptotypes' discussed in Chapter 2). Therefore, even in secular contexts, religion can be championed actively or embedded indirectly, even unconsciously through the work of the actors involved in TJ initiatives.

This consideration leads to the second element of the encounter between religion and TJ, namely the role and authority of religious actors. In the context of what Colleen Murphy terms the 'fundamental uncertainty about authority' that characterises the period before (and during) transition, religious actors

[248] AA An-Na'im, 'The Best of Times and the Worst of Times: Human Agency and Human Rights in Islamic Societies' (2004) 1(1) *Muslim World Journal of Human Rights*, cited in Baderin (n 244) 658.

[249] As background, see A Omer, 'Can a Critic Be a Caretaker Too? Religion, Conflict, and Conflict Transformation' (2011) 79(2) *Journal of the American Academy of Religion* 459.

[250] Baderin (n 244) 643ff.

[251] M Bohlander, 'Political Islam and Non-Muslim Religions: A Lesson from Lessing for the Arab Transition' (2014) 25(1) *Islam and Christian–Muslim Relations* 27, 32.

[252] A Podgorecki, 'Unrecognized Father of Sociology of Law: Leon Petrazycki – Reflections Based on Jan Gorecki's Sociology and Jurisprudence of Leon Petrazycki' (1980–81) 15 *Law & Society Review* 183, 189.

[253] ibid, 191ff. This article elaborates on L Petrażycki, *Law and Morality* (Somerset, Transaction Publishers, 2011) (based on previous works of the early 1900s) and Jan Gorecki, *Sociology and Jurisprudence of Leon Petrazycki* (Urbana, IL, University of Illinois Press, 1975).

'frequently play a critical role in the promotion of transitional justice'.[254] Often this occurs against a backdrop of state fragility, where confidence in state institutions and government is marred by recent violence so turning to the divine – and its human representatives – may hold special allure. Religious actors can help fill the gap left by state structures, with the potential to provide capacity and legitimacy to TJ initiatives (and local ownership).[255] Their role, however, remains contested: they may participate in or be absent from TJ initiatives for a variety of reasons, and consequently may enable or spoil the processes.[256] Ioana Cismas identifies the legitimacy of religious actors as 'ascribed on traditional or charismatic grounds', as opposed to international law's rational connotations in TJ.[257] As Cismas, Philpott and others indicate, the 'authoritative pull' of the specialised regimes of international law that underpin TJ (and in particular human rights) can be enhanced by their grounding in religious principles.[258] The ways in which religious actors operate on the international stage to promote competing or complementary religious norms mirrors their role in dealing within the space of international law more broadly.[259]

Because they are civil society actors, religious actors can influence TJ according to the degree of their 'institutional autonomy from the state' before and after the transition.[260] Aaron Boesenecker and Leslie Vinjamuri have argued that 'local faith-based actors' have 'played a pivotal role in adapting international accountability norms and embedding them in local practice'.[261] Despite the spiritual connotations of their raison d'être, religious actors operate politically in ways that compare to secular actors, and should also be similarly scrutinised. Some religious actors have played important political roles fostering transitions, such as Father Alec Reid in Belfast.[262] Others, such as Archbishop Tutu in South Africa and Bishop Gerardi in Guatemala, were crucial in setting up specific TJ initiatives, being sufficiently independent of local authorities,

[254] Murphy (n 241) 195.
[255] Cismas (n 237) 343, 306.
[256] ibid 303.
[257] ibid 305.
[258] ibid 307; D Philpott, *Just and Unjust Peace: An Ethic of Political Reconciliation: An Ethic of Political Reconciliation* (Oxford, Oxford University Press, 2012); MC Bassiouni, *The Shari'a and Islamic Criminal Justice in Time of War and Peace* (Cambridge, Cambridge University Press, 2013) and others.
[259] On this, see I Cismas, *Religious Actors and International Law* (Oxford, Oxford University Press, 2014).
[260] Philpott, 'What Religion Brings to the Politics of Transitional Justice' (n 236) 102, 107. Similar themes are discussed in L Vinjamuri and AP Boesenecker, 'Religious Actors and Transitional Justice' in T Banchoff (ed), *Religious Pluralism, Globalisation and World Politics* (Cambridge, Cambridge University Press, 2008).
[261] AP Boesenecker and L Vinjamuri, 'Lost in Translation? Civil Society, Faith-Based Organizations and the Negotiation of International Norms' (2011) 5 *International Journal of Transitional Justice* 345.
[262] See account in BBC documentary, *14 Days*, and related content available at www.bbc.co.uk/news/uk-28812366.

but enjoying a good degree of popular support and so able to promote truth commissions (notwithstanding the scepticism of others who did not share their religious faith).[263] Nevertheless, bringing religious norms into the space of TJ is not always considered an appropriate or welcome move by all involved. For instance, the emphasis on Christian forgiveness in the South African Truth and Reconcilation Commission (TRC) has been assessed as ambiguous, and might have alienated those of other faiths or other views on forgiveness.[264] In other contexts, religious leaders have 'acquiesced to tyranny, civil war and genocide and were impotent in the aftermath', or were too closely incorporated into the state apparatus to take on a constructive role in transitions, as was the case of the Catholic Church in Argentina and the three religious communities in former Yugoslavia.[265] In the Arab region, al-Azhar, the leading centre for (Sunni) Islamic jurisprudence, has participated in some of the TJ debates, revealing its dual spiritual and political character both in Egypt and across Muslim-majority societies (as discussed in Chapter 6).[266] These summary examples should remind observers to evaluate the role of religious actors in TJ as a secular and not merely spiritual force.

Transitional justice is generally the product of entrepreneurial individuals, groups or organisations at local, regional and international level (including the UN, discussed earlier in this chapter[267]).[268] With regard to their potential engagement with TJ, religious leaders as civil society actors fall into four broad categories as identified by Boesenecker and Vinjamuri: norm makers, norm adaptors, norm facilitators and norm reflectors in 'bridg[ing] the gap between international norms and local practice'.[269] Faith-based organisations are primarily norm-makers, governed by values embedded in organisational 'beliefs and practices' and 'faith doctrines'; as such, when facing a tension between theological principles and IHRL, they tend to defend the ostensibly spiritual norms, regardless of their temporal facets.[270] Norm adaptors are 'highly pragmatic actors' and negotiators operating at 'the interface of the local and the international, seeking to adapt the international accountability norm to fit with local political constraints and culture'.[271] Norm facilitators 'embrace,

[263] Philpott, 'What Religion Brings to the Politics of Transitional Justice' (n 236) 107.

[264] See eg M Shore, *Religion and Conflict Resolution: Christianity and South Africa's Truth and Reconciliation Commission* (London, Routledge, 2009).

[265] Philpott, 'What Religion Brings to the Politics of Transitional Justice' (n 236) 104.

[266] The al-Azhar Declaration in Support for the Arab Revolutions, 31 October 2011, translated by A Maged and A Panepinto, available at www.dur.ac.uk/ilm.

[267] Grover (n 12).

[268] See T Madlingozi, 'On Transitional Justice Entrepreneurs and the Production of Victims' (2010) 2(2) *Journal of Human Rights Practice* 208; van der Merwe and Lykes (n 16); P Gready and S Robins, 'Rethinking Civil Society and Transitional Justice: Lessons from Social Movements and "New" Civil Society' (2017) 21(7) *International Journal of Human Rights* 956.

[269] Boesenecker and Vinjamuri (n 263) 352ff.

[270] ibid 353.

[271] ibid 355ff.

embody and disseminate international expectations for accountability', acting as 'agents of the international human rights community' seeking to 'ensure that local practices governing peace, justice and accountability are consistent with international standards'.[272] Finally, highly localised norm reflectors closely reflect the culture of their environment, and may resist engagement with international law or any other norms perceived as foreign.[273] Norm adaptors and norm facilitators are therefore the most likely to develop conceptions of TJ that meet international law standards and that are also inclusive of local justice and religious principles. In light of the inherent pluralism of TJ, which relies on a variety of sources including 'intuitive unofficial law', these actors may play an important role in synthesising and balancing competing norms. A critical awareness of the composite legal framework of TJ may overcome standoffs between different actors as championing competing normative systems, and carries the potential to include multiple perspectives in the TJ process. By recognising that the normative framework for TJ rests on a variety of laws, international law and religious principles can coexist more explicitly, offering deeper societal meaning to the abstractions of IHRL, IHL and ICL and contributing to greater local ownership of the process.

In sum, TJ based on international law cannot solely rely on international law, because local actors and understandings of justice, including religious leaders and normative values, permeate each process. The relationship between religion and the international law sources of TJ plays out at two levels: the first is doctrinal and relates to principles, and the second relates to the actors that determine the dialogue between the two sets of rules. The latter level also brings to the fore the profane and flexible character of religious law when it meets political interests in the context of TJ. As the next chapter will explore, the theoretical lens of legal pluralism and the methods of comparative law can help make greater sense of the 'mess' of the sources of TJ, and navigate competing directional pulls based on normative principles as well as the actors that drive them.

V. CONCLUSION

This chapter argued that the normative framework of TJ is a relatively fluid combination of differing levels and types of norms juxtaposed and variously applied by a range of actors in specific contexts. As such, an enquiry into the norms that underpin TJ cannot be oblivious to the politics, power structures and cultural dimension of each scenario, as this will inform the ways in which laws are selected, combined and applied, to the relative benefit or detriment for those affected. This framing problematises the book's two core research questions:

[272] ibid 359ff.
[273] ibid 361ff.

How can the truth-seeking element of the international legal framework for TJ be embedded in Muslim-majority societies? To what extent does Islamic law and jurisprudence support the notion of the right to truth about past violence, as emerging in international law? In particular, it probes the very notion of a clearly defined, discrete international legal framework for TJ, suggesting instead that the mess of the law of TJ is an opportunity for a more in-depth, critical evaluation of the normative (and political) forces that guide any given initiative in its unique context.

As an example of legal pluralism (discussed in more detail in Chapter 2) the international legal framework of TJ draws on ICL, IHL and IHRL and is enmeshed with other norms that may include elements or philosophies of local, traditional, customary justice, including religious law – and its proponents. Therefore, in Muslim-majority contexts, it would be amiss to ignore a priori the possible normative influence of the *shari'ah* as a complementary, antagonist or casual bedfellow of the international (and where relevant, domestic) laws (as discussed in Chapters 5 and 6).

Ultimately, the balance between global and local norms in TJ is contextual and informed by different factors specific to each setting – though it may reflect political manipulations, exacerbate structural inequalities, or establish new forms of social violence. With regards to reconstructing narratives of the past through specific laws (as discussed in Chapters 3 and 4), tensions between different norms may in fact conceal competition between different actors and interest groups involved in shaping the process. For this reason, to avoid the entrenchment or marginalisation of certain individuals and communities during TJ processes and also in the post-transitional society, diverse participation under a framework of legal pluralism is more likely to capture the complexities of ensuring accountability, serving justice and achieving reconciliation. The following chapter will explore the theoretical and methodological approaches through which international lawyers working in the field of TJ may engage with local, unofficial norms, including religious principles.

2

Localising the International Law Framework of Transitional Justice in Muslim-Majority Societies: Theoretical and Methodological Considerations

I. INTRODUCTION

IN THE WAKE of the Arab uprisings and ongoing and recent conflicts in Muslim-majority societies[1] in other parts of the world, there is a pressing need to reassess the international law framework of TJ in relation to Islamic legal thought and practices. This task is caught between two competing draws: on the one hand, the wholesale top-down imposition of the (still emerging) global paradigm of TJ premised on international law; and on the other, the apologetic deference to local formal and informal norms inspired by tradition, religion and custom in vernacular settings. Embedding the emerging global normative framework for TJ based on PIL in local conceptions of justice that take into account the specificities and complexities of each setting is firmly on the UN agenda[2] and widely recognised in scholarship as discussed in the previous chapter.[3] How this operates in practice for specific communities facing transition is a crucial question for academics and practitioners alike. But there are deeper theoretical and methodological questions that require closer attention. This chapter tackles the oft-overlooked preliminary issues around concepts and methods that underpin the localisation of the international law framework of TJ, including for truth seeking, in Muslim-majority societies.

[1] To recall what I intend by 'Muslim-majority societies' or 'settings' or 'contexts', see discussion in the Introduction.

[2] United Nations Security Council, 'The Rule of Law and Transitional Justice in Conflict and Post-conflict Situations: Report of the Secretary General' (23 August 2004) S/2004/616, para 36.

[3] Notably R Shaw and L Waldorf (eds), *Localising Transitional Justice: Interventions and Priorities after Mass Violence* (Stanford, CA, Stanford University Press, 2010); L Viaene and E Brems, 'Transitional Justice and Cultural Contexts: Learning from the Universality Debate' (2010) 28(2) *Netherlands Quarterly of Human Rights* 199.

In order to strike an appropriate balance between the global and the local, it is important to consider the opportunities and limitations of this encounter carefully. Indeed, while some concepts may in principle 'travel well' across different jurisdictions, traditions and cultures, the 'dangers of ethnocentric projections' (from both the global and the local), to borrow from Twining,[4] can distort TJ initiatives. This is especially true where there are idealised visions of what TJ, and in particular truth seeking, might look like and be able to deliver.[5] Likewise, embracing local understandings of justice without critical thinking may bring about, make invisible or legitimise other forms of violence or discrimination. In particular, the continuities between the colonial past and postcolonial present may perpetuate structural injustices and stifle the transformative potential of TJ.[6] Hakeem Yusuf pertinently explains that 'it is possible to miss how local elites, who mobilized for and secured power through the doctrine of self-determination, ended up adopting the template of colonial rule for governance in the postcolony'.[7] This admonishment mirrors some of the preoccupations expressed in the critiques to the 'turn to the local' discussed in the previous chapter,[8] and guides the entire book.

This chapter posits, in the first part, that the analytical lens of legal pluralism helps interpret the hybridity and complexities of the (purportedly) universal normative framework for TJ, as well as any given local setting in which multiple normative elements coexist – and the potential interaction between them. Acknowledging legal pluralism reveals how both positive (international) law and unofficial law and discourses about the legal 'can enrich our understanding

[4] W Twining, 'Have Concepts, Will Travel: Analytical Jurisprudence in a Global Context' (2005) 1(1) *International Journal of Law in Context* 5, 34.

[5] On the idealisations of truth seeking, see eg the discussion of the ideal of TJ in JR Rowen, '"We Don't Believe in Transitional Justice": Peace and the Politics of Legal Ideas in Colombia' (2018) 42(3) *Law & Social Inquiry* 622, 637. For a general review of the most common idealisations of TJ, see M Krotoszyński, 'Transitional Justice Models and Analytic Philosophy: Towards Theory' (2017) 42(2) *Polish Political Science Yearbook* 9, 15–16: (1) idealisation connected to dealing with the past, which can be retributive/punitive, or driven by truth and acknowledgement; (2) idealisation based on upholding the rule of law, which can result in three broad sets of initiatives (individualised legal sanctions, historical clarification through truth seeking, or social inclusion); (3) adherence to international human rights law whereby 'punishment is required for certain crimes under international law, including genocide, torture or forced disappearance' (limiting the scope of amnesties) and the limitations imposed on the forms of punishment.

[6] HO Yusuf, 'Colonialism and the Dilemmas of Transitional Justice in Nigeria' (2018) 12(2) *International Journal of Transitional Justice* 257.

[7] ibid 260.

[8] Summed up in P McAuliffe, 'Romanticization versus Integration: Indigenous Justice in Rule of Law Reconstruction and Transitional Justice Discourse' (2013) 5 *Goettingen Journal of International Law* 41; DN Sharp, 'What Would Satisfy Us? Taking Stock of Critical Approaches to Transitional Justice' (2019) 13(3) *International Journal of Transitional Justice* 580; and A Kochanski, 'The "Local Turn" in Transitional Justice: Curb the Enthusiasm' (2020) 22(1) *International Studies Review* 2; and J Obradovic-Wochnik, 'Hidden Politics of Power and Governmentality in Transitional Justice and Peacebuilding: The Problem of "Bringing the Local Back in"' (2020) 23(1) *Journal of International Relations and Development* 117.

of the legal both philosophically, as it concerns itself with the substantive content of norms, but also sociologically, to the extent that it is attentive to the social relevance of these norms'.[9] With this in mind, this chapter builds on a critical understanding of the international legal framework of TJ (presented in the previous chapter), and considers the contributions to that paradigm of official and unofficial local norms imbued with normative elements of cultures, customs, traditions and religions of affected communities. In order to appreciate the hybrid, shifting and pluralistic nature of the legal framework of TJ, scholars and practitioners must borrow tools from other disciplines to grasp the contextual meaning of what constitutes 'law' in any given setting. In the second half, this chapter argues that comparative legal methods, and in particular Sacco's theory of legal formants reinterpreted through a more critical postcolonial lens,[10] offer helpful tools to capture and make sense of the different normative forces within a given context, including official and unofficial law, as well as invisible normative elements. Given that the evolving global law of TJ is infused with elements of local norms, the field as a whole would do well to engage more explicitly with the broader range of normative forces at all levels through the interdisciplinary tools of comparative legal methods. Building on these considerations, the process of localisation of the international paradigm of TJ in specific contexts, such as in Muslim-majority settings, can reveal a valuable cross-fertilisation between global and local whereby international norms are localised, and local norms feed into the global framework of TJ.

II. TRANSLATING THE INTERNATIONAL PARADIGM OF TRANSITIONAL JUSTICE INTO LOCAL SETTINGS: CONCEPTS AND THEORETICAL CONSIDERATIONS

The first part of this chapter revisits the hybrid international framework of TJ in light of legal pluralism,[11] taking stock of the complex relationship between law, culture and society, informing broader normative elements that can be identified through comparative law (discussed in the second part of this chapter).

[9] E Melissaris, 'The More the Merrier? A New Take on Legal Pluralism' (2004) 13(1) *Social & Legal Studies* 57, 58.

[10] On these comparative law concepts, R Sacco, 'Legal Formants: A Dynamic Approach to Comparative Law', Instalments I and II (1991) 39 *American Journal of Comparative Law* 1 and 343. On the critical postcolonial way of doing comparative law, see J Schacherreiter, 'Postcolonial Theory and Comparative Law: On the Methodological and Epistemological Benefits to Comparative Law through Postcolonial Theory' (2016) 49(3) *Verfassung und Recht in Übersee/Law and Politics in Africa, Asia and Latin America* 291.

[11] On legal pluralism, see the classic texts by J Griffiths, 'What Is Legal Pluralism?' (1986) 24 *Journal of Legal Pluralism and Unofficial Law* 1; and SE Merry, 'Legal Pluralism' (1988) 22 *Law & Society Review* 869; and more recently, G Swenson, 'Legal Pluralism in Theory and Practice' (2018) 20(3) *International Studies Review* 438.

The discussion builds on the classic notion of 'vernacularisation' proposed by Sally Engle Merry, whereby procedures, rules and practices are imported across legal systems and translated into different contexts,[12] cross-fertilising between international and local dimensions. This supports one of the overall arguments of the book: the malleability of the international paradigm of TJ and its interaction with local normative dimensions is a circular process. Embedding Dustin Sharp's 'deconstruction of the concept of the local' which 'tends to destabilize, breaking down simple binary notions of global and local' is essential.[13] In this light, the international framework of TJ is permeable to the laws and normative principles of local settings, including those emanating from culture and religion. For these reasons scholars and practitioners should pay close attention to what is normative in each setting beyond black-letter law: the localisation process reveals the inherent pluralism of the evolving law of TJ at both global and local level.

A. The International Framework of Transitional Justice through the Lens of Legal Pluralism

The very notion of the international paradigm of TJ often used as a placeholder concept requires careful scrutiny, as outlined in the first chapter. The variety of norms, including official and unofficial law, underpinning TJ appears more clearly through the lens of legal pluralism. TJ has been heavily influenced by 'international legal regulation, particularly in the field of human rights',[14] as well as international humanitarian law[15] and developments of international criminal tribunals.[16] Moreover, as one of the key promoters of TJ, the UN has championed the global primacy of international law and its institutions; but this has overstated the coherence of the international framework of TJ and overshadowed the localities where TJ occurs.[17] For these reasons, Christine Bell's

[12] SE Merry, *Human Rights and Gender Violence: Translating International Law into Local Justice* (Chicago, IL, University of Chicago Press, 2006); see also discussion in SE Merry, 'What Is Legal Culture – An Anthropological Perspective' (2010) 5 *Journal of Comparative Law* 40, 54.

[13] DN Sharp, 'Addressing Dilemmas of the Global and the Local in Transitional Justice' (2014) 29 *Emory International Law Review* 71.

[14] C Turner, 'Delivering Lasting Peace, Democracy and Human Rights in Times of Transition: The Role of International Law' (2008) 2 *International Journal of Transitional Justice* 126.

[15] E Salmón, 'Reflections on International Humanitarian Law and Transitional Justice: Lessons to be Learnt from the Latin American Experience' (2006) 88 *International Review of the Red Cross* 327.

[16] L Vinjamuri and J Snyder, 'Advocacy and Scholarship in the Study of International War Crime Tribunals and Transitional Justice' (2004) 7 *Annual Review of Political Science* 345.

[17] L Grover, 'Transitional Justice, International Law and the United Nations' (2019) 88 *Nordic Journal of International Law* 359; and LE Gissel, 'Contemporary Transitional Justice: Normalising a Politics of Exception' (2017) 31(3) *Global Society* 353.

description of transitional justice as a 'mess' captures the indeterminacy of the law of TJ.[18] As such, a more blurred, discursive vision of the international paradigm of TJ emerges, characterised by a plurality of sources and actors at all levels.

The universal 'paradigm of transitional justice', contend Rosalind Shaw and Lars Waldorf, is 'increasingly destabilized by its local applications'.[19] On the one hand, TJ is pulled by some actors towards the international legal framework, and by others, towards localisation.[20] Moreover, the concept of exceptionality has always been a feature of TJ, premised on the need to adopt exceptional approaches that may deviate from universal norms or the normal application of domestic law in order to meet the exceptional challenges in specific transitional societies – despite more recent attempts to 'normalise' TJ.[21] Reckoning with the perceived tensions between universal and particular norms is unavoidable when relocating international understandings of TJ to local settings. Moreover, as TJ relies heavily on instruments and discourses of international human rights law (IHRL), aspects of the universality versus relativism debate have been imported into the field.[22] Taking stock of this, Lieselotte Viaene and Eva Brems suggest that TJ is better placed in facing this deadlock for four reasons: TJ has emerged in developing contexts and

[18] C Bell, 'The "New Law" of Transitional Justice' in K Ambos et al (eds), *Building a Future on Peace and Justice: Studies on Transitional Justice, Peace and Development* (Berlin, Springer-Verlag, 2009).

[19] Shaw and Waldorf (n 3) 4.

[20] ibid 5.

[21] See Gissel (n 17) discussing the 'three macro-level causes of normalisation: the legalisation, internationalisation and professionalisation of the field'. The conception of justice in transition as extraordinary, contextualised and partial is one of the founding ideas of TJ, as argued in RG Teitel, *Transitional Justice* (New York, Oxford University Press, 2000) 6. However, the validity of this exceptionality premise has been called into question by (1) the push towards legalism within the field (see, for instance, the critical discussion around the seduction of legalism and the triumph of human rights in K McEvoy, 'Beyond Legalism: Towards a Thicker Understanding of Transitional Justice' (2007) 34(4) *Journal of Law and Society* 411) and (2) the expansion of TJ into non-transitional settings (see the notion of 'steady-state TJ' in RG Teitel, 'Transitional Justice Genealogy' (2003) 16 *Harvard Human Rights Journal* 69, and elsewhere) including in established democracies. See also S Winter, *Transitional Justice in Established Democracies* (London, Palgrave MacMillan, 2014); JR Quinn, 'Whither the Transition of Transitional Justice' (2014) 8 *Interdisciplinary Journal of Human Rights Law* 63; AÁ Berastegi, 'Transitional Justice in Settled Democracies: Northern Ireland and the Basque Country in Comparative Perspective' (2017) 10(3) *Critical Studies on Terrorism* 542.

[22] On TJ and IHRL, see P Arthur, 'How Transitions Reshaped Human Rights: A Conceptual History of Transitional Justice' (2009) 31 *Human Rights Quarterly* 321. On the relativism–universality debate, see also J Donnelly, 'Cultural Relativism and Universal Human Rights' (1984) *Human Rights Quarterly* 400; J Donnelly, 'The Relative Universality of Human Rights' (2007) 29(2) *Human Rights Quarterly* 281; M Goodhart, 'Neither Relative nor Universal: A Response to Donnelly' (2008) 30(1) *Human Rights Quarterly* 183; AD Renteln, *International Human Rights: Universalism versus Relativism* (New Orleans, Quid Pro Books, 2013); E Brems, *Human Rights: Universality and Diversity* (The Hague, Martinus Nijhoff, 2001); and, in relation to Islamic law, AA An-Na'im, 'Islam and Human Rights: Beyond the Universality Debate' (2000) *American Society of International Law*, Proceedings of the 94th Annual Meeting.

not in the West; the unacceptability of past harm is (generally) uncontested;[23] cultural specificity claims are mostly external and academic; and, finally, the international law of TJ is at a (relatively) early stage and thus can still integrate cultural diversity.[24] This final point is especially interesting because it acknowledges that the international TJ paradigm is capable of incorporating local conceptions of law and justice (despite the supremacist tendencies of the international law/human rights project). Through the lens of legal pluralism a more holistic analysis of the evolving hybrid configuration of the global paradigm of TJ is possible, and thus its current and potential engagements with norms originating from different sources become apparent.

The UN has long acknowledged the potential relevance of multiple norms in any given TJ context. The 2004 UN Secretary-General's Report on 'The Rule of Law and Transitional Justice' highlights the need to take into account 'indigenous and informal traditions for administering justice or settling disputes' to ensure conformity with both international standards and local tradition.[25] Warning against prepackaged solutions imposed from external actors, the Report stresses how TJ must be localised at all stages to empower national actors and facilitate local ownership.[26] The Report considers that international law and standards set out by the UN are 'accommodated by the full range of legal systems of Member States, whether based in common law, civil law, Islamic law, or other legal traditions'.[27] This statement recognises that every TJ initiative operates in a context of legal pluralism combining international and local norms – as numerous experiences suggest.[28] However, what this means in practice faces the challenge of identifying what actually constitutes law, as discussed in the second part of the chapter.

Legal pluralism has emerged in the literature as an important interpretative lens to study TJ experiences in specific local settings as well as in general. Rosemary Nagy describes TJ as the 'archetype of the "new" legal pluralism

[23] However, a caveat is required on the general unacceptability of past harm, given harms are often contested, for instance through denial or through narratives of heroism and sacrifice. See eg S Cohen, *States of Denial: Knowing About Atrocities and Suffering* (Cambridge, Polity Press, 2001).

[24] Viaene and Brems (n 3) 202ff.

[25] United Nations Security Council (n 2) para 36.

[26] ibid 16ff.

[27] ibid 5.

[28] On the subject of legal pluralism in general, see Merry (n 11) and BZ Tamanaha, 'Understanding Legal Pluralism: Past to Present, Local to Global' (2008) 30 *Sydney Law Review* 375. The concept is discussed in relation to TJ in L Waldorf, 'Mass Justice for Mass Atrocity: Rethinking Local Justice as Transitional Justice' (2006) 79 *Temple Law Review* 1; P Sullo, 'To Repair the Irreparable: Post-genocide Justice, Legal Pluralism and Rule of Law' in L Zagato (ed), *Genocidio: declinazioni e risposte di inizio secolo* (Torino, Giappichelli, 2018); and in relation to specific TJ initiatives, see inter alia P Clark, 'Hybridity, Holism, and Traditional Justice: The Case of the Gacaca Courts in Post-genocide Rwanda' (2007) 39 *George Washington International Law Review* 765. On other localities, see eg P McAuliffe, 'East Timor's Community Reconciliation Process as a Model for Legal Pluralism in Criminal Justice' (2008) 12 *Law, Social Justice & Global Development Journal* 1; P Manning, *Transitional Justice and Memory in Cambodia: Beyond the Extraordinary Chambers* (London, Routledge, 2017) 28.

insofar as it takes place through the interpenetration of a variety of legal and normative orders across different socio-legal fields at the international, transnational, state and community level'.[29] This echoes Bell's understanding of TJ as a pluralist conception of law encompassing 'multiple legal and quasi-legal orders all with a claim to autonomy, and none acknowledging the higher authority of the other', which includes 'law and other forms of normativity' that combine legal and political elements.[30] Also presenting TJ as a pluralist process, Jaya Ramji-Nogales rejects the assumption of 'one transcendental legal standard and one preferred legal mechanism for performing transitional justice', in favour of 'an inclusive process that asks what form accountability should take in order to increase legitimacy within a particular society'.[31] Therefore, as noted by Geoffrey Swenson, legal pluralism allows for a fuller analysis of relevant norms given that 'post-conflict situations are fluid and can feature a wide range of relationships between state and non-state actors'.[32]

The gradual acknowledgement of the pluralist normative underpinnings of TJ illustrates how critiques can shape the field, even if the shift from academic analysis to practical change is in its infancy. Taking stock of critical approaches, Dustin Sharp describes

> a common vision of a renewed transitional justice that is bottom-up, locally owned, victim-centered, contextually tailored, politically and culturally grounded in ways that foreground an array of options, oriented towards root causes and a broad array of structures of power and domination, and better coordinated with development and peacebuilding work.[33]

Each one of these elements carries normative potential in the formulation and implementation of any given TJ experience, which emerges as the outcome of a complex web of guiding principles and ideas about what TJ should do, generally, and specifically in a particular context, as shaped by specific actors. The adoption of a pluralistic lens also helps reveal the problematic 'legacy of colonialism as a political backdrop' to TJ initiatives, and the perpetuation of north–south dynamics through the field.[34] Nonetheless, the 'models of 'best practices' anchored in global power structures have become 'standardized', and

[29] R Nagy, 'Centralizing Legal Pluralism? Traditional Justice in Transitional Contexts' in CL Sriram et al (eds), *Transitional Justice and Peacebuilding on the Ground* (Abingdon, Routledge, 2012) 83.

[30] C Bell, *On the Law of Peace: Peace Agreements and the Lex Pacificatoria* (Oxford, Oxford University Press 2008) 295.

[31] J Ramji-Nogales, 'Designing Bespoke Transitional Justice: A Pluralist Process Approach' (2010) 32(1) *Michigan Journal of International Law* 1, 68.

[32] Swenson (n 11).

[33] Sharp (n 8) 579.

[34] LE Fletcher and HM Weinstein, 'How Power Dynamics Influence the "North–South" Gap in Transitional Justice' (2018) 37(1) *Berkeley Journal of International Law* 1.

thus 'may not accord with the specifics of local context or the demands of local social movements'.[35] Donors seem to drive much of the standardisation: in the quest for TJ approaches which are 'transparent, universal and fair' and, especially, 'apolitical', the result is in fact 'rooted in political "mythologies" within international institutions that allow for the "reproduction" and "stabilization" of standardized interventions'.[36] This normativity emerging from donor practices and preferences influences how TJ operates locally. Nonetheless, local norms and conceptions of justice cannot be engineered out of a given context, and as such legal pluralism remains a central feature of TJ and how it is reproduced – and produced differently – in different localities.

The coexisting – and sometimes competing – different legal orders within the same jurisdiction or (informal) normative space can be captured through the theoretical lens of legal pluralism.[37] The project of 'global legal pluralism' chips away at the notion of a single, uniform governing law applicable to all: for Paul Schiff Berman, it is 'clear that the global legal system is an interlocking web of jurisdictional assertions by state, international, and non-state normative communities'.[38] Manifestations of legal pluralism include the inherently pluralistic notion of international law,[39] the challenge posed by international human rights norms to domestic law, local customs and cultural practices,[40] the

[35] V Nesiah, 'Transitional Justice Practice: Looking Back, Moving Forward' in Impunity Watch Scoping Study (May 2016) available at www.impunitywatch.org/post/transitional-justice-practice-looking-back-moving-forward.

[36] A Macdonald, '"Somehow This Whole Process Became So Artificial": Exploring the Transitional Justice Implementation Gap in Uganda' (2019) 13(2) *International Journal of Transitional Justice* 225, 230.

[37] For an overview on this topic, see inter alia: Merry (n 11); Griffiths (n 11); G Teubner, 'The Two Faces of Janus: Rethinking Legal Pluralism' (1991) 13 *Cardozo Law Review* 1443. The notion of normative space in relation to legal pluralism is discussed by B de Sousa Santos, 'Law: A Map of Misreading. Toward a Postmodern Conception of Law' (1987) 14 *Journal of Law & Society* 279; in A Griffiths, F von Benda-Beckmann and K von Benda-Beckmann 'Space and Legal Pluralism: An Introduction' in A Griffiths, F von Benda-Beckmann and K von Benda-Beckmann (eds), *Spatializing Law: An Anthropological Geography of Law in Society* (Farnham, Ashgate, 2009), 1; and in K Von Benda-Beckmann and B Turner, 'Legal Pluralism, Social Theory, and the State' (2018) 50(3) *Journal of Legal Pluralism and Unofficial Law* 255.

[38] PS Berman, 'Global Legal Pluralism' (2006–07) 80 *Southern California Law Review* 1155, 1159; and also PS Berman, 'From Legal Pluralism to Global Legal Pluralism' in R Nobles and D Schiff (eds), *Law, Society and Community: Socio-legal Essays in Honour of Roger Cotterrell* (London, Routledge 2014); and SE Merry, 'Human Rights and Global Legal Pluralism: Reciprocity and Disjuncture' in F von Benda-Beckmann and K von Benda-Beckmann (eds), *Mobile People, Mobile Law: Expanding Legal Relations in a Contracting World* (Abingdon, Routledge, 2005).

[39] Tamanaha (n 28) 386ff, citing WW Burke-White, 'International Legal Pluralism' (2003–04) 25 *Michigan Journal of International Law* 963 and A Fischer-Lescano and G Teubner, 'Regime Collisions: The Vain Search for Legal Unity in the Fragmentation of Global Law' (2003–04) 25 *Michigan Journal of International Law* 999.

[40] Tamanaha (n 28), citing SE Merry, 'Global Human Rights and Local Social Movements in a Legally Plural World' (1997) 12 *Canadian Journal of Law and Society* 247. On navigating cultural relativism challenges of the meeting between human rights and legal pluralism, see also H Quane, 'Legal Pluralism and International Human Rights Law: Inherently Incompatible, Mutually Reinforcing or Something in Between?' (2013) 33(4) *OJLS* 675.

self-creating legal orders established by 'NGOs …, various subject-based international agencies, and lawyers who serve them', transgovernmental networks, and the global movements of people.[41] Understanding what exactly constitutes law can be complicated.[42] Moreover, in postcolonial settings, identifying 'customary law' in the tapestry of legal pluralism is problematised further: the designation of a norm as 'custom' is 'an invention of the colonial state' but it is 'not purely a state invention'.[43] Turning to transitional contexts, Laura Grenfell suggests that while the 'rule of law is deficient when there is confusion within communities as to the applicable law due to inconsistencies between local law and the formal legal system', legal pluralism is helpful in 'weak state legal systems'.[44] Indeed, when state law and institutions are part of the problem during transition, accepting the pluralistic foundations of TJ can provide other useful tools.

In addition to capturing the normative complexities and hybrid law of TJ, the lens of legal pluralism can also help reveal international law itself as a site of multiple proliferating rules, institutions and practices, incorporating a 'range of different and equally legitimate normative choices by national governments and international institutions and tribunals', within the framework of a universal system.[45] Much of this is amply analysed in the Third World approaches to international law (TWAIL) literature with regards to the peoples of the Global South.[46] An 'implicitly monist understanding of law', argues Ruth Buchanan, 'stands in the way of a meaningful engagement with the legal pluralism that many TWAIL scholars nonetheless recognize as necessary'.[47] A radical re-reading of the origins of international law in this sense is provided by Arnulf Becker Lorca: the concept of 'mestizo international law' juxtaposes the conventional Eurocentric assumptions and the distinctive contributions to the history of international law from 'a larger number of nations and lawyers across the globe'.[48]

41 Tamanaha (n 28) 388.

42 ibid 392.

43 Von Benda-Beckmann and Turner (n 37).

44 L Grenfell, 'Legal Pluralism and the Rule of Law in Timor Leste' (2006) 19 *Leiden Journal of International Law* 305, 335.

45 Burke-White (n 39) 963 and 977.

46 See eg L Eslava and S Pahuja, 'Beyond the (Post) Colonial: TWAIL and the Everyday Life of International Law' (2012) 45(2) *Verfassung und Recht in Übersee/Law and Politics in Africa, Asia and Latin America* 195; V Nesiah, 'Decolonial CIL: TWAIL, Feminism, and an Insurgent Jurisprudence' (2018) 112 *AJIL Unbound* 313; JT Gathii, 'TWAIL: A brief History of its Origins, its Decentralized Network, and a Tentative Bibliography' (2011) 3 *Trade Law & Development* 26; L Ramina, 'Framing the Concept of TWAIL: "Third World Approaches to International Law"' (2018) 32(1) *Revista Justiça do Direito* 5.

47 R Buchanan, 'Writing Resistance into International Law' (2008) 10(4) *International Community Law Review* 445, 454.

48 AB Lorca, *Mestizo International Law: A Global Intellectual History 1842–1933* (Cambridge, Cambridge University Press, 2014).

Moreover, not only states participate in international law.[49] International law developments – such as in the case of the framework for TJ – are characterized by overlapping legal and quasi-legal communities including traditional actors alongside NGOs, indigenous actors and many others.[50] Civil society, in particular, offers a good example of the reach of global, regional, domestic and local actors involved in TJ.[51] Pluralism looks beyond state law and state practice, taking stock of 'multiple sites of normative authority in the global legal system as a set of inevitable interactions to be understood, not as a "problem" to be "solved"'.[52] The resulting 'dialectical and iterative processes' depart from traditional hierarchies,[53] and as such offer a less constricted way of understanding international law. The hybridity – and messiness – of this picture emerges as a reality to be managed, not eliminated, in a manner that allows for contestation and creativity in each context.[54] Thus, the international framework of TJ is embedded in the realities of pluralism, and as such, combines a variety of potentially legitimate normative choices resulting in a highly adaptable hybrid paradigm.

Drawing on the classic text by Sally Engle Merry (talking about state law specifically, but applicable to all official law), legal pluralism allows the 'study of law as a system of meanings' like an interpretative cultural code.[55] The dialectic between legal systems 'constitutes and reconstitutes the other in some way' and, as such, plural normative orders can persist 'by appeals to tradition'

[49] Critiquing the persistence of the state, see M Kleinhans and A Macdonald, 'What Is a Critical Legal Pluralism' (1997) 12 *Canadian Journal of Law and Society* 25, 34; and earlier Merry (n 11) 889. There is a rich literature on non-state actors' participation in international law: see inter alia A Bianchi (ed), *Non-state Actors and International Law*, 1st edn (London, Routledge, 2009); M Noortmann, A Reinisch and C Ryngaert (eds), *Non-state Actors in International Law* (Oxford, Hart, 2015); CM Bailliet (ed), *Non-state Actors, Soft Law and Protective Regimes: From the Margins* (Cambridge, Cambridge University Press, 2012).

[50] Berman, 'Global Legal Pluralism' (n 38) 1175. See also I Cismas, 'Reflections on the Presence and Absence of Religious Actors in Transitional Justice Processes: On Legitimacy and Accountability' in R Duthie and P Seils (eds), *Justice Mosaics: How Context Shapes Transitional Justice in Fractured Societies* (New York, ICTJ, 2017); I Cismas, *Religious Actors and International Law* (Oxford, Oxford University Press, 2014).

[51] This is widely discussed in the literature, see eg D Backer, 'Civil Society and Transitional Justice: Possibilities, Patterns and Prospects' (2003) 2(3) *Journal of Human Rights* 297; E Brahm 'Transitional Justice, Civil Society, and the Development of the Rule of Law in Post-conflict Societies' (2006–07) 9(4) *International Journal of Not-for-Profit Law* 62; T Madlingozi, 'On Transitional Justice Entrepreneurs and the Production of Victims' (2010) 2(2) *Journal of Human Rights Practice* 208; J Subotić, 'The Transformation of International Transitional Justice Advocacy' (2012) 6(1) *International Journal of Transitional Justice* 106; P Gready and S Robins, 'Rethinking Civil Society and Transitional Justice: Lessons from Social Movements and "New" Civil Society' (2017) 21(1) *International Journal of Human Rights* 956; H Van der Merwe and M Schkolne, 'The Role of Local Civil Society in Transitional Justice' in C Lawther et al (eds), *Research Handbook on Transitional Justice* (Cheltenham, Edward Elgar, 2017).

[52] Berman, 'Global Legal Pluralism' (n 38) 1176–77.

[53] ibid 1197.

[54] ibid 1237.

[55] Merry (n 11) 886.

or change through a process of gradual reinterpretation.[56] The presumed dichotomy between national and international law typifies this paradox: the two are less clear-cut than is commonly believed, as attested by the fact that many of the domestic legal systems emerging in postwar Europe were already 'infused by international law' and not in fact sealed within national borders.[57] These blurred boundaries between legal orders apply to the international framework of TJ as well. As the TJ paradigm has developed, it has engaged with local experiences continuously, but in different ways. For example, the centrality of truth commissions in TJ[58] embedded in specific local experiences (in particular, in South Africa and Latin America) has shaped global understandings of what TJ is. Another example of how local experiences have infused the global paradigm of TJ is found in the (contested) notion of forgiveness emerging from the South African experience,[59] alongside the possibility of (contested) amnesty emerging from the Latin American TJ processes,[60] in relation to the international law principle of accountability and the emerging right-to-truth norm.[61] In this light, earlier TJ initiatives were uniquely bottom-up, original and localised, whereas as the field developed the global paradigm emerged as a blend of international and local experiences, synthesised and promoted as a global framework of reference for subsequent TJ initiatives. As such, the international framework of TJ, as a whole, is a product of the dialectic between global and local norms, experiences and understandings of justice over time and space – continuously informed and renegotiated in light of the specific experiences of harm arising from conflict and authoritarianism.

B. Bridging Global and Local: Law, Culture and Society

The importance of legal culture and its role in the social construction of (the rule of) law emerges in Ruti Teitel's classic work on TJ.[62] Culture – a complex and contested notion – has been described as the 'missing link' of TJ.[63]

[56] ibid 889.

[57] C Thornhill, *A Sociology of Transnational Constitutions: Social Foundations of the Post-national Legal Structure* (Cambridge, Cambridge University Press, 2016), 420.

[58] On truth commissions, see PB Hayner, *Unspeakable Truths: Confronting State Terror and Atrocity* (London, Routledge, 2001).

[59] Discussed inter alia in R Saunders, 'Questionable Associations: The Role of Forgiveness in Transitional Justice' (2011) 5(1) *International Journal of Transitional Justice* 119.

[60] inter alia, N Roht-Arriaza, "Truth Commissions and Amnesties in Latin America: The Second Generation" (1998) 92 *Proceedings of the Annual Meeting (American Society of International Law)* 313.

[61] See A Panepinto, 'The Right to the Truth in International Law: The Significance of Strasbourg's Contributions' (2017) 37(4) *Legal Studies* 739.

[62] Teitel, *Transitional Justice* (n 21) 19.

[63] C Bollaert, 'Culture: The Missing Link in Transitional Justice; An Imperative for Transformative Justice' in M Evans (ed), *Transitional and Transformative Justice: Critical and International Perspectives* (Abingdon, Routledge, 2019).

Legal pluralism (as well as comparative law and related disciplines) can help understand the role of culture in relation to the normative framework of TJ. The theme of culture as an interpretative tool of law emerges throughout the literature.[64] As David Nelken famously noted, legal culture 'is both hard to pin down and, at the same time, difficult to escape'.[65] The invocation of culture is embedded in the highly complex tension between ethnocentrism and cultural relativism, and the tendency to essentialise culture (both of the Self and of the Other); the critique of postcolonialism presented by Judith Schacherreiter is very helpful in navigating the problems:

> The critique of postcolonial theory is directed not only against creating hierarchies between different cultures but also against essentialist conceptions of cultures that underlie not only ethnocentrism but also cultural relativism. Hence, it questions strictly binary oppositions of Self and Other, no matter whether this manifests as ethnocentrism or cultural relativism.[66]

Given its complexities and political context, the concept of culture requires a 'self-reflective methodological and critical application of legal culture'; Balázs Fekete identifies three main ways in which legal culture is invoked: '(i.) background, (ii.) interactions around law, and (iii.) a sum of attitudes towards law'.[67] In each of these uses it is vital to consider the dangers of cultural essentialisation, ethnocentrism and cultural relativism, and embed the critique of postcolonial theory. Therefore, sustained critical thinking is required whenever invoking the notion of culture as a way to interpret normative phenomena, including in TJ as well as the international law elements that underpin part of its framework of reference.

Turning again to the international framework of TJ, a variety of legal discourses embedded in different areas of PIL and pursued by different actors can be identified. In a 'world of hybrid legal spaces', Paul Schiff Berman invokes a 'cultural analysis of law, which argues that law both reflects and constructs social reality'.[68] Building on that, (critical) legal pluralism challenges the supposition of 'reified cultures and communities' as well as legal

[64] See on culture and legal pluralism, SE Merry, 'Legal Pluralism and Legal Culture: Mapping the Terrain' in B Tamanaha, C Sage and M Woolcock (eds), *Legal Pluralism and Development: Scholars and Practitioners in Dialogue* (Cambridge, Cambridge University Press, 2012); WA Adams, *Popular Culture and Legal Pluralism: Narrative as Law*, 1st edn (London, Routledge, 2016); SG Abebe, 'The Relevance of African Culture in Building Modern Institutions and the Quest for Legal pluralism' (2012) 57 *Louis University Law Journal* 429.

[65] D Nelken, 'Disclosing/Invoking Legal Culture: An Introduction' (1995) 4 *Social & Legal Studies* 435.

[66] Schacherreiter (n 10) 292, 294, discussing E Said, *Orientalism* (New York, Vintage Books, 1978), F Fanon, *The Wretched of the Earth*, trans C Farrington (London, Penguin, 2001), and HK Bhabha, *The Location of Culture*, 2nd edn (London, Routledge, 2004).

[67] B Fekete, 'Inconsistencies in the Use of Legal Culture in Comparative Legal Studies' (2018) 25(5) *Maastricht Journal of European and Comparative Law* 551.

[68] PS Berman, *Global Legal Pluralism: A Jurisprudence of Law Beyond Borders* (Cambridge, Cambridge University Press, 2012) 11–14 and 21.

positivism, suggesting that 'subjects control law as much as law controls subjects', collapsing the distinction between normative spheres.[69] As such, 'legal meaning moves through a circle of narrative construction by a dynamic, creative subject' (or subjects).[70] This involves a shift from talking about legal systems to considering legal discourses.[71] This allows the possibility of incorporating additional legal discourses taken from outside the confines of international law and its traditional actors in specific TJ settings to include unofficial law and the normative principles emanating from indigenous and religious communities.

The determination of the most appropriate type and combination of TJ mechanisms depends on 'knowledge of local population preferences and a deep understanding of local cultures'.[72] But these considerations require a degree of caution:[73] traditional justice invocations in TJ may emerge from 'the interaction with international TJ as mediated by the state', which it turn may 'consolidate[e] state power at the expense of truth, justice, reconciliation and durable peace'.[74] Moreover, tendencies to romanticise the attributes of (rarefied) indigenous justice in TJ vis-à-vis international or state-centred understandings of justice are deeply problematic and overlook the cross-fertilisation that occurs in practice.[75] Invocations of traditional justice also run the risk of Orientalist essentialisations and colonial romanticisation.[76] These premises will inform the discussion of Islamic law set out in Chapters 5 and 6.

Legal pluralism helps make sense of the relationships between multiple legal spheres, and the 'dialectic, mutually constitutive link between state law and other normative orders'.[77] This is also true for the international framework of TJ, informed by traditional PIL norms and other forms of law. And just as 'state law may borrow the symbols of other normative orders',[78] the international framework of TJ can draw on local forms of justice.[79] Despite the risks outlined above, embracing this pluralist approach can help engage grassroots levels, including survivors of violence, and eschew universalist visions of justice.[80] Abdullahi Ahmed An-Na'im has critically discussed how international

[69] Kleinhans and Macdonald (n 49) 38–40.
[70] ibid 45.
[71] Melissaris (n 9) 58.
[72] Ramji-Nogales (n 31) 68 and 71.
[73] Recalling the critiques of McAuliffe (n 8); Sharp (n 13); Kochanski (n 8); Obradovic-Wochnik (n 8); Yusuf (n 6).
[74] Nagy (n 29) 82.
[75] McAuliffe (n 8).
[76] ibid 67.
[77] Merry (n 11) 879–80.
[78] ibid 882.
[79] An example of how more plural understandings of justice are described and justified in TJ is the (uncritical) import of local/indigenous forms of justice within 'restorative justice'. See inter alia McAuliffe (n 8) 63–64.
[80] On this point, Ramji-Nogales (n 31) discussed in A Panepinto, 'Transitional Justice: International Criminal Law and Beyond' (2014) 3 *Archivio Penale* 1, 24.

standards tend to prevail over indigenous or traditional practices deemed unacceptable according to human rights criteria.[81] Indeed, 'cultural challenges are part of a critical evaluation and reflection that is going on as part of the maturation process of the field', although it is also vital to avoid oversimplified notions of culture and tradition, and see through attempts to misuse cultural arguments to avoid dealing with the past.[82] Thinking beyond norms, it is important to recall the role of the various actors in TJ: clashes among normative systems can be driven by tensions between the systems themselves, but also between their strategic actors.[83]

Within the framework of legal pluralism that underpins TJ, customary forms of justice can contribute to TJ initiatives in a variety of ways. As summarised by Deborah Isser, customary justice systems, firstly, 'are and will likely remain far more accessible and effective than the broken and mostly distrusted formal systems'; secondly, 'they offer a paradigm of justice preferred by much of the population and can often resolve problems that the formal justice system cannot', such as 'root causes of conflict, ending cycles of blood vengeance, resolving sociospiritual problems, and promoting social reconciliation'; thirdly, 'constructively engaging customary justice systems can improve the legitimacy of the state and its formal institutions'.[84] Through the lens of legal pluralism, Isser sees the potential of the 'sociocultural basis of customary justice systems', its limitations, and the relationship between customary and formal justice systems.[85] The way in which juxtaposition and dialogue between different norms and approaches to justice operate requires close scrutiny to avoid apologetic stances towards both global and local normative sources and ways of thinking about justice.

Tensions may arise between customary forms of justice and the standards set out in international law in the localisation of TJ. Just as formal state law can be an expression of previous or successor repressive governments, customary law may be a tool of state or non-state actors promoting specific agendas.

[81] AA An-Na'im, 'Editorial Note: From the Neocolonial "Transitional" to Indigenous Formations of Justice' (2013) 7 *International Journal of Transitional Justice*, 19, 197. A prominent example of the tension between local and international conceptions of justice is the poor reception of the *gacaca* in Rwanda by prominent human rights NGOs, such as Human Rights Watch, described inter alia in P Clark, 'How Rwanda Judged its Genocide' (2012) Africa Research Institute, available at africaresearchinstitute.org/newsite/wp-content/uploads/2013/03/How-Rwanda-judged-its-genocide-E6QODPW0KV.pdf.

[82] Viaene and Brems (n 3) 211.

[83] Tamanaha (n 28) 400–01.

[84] D Isser (ed), *Customary Justice and the Rule of Law in War-torn Societies* (Washington, DC, United States Institute of Peace Press, 2011) 326ff. Studies indicate that over 80 per cent of disputes are resolved through informal justice mechanisms in some countries (see E Wojkowska, *How Informal Justice Systems Can Contribute* (Oslo, UNDP Oslo Governance Centre, 2006); the OECD estimates that as much as 80 per cent of the people in today's fragile states rely on non-state actors for various forms of justice and security (cited in T Allen and A Macdonald. 'Post-conflict Traditional Justice: A Critical Overview' (2013) LSE Justice and Security Research Programme, paper 3).

[85] Isser (n 84) 327ff.

For instance, Isser describes customary justice systems as 'guardians of the dominant social and cultural beliefs of their societies', which preserve a 'conservative social order often characterised by a patriarchal hierarchy and social inequalities'.[86] She suggests taking into account the purpose and broader social significance of normative principles that are, or appear to be, at odds with basic IHRL standards, and working through them consciously. Moreover, during the TJ process there may be fresh opportunities to consider new interpretations of customary justice that could be reoriented towards the substance of IHRL, including in relation to truth seeking.

In any given context the indeterminacy of the international legal framework of TJ is enmeshed with various normative forces at local level, which include unofficial norms, but also the ways those laws are understood and deployed by key actors. The complex relationship between law, culture and society is key to understanding how TJ is localised.[87] As the discussion reveals, acknowledging the pluralistic foundations of TJ is the first step towards recognising contested concepts such as culture and custom and their normative force. Law alone cannot comprehensively and critically make sense of these complexities, so drawing from sister disciplines is essential. Alexander Laban Hinton uses an 'anthropology of transitional justice' to navigate how TJ meets the vernacular and the ways in which TJ initiatives 'foreground and background different groups and perspectives'.[88] The critical tools of anthropology help make sense of the problematic normative connotations of the evolving global framework of TJ and the (assumed) 'hierarchy and teleology' of processes through which societies develop into 'a more modern, "civilised", liberal and democratic state'.[89] Austin Sarat and Jonathan Simon have called for legal scholarship to 'embrace cultural analysis and cultural studies',[90] as a 'kind of epistemological corrective to the plethora of problems posed for postrealist legal studies by the crisis of the social liberal state'.[91]

[86] ibid 334.

[87] For a background on this relationship, see L Nader (ed) *Law in Culture and Society* (Chicago, IL, Aldine, 1969).

[88] AL Hinton, 'Introduction: Toward an Anthropology of Transitional Justice' in AL Hinton (ed) *Transitional Justice: Global Mechanisms and Local Realities after Genocide and Mass Violence* (New Brunswick, NJ, Rutgers University Press, 2010), 2.

[89] ibid 6–8.

[90] A Sarat and J Simon, 'Cultural Analysis, Cultural Studies, and the Situation of Legal Scholarship' in A Sarat and J Simon (eds), *Cultural Analysis, Cultural Studies, and the Law: Moving Beyond Legal Realism* (Durham, NC, Duke University Press, 2003) 4. For present purposes, 'cultural studies' is 'a tendency across disciplines, rather than a discipline itself', as expressed by T Miller, 'What It Is and What It Isn't: Cultural Studies Meets Graduate Student Labour' in A Sarat and J Simon (eds), *Cultural Analysis, Cultural Studies, and the Law: Moving Beyond Legal Realism* (Durham, NC, Duke University Press, 2003), 73.

[91] Sarat and Simon, 'Cultural Analysis' (n 90). For a background on legal realism, see also R Pound, 'The Call for a Realist Jurisprudence' (1931) 44(5) *Harvard Law Review* 697; KN Llewellyn, 'Some Realism about Realism: Responding to Dean Pound' (1931) 44(8) *Harvard Law Review* 1222; LL Fuller, 'American Legal Realism' (1934) 82(5) *University of Pennsylvania Law Review and American Law Register* 429. In brief: 'What judges really do, according to the realists, is decide

Despite its potential, making sense of culture unearths other issues: much like the notion of tradition analysed by Hobsbawm and Ranger,[92] the very 'idea of cultural authenticity' is questionable,[93] and risks essentialising foreign legal cultures instead of recognising that societies and states (including our own) are not culturally homogeneous, monolithic or static.[94] Dynamics of power and subjectivity emerge,[95] challenging traditional ideas of culture and advancing new (and alternative) conceptions of law,[96] instead of returning to a romanticised golden era of an unadulterated, authentic distant past and imposing its rules on contemporary societies (and the colonial connotations that might entail). Moreover, as (all) law proposes a 'distinctive manner of imagining the real', it is itself constitutive of culture.[97] Thinking about all law in cultural terms is intellectually liberating for trained lawyers: this perspective allows an interpretation of the international legal framework of reference of TJ itself as a form of legal culture that continues to shape the field.

Borrowing from the ethnographic method, which rejects the artificial separation between law and culture, Naomi Mezey has conceptualised 'law as culture and culture as law', whereby 'specific cultural practices or identities coincide or collide with specific legal rules or conventions' thus 'altering the meanings of both'.[98] Ethnography can provide both explanation and 'cultural interpretation' of the law: (1) interpretation of law at a site of production discernible through

cases according to how the facts of the cases strike them, and not because legal rules require particular results; judges are largely "fact-responsive" rather than "rule-responsive" in reaching decisions. How a judge responds to the facts of a particular case is determined by various psychological and sociological factors, both conscious and unconscious', as summarised by B Leiter, 'Legal Realism' in D Patterson (ed), *A Companion to Philosophy of Law and Legal Theory* (Blackwell 1999). For a summary of legal postrealism, see N Duxbury, 'Post-realism and Legal Process' in D Patterson (ed), *A Companion to Philosophy of Law and Legal Theory* (Malden, MA, Blackwell, 1999), exploring two variants: policy science and legal process, both concerned with the links between law and politics.

[92] E Hobsbawm and T Ranger, *The Invention of Tradition* (Cambridge, Cambridge University Press, 1983).

[93] Sarat and Simon, 'Cultural Analysis' (n 90) 12, citing J Clifford, *The Predicament of Culture: Twentieth-Century Ethnography, Literature and Art* (Harvard, MA, Harvard University Press, 1988) and TM Luhrmann, 'Review of Hermes' Dilemma and Hamlet's Desire: On the Epistemology of Interpretation' (1993) 95 *American Anthropologist* 1058. See also the articulate critical discussion in Schacherreiter (n 10).

[94] HP Glenn, 'Legal Cultures and Legal Traditions' in M Van Hoeck (ed), *Epistemology and Methodology of Comparative Law* (Oxford, Hart 2004), 18, also referencing Said (n 66). See also the articulate critical discussion in Schacherreiter (n 10).

[95] ibid 8, citing S Hall, 'Cultural Studies: Two Paradigms', in NB Dirks et al (eds) *Culture/Power/History: A Reader in Contemporary Social History* (Princeton, NJ, Princeton University Press, 1993).

[96] ibid 9, citing C Weisbrod, *Emblems of Pluralism: Cultural Differences and the State* (Princeton, NJ, Princeton University Press, 2002).

[97] Sarat and Simon, 'Cultural Analysis' (n 90) 13ff, citing C Geertz, *Local Knowledge: Further Essays in Interpretative Anthropology* (New York, Basic Books 1983), and S Silby, 'Making a Place for a Cultural Analysis of Law' (1992) 17 *Law and Society Inquiry 39*.

[98] N Mezey, 'Law as Culture' in Sarat and Simon, 'Cultural Analysis' (n 90) 38 and 54, 56, citing C Geertz, *The Interpretation of Cultures* (New York, Basic Books, 1973).

traditional and non-traditional modes of legal interpretation; (2) interpretation of the cultural practices 'that might be said to inspire the law and those that the law confronts when applied'; and (3) 'interpretation of the interventions of culture in law and law in culture, of the dissolution of production and reception into a circulation of the interdependencies, contradictions, and conspiracies in meaning'.[99] These insights allow a frank engagement with law and 'the normative' which can emerge outside the confines of positive law, as occasionally happens with TJ; moreover, international law practices in the specific field of TJ emerge as a form of culture of TJ that over time and reiteration acquires its own distinctive normativity. By setting aside the (positivist) need for discreteness and determinacy,[100] a complex, varied and improvised relationship between *all* law and *all* culture emerges. This necessarily includes the international and global laws and practices of TJ which are generally treated as deculturalised when in fact they embody a distinctive culture of their own. This realisation offers a more accurate picture of the contexts in which TJ is localised, taking stock of the fact that law and culture, and politics and power structures, cannot be easily disentangled. Legal pluralism complemented by non-law critiques offers a useful theoretical starting point for understanding how TJ localisation might operate and the challenges it faces.

The relationship between law and culture reaches a peak of complexity in relation to human rights, which underpin a significant part of the law of TJ including truth seeking. Culture connects to human rights in ways that both enhance and restrict the realisation of those rights;[101] but culture may also hinder the enjoyment of human rights and promote harmful practices.[102] Rejecting the tendency to 'demonise culture' in human rights circles, Sally Engle Merry argues that culture is not necessarily 'a barrier to progress' as opposed to 'modernity and the norms of human rights' which are presented as purportedly 'culture-free'.[103] Drawing instead on anthropology, the 'human rights legal system produces culture' by identifying problems and articulating 'normative visions of a just society' (and the related procedural rules to make complaints) and imposing them at national and international levels.[104] An example of the

[99] ibid 57.

[100] ibid 60.

[101] For example, culture is presented as an inhibitive force to the enjoyment of human rights in CEDAW, UN General Assembly, 'Convention on the Elimination of All Forms of Discrimination Against Women' (18 December 1979) United Nations Treaty Series, vol 1249, 13 in the Preamble and Art 5(a): 'To modify the social and cultural patterns of conduct of men and women, with a view to achieving the elimination of prejudices and customary and all other practices which are based on the idea of the inferiority or the superiority of either of the sexes or on stereotyped roles for men and women.'

[102] Discussed in J Almqvist, *Human Rights, Culture, and the Rule of Law* (Oxford, Hart, 2005) 8ff.

[103] SE Merry, 'Human Rights Law and the Demonization of Culture (And Anthropology Along the Way)' (2003) 26(1) *PoLAR* 55, 60, 62 and 70.

[104] ibid 70ff.

encounter is the infusion of a human rights culture in Argentinian society through the TJ experience.[105] Both Merry and Jessica Almqvist link culture to power dynamics and political appropriation; moreover, culture carries normative effects even if these are generally invisible to a legally trained eye. In light of its persuasiveness, culture (much like law) is ambiguous: it may be used to shield perpetrators of violations, but also to further human rights enjoyment.[106] To understand the relationship between culture and human rights, Almqvist cautions against excessive reliance on controversial propositions, idealism, simplicity and particularism.[107] Rejecting essentialisations of what law is and what constitutes culture, the meeting between laws and cultures, including in ways that change the dominant legal culture, is a multifaceted and shifting process that can feed into the localisation of TJ within the framework of legal pluralism. In considering the overarching research question of this project, the localisation of TJ from international law cannot ignore the cultural context altogether or adopt a static, essentialised view of what law and culture are. Therefore, international standards will inevitably coexist in the framework of legal pluralism alongside other forms of culturally specific norms that characterise a given society experiencing transition.

C. 'Seeing' the Relevant Laws in Pluralistic TJ: Borrowing the Tools of Comparative Legal Studies

Having discussed the relative indeterminacy of the international framework for TJ in Chapter 1 and the possibilities (and risks) of adopting the lens of legal pluralism and law-and-culture (and law-as-culture) to bridge the local and global in this section, we now turn to how to identify the laws that fall short of official, written qualities. Recognising law's existence outside the formal confines of official and written state law is a feature of legal pluralism and sociolegal analysis.[108] For Roger Cotterrell, law is understood as an 'institutionalized doctrine … created, interpreted or enforced in certain socially established ways, through the use of recognized procedures and agencies'.[109] Not only is 'the state legal system' far from a unified, coherent whole, but 'there is more to law

[105] See inter alia E Jelin, 'The Politics of Memory: The Human Rights Movements and the Construction of Democracy in Argentina' (1994) 21(2) *Latin American Perspectives* 38; K Sikkink, 'From Pariah State to Global Protagonist: Argentina and the Struggle for International Human Rights' (2008) 50(1) *Latin American Politics and Society* 1.

[106] Almqvist (n 102) 40 and 219ff.

[107] ibid 25ff.

[108] See inter alia R Michaels, 'The Re-state-ment of Non-state Law: The State, Choice of Law, and the Challenge from Global Legal Pluralism' (2005) 51 *Wayne Law Review* 1209.

[109] R Cotterrell, *Law, Culture and Society: Legal Ideas in the Mirror of Social Theory* (Burlington, VT, Ashgate, 2006) 1.

than the legal doctrine that lawyers recognize and work with': it 'can be found "outside" the official legal system of the state' and 'may flourish in social sites and settings where lawyers ... never venture'.[110] We have seen in Chapter 1 that the same is true of the international law that underpins the framework of reference of TJ. Translating the international framework of TJ into local settings, including Muslim-majority societies, requires a critical approach to all forms of law, including international law. Given its self-consciously civilising mission inherited from its imperial heritage,[111] international law tends to assert itself over local, unofficial norms, including alternative conceptions of justice that emerge from religion and other life philosophies. Unseeing or erasing all other context-specific norms relevant to TJ is problematic: the pluralistic legal system in which TJ occurs must be understood in its entirety.

The tension between international law and unofficial norms has been exacerbated by a strand of international relations which blames cultural identity for violence and conflict.[112] Since 9/11, in particular, misrepresentations of Islam and *shari'ah* law as antagonistic to human rights and international law standards have abounded in the West.[113] When discussing the localisation of the international framework of TJ into Muslim-majority societies, the lens of legal pluralism helps to navigate competing normative foundations and justifications and to identify synergies and potential tensions. To identify and evaluate these possibilities, comparative law offers a range of methods to analyse links between law and culture,[114] and can help lawyers to become '"culturally fluent" in another legal language'.[115] In particular, as the next section will explore in more detail,

[110] ibid.

[111] See generally M Koskenniemi, *The Gentle Civilizer of Nations: The Rise and Fall of International Law 1870–1960* (Cambridge, Cambridge University Press, 2001).

[112] In that regard, the theorisation of post-Cold War world orders has heavily relied on perceptions of culture. See also F Fukuyama, *The End of History and the Last Man* (New York, Penguin, 1992) xiii, xv, xix; and S Huntington, 'Clash of Civilisations?' (1993) 72(3) *Foreign Affairs* 22, 23: 'It is far more meaningful now to group countries not in terms of their political or economic systems or in terms of their level of economic development but rather in terms of their culture and civilization.' The theme of culture in Huntington is discussed by comparative lawyers, inter alia Glenn (n 95) 17.

[113] See generally, J Rehman, *Islamic State Practices, International Law and the Threat from Terrorism: A Critique of the 'Clash of Civilizations' in the New World Order* (Oxford, Hart, 2005); S Sardar Ali and J Rehman, 'The Concept of Jihad in International Islamic Law' (2005) 10(3) *Journal of Conflict & Security Law* 321.

[114] For an overview on the discipline of comparative law, see inter alia A Riles (ed), *Rethinking the Masters of Comparative Law* (Oxford, Hart, 2001); K Zweigert and H Kötz, *An Introduction to Comparative Law*, 3rd edn (Oxford, Oxford University Press, 1998); and U Mattei, T Ruskola and A Gidi, *Schlesinger's Comparative Law* (Foundation Press, 2009), in celebration of R Schlesinger, author of *Comparative Law Cases and Materials* (Mineola, The Foundation Press, 1950). For an overview of the history of comparative law, see inter alia R Sacco, 'One Hundred Years of Comparative Law' (2000–01) 75 *Tulane Law Review Review* 1159.

[115] N Jansen, 'Comparative Law and Comparative Knowledge' in M Reimann and R Zimmermann (eds) *The Oxford Handbook of Comparative Law* (Oxford, Oxford University Press, 2006) 306, referencing, inter alia, P Legrand, *Fragments on Law as Culture* (Deventer, Tjeenk Willink, 1999).

comparative law builds on the premises of legal pluralism and law-and-culture to help translate this interdisciplinary knowledge into methods lawyers can relate to. The pluralism embedded in TJ initiatives allows for a deeper engagement with the multiple norms relevant to a particular setting, enabling scholars and practitioners to 'see' the legal framework of TJ more holistically. Like legal pluralism, comparative law borrows from other disciplines, including anthropology, to understand and interpret the distinctive cultural, social and political features that influence a legal system.[116] This interdisciplinary angle is more likely to provide the basis for constructively engaging local norms in designing relevant TJ processes. As such, attempts to localise TJ from international law to Islamic settings benefit from a joint toolkit of legal pluralism and comparative methods, as well as the critical self-awareness of the people and organisations who take on this task.

III. UNDERSTANDING LOCAL SETTINGS IN THE DEVELOPMENT OF A GLOBAL PARADIGM OF TRANSITIONAL JUSTICE: METHODS

The second half of this chapter discusses the potential of comparative law, and in particular Sacco's theory of legal formants understood critically, in navigating the interaction between local norms and the international framework of TJ, and offers preliminary reflections in relation to Muslim-majority contexts (developed in greater detail in Chapters 5 and 6). After briefly reflecting on the potential of comparative law, this part first considers some of its potential limitations; it then argues that the theory of legal formants offers a toolkit to look beyond black-letter law and essentialised notions of traditional justice, and concludes by evaluating how comparative law thinking might help develop the global paradigm of TJ.

The core benefit of adopting comparative law tools within the framework of legal pluralism is the fact that taken together they look beyond official state law and other types of formal law. Informed by the law-and-society approach, which understands different types of law as a product of society,[117] comparative law looks for 'legal matter' in all aspects of human experience. Sacco's approach, in particular, lends itself to importing key sociolegal ideas such as legal consciousness, seeing 'threads of law and legality within the tapestry of ordinary lives

[116] R Sacco, 'Legal Formants' Instalment I (n 10) 7ff. Also, Sacco, 'One Hundred Years' (n 114) 1174ff, in which he argues that 'anthropologists are in the process of teaching [lawyers] to reflect on the law and its manifestations', as they 'speak more to the comparativists than to the jurists in general' and precede them 'when it comes to penetrating certain domains'.

[117] On law and society, see inter alia K Calavita, *Invitation to Law and Society: An Introduction to the Study of Real Law* (Chicago, IL, University of Chicago Press, 2016) 12 and elsewhere. The academic literature in law and society is vast; see also S Vago, *Law and Society* (London, Routledge, 2015) for a helpful overview of the field.

and everyday events'.[118] This analytical lens has often been used to study the gaps between Islamic law principles and its popular perceptions, illustrating the deeply contextual variations of what is understood as *shari'ah* in different settings and by different groups.[119] Moreover, comparative law does not ignore the normative value of impressions of law in individuals and groups, such as the process and effects of legal socialisation.[120] For these reasons, comparative law can enable a fuller analysis of both the international framework of TJ, and Islamic law, as examples of composite law made up of explicit and implicit elements, specific ways of thinking about law in different settings, and invisible normative forces.

Comparing different legal systems can include juxtaposing international law with local understandings of law, as attested in the developments in comparative international law.[121] This echoes some of the normative, methodological and political preoccupations of the project of 'global legal pluralism'.[122] Much like legal pluralism, comparative law lends itself to seeing and understanding the complexities of the international framework of TJ and its relocation in local settings, including Muslim-majority societies. It looks at broad patterns of social order and rules which have yet to be formalised, even in the absence of centralised state power,[123] considering 'whatever gives individuals incentives strong enough to affect their social behaviour'.[124] Sacco terms these abstract normative principles 'genotypes' (theoretical norms) and their contextual tangible expressions 'phenotypes'.[125] These twin concepts identify the prescriptive force of culture and customary forms of justice alongside other rules that make up a legal system, and as such can help inform the process of relocating TJ in a culturally responsive manner (and will be discussed in

[118] On legal consciousness, P Ewick and S Silbey, 'Conformity, Contestation, and Resistance: An Account of Legal Consciousness' (1991) 26 *New England Law Review* 26, 731; P Ewick and S Silbey, *The Common Place of Law: Stories from Everyday Life* (Chicago, IL, University of Chicago Press, 1998); and S Silbey, 'After Legal Consciousness' (2005) 1 *Annual Review of Law and Social Science*. 323.

[119] T Moustafa, 'Islamic Law, Women's Rights, and Popular Legal Consciousness in Malaysia' (2013) 38(1) *Law & Social Inquiry* 168.

[120] J Louin-Tapp, 'The Geography of Legal Socialisation: Scientific and Social Markers' (1991) 19(1) *Droit et société* 329; CI Kourilsky-Augeven, 'Legal Socialisation: From Compliance to Familiarisation Through Permeation' (2007) 1 *European Journal of Legal Studies* 265.

[121] A Roberts et al, 'Comparative International Law: Framing the Field' (2015) 109 *American Journal of International Law* 467.

[122] See PS Berman, 'Global Legal Pluralism as a Normative Project' (2018) 8 *UC Irvine Law Review* 149 (and his other work on the topic); R Michaels, 'Global Legal Pluralism' (2009) 5 *Annual Review of Law and Social Science* 5 243; W Twining, 'Normative and Legal Pluralism: A Global Perspective' (2009) 20 *Duke Journal of Comparative & International Law* 473; and also A Peters and H Schwenke, 'Comparative Law Beyond Post-modernism' (2000) 49(4) *ICLQ* 800.

[123] Sacco 'Legal Formants' Instalment I (n 10) 7, 9.

[124] U Mattei, 'Three Patterns of Law: Taxonomy and Change in the World's Legal Systems' (1997) 45 *American Journal of Comparative Law* 5, 13.

[125] Sacco 'Legal Formants' Instalment I (n 10).

greater detail later in this section). Nonetheless, as already discussed in relation to legal pluralism, the invocation of culture can be problematic and should be understood in the context of other potential limitations of comparative legal methods.

A. Comparative Law between Creative Thinking and Questionable Legacies

In translating TJ into local settings, multiple actors (including civil society and international organisations) invoke law and legal principles that do not exist in a vacuum. In principle, comparative legal methods are well placed to capture the 'diversity, change, or history' in which TJ occurs, searching for 'all the factors that, by nature, influence the creative process of law and shape the rule and the life of law'.[126] This enables deeper insights into the law and tools to see beyond black-letter law to consider social and political contexts.[127] As such, comparative law ought to 'become part of interdisciplinary research and serve the scholar concerned with problems of sociology and politics'.[128] Power structures and subjectivities (both individual and collective) feed into the process of comparison, and the risks of ethnocentrism, uncritical deference to international law or romanticisation of local law (discussed above) are an embedded risk of comparative legal methods. Scholars and practitioners approaching the task of localising TJ from international law to local settings should be mindful of these considerations – including in the legal systems of Muslim-majority societies discussed in Chapters 5 and 6.

Comparative law and its proponents have often been described through metaphors of travel and exploration.[129] But observing 'a foreign legal system from the outside' is complicated, and requires responsible engagement with the object of study and an appreciation of the risks of essentialisation and hierarchies ascribed to the Self and the Other.[130] The comparison between different legal systems helps engage 'the unspoken, taken-for-granted body of assumptions and beliefs that inform and motivate the law in different societies', but

[126] Sacco (n 114) 1170.

[127] O Kahn-Freund, 'On Uses and Misuses of Comparative Law' (1974) 37(1) *MLR* 1, 27, and Zweigert and Kötz (n 114) 33ff. Sacco also considers how comparative law fosters critical approaches in Sacco (n 114) 1159.

[128] Sacco, 'Legal Formants' Instalment II (n 10) 388ff. Sacco notes: 'Comparative law can offer its conclusions to sociology. If sociology does not utilise them, it is not the comparativist's fault.'

[129] Sacco (n 114) 1175. Sacco's legacy in comparative law is notable; as a drafter of the Tesi di Trento (Trento, 3 June 1987), he contributed to developing the contemporary understanding of comparative law. The Tesi di Trento can be found in the original version at www.jus.unitn.it/cardozo/Review/2008/Trento2.pdf. Also G Frankenberg, 'Critical Comparisons: Re-thinking Comparative Law' (1985) 26 *Harvard International Law Journal* 411.

[130] M De S-O-L'E Lasser, 'The Question of Understanding' in P Legrand and R Munday (eds), *Comparative Legal Studies: Traditions and Transitions* (Cambridge, Cambridge University Press, 2003) 221 and 235ff. And also Schacherreiter (n 10).

should not succumb to a purely apologetic stance towards any of them.[131] One's cultural starting point is likely to influence how norms are understood:[132] this could take the form of 'the 'inner' perspective',[133] bringing an outside view, or focusing on 'trans-cultural unity'.[134] In the context of legal pluralism presented earlier, it is vital not to assume the hegemony of international standards, or the primacy of local ways of thinking about law. In the context of one's cultural starting points, anthropologist Lila Abu-Lughod warns that this way of thinking may enforce 'separations that inevitably carry a sense of hierarchy', when actually 'the boundaries between self and other' are unsettled.[135] The same challenges have been identified in comparative law: in order to avoid dichotomies and homogenisations Judith Schacherreiter considers:

> The problematic simplification … in placing the Self and the Other as homogenous entities in a rigidly binary opposition. Such an approach obscures the presence of the Self *in* the Other (and vice versa), the side-by-side presence of differences and similarities, and the instances of mutual influence and mixing.[136]

In comparative legal studies these distinctions are partly driven by 'functionality' as one of the core aims of the comparative law project and its evolution, which rely on having a clear difference between the two norms to juxtapose.[137] Critics of the functionalist position are sceptical of oversimplifications that negate or marginalise 'the effects of legal forms and ideas in the realm of consciousness as ideologies and rituals' for the sake of problem solving.[138] One example of this oversimplification is the classic legal systemology as proposed by Rene David, which classifies laws into families based on conceptual structures ('the theory of the sources of the law') and the 'social objectives to be achieved with the help of the legal system or the place of law itself within the social order'.[139]

[131] J Whitman, 'The Neo-romantic Turn' in P Legrand and R Munday (eds), *Comparative Legal Studies: Traditions and Transitions* (Cambridge, Cambridge University Press, 2003) 315 and 334. For a background on hermeneutics, see inter alia RJ Dostal (ed), *The Cambridge Companion to Gadamer* (Cambridge, Cambridge University Press, 2002); H Gadamer, *Philosophical Hermeneutics* (Berkeley, University of California Press, 2008).

[132] Nelken (n 65) 444.

[133] Whitman (n 131) 314ff, referencing W Ewald 'Comparative Jurisprudence (II): The Logic of Legal Transplants' (1995) *American Journal of Comparative Law* 489.

[134] GP Fletcher, 'Comparative Law as a Subversive Discipline' (1998) *American Journal of Comparative Law* 683, 691 and 693ff.

[135] L Abu-Lughod, 'Writing Against Culture' in T Oakes and PL Price (eds), *The Cultural Geography Reader* (London, Routledge, 2008). Related themes are discussed in RG Fox, *Recapturing Anthropology: Working in the Present* (Santa Fe, NM, School of American Research Press, 1991) 137.

[136] Schacherreiter (n 10) 303.

[137] Zweigert and Kötz (n 114) 34ff.

[138] Frankenberg (n 129) 434ff. Similar objections to functionalism are found in M Graziadei, 'The Functionalist Heritage' in P Legrand and R Munday (eds), *Comparative Legal Studies: Traditions and Transitions* (Cambridge, Cambridge University Press, 2003) 113.

[139] R David and EC Brierley, *The Major Legal Systems of the World Today* (London, Stevens and Sons, 1985) 20. Relatedly, HP Glenn, *Legal Traditions of the World: Sustainable Diversity in Law*, 4th edn (Oxford, Oxford University Press, 2010).

The portrayal of legal families as relatively linear and homogeneous legal traditions, which relies on Eurocentric notions of what constitutes a legal system, is now received with scepticism but has not been completely abandoned.[140] The search for 'ideal law'[141] is infused with the preconceived notions and identities of those involved in the search.

Günter Frankenberg has lamented that some comparativists 'suppress their subjectivity and hide their peculiar perspective behind the rhetoric of objectivity and neutrality', 'camouflaging their politics' and avoiding 'immersion into the other' until they recognise their own prevailing culture.[142] This is a flaw of the entire project: the origins of comparative law reveal entrenched colonial attitudes towards foreign (ie 'native' or 'primitive') legal systems,[143] much like the hegemonic histories of international law.[144] Both the early international and comparative schools were based on the racist notion that some nations and cultures were more civilised that others. The troubling subtext of that approach is the misguided belief that some legal systems (ie those of the Global South) incorporate more culture than law, so are not equivalent comparators: that type of law is not seen as real law, so it can be treated as an object to be civilised by the categories of Western law, including international law.[145] Therefore, when adopting comparative law approaches to localising the international framework of TJ into Muslim-majority settings it is vital for those contributing to the process to reject any notion of objectivity and neutrality in their project, recognising and engaging with their own unconscious bias (and that of the disciplines of international law and comparative methods) and their assumptions about what law is, should look like and do.

Other models of classification have emerged that account more explicitly for the competing normative forces within given contexts and allow for greater degrees of problematisation. For instance, Ugo Mattei adopts a notion of 'law as a tool of social organisation' to evaluate the balance between law, politics, religious and philosophical traditions in shaping three patterns of rule of law: professional (legal and political arenas are separate and secularised),

[140] See eg the informative discussion in Schacherreiter (n 10) 297ff; M Pargendler, 'The Rise and Decline of Legal Families' (2012) 60(4) *American Journal of Comparative Law* 1043; J Husa, 'The Future of Legal Families' in *Oxford Handbooks Online* (Oxford, Oxford University Press, 2016).

[141] G Frankenberg, 'Stranger than Paradise: Identity and Politics in Comparative Law' (1997) 2 *Utah Law Review* 259, 262ff.

[142] ibid and 269ff.

[143] U Baxi, 'The Colonial Heritage' in P Legrand and R Munday (eds), *Comparative Legal Studies: Traditions and Transitions* (Cambridge, Cambridge University Press, 2003) 46ff. In particular, the First International Congress for Comparative Law in 1900 in Paris sought to develop a common law of humanity, as a consequence of human progress aided by the comparative method, as discussed in Zweigert and Kötz (n 114) 2ff. For a critical overview of the history of comparative law, see inter alia, Sacco (n 114) 1159.

[144] See eg A Anghie, 'Finding the Peripheries: Sovereignty and Colonialism in Nineteenth-century International Law' (1999) 40 *Harvard International Law Journal* 1; and A Anghie, *Imperialism, Sovereignty and the Making of International Law* (Cambridge, Cambridge University Press, 2007).

[145] On these themes, see inter alia Koskenniemi (n 111).

political (law and politics are not completely separate and authorities may live above the rule of law – typical of transitional and development contexts) or traditional (in which religion or a transcendental philosophy have a prominent role).[146] The political rule-of-law system (described as typical of transitions) is also characterised by the competition between the rule of professional law and the rule of traditional law in dominating a legal setting.[147] The tripartite classification set out by Mattei and the explicit mention of transitions suggest that while the rule of politics temporarily prevails, the rule of professional law and the rule of traditional law struggle to project their respective weight in the process. The ways in which foreign models are imported into any given context is also relevant: legal borrowing and 'transplants'[148] bring to light how elites draw on foreign law (either by choice, self-interest or influenced by other actors).[149] This intricate tapestry of the normative force of professional (official) law, politics and tradition can be broadly captured by Sacco's theory of legal formants – which underpins the comparative analysis set out in Chapters 5 and 6.

B. The Theory of Legal Formants Meets the Localisation of Transitional Justice

Having set out the caveats in adopting the comparative law method, the discussion now turns to the merits of the theory of legal formants proposed by Sacco. This underutilised method can help explore the localisation of the international legal framework in TJ in Muslim-majority settings, discussed in more detail in the final section of this chapter and again in Chapter 6 (specifically, the truth-seeking element). We have already seen that no given legal system – including the international law framework of TJ – is based on a single set of cohesive norms.[150] Instead, a plethora of legal material, interpretations and conflicting pulls indicate multiple 'legal formants' within a given legal system; sometimes they coexist in harmony, other times in conflict.[151] Legal formants are defined as:

> All those formative elements that make any given rule of law amidst statutes, general propositions, particular definitions, reasons, holdings, etc. All of these

[146] Mattei (n 124), citing M Weber, *On Law in Economy and Society* (Cambridge, MA, Harvard University Press, 1954) 12 and 16ff.

[147] ibid 35.

[148] On legal transplants, see inter alia A Watson, *Legal Transplants: An Approach to Comparative Law* (Athens, University of Georgia Press, 1974); A Watson, 'Aspects of Reception of Law' (1996) *American Journal of Comparative Law* 335; Ewald (n 134) 4; E Stein, 'Uses, Misuses – and Nonuses of Comparative Law' (1977) 72 *Northwestern University Law Review* 198.

[149] Graziadei (n 138) 124ff.

[150] Sacco, 'Legal Formants' Instalment I (n 10) 21ff.

[151] ibid 23ff.

> formative elements are not necessarily coherent with each other within each system. … To the contrary, legal formants are usually conflicting and can better be pictured in a competitive relationship with one another.[152]

According to Sacco's theory, multitudes of facts influence how scholars or judges interpret legal provisions, including factors extraneous to the law and norms borrowed and transplanted from elsewhere. Competing interpretations and options can all be valid by virtue of their very existence, based on 'the actual observation of the elements at work in a given legal system'.[153] The number of legal formants is not finite (or limited to statute/judicial decisions/scholarly writings).[154] A key distinction, however, is between 'legal formants that are themselves rules of conduct and others that are developed in order to provide abstract formulations or justifications of rules and conduct'.[155] In the international framework of TJ, an example of this could be the right to truth for violations of the right to life and prohibition of torture (rule of conduct), and the normative principle of accountability for past harm (justification of the rule of conduct). Sacco also distinguishes between 'enacted legal formants' (eg in constitutions) and 'those which have grown up without formal enactment'.[156] An example of this would be the explicit references to Islamic law in the jurisdictions of some countries, and the normative principles of *shari'ah* that might inform a legal system indirectly without formal enactment in other jurisdictions (as discussed in Chapters 5 and 6).

Interpretation of the law and 'whatever affects the convictions of the interpreter' is also a source of law.[157] Scholarly work is one of the supreme sources of law, also evidenced in relation to Islamic law where scholarly interpretation fills the gaps of more abstract legal propositions based on infallible divine revelation (discussed in Chapter 5).[158] In this context, scholars (and especially early jurists) are recognised as the 'architect[s] of this immense framework of rules', given there is little space accorded to judicial precedent; moreover, in Sunni Islamic law and theology, there is no supreme interpretative authority.[159] Even when the nationalisation of law limits the scholar's capacity to create law, scholarly authority may play an important role in the legal system. For example, in Egypt, the Grand Sheykh of Al-Azhar, the leading scholarly institution in Sunni Islam, is held in high esteem by state institutions,

[152] M Bussani and U Mattei, 'The Common Core Approach to the European Private Law' (1997/1998) 3 *Columbia Journal of European Law* 339, 344.
[153] Sacco, 'Legal Formants' Instalment I (n 10) 25.
[154] ibid 32ff.
[155] ibid 34.
[156] Sacco, 'Legal Formants' Instalment II (n 10) 344.
[157] ibid 345.
[158] ibid 347ff.
[159] ibid 348.

and has sought a role in the public debate around the law – also during the Arab Spring uprisings.[160]

Not all formants are articulated explicitly.[161] There are numerous implicit, non-verbalised rules and patterns, termed 'cryptotypes' by Sacco, which may diverge from 'the explicit formulations of a system' and yet still have significant outward normative consequences.[162] The more general a cryptotype, the harder it is to identify, although 'they may form the conceptual framework for the whole system'.[163] This notion seems to echo the psychological and sociological concept of 'legal impulsions' giving rise to 'intuitive unofficial law' discussed in Chapter 1.[164] It also builds on some of the more general and foundational ideas about the force of law as expressed in the sociology of law of Pierre Bourdieu.[165] More specifically, Sacco talks about the 'mentality' of jurists of given countries as linked to contextual cryptotypes,[166] and the 'cultural baggage' of judges and lawyers.[167] Previous parts of this chapter considered the difficulties in defining and using the concept of legal culture, so extreme caution in adopting this lens is required, but it may still be useful. An example of the mentality of jurists in a specific context is offered by the Turkish legal system, which is largely secular, but embedded in the social and political realities of a Muslim-majority society, which in turn might inform the interpretation of the positive secular laws enacted by the secular state.[168] Therefore, elements of what can be termed 'mute law' coexist with, albeit are overshadowed by, spoken (ie explicit) legal sources.[169] The role of *shari'ah* in the legal systems of Muslim-majority states is a fitting example of a cryptotype that might coexist, though not necessarily in a dominant fashion, alongside numerous other normative forces (as will be discussed in Chapter 5).

A flaw of this theory is Sacco's belief that certain rules survive 'because they do not represent any value, do not correspond to any ideology, are foreign to any moral systems and respond to an elementary necessity of social

[160] See NJ Brown, *Post-Revolutionary Al-Azhar* (Washington, DC, Carnegie Endowment for International Peace, 2011) 5.

[161] Sacco, 'Legal Formants' Instalment II (n 10) 385ff.

[162] ibid.

[163] ibid 386.

[164] See discussion of A Podgorecki, 'Unrecognized Father of Sociology of Law: Leon Petrazycki – Reflections Based on Jan Gorecki's Sociology and Jurisprudence of Leon Petrazycki' (1980–81) 15 *Law & Society Review* 183 in ch 1.

[165] P Bourdieu, 'The Force of Law: Toward a Sociology of the Juridical Field' (1986) 38 *Hastings Law Journal* 805.

[166] Sacco, 'Legal Formants' Instalment II (n 10) 387.

[167] Sacco (n 114) 1171.

[168] On the effects of a Muslim-majority population in the secular state and law, see AA An-Na'im, *Islam and the Secular State: Negotiating the Future of Shari'a* (Cambridge, MA, Harvard University Press, 2008) 182ff: 'The Islamic identity of Turkey is rooted in its culture, tradition, and the religious affiliation of the vast majority of its population, while the secular nature of the state is entrenched in its constitution.'

[169] R Sacco, 'Mute Law' (1995) 43 *American Journal of Comparative Law* 455, 465ff.

organization' (or pose a threat to dominant interests).[170] By presenting itself as a neutral interpretative lens to identify legal formants of a given system, his analysis ignores deep-rooted structural imbalances. It is evident that cryptotypes underpinning a legal system are intimately linked with the prevailing social structures and power dynamics. The role of positive law in this regard may be duplicitous: one the one hand, enacted laws may both shield and be shielded by certain negative practices that determine the cryptotype; on the other, the law (eg IHRL) may provide the very tools to bring about positive change that may contribute to minimising or eradicating the effects of an 'unethical' cryptotype (eg international or local social norms condoning certain forms of violence). In the context of TJ, (newly) enacted law may carry this transformative potential, breaking with an illiberal past, or imposing silence and new violence.

Taking stock of the discussion, the important contribution of comparative law, and in particular Sacco's theory of legal formants to the relocation of TJ from international law to Muslim-majority settings, is the attention it affords to the hidden normative forces that might inform a legal system. With reference to the evolution of the international framework of TJ, comparative methods can help identify local normative principles to complement global rules. Mindful of the structural inequalities that may be enshrined and perpetuated by legal formants and cryptotypes, international law approaches to TJ may find a valuable ally in comparative law's ability to see the nuances of the legal systems of countries undergoing transition.

C. Comparative Law for Developing International Law and the Global Paradigm of Transitional Justice

Comparative legal analysis can help develop international law – including the global framework of TJ. For instance, the meaning and content of 'general principles of law recognised by civilised nations' as a source of international law under Article 38 of the ICJ Statute can be clarified through comparative law methods;[171] this in turn is relevant for other areas of PIL, such as the Rome Statute of the ICC (although the actual use of comparative law by that Court beyond civil/common law is limited).[172] In principle, PIL and the work of the United Nations may help bridge gaps between legal systems;[173] but thinking

[170] Sacco, 'Legal Formants' Instalment II (n 10) 392.

[171] Zweigert and Kötz (n 114) 7ff. Reference to Art 38 ICJ Statute is also made in David and Brierley (n 139) 9ff.

[172] M Siems, *Comparative Law* (Cambridge, Cambridge University Press, 2014) 225. See Art 21 (1)(c) of the Rome Statute of the ICC. The ICC Office of the Prosecutor, Policy Paper on the Interests of Justice (September 2007) 7–8, offers some recognition to 'other forms of justice', available at www.icc-cpi.int/NR/rdonlyres/772C95C9-F54D-4321-BF09-73422BB23528/143640/ICCOTPInterestsOfJustice.pdf.

[173] Sacco, 'Legal Formants' Instalment I (n 10) 6.

more critically about international law reveals that it is a legal system itself, with a distinctive legal culture (albeit informed by many others) and its key champions (first and foremost, the UN). David Kennedy sums up some of the tensions between the two disciplines: while international law focuses on a 'universal claim or project' aimed at 'governing', comparative law concerns itself more with 'understanding' – and comparative lawyers are 'legal specialists in difference'.[174] International lawyers tend to equate culture with the nation, inhabiting a different frame from law.[175] In principle, therefore, PIL is well equipped to respond to comparative law, but in practice 'intra-Western' debates about civil and common law and existing political hegemonies have marginalised other legal traditions on the international plane, including Islamic law.

Given the 'indivisibility of the local and international dimensions of transitional justice', comparative law (if used correctly) can operate as a shuttle between the global and the various particular applications of TJ that in turn feed back into the global.[176] Moreover, comparative analysis can feed into the development of the global paradigm of TJ within the 'steady state of transitional justice', normalised in permanent institutions set out under international law, such as the ICC,[177] that can potentially embed comparative law in their work. The globalisation of human rights through international organisations can also help promote comparative understandings.[178] Soft law can also be fertile ground for legal developments.[179] Cross-cultural communication based on general concepts such as human dignity might foster a 'deeper and more genuine universality' in which common principles adapt to different local settings.[180] This could support a *jus commune* for TJ that accommodates and includes international law principles as well as local norms. The emerging global framework of TJ, if predicated on international law alongside domestic and local norms, could be framed in relation to the notion of *jus gentium*: international law understood as the law of nations (ie peoples, not states).[181] This argument could in principle be adopted in the context of the design and development of TJ initiatives that embed multiple normative forces.

[174] D Kennedy, 'New Approaches to Comparative Law: Comparativism and International Governance' (1997) *Utah Law Review* 545, 548 and 551. Some of the themes presented in Kennedy's 1997 work were further discussed in D Kennedy, 'The Methods and the Politics' in P Legrand and R Munday (eds) *Comparative Legal Studies: Traditions and Transitions* (Cambridge, Cambridge University Press, 2003) 345ff.

[175] ibid, 'New Approaches' 552ff.

[176] Viaene and Brems (n 3) 215.

[177] Teitel, 'Transitional Justice Genealogy' (n 21) 89ff.

[178] Siems (n 172) 214ff.

[179] CM Chinkin, 'The Challenge of Soft Law: Development and Change in International Law' (1989) 38 *ICLQ* 850.

[180] P Carozza, '"My Friend is a Stranger": The Death Penalty and the Global Ius Commune of Human Rights' (2003) 81 *Texas Law Review* 1031, 1084ff.

[181] J Waldron, 'Foreign Law and the Modern Jus Gentium' (2005) 119(1) *Harvard Law Review* 129, 132ff.

Dialogue on best practices in relation to TJ is commonplace, and encompasses South–South conversations as well as classic North–South interaction (which may be problematic for the reasons discussed). For instance, in 2013, Libyan delegations attended meetings in Kosovo to discuss disarmament, demobilisation and reintegration (DDR) solutions, with a view to learning from best practices in another Muslim-majority transitional society.[182] Likewise, the official proponents of the draft TJ law for Egypt[183] have sought to consult with foreign lawyers, academics and policymakers with experience of TJ to discuss the aims, legal framework and challenges of this type of process.[184] Conversations with Egyptian officials involved in the tentative design of TJ mechanisms for the country have also illustrated awareness and interest in foreign experiences as disparate as the South African TRC, the experience of Sierra Leone, and the case law of the Inter-American Court of Human Rights.[185] These encounters can be fruitful in promoting the circulation of certain ideas – but any comparison between transitions is limited by the differences in each setting.

When the international framework of TJ meets Muslim-majority societies, the question of what role Islamic law – regardless of its formal recognition in the legal system – might play is hard to ignore. While this book does not offer a specific analysis of national settings, the theory of legal formants conceptualised by Rodolfo Sacco may assist the understanding of how Islamic law concepts dialogue with the international framework of TJ – and what role different actors might have in negotiating that process. Moreover, when observing contexts in which Islamic law and jurisprudence play some sort of role in a legal system where the majority of the population identifies as Muslim, it is important to consider the possible divergence between the normative force of formal state-declared religious law, and the more fluid normativities emanating from individual spiritual identities.[186] As such the positive laws of self-declared Islamic states (such as Saudi Arabia or Iran) or of Muslim-majority communities not in self-defined Islamic states are the outcome of 'ordinary' political processes of a given historical and geographic context which interprets what is 'Islamic'. Therefore, it is important to consider that the 'Islamic' label might be used strategically, cynically and at times naively to further specific political

[182] For coverage, see F Aliu, 'Libya Seeks Kosovo's Help in Peace Transition' in *Balkan Insight*, 21 March 2012, available at balkaninsight.com/2012/03/21/libya-interested-in-kosovo-demilitarization-model.

[183] For coverage, see inter alia F Salah, 'NSF Calls for Transitional Justice Law' *Daily News Egypt* (Cairo, 1 April 2013) www.dailynewsegypt.com/2013/04/03/nsf-calls-for-transitional-justice-law and M El-Shewy 'And Justice for All?' *Sada* (19 March 2013) carnegieendowment.org/sada/2013/03/19/and-justice-for-all/frm9.

[184] On this matter, the author acknowledges the programme at the ZIF/UN-DPKO/CCCPA Expert Conference on Criminal Justice and Accountability in Arab Transition Processes held in September 2012 in Cairo, Egypt, which she attended.

[185] ibid.

[186] On this point, see inter alia Rehman (n 113) 26ff.

interests, which may not necessarily chime with the aims of transition or the requirements of international law (or indeed the noble aims of the *shari'ah*). This will be discussed in Chapters 5 and 6 in more detail.

As illustrated in Chapter 1, ways in which international law and religion may interact offer useful ideas for comparative lawyers.[187] Baderin argues that 'religion is like a double-edged sword that could be utilised either positively or negatively in its relationship with international law'.[188] Accordingly, Islamic law can be used in various constructive as well as destructive ways in relation to international law, and consequently in relation to the global TJ paradigm – much like international law can be used constructively or destructively in relation to local norms.

The dialogue between the international framework of TJ and Islamic law faces the additional challenge of the interpenetration between theology and jurisprudence. Nonetheless, this is not a barrier for comparative lawyers operating as secular thinkers. Firstly, the 'Islamic' element may be employed as a convenient label for political gain and populist gratification. The social significance of the Islamic label – unchallenged and unchallengeable as 'divine' – is thus a potent political tool for oppression as well as liberation. Secondly, to serve certain political interests, the 'Islamic' element may be based on contentious exegesis. Thirdly, the sources of Islamic law are often quite general: as such, drawing on abstract notions of *shari'ah* is based on a vision of law of an idealised, non-existent Muslim society. This will be explored in greater detail in Chapters 5 and 6.

The study of the synergies between principles of the Islamic legal tradition and the objectives of TJ is necessary for both theoretical and practical purposes. A critical comparative study might help localise international/human rights conceptions of TJ in Muslim-majority settings, by widening the view of relevant sources to incorporate Islamic law, thereby strengthening the implementation of TJ in Muslim-majority societies through local conceptions of law. With regards to relocating TJ from international law to Muslim-majority legal systems, comparative law may reveal how PIL and Islamic law (as a formant of Muslim-majority legal systems undergoing transition) cross-fertilise, thus strengthening the normative framework both in its abstract global dimension and in its local applications. Moreover, this could lead to future exploration of regional approaches to TJ in the Arab region and other Muslim-majority contexts, taking stock of the potential influence of Islamic law. This approach also provides a toolkit for the developing global legal framework of TJ to draw creatively from the elements of Islamic law. While proponents of legal purism – either in international law or in Islamic law – are likely to be critical

[187] M Baderin, 'Religion and International Law: Friends or Foes?' (2009) 5 *European Human Rights Law Review* 637.

[188] ibid 649.

of these suggestions, considering the synergies and cross-fertilisation between the two sets of norms seems pragmatic in Muslim-majority settings, and potentially beneficial in general. As such, a critically aware, constructive comparative approach to the international framework of TJ may engage fully and frankly with the Islamic law formants (and cryptotypes) of Muslim-majority legal systems as discussed in the final two chapters.

IV. CONCLUSION

This chapter built on the premise that in any given context the framework of TJ is informed by international law as well as by multiple local normative forces that are both official and unofficial, as well as enacted and invisible. As such, IHRL standards, customary forms of justice and cultural practices coexist in TJ, which is more likely to reflect the aspirations of a broader range of stakeholders and beneficiaries if different normative principles are recognised and included in the process. The first part of this chapter argued that the inherent pluralism of the international framework of TJ is a useful way to interpret the indeterminacy of the law of TJ. It also considered the dynamic relationship between law, culture and society in any given TJ setting where the global paradigm faces a local context informed by different normative forces – including norms emanating from religious and traditional sources and practices (such as the case with Islamic law). Resisting the pitfalls of essentialisation and hierarchies, the second part of this chapter explored how comparative legal methods offer useful tools to identify and understand the role of (and tensions between) different normative forces within the process of localising TJ in any given setting. Comparative law methods (and in particular, Sacco's theory of legal formants) are well-suited to capturing and critically interpreting the full range of normative elements in a given context including other – often unseen – normative forces in societies and the political context in which they operate.

The theoretical and methodological approach illustrated in this chapter is adopted throughout the project to answer the two interrelated questions: How can the truth-seeking element of the international legal framework for TJ be localised in Muslim-majority societies? And to what extent does Islamic law and jurisprudence support the notion of the right to truth about past violence, as emerging in international law? The theoretical premise of legal pluralism and the comparative legal method will underpin the analysis of the truth-seeking element of TJ and the right to truth in international law, and the notion and role of Islamic law in Muslim-majority societies, and the extent to which the *shari'ah* accommodates and promotes truth seeking and the right to truth. Legal pluralism and comparative law lend themselves to a critical analysis of the object of study, inasmuch as they do not settle for rarefied, decontextualised and hierarchical notions of law, but instead are able to address the complex social, cultural and political contexts (and their key actors) in which norms emerge and operate. By reinterpreting the international law framework of TJ from a critical comparative perspective, local norms may facilitate the translation of global principles of TJ (such as the right to the truth discussed in Chapter 4) into local settings; this also contributes to the formation of the international framework of TJ itself by drawing on a broader range of ways of thinking about justice and normative factors that emerge organically.

3

Legal Truths, Judicial Rituals and Transitional Justice

I. INTRODUCTION

UNCOVERING TRUTHS, SHAPING collective memories and acknowledging competing narratives about past harm feature as central themes of TJ premised on human rights.[1] Much of the literature on transitional truth seeking is informed by memory studies, including memory laws, evidencing the complex, contested and interdisciplinary nature of the topic and its centrality.[2] The belief that 'the past must be dealt with' has emerged as 'the memory assumption' in TJ.[3] Confronting the view that there ought to be a standard

[1] RG Teitel, *Transitional Justice* (Oxford, Oxford University Press, 2000) 88ff.

[2] The literature in this area is immense. On reckoning with the past, see inter alia MS Grindle and EE Goodman (eds), *Reflections on Memory and Democracy* (Cambridge, MA, Harvard University Press, 2016); DA Crocker, 'Reckoning with Past Wrongs: A Normative Framework' (1999) 13 *Ethics and International Affairs* 43; J Elster, 'Coming to Terms with the Past. A Framework for the Study of Justice in the Transition to Democracy' (1998) 39 *European Journal of Sociology* 7; E Jelin, *State Repression and the Labors of Memory* (Minneapolis, University of Minnesota Press, 2003). On collective memory, see inter alia E Apfelbaum, 'Halbwachs and the Social Properties of Memory' in S Radstone and B Schwarz (eds), *Memory: Histories, Theories, Debates* (New York, Fordham University Press, 2010); A Barahona de Brito, 'Introduction' in A Barahona de Brito, C Gonzalez Enriquez and P Aguilar (eds), *The Politics of Memory: Transitional Justice in Democratizing Societies* (Oxford, Oxford University Press, 2001); I Irwin-Zarecka, *Frames of Remembrance: The Dynamics of Collective Memory* (London, Routledge, 2007); M Osiel, *Mass Atrocity: Collective Memory, and the Law* (New Brunswick, NJ, Transaction Publishers, 1997); S Karstedt (ed), *Legal Institutions and Collective Memories* (Oxford, Hart 2009); JK Olick, V Vinitzky-Seroussi and D Levy (eds), *The Collective Memory Reader* (New York, Oxford University Press, 2011); R López, 'Legalising Collective Remembrance after Mass Atrocities' in FM Ottanelli and SE Bird (eds), *The Performance of Memory as Transitional Justice* (Cambridge, Intersentia, 2014). On memory laws specifically, see inter alia N Koposov, *Memory Laws, Memory Wars: The Politics of the Past in Europe and Russia*, (Cambridge, Cambridge University Press, 2018); U Belavusau and A Gliszczyńska-Grabias, 'Memory Laws Mapping a New Subject in Comparative Law and Transitional Justice' in U Belavusau and A Gliszczynska-Grabias (eds), *Law and Memory: Towards Legal Governance of History* (Cambridge, Cambridge University Press, 2017); U Belavusau and A Gliszczyńska-Grabias, 'The Remarkable Rise of "Law and Historical Memory" in Europe: Theorizing Trends and Prospects in the Recent Literature' (2020) 47(2) *Journal of Law and Society* 325; Y Gutman, 'Memory Laws: An Escalation in Minority Exclusion or a Testimony to the Limits of State Power?' (2016) 50(3) *Law & Society Review* 575.

[3] JV Rotondi and N Eisikovits, 'Forgetting after War: A Qualified Defence' in C Corradetti, N Eisikovits, and JV Rotondi (eds), *Theorising Transitional Justice* (Abingdon, Routledge, 2016) 24.

'proper' way to remember past atrocities, Lea David challenges the 'unquestionable assumption' held by (many) human rights advocates 'that a proper memorialisation of a difficult past is essential for both democracy and human rights'.[4] Based on the links between truth seeking and the transitional aims of accountability, justice and reconciliation (and non-recurrence), the quest for the truth emerges as an ever-present and cross-cutting – albeit contested – theme that is declined in different ways across time and place.

Denial, as famously articulated by Stanley Cohen drawing on sociology, psychology and many other disciplines, intertwines micro-denial (featuring personal and psychological connotations) and 'macro-denial' (with social and historical connotations).[5] Uncovering the truth about mass violence, and making it publicly accessible and debatable across political and social settings, is clearly an interdisciplinary endeavour.[6] With that in mind, law offers an important, yet somewhat blunt, set of tools to pursue and contest truth(s) about past violence, including the emerging right to truth discussed in the next chapter. For Elizabeth Jelin, the production of memory is situated within the 'struggle for public recognition of past suffering'; its pedagogic purpose seeks to convey meaning to others and future generations, despite ambiguities and subjective interpretations.[7] Given the limitations and distortions that can be produced through law, however, it is important to consider how 'the memories of the recent past, memories of suffering and political violence, elicit a great diversity of rituals and cultural productions, as well as a search for interpretations and explanations'.[8] When transitional truth seeking is pursued through legal/legalised tools, the processes that seek to uncover and produce memory are shaped by law and extralegal factors, and in turn, contribute to shaping collective memories of fraught pasts.

Building on these premises, this chapter investigates the formation, significance and limitations of truth seeking through formal legal/legalised proceedings, focusing in particular on the value and ambiguities of legal truth in transitional contexts. It does not consider the philosophical foundations of the truth directly.[9] Nor does it consider the 'appropriate standards of justice'

[4] L David, *The Past Can't Heal Us: The Dangers of Mandating Memory in the Name of Human Rights* (Cambridge, Cambridge University Press, 2020) 3.

[5] S Cohen, *States of Denial: Knowing about Atrocities and Suffering* (Cambridge, Polity, 2001).

[6] For instance, artistic expressions that describe past sufferings through literature, drama, visual arts and music may all contribute to truth seeking. See the fascinating account offered in L Bisschoff and S Van de Peer (eds), *Art and Trauma in Africa: Representations of Reconciliation in Music, Visual Arts, Literature and Film* (London, IB Tauris, 2013).

[7] E Jelin, 'Memory and Democracy Toward a Transformative Relationship in P Gready and S Robins (eds), *From Transitional to Transformative Justice* (Cambridge, Cambridge University Press, 2019) 173.

[8] ibid 172.

[9] For a summary of some philosophical foundations of truth, see inter alia G Girelli, *Understanding Transitional Justice: A Struggle for Peace, Reconciliation, and Rebuilding* (London, Palgrave Macmillan, 2017) 44–48.

in evaluating the legal responses to wrongdoing: other studies engage these complex questions.[10] This work builds on the understanding of truth emerging from Heidegger's interpretation of Plato's Allegory of the Cave: the truth is 'that which is unhidden', as in not concealed (for instance, by those interested in keeping the truth hidden), and capable of being comprehended.[11] This twofold appreciation of the truth is particularly suited to the context of TJ, where efforts to obscure the past or distort its meaning can shape not only truth seeking but also justice and reconciliation prospects. While both moments presented in Heidegger's conceptualisation of truth are inherently political, they differ in their historical focus: the act of uncovering the truth is a backward-facing endeavour, whereas its interpretation is forward-looking.

This chapter investigates and situates the legal truth as a key, yet contested, element of TJ, distinct (but related to) other forms of truth. It argues that the legal truth is a distinctive element of TJ that emerges from a range of legal/legalised truth-seeking mechanisms, including trials and truth commissions, and despite its limitations, it feeds into the formation of collective memories in various ways – including through archival outcomes. The overall discussion builds loosely on Deborah Posel's 'rainbow of truths' metaphor, drawing on the South African TRC's four notions of truth: factual/forensic; personal/narrative; social/dialogue; and healing/restorative.[12] This list of truths, however, is not clear-cut and conclusive; moreover, the formulation of historical records of the past might include 'various 'truths' or interpretations' that combine some of the TRC's four notions with other forms of knowledge of contested pasts.[13] This study is informed by Alexandra Barahona de Brito's description of 'ongoing "cognitive battles" over memory' that 'highlight that there is not one "truth" but various competing "truths" that will jostle to gain ascendancy, and the dominance of one "narrative" over another may shift with the passage of time' and may be interrupted by 'events that spark off new battles over memory'.[14] By exploring the notion of 'legal truth' from this perspective, this chapter illustrates that the distinction between 'judicial truth' and 'truth commission truth' – and other truths emanating from quasi-judicial, legalised mechanisms – is not clear cut;[15]

[10] C Murphy, *The Conceptual Foundations of Transitional Justice* (Cambridge, Cambridge University Press, 2017) 5.

[11] M Heidegger, *The Essence of Truth* (New York, Continuum, 2002) 47ff.

[12] D Posel, 'The TRC Report: What Kind of History? What Kind of Truth?' (1999) 10, quoting the TRC Report, vol I, ch 5, paras 29–30, available at wiredspace.wits.ac.za/bitstream/handle/10539/8046/HWS-341.pdf.

[13] W Lambourne, 'Transitional Justice and Peacebuilding After Mass Violence' (2009) 3(1) *International Journal of Transitional Justice* 28, 39.

[14] A Barahona de Brito, 'Transitional Justice and Memory: Exploring Perspectives' (2010) 15 *South European Society and Politics* 359, 365

[15] For a helpful overview of the judicial truth, see D Accatino and C Collins, 'Truth, Evidence, Truth: The Deployment of Testimony, Archives and Technical Data in Domestic Human Rights Trials' (2016) 8(1) *Journal of Human Rights Practice* 81, 82.

as such, discussions about the merits and limitations of truths emerging from those initiatives benefit from a joint critique, which collapse assumptions about both. This proposition is based on Sacco's comparative law approach outlines in Chapter 2, which posits that law, legal categories and processes, and legal actors must be understood by virtue of their substance, not only based on their form. In other words, truth seeking based on legal sources and championed by actors whose decisions become normative must be approached factually, not on the basis of a largely artificial dichotomy.

The first part of this chapter reviews some of the main issues and legal/legalised mechanisms of truth seeking in TJ. The second part explores the notion of legal truth, its formation and limitations. It considers how the legal truth shapes historical accounts, and considers the influence of key stakeholders in the process. The final part examines the ritual and performative characteristics of formal truth seeking such as trials and truth commissions – in addition to other mechanisms – in forming collective memories. The ritual character of legal/legalised truth-seeking mechanisms can play an important role in TJ, if situated within the cultural and political expectations of the beneficiary communities (and other key stakeholders).

II. TRUTH SEEKING AND TRANSITIONAL JUSTICE: ISSUES, AMBITIONS AND LIMITATIONS

Truth seeking has emerged as a core – yet contested – theme in TJ. Doctrinally, argues Ruti Teitel, truth is 'a virtue of justice', neither synonymous nor independent of it, and because of this, interesting synergies may develop between criminal investigations, historical inquiries and other initiatives.[16] Taking stock of the central cross-cutting role of truth seeking in transition, former UN Special Rapporteur Pablo de Greiff identifies three strands of TJ that link to historical justice: (1) recognition of victim status; (2) promotion of civic trust (both horizontal, between citizens, and vertical, between citizens and state institutions); and (3) the strengthening of the democratic rule of law.[17] The public and collective aspect of truth seeking engages the social and political domains and indicates the state obligation to uncover the truth not solely for the benefit of individual victims and families (who may have a range of psychological and

[16] Teitel (n 1) 89. In this context, Teitel notes how 'truth inquiries in some countries have been considered not a prelude but an alternative to punishment'.

[17] P de Greiff, 'Some thoughts on the Development and Present State of Transitional Justice' (2011) 5(2) *Journal for Human Rights/Zeitschrift fur Menschenrechte* 98, 114ff. In relation to the promotion of civic trust, however, some transitional justice policies, such as forced DNA testing, may in fact impede civic trust insofar as it contravenes the right to privacy; for a discussion of this issue, see EBL King, 'A Conflict of Interests: Privacy, Truth and Compulsory DNA Testing for Argentina's Children of the Disappeared' (2011) 44 *Cornell International Law Journal* 535.

economic needs as well as the 'reasonable expectation of justice') but also the principle of 'good governance in a democratic society'.[18] Separately, but relatedly, the right to truth as an emerging actionable tool (discussed in greater detail in Chapter 4) offers individual victims and their families, as well as society more broadly, the opportunity to demand information about past harm. This section explores the core role and tensions of truth seeking in TJ and the complexities of legal and legalised mechanisms to pursue those aims. It argues that despite the differences between the two typologies of mechanisms, truth produced by trials and truth commissions is similarly contextual, political and circumscribed by design; this sets the scene for the discussion of legal truths and collective memories in subsequent parts of this chapter.

In considering knowledge of the past a useful (and sometimes necessary) but contested step to build the future, transitional truth seeking reflects Ruti Teitel's dual vision of TJ as both backward and forward looking.[19] Broadly speaking, the adoption of a 'presentist' perspective of the past overcomes the 'pastness of the past'.[20] In transitions especially, 'truth is relative to present interest' and may take on different meanings according to time and context.[21] Discussions around why and how to uncover the truth about past violence while moving forward abound in the literature.[22] As Susanne Buckley-Zistel aptly sums up: 'events belong to the past, narratives about them to the present'.[23] Contemporary political considerations motivate the politics of memory and 'the desired communicative effect of these discourses'.[24] Thus, memory emerges as a 'site of conflict, in which many contrary forces converge and in which the interactions between memory and forgetting are contingent as much as they are systemic'.[25] Accordingly, in interpreting the past, 'law is more concerned with the subjection of past pronouncements to present social needs'.[26] In this way, transitional truth seeking and the truth itself join up past, present

[18] M Klinkner and H Davis, *The Right to the Truth in International Law: Victims' Rights in Human Rights and International Criminal Law* (Abingdon, Routledge, 2020) 66–74.

[19] Teitel (n 1) 7.

[20] See discussion of HG Gadamer, *Truth and Method* (London, Sheed and Ward, 1975) cited in P O'Callaghan, 'Collective Memory in Law and Policy: The Problem of the Sovereign Debt Crisis' (2012) 32(4) *Legal Studies* 642, 649.

[21] Naqvi, 'The Right to Truth in International Law: Fact or Fiction?' (2006) 88 (862) *International Review of the Red Cross* 245, 251.

[22] See eg B Bevernage, 'Writing the Past Out of the Present: History and the Politics of Time in Transitional Justice' (2010) 69(1) *History Workshop Journal* 111.

[23] S Buckley-Zistel, 'Narrative Truths: On the Construction of the Past in Truth Commissions' in S Buckley-Zistel, TK Beck, C Braun and F Mieth (eds), *Transitional Justice Theories* (London, Routledge, 2014) 144.

[24] PJ Verovšek, 'Collective Memory, Politics, and the Influence of the Past: The Politics of Memory as a Research Paradigm' (2016) 4(3) *Politics, Groups, and Identities* 529, 530.

[25] S Radstone and B Schwarz (eds), *Memory: Histories, Theories, Debates* (New York, Fordham University Press 2010) 4.

[26] W Weyrauch, 'Law as Mask – Legal Ritual and Relevance' (1978) 66(4) *California Law Review* 699, 723.

and future; the choices and uses of law to ground those processes carry consequences that may be felt individually and across society over time.

The centrality of the theme of truth seeking in TJ discourse is unquestionable, although its purpose and value are contextual and debated. Truth seeking relates to a broad range of initiatives surrounding accountability and amnesty for past harm, victims' right to truth about the abuse suffered, the formation of collective memories of contested pasts and society's need to reckon with legacies of violence – or not – to move forward. The purported benefits of uncovering the truth include social healing and reconciliation, the promotion of justice, the establishment of official records, public education, institutional reforms, the promotion of democracy and deterrence,[27] as well as carrying a reparative effect.[28] Knowing the truth about events and responsibilities related to gross human rights violations and details of the abuse itself is often 'seen as an important precondition for transitional justice goals'.[29] For truth 'enthusiasts',[30] the processes of truth seeking and acknowledgement of past harm carry individual and collective significance, with important political repercussions in broken societies. Reconstruction and public recognition of truths may encourage 'other legal responses, such as sanctions against perpetrators, reparations for victims, and institutional change'.[31] In addition to the political significance of truth seeking, acknowledgement of truths about gross and widespread abuse may support psychological and social recovery of victims and survivors.[32] Empowerment, catharsis and social acknowledgement emerge as some of the main 'pathways to healing' for victims who have a 'voice within the context of their country's national truth commission public hearings'.[33] Raquel Aldana summarises the

[27] Radstone and Schwarz (n 25) Also D Mendeloff, 'Truth-seeking, Truth-telling, and Postconflict Peacebuilding: Curb the Enthusiasm?' (2004) 6 *International Studies Review* 355.

[28] M Lawry-White, 'The Reparative Effect of Truth Seeking in Transitional Justice' (2015) 64(1) *ICLQ* 141.

[29] Klinkner and Davis (n 18) 13.

[30] To borrow the concept from Mendeloff (n 27).

[31] Teitel (n 1) 88 ff.

[32] On truth and the social-psychological healing of victims, see inter alia: I Amadiume and A An-Na'im (eds), *The Politics of Memory: Truth, Healing, and Social Justice* (London, Zed Books, 2000); N Roht-Arriaza, 'The New Landscape of Transitional Justice' in N Roht-Arriaza and J Mariezcurrena (eds), *Transitional Justice in the Twenty-first Century: Beyond Truth versus Justice* (Cambridge, Cambridge University Press, 2006) 4; R David and SYP Choi, 'Getting Even or Getting Equal? Retributive Desires and Transitional Justice' (2009) 30(2) *Political Psychology* 161; J Doak, 'The Therapeutic Dimension of Transitional Justice: Emotional Repair and Victim Satisfaction in International Trials and Truth Commissions' (2011) 11(2) *International Criminal Law Review* 263; JL Gibson, 'The Contributions of Truth to Reconciliation Lessons From South Africa' (2006) 50(3) *Journal of Conflict Resolution* 409; M Minow, *Breaking the Cycles of Hatred: Memory, Law and Repair* (Princeton, NJ, Princeton University Press, 2002). For a more critical appraisal of the healing and reconciliatory power of truth seeking in TJ, see K McEvoy, *The Trouble with Truth: Struggling with the Past in Northern Ireland* (London, Routledge, 2011), and K McEvoy, 'What Did the Lawyers Do During the "War"? Neutrality, Conflict and the Culture of Quietism' (2011) 74(3) *MLR* 350, fn 195.

[33] HL Guthrey, *Victim Healing and Truth Commissions: Transforming Pain Through Voice in Solomon Islands and Timor-Leste* (Heidelberg, Springer, 2015) 5–6.

potential importance, for victims, of truth (forensic truth/hard facts; emotional truth; general truth) emerging from criminal trials and truth commissions:

> To (1) alleviate the suffering of the surviving victims, (2) vindicate the memory or status of the direct victim of the violation; (3) increase the surviving victims' depth of understanding into the circumstances and causes that led to the atrocity, and (4) encourage society to confront its dark past and through it to seek reform.[34]

However, when victims' testimonies form part of truth-seeking initiatives such as truth commissions there are difficult questions to navigate about disclosure and confidentiality, which problematise some of the assumptions around the net benefits for victims.[35] Moreover, there are 'somewhat mixed responses from victims about the therapeutic potential of truth telling' in the context of truth commissions, and evidence of 'even greater psychological cost to victims' participating in criminal proceedings.[36] As Simon Robins suggests, 'the real goal of a truth commission is the transformation of traumatic memory into therapeutic history' through 'victims' testimony, legitimated by their suffering, creating new narratives for states to build their legitimacy upon'.[37] In this light, 'truth commissions operate through the continuing objectification of the victim to support the broader aims of the state'.[38] Echoing these worries, Juan Carlos Urquidi Herrera admonishes (in relation to Latin American truth commissions), 'the truth cannot be obtained at the expense of the victims': at times, 'public disclosure of the facts can mean a step backward in the healing process for some victims', and in many cases 'some victims do not want to tell their stories to the world, or to their country, or even to their closest loved ones', despite there being a collective interest in knowing the truth about past harm.[39]

The value placed on truth seeking in times of transition is relative: 'the truth neither is nor does all that we expect of it' and is not 'monolithic, objective or verifiable as we would like it to be'.[40] There is significant scepticism around the reconciliatory powers of truth seeking.[41] Moreover, given that a group's collective memory is 'shaped and influenced by many factors including the state's manipulation, social narratives, school education, and popular culture', Zheng Wang

[34] R Aldana, 'A Victim-centered Reflection on Truth Commissions and Prosecutions as a Response to Mass Atrocities' (2006) 5(1) *Journal of Human Rights* 107, 109.

[35] See eg the discussion in JC Urquidi Herrera, 'Victims' Testimonies in Truth Commissions: Who Owns the Memory' (2018–19) 20 *Oregon Review of International Law* 79.

[36] Aldana (n 34) 114.

[37] S Robins, 'Failing Victims? The Limits of Transitional Justice in Addressing the Needs of Victims of Violations' (2017) (2) *Human Rights and International Legal Discourse* 41, 47.

[38] ibid.

[39] Urquidi Herrera (n 35) 111.

[40] E Daly, 'Truth Skepticism: An Inquiry into the Value of Truth in Times of Transition' (2008) 2 *International Journal of Transitional Justice* 23, 23. See also Mendeloff (n 27) outlining critiques.

[41] eg JN Clark, 'Transitional Justice, Truth and Reconciliation: An Under-explored Relationship' (2011) 11(2) *International Criminal Law Review* 241.

reminds us that it 'is not realistic to expect a brand-new master narrative or national story to be created out of nothing'.[42] As the truth carries an 'inevitably political and contested character', it should be 'approached and pursued as a dynamic, long-term process, embracing – rather than resisting – its limitations and tensions'.[43] At times truth seeking is knowingly avoided or deferred.[44] Indeed, there may be some instances when forgetting about the past might be wise.[45] Even when truth-seeking efforts are made, 'all remembering involves forgetting' and a 'degree of editing'.[46] David's warning that the emergence of 'moral remembrance', prescribing standards for a 'proper way' for states to remember and deal with legacies of mass human rights abuses, can be ineffective or counterproductive in seeking to reconcile a fraught past, is particularly pertinent.[47] As such, viewing the 'human rights memorialization agenda as a universal and indisputable moral code' fails to acknowledge political and historic contexts.[48] Moreover, as Sharon Hom and Eric Yamamoto summarise:

> Individuals, social groups, institutions, and nations filter and twist, recall and forget 'information' in reframing shameful past acts (thereby lessening responsibility) as well as in enhancing victim status (thereby increasing power). Collective memory not only vivifies a group's past, it also reconstructs it and thereby situates a group in relation to others in a power hierarchy.[49]

Focusing on these legalised avenues for truth seeking, Melanie Klinkner and Howard Davis list some of the limitations of truth seeking, in relation to peacebuilding, retraumatisation of victims and the delicate balance between knowing and forgetting in order for society to reconcile; indeed, 'there may be cultural, political or religious reasons for rejecting elements of truth-finding'.[50] Despite their different aims, international criminal trials and truth commissions may both contribute to 'the development of a collective memory by establishing a version of history that informs, and is informed by, the memories of those involved'.[51] Aldana explains that 'both truth commissions and trials present different benefits to the revelation of forensic truth' – although neither is sufficient 'to address the complexities of victims' "healing"'.[52] For instance, truth

[42] Z Wang, *Memory Politics, Identity and Conflict: Historical Memory as a Variable* (Cham, Palgrave Macmillan, 2018) 32.

[43] Girelli, (n 9) 43–44.

[44] See I Kovras, *Truth Recovery and Transitional Justice: Deferring Human Rights Issues* (Abingdon, Routledge, 2014).

[45] Rotondi and Eisikovits (n 3) 24.

[46] ibid.

[47] David (n 4) 1–2.

[48] ibid 12.

[49] SK Hom and EK Yamamoto, 'Collective Memory, History, and Social Justice' (2000) 47 *UCLA Law Review* 1747, 1758.

[50] Klinkner and Davis (n 18) 13–15, 17–18.

[51] C Brants and K Klep, 'Transitional Justice: History-telling, Collective Memory and the Victim-Witness' (2013) 7(1) *International Journal of Conflict and Violence* 36, 37.

[52] Aldana (n 34) 107–09.

commissions 'can lead to the identification of many more perpetrators more quickly than is sometimes possible through prosecutions', but confessions 'are subject to the good will and trustworthiness of the confessor'.[53] In contrast, trials are 'often slow and cumbersome', but the 'factual discovery process can enhance victims' trust in the reliability' of the findings.[54] Moreover, compared to trials, truth commissions lend themselves to uncovering more comprehensive, historical and contextual truths – but there is evidence of trials (such as the Nuremberg trials) producing a significant volume of documentation that 'consolidates memories'.[55] Both mechanisms, however, carry risks, as outlined by Bronwyn Leebaw:

> Because truth commissions and criminal tribunals investigate extremely divisive and violent histories, they have often been viewed as obstacles to reconciliation and charged with 'opening old wounds,' generating political instability and interfering with forward-looking political change.[56]

These reflections echo the fraught relationships between truth, justice and reconciliation.[57] There is extensive literature on the synergies and tensions between truth seeking and the (retributive) justice aims of transition.[58] Focusing only on criminal retribution misrepresents the broader aims of TJ, which encompass a collective forward-looking dimension as much as a backward-looking premise, as well as responding to the specific needs of each given scenario.[59] At the same time, truth seeking outside trials (alone and in conjunction with prosecutions) may be subjected to the interests of reconciliation, leading to

[53] ibid.

[54] ibid.

[55] ibid 112–13.

[56] BA Leebaw, 'The Irreconcilable Goals of Transitional Justice' (2008) 30(1) *Human Rights Quarterly* 95, 96.

[57] See eg RI Rotberg and D Thompson (eds), *Truth v Justice: The Morality of Truth Commissions* (Princeton, NJ, Princeton University Press, 2000); P McAuliffe, 'Transitional Justice and the Rule of Law: The Perfect Couple or Awkward Bedfellows?' (2010) 2 *Hague Journal of the Rule of Law* 127; Roht-Arriaza (n 32).

[58] See inter alia JE Mendez, 'In Defense of Transitional Justice' in J McAdams (ed), *Transitional Justice and the Rule of Law in New Democracies* (Notre Dame, IN, University of Notre Dame Press, 1997); NJ Kritz, 'The Dilemmas of Transitional Justice' in NJ Kritz (ed) *Transitional Justice* (Washington, DC, United States Institute of Peace Press, 1995) xix; J Zalaquett, 'Balancing Ethical Imperatives and Political Constraints: The Dilemma of New Democracies Confronting Past Human Rights Violations' (1992) 43 *Hastings Law Journal* 1425. On the truth v justice debate specifically, M Popkin and N Roht-Arriaza, 'Truth as Justice: Investigatory Commissions in Latin America' (1995) 20(1) *Law & Social Inquiry* 79; N Roht-Arriaza, and J Mariezcurrena (eds), *Transitional Justice in the Twenty-first Century: Beyond Truth versus Justice* (Cambridge, Cambridge University Press, 2006).

[59] For an interesting discussion on balancing sentencing and leniency in the context of the ICTY, see L Mallinder, 'Retribution, Restitution and Reconciliation: Limited Amnesty in Bosnia-Herzegovina' (2009) Working Paper No 3 from 'Beyond Legalism: Amnesties, Transition and Conflict Transformation', Institute of Criminology and Criminal Justice, Queen's University Belfast, November 2009, 49ff. On balancing retributive and restorative models in transitional contexts, see inter alia K McEvoy and T Newburn (eds), *Criminology, Conflict Resolution and Restorative Justice* (London, Palgrave Macmillan 2003).

'selection and championing of only those truths useful in a reconciliation-focused teleology'.[60] Moreover, the topic of amnesties poses additional challenges, reflecting concerns driven by reconciliation aims, but without necessarily excluding forms of accountability outside the confines of criminal justice (such as truth commissions).[61] The 2013 *Belfast Guidelines on Amnesty and Accountability* provide a helpful overview on how to balance competing factors in the light of multiple human rights obligations.[62] Different types of amnesties problematise the aims and applications of truth seeking, as amply illustrated in the volume of academic writing on the topic.[63] Reflecting on the transitions in Latin America and Eastern Europe, Naomi Roht-Arriaza has considered amnesties as trading 'justice for the past in exchange for justice for the future'.[64] Nevertheless, the uniqueness of each context may lead to novel solutions. To cite a textbook example,[65] with the 1984 *Nunca Más* report by the Argentine National Commission of the Disappeared (the CONADEP truth commission),[66] the fate of many disappeared persons emerged.[67] However, the introduction of amnesty laws prevented victims, family members and the general public from seeking the truth through formal judicial means.[68] As a reaction, a creative judiciary and a proactive civil society found an alternative route: truth-finding trials/truth-trials (*juicios por la verdad*).[69] Moreover, thanks to petitions to the Inter-American

[60] C Campbell and C Turner, 'Utopia and the Doubters: Truth, Transition and the Law' (2008) 28(3) *Legal Studies* 374, 381ff.

[61] On some of the key complexities, see inter alia L Mallinder and K McEvoy 'Rethinking Amnesties: Atrocity, Accountability and Impunity in Post-conflict Societies' (2011) 6(1) *Contemporary Social Science* 107.

[62] Transitional Justice Institute, University of Ulster, *The Belfast Guidelines on Amnesty and Accountability* (2013) available at www.ulster.ac.uk/__data/assets/pdf_file/0005/57839/TheBelfastGuidelinesFINAL_000.pdf.

[63] Inter alia, L Mallinder, *Amnesty, Human Rights and Political Transitions: Bridging the Peace and Justice Divide* (Oxford, Hart, 2008); L Mallinder, 'Can Amnesties and International Justice Be Reconciled?' (2007) 1(2) *International Journal of Transitional Justice* 208; LJ Laplante. 'Outlawing Amnesty: The Return of Criminal Justice in Transitional Justice Schemes' (2009) 49 *Virginia Journal of International Law* 915; F Lessa and LA Payne (eds), *Amnesty in the Age of Human Rights Accountability: Comparative and International Perspectives* (Cambridge, Cambridge University Press, 2012); U Egbai and J Chimakonam, 'Protecting the Rights of Victims in Transitional Justice: An Interrogation of Amnesty' (2019) 19(2) *African Human Rights Law Journal* 608.

[64] Roht-Arriaza (n 32) 3.

[65] For arguments as to why the Argentine example is noteworthy, see K Sikkink and CB Walling, 'Argentina's Contribution to Global Trends in Transitional Justice' in N Roht-Arriaza, and J Mariezcurrena (eds), *Transitional Justice in the Twenty-first Century: Beyond Truth versus Justice* (Cambridge, Cambridge University Press, 2006) 301.

[66] K Sikkink, 'From Pariah State to Global Protagonist: Argentina and the Struggle for International Human Rights' (2008) 50(1) *Latin American Politics and Society* 1, 6ff.

[67] E Crenzel, 'Argentina's National Commission on the Disappearance of Persons: Contributions to Transitional Justice' (2008) 2 *International Journal of Transitional Justice* 173, 184ff.

[68] The Full Stop Law (Ley de Punto Final) and the Due Obedience Law (Ley de Obediencia Debida).

[69] On the Argentine truth-finding trials, see E Maculan, 'Prosecuting International Crimes at National Level: Lessons from the Argentine "Truth-Finding Trials"' (2012) 8(1) *Utrecht Law Review* 106ff. See also S Garibian, 'Ghosts also Die: Resisting Disappearance through the "Right to the Truth" and the Juicios por la Verdad in Argentina' (2014) 12 *Journal of International Criminal Justice* 515.

Commission of Human Rights, further investigations were instigated.[70] This example typifies how truth seeking in any given context is affected by multiple factors and can evolve as a result of a new law, political events and impetus from certain actors. Building on these considerations, the following section considers legal/legalised truth-seeking mechanisms in more detail before analysing the distinctive category of legal truth.

A. Legal/Legalised Truth-Seeking Mechanisms

There are multiple mechanisms through which truth seeking (and truth telling) occurs, resulting in both truth as the direct aim, as well as the incidental outcome of other justice-related goals. The scope, focus and content of the truths produced by different legal/legalised mechanisms reflect the mandate of each body tasked with truth seeking and broader sociopolitical context. These 'multiple representations of the "truth"' and the extent to which societies and leaders deal with that multiplicity are a feature, not a flaw, of transitional truth seeking.[71] Criminal trials at domestic and international level, as well as truth commissions (including commissions of inquiry[72]), constitute the core legal/legalised tools of transitional truth seeking.[73] Additionally, other, non-criminal trials have emerged as important sites of truth production; these include regional human rights courts (as analysed in greater detail in Chapter 4 regarding the Inter-American and European human rights systems[74]) and domestic human rights and civil trials (not discussed directly in this book[75]). Sometimes, international human rights instruments have the potential to activate trial-based truth seeking by triggering criminal prosecutions.[76] But while trials (criminal

[70] Maculan (n 69) 109ff.

[71] Teitel (n 1) 89.

[72] Commissions of inquiry occur both in transitional contexts as well as non-transitional contexts. See inter alia F Schmid, 'The Diversity of Truth Commissions and Commissions of Inquiry' (January 2012) US Institute of Peace: Peace Brief 118; and in relation to 'steady state democracies' P Scraton, 'The Legacy of Hillsborough: Liberating Truth, Challenging Power' (2013) 55(2) *Race and Class* 1.

[73] A Bisset, *Truth Commissions and Criminal Courts* (Cambridge, Cambridge University Press, 2012) 1ff, also discussing inter alia Roht-Arriaza and Mariezcurrena (n 58) and C Villa-Vicencio, 'Why Perpetrators Should Not Always Be Prosecuted: Where the International Criminal Court and Truth Commissions Meet' (2000) 49 *Emory Law Journal* 205.

[74] Klinkner and Davis (n 18) 79–86.

[75] On the potential of private law in addressing historic wrongs, see inter alia S Degeling and K Barker, 'Private Law and Grave Historical Injustice' (2015) 41(2) *Monash University Law Review* 377 and M Moran, 'The Problem of the Past: How Historic Wrongs Became Legal Problems' (2019) 69(4) *University of Toronto Law Journal* 421.

[76] F Tulkens, 'The Paradoxical Relationship between Criminal Law and Human Rights' (2011) 9 *J International Criminal Justice* 577.

and non-criminal) and truth commissions as the two core legalised mechanisms for truth seeking are conceptually and practically distinct, the 'legal' truths they produce – and their limitations – are closer than generally assumed, as this section illustrates. It is, therefore, important to consider, in view of the theoretical and methodological considerations set out in Chapter 2, how the two categories of legalised truth-seeking instruments are more comparable than is generally assumed.

The refrain in the literature is that trials and truth commissions 'are different, and that each has its own, limited role to play in transitional justice', with neither better than the other.[77] There can be a division of labour of sorts between trials and truth commissions, but this is not always the case.[78] The essentialising dichotomy between criminal trials delivering justice and truth commissions uncovering truth has long been rejected.[79] This differentiation is based on the presumption that the 'verdict of a court is definite and authoritative' and offers 'closure', ends debate 'about what it has established as the truth' and carries a limited 'contribution to history-telling, collective memory, and justice for victims' – the domain of truth commissions.[80] Among the key distinctions, truth commissions consist of an 'investigation and reporting of facts'; significantly, their recommendations are not legally binding in the same way as judgments, and tend to engage in the wider context in which harm occurred.[81] However, upon closer scrutiny of the mandates and operations of truth commissions, and the possibility to recommend prosecutions in some cases, the 'false duality' and assumed trade-offs between truth and justice are more nuanced, as already illustrated in Priscilla Hayner's classic study.[82]

Truth commissions and trials, then, 'are not airtight analytical categories' and might partly overlap, given 'trials may have functions as recorders of truth or may include victim forums while truth commissions may have justice functions'.[83] Drawing on the tools of comparative law, the clear distinction between trials

[77] Brants and Klep (n 51) 48.

[78] See eg MVS Sirleaf, 'Beyond Truth and Punishment in Transitional Justice' (2014) 54 *Virginia Journal of International Law* 223.

[79] A Bisset (n 73) 12ff.

[80] ibid.

[81] M Freeman, *Truth Commissions and Procedural Fairness* (Cambridge, Cambridge University Press, 2006) 71–72.

[82] PB Hayner, *Unspeakable Truths: Transitional Justice and the Challenge of Truth Commissions*, 2nd edn (London, Routledge, 2010) 93ff. Her examples include Argentina, Peru and Chad. On Peru, see inter alia EG Cueva, 'The Peruvian Truth and Reconciliation Commission and the Challenge of Impunity' in N Roht-Arriaza, and J Mariezcurrena (eds), *Transitional Justice in the Twenty-first Century: Beyond Truth versus Justice* (Cambridge, Cambridge University Press, 2006) 70ff and Roht-Arriaza (n 32) 9. Among other examples, note also Mexico, discussed in M Acosta and E Ennelin, 'The "Mexican Solution" to Transitional Justice' in N Roht-Arriaza, and J Mariezcurrena (eds), *Transitional Justice in the Twenty-first Century: Beyond Truth versus Justice* (Cambridge, Cambridge University Press, 2006) 105.

[83] A Dukalskis, 'Interactions in Transition: How Truth Commissions and Trials Complement or Constrain Each Other' (2011) 13(3) *International Studies Review* 432, 433.

and truth commissions collapses if both are appreciated as normative initiatives based on a set of socially relevant rules promoted by actors exercising (and to a degree, enjoying) some authority in their communities. For transitional truth-seeking aims, some of the findings of courts, if produced 'to a high standard of proof', may be 'of historical interest'.[84] In fact, a greater 'incorporation of collective memory into certain judicial proceedings' would facilitate a more holistic and less individualised understanding of past harms and advance reconciliation.[85] At the same time, truth commissions are based on rules and procedures, which makes them much closer to trials than might be presumed; questions around procedural fairness towards 'victims and their families, witnesses and perpetrators' illustrate how basic fair-trial guarantees have seeped into how this mechanism is assessed as well.[86] Moreover, the public, quasi-judicial nature of truth commissions, some of which 'resemble court proceedings', generally 'brings in the legitimacy of the state, which makes these bodies seem more capable of ensuring social and political change' even when they fail to do so.[87] The range of relationships and possibilities of cross-fertilisation between trials (including international prosecutions) and truth commissions add to the converging outcomes of transitional truth-seeking endeavours.[88] In particular, truth commissions may connect with other TJ mechanisms, including prosecutions (as well as 'initiating meaningful institutional reform').[89] So despite significant differences between the two mechanisms, the truths they produce carry comparable possibilities and limitations, and as such fall collectively under the rubric of 'legal truth' discussed later.

While trials carry an enduring appeal as truth-seeking mechanisms, 'criminal convictions for perpetrators of violence are rare (and amnesties frequent)'.[90] Much has been written on the challenges and possibilities of dealing with mass atrocities through domestic and international prosecutions.[91] A key problem of trials as truth-seeking mechanisms is that 'trials tend to put to the fore certain narratives as legitimate readings, while excluding many others', thus offering a relatively limited scope of analysis of anything beyond the narrow confines of the proceedings.[92] Against this backdrop, truth commissions have emerged

[84] Klinkner and Davis (n 18) 194–95.
[85] López (n 2).
[86] Freeman (n 81).
[87] J Rowen, *Searching for Truth in the Transitional Justice Movement* (Cambridge, Cambridge University Press, 2017) 151.
[88] ibid 438.
[89] L Bickford, 'Unofficial Truth Projects', (2007) 29 *Human Rights Quarterly* 994, 997.
[90] S Gensburger and S Lefranc, *Beyond Memory: Can We Really Learn from the Past?* (Cham, Palgrave Macmillan, 2020) 30.
[91] See inter alia MA Drumbl, *Atrocity, Punishment, and International Law* (Cambridge, Cambridge University Press, 2007).
[92] M Rauschenbach, 'Individuals Accused of International Crimes as Delegitimized Agents of Truth' (2018) 28(4) *International Criminal Justice Review* 29.

as the transitional truth-seeking mechanism par excellence.[93] The academic and practitioner literature on truth commissions abounds and includes a significant critical awareness of their function and possibilities.[94] Compared to trials, perceptions of truth seeking range from the belief that they offer a lesser alternative that allows alleged perpetrators to escape accountability, to the hope that they might act as a precursor to prosecutions.[95] As summarised by Onur Bakiner:

> Truth commissions have emerged in political contexts where societies' conventional mechanisms for investigating serious crimes and writing unbiased accounts of the past (the judiciary and the media, chief among them) had ceased to function. They face the twofold task of discovering forensic facts and forging societal consensus over the meaning of the past.[96]

The definitions of truth commissions continue to evolve. There are calls for a broader and more inclusive 'backward-looking definition that is used reflectively to contrast, compare and research past and present truth commissions', as well as 'a non-prescriptive explanatory forward-looking definition focusing on the compositional elements of a [truth commission]'.[97] In general terms, truth commissions 'encourage a compromise between former enemies, as well as the recognition of victims'; they cross-fertilise with the work of historians.[98]

[93] For a summary of truth commissions and transitional justice, see inter alia N Mncwabe 'Truth Commissions' in L Stan and N Nedelsky (eds), *Encyclopedia of Transitional Justice*, vol 1 (Cambridge, Cambridge University Press, 2013) 98ff; M Minow, 'The Hope for Healing: What Can Truth Commissions Do?' in R Rotberg and D Thompson (eds), *Truth v Justice: The Morality of Truth Commissions* (Princeton, NJ, Princeton University Press, 2010); S Parmentier and M Aciru, 'The Whole Truth and Nothing but the Truth? On the Role of Truth Commissions in Facing the Past' in P Malcontent (eds) *Facing the Past: Amending Historical Injustices through Instruments of Transitional Justice* (Cambridge, Intersentia, 2016).

[94] Inter alia, Hayner (n 82); MU Walker, 'Troubles with Truth Commissions: Putting the Moral Aims of Truth Commissions to the Fore' in E Bird and FM Ottanelli (eds), *The Performance of Memory as Transitional Justice* (Cambridge, Intersentia, 2015); E Wiebelhaus-Brahm, *Truth Commissions and Transitional Societies: The Impact on Human Rights and Democracy* (New York, Routledge, 2010); J Perry and TD Sayndee, *African Truth Commissions and Transitional Justice* (Lanham, MD, Lexington Books, 2015); L Stan and N Nedelsky (eds) *Post-Communist Transitional Justice* (Cambridge, Cambridge University Press, 2015); Rowen (n 87); K Zvobgo, 'Demanding Truth: The Global Transitional Justice Network and the Creation of Truth Commissions' (2020) 64(3) *International Studies Quarterly* 609; C Lawther, 'Transitional Justice and Truth Commissions' in C Lawther et al (eds), *Research Handbook on Transitional Justice* (Cheltenham, Edward Elgar, 2017); E Wiebelhaus-Brahm, 'Global Transitional Justice Norms and the Framing of Truth Commissions in the Absence of Transition' (2020) *Negotiation and Conflict Management Research* (online first).

[95] Rowen (n 87) 9, 151 and elsewhere.

[96] O Bakiner, *Truth Commissions: Memory, Power, and Legitimacy* (Philadelphia, University of Pennsylvania Press, 2016) 63.

[97] J Sarkin, 'Redesigning the Definition a Truth Commission, but Also Designing a Forward-Looking Non-prescriptive Definition to Make Them Potentially More Successful' (2018) 19(3) *Human Rights Review* 1.

[98] Gensburger and Lefranc (n 90) 30.

They seek to uncover the truth through (somewhat) formalised, yet non-judicial, proceedings characterised by a non-punitive primary intent.[99] They offer the possibility of designing a bespoke, flexible and malleable tool to investigate the past distinct from trials – but not totally divorced from criminal and non-criminal proceedings.[100] Moreover, upon closer scrutiny, the degree to which truth commissions promote political, institutional, societal and judicial transformations is not always as significant as commonly assumed.[101] Inhabiting the space between state institutions and NGOs, truth commissions possess a 'quasi-official character', and as such may have a 'direct political impact'; but it is their relationship with civil society involved in 'activism to keep politicians accountable to otherwise nonbinding recommendations' that seems to be more significant in bringing about 'delayed political impact' as well as 'generating long-term judicial and normative impact'.[102] As such, truth commissions do not exist in an abstract, rarefied and idealised context, and the degree to which they connect to other mechanisms, including trials, and other actors, in particular civil society, will impact on the truths they produce and their uses.

A specific aspect to consider in truth commissions is the combination of elements of 'private/individual truth of those who have been victims of human rights violations' and the 'public/social level truth'.[103] This echoes the dual individual/collective dimensions of the right to truth as emerging in international law, and discussed in Chapter 4. The public nature of their findings helps 'transform what is often widely-known about violent past events – common knowledge – into official acknowledgment', which is 'important both for its symbolic value and for its practical effects'.[104] While truth commissions aspire to 'creating an accurate historical record of the violence, enabling survivors to share their stories, and making recommendations for social and political change', results are often disappointing.[105] Multiple typologies of truth commissions have been designed and tested, with a range of outcomes.[106] Some are official, state-driven, or promoted by international organisations, while others emerge from civil society.[107] Given their popularity,[108] the disparate geographic, political and social contexts in which they have been set up, their varying mandates and driving actors, truth

[99] In general, see Hayner (n 82).

[100] On the malleability of truth commissions, see generally Rowen (n 87).

[101] O Bakiner, 'Truth Commission Impact: An Assessment of How Commissions Influence Politics and Society' (2014) 8(1) *International Journal of Transitional Justice* 6.

[102] ibid 29.

[103] AR Chapman and P Ball, 'The Truth of Truth Commissions: Comparative Lessons from Haiti, South Africa, and Guatemala' (2001) 23 *Human Rights Quarterly* 1, 7.

[104] Bickford (n 89) 997.

[105] Rowen (n 87) 3. On the problems with truth commissions and the difficulty in measuring success, see inter alia E Brahm, 'Uncovering the Truth: Examining Truth Commission Success and Impact' (2007) 8(1) *International Studies Perspectives* 16.

[106] A Kochanski, 'Mandating Truth: Patterns and Trends in Truth Commission Design' (2020) 21 *Human Rights Review* 113, 133.

[107] Bickford (n 89).

[108] Rowen (n 87) 3 reports between forty and ninety truth commissions, depending on definitions.

commissions uncover the truth about past harm in different ways. What they all seem to have in common, however, is the gap between ambitions and what truth they actually deliver. As a result, 'truth projects' have been famously described as 'narrowing the range of permissible lies',[109] 'limit[ing] the possibility of denial or trivialization of victims' experiences',[110] rather than a perfect mechanism. A range of constraints, including time and resources, restrict the ability of truth commissions to recover the truth; not all harm will be acknowledged, and not all victims will have the chance to give their testimony. The finite number of 'window cases' and 'illustrative cases' heard by the truth commissions in South Africa and Guatemala are famous examples of the limitations of these mechanisms.[111] Taking stock of this brief overview, it emerges that the operation of truth commissions (understood in the political and social contexts in which they emerge) provides a relatively slim chance to produce the complete truth about past harm. As such, and despite differences, the truths emerging from truth commissions should be qualified as 'legal truths' similar to the truths emerging from international or domestic trials.

When international crimes have taken place and the domestic justice system has been unable and unwilling to investigate, international prosecutions have also participated in transitional truth-seeking endeavours. While the number of cases before the two ad hoc tribunals for the former Yugoslavia and Rwanda, and more recently the ICC, are minimal, they may enjoy a greater degree of authoritativeness given the higher standard of proof required (beyond reasonable doubt) and more articulate procedural rules (and guarantees) that guide judicial fact-finding, reporting and judgments.[112] The truth in the (international and domestic) criminal justice context 'emerges as a by-product of the criminal process' that focuses more narrowly on the individual criminal responsibility of the alleged perpetrators of the most serious crimes that fall within the jurisdictional scope of the court's mandate.[113] More generally, the punitive intent of criminal trials contributes to the formal recognition of details and accountability for past harm, which in turn might be 'capable of serving the needs of the victims'.[114] While the literature surveyed here suggests this claim is open to debate, there is an important public function of international trials that cannot be overlooked.

International prosecutions carry an important collective function in stating an official version of the truth. This is a feature of high-profile cases even in domestic non-transitional settings,[115] and acquires greater significance in

[109] M Ignatieff, 'Articles of Faith' (1996) 25(5) *Index on Censorship* 113.
[110] Bickford (n 89) 997.
[111] Chapman and Ball (n 103) 22.
[112] Klinkner and Davis (n 18) 96–99.
[113] ibid.
[114] Elster (n 2) 24.
[115] A notable example of this kind of legal truth in a political setting is provided in the ominous 21,000-word Italian Court of Cassation case involving seven-time Prime Minister Giulio Andreotti: the nine-judge panel painstakingly described his dealings with senior mafia bosses, regardless of the

transitional contexts. There is, however, an enduring tension between the narrow adjudicative function and broader sociopolitical conceptions of justice that coexist in the work of international criminal courts, including the ICC.[116] These competing approaches to the historical function of international criminal courts, as outlined by Barrie Sander, inform jurisdictional practices in different ways, suggesting that the social actors involved in the day-to-day operations of these courts play an important role in weaving – or not – the dual adjudicative and sociopolitical function inherent in the implementation of their mandates.[117] This echoes what is well known about the explicit and hidden politics of international criminal trials.[118] The truth emerging from international prosecutions, then, is shaped by a myriad of structural, contextual and political factors, in addition to the choices of its key human and institutional stakeholders. Compared to the truth produced by truth commissions, the truth emerging from international criminal tribunals is not better placed to reflect the realities of past harm fully or accurately. To misquote Tolstoy, 'Happy truths are all alike; every unhappy truth is unhappy in its own way.'[119] This is, perhaps, because the happy, perfect truth envisaged by victims and (some) architects of truth-seeking mechanisms is imagined; once it is pursued through trials and truth commissions (or other 'mundane' mechanisms that may exist in the arsenal of legalised truth seeking), its abstract, idealised perfection is polluted by the constraints of reality. Legalised truth-seeking mechanisms are only capable of uncovering and producing truths within the scope of their mandate and procedures.

B. The Product of Legal/Legalised Truth-Seeking Mechanisms

All truths emerging from legalised truth-seeking mechanisms reveal the contextual and constructed dimension of truth, its politically contested nature and its relationship to power. Returning to Deborah Posel's 'rainbow of truths' reading

fact that an applicable statute of limitations (prescription) prevented the court from formally finding the defendant guilty. The point of the exercise was not the conviction of Andreotti, which was impossible given the procedural limitations of the case; instead, the court handed the Italian public a formal yet accessible document describing years of corrupt politics. See Corte di cassazione, Sezioni unite penali, Sentenza 24 novembre 2003, no 45276, available in Italian at www.eius.it/giurisprudenza/2003/140.asp.

[116] B Sander, 'Unveiling the Historical Function of International Criminal Courts: Between Adjudicative and Sociopolitical Justice' (2018) 12 *International Journal of Transitional Justice* 334, 336.

[117] ibid 341.

[118] eg T Krever, 'Unveiling (and Veiling) Politics in International Criminal Trials' in C Schwöbel (ed), *Critical Approaches to International Criminal Law: An Introduction* (Abingdon, Routledge, 2014).

[119] The first sentence of Tolstoy's novel *Anna Karenina* (1877) is: 'Happy families are all alike; every unhappy family is unhappy in its own way.'

of the South African TRC's four notions of truth (factual/forensic; personal/narrative; social/dialogue; and healing/restorative) discussed in the introduction is helpful.[120] Onur Bakiner links forensic truth, defined as 'the totality of corroborated facts about human rights violations' to 'historical truth, which incorporates these facts into explanations about conflict onset, patterns of violations, and their consequences'.[121] But the range of interpretations can be problematised further. Philosophically, Frederick Schmitt outlines four types of truth: correspondent, pragmatist, coherent and deflationary.[122] The latter is different from the first three as it posits that 'truth talk is expressive (enhances the expressive power of language) rather than descriptive'.[123] This suggests that talking about the truth may actually contribute to constructing the truth, reflecting Austin's theory of 'performative utterances', discussed in the next chapter.[124] With regards to transitional truth seeking, this highlights the constructive force of official accounts – such as those emerging from trials and truth commissions – about the past in establishing and promoting certain narratives over others. As a social matter, truth 'may be generated by social procedures and structures' and it is possible for it to be 'agreed upon' or deeply contested.[125] In other words, truth can be presented as a construction of knowledge, or 'manufactured'.[126] Borrowing from Derrida's aphorism that 'nothing is outside the text', Yasmin Naqvi connects truth seeking to a 'right to an official statement about what happened'.[127] This illustrates Schmitt's point that truth is expressive, rather than descriptive, and talking about the truth in certain ways, and through specific truth-seeking mechanisms, contributes to its construction. These considerations underpin the analysis of the distinctive category of legal truth analysed in the next section.

A way to interpret the circumscribed and contextual nature and scope of the truth produced through both international trials as well as truth commissions is to reflect on the distinctiveness of truth resulting from legal/legalised mechanisms. Within transitional truth seeking the distinctive notion of legal truth is separate from the notion of historical (and other forms of) truth.[128] As discussed later in this chapter, trials and other quasi-judicial mechanisms, such

[120] Posel (n 12) 10.
[121] O Bakiner, 'One Truth Among Others? Truth Commissions' Struggle for Truth and Memory' (2015) 8(3) *Memory Studies* 345, 347.
[122] F Schmitt, *Theories of Truth* (Malden, MA, Blackwell, 2004).
[123] ibid 28.
[124] JL Austin, *How to Do Things with Words* (Oxford, Oxford University Press, 1962).
[125] Naqvi (n 21) 253.
[126] MC Okello, 'Afterward: Elevating Transitional Local Justice or Crystallizing Global Governance?' in R Shaw and L Waldorf (eds), *Localizing Transitional Justice: Interventions and Priorities after Mass Violence* (Stanford, CA, Stanford University Press, 2010) 276.
[127] Naqvi (n 21) 250ff, citing J Derrida, *Prophets of Extremity* (Berkeley, University of California Press, 1985); J Derrida, *Of Grammatology*, trans Gayatri Chakravorty Spivak (Baltimore, MD, Johns Hopkins University Press, 1976).
[128] M Koskenniemi, 'Between Impunity and Show Trials' (2002) 6 *Max Planck Yearbook of United Nations Law* 1, 10.

as truth commissions, produce records, statements and judgments that respond to a certain set of procedural rules that despite significant limitations generally command a higher degree of authoritativeness than non-legal mechanisms. International law seems to envisage two types of (interrelated) truth, which Sam Szoke-Burke terms 'incident-specific truth' and 'structural truth'.[129] The former pertains, as the name suggests, to a specific incident, 'including the human rights violations suffered, the identity of the victim, the identity and responsibility of the perpetrator and, for disappearances, the victim's whereabouts'; the latter instead indicates that the 'victims and the general public are also entitled to the "full and complete truth" about the systemic and structural causes and circumstances of the events' and 'any patterns of abuse'.[130] Much like narrative truths that emerge from other transitional truth-seeking mechanisms, including the less legalised dimensions of truth commissions, legal truths are a 'social construction' separate from factual and forensic truth.[131] Narrative theory, as proposed by Buckley-Zistel in relation to truth commissions,[132] offers a more nuanced understanding of the truth that extends to legal truths as well, inasmuch as they are produced in specific institutional and sociopolitical contexts.

Despite the apparent differences in aims, setup and actors of trials and truth commissions, the distinction between the truth emerging from the two truth-seeking mechanisms is blurred if approached through narrative theory. The 'mode of construction and production' informs the meanings of individual and collective narratives;[133] this occurs in both truth commissions (the context of Buckley-Zistel's theorisation), but also in trials, because the truth emerging from a 'process' and as a 'product' of a trial is also constructed in specific contexts and surroundings. The 'packaging' of the legal truth, however, is different from other forms of truth, which present narratives under a particular guise. Legal truths are formalised through the judiciary in trials or comparable actors in truth commissions, and archived explicitly or implicitly through specific procedures that possess normative character. This adds a layer of complexity deriving from the power dynamics underpinning the place and function of the judiciary and key actors in truth commissions during transitions, which impacts perceptions (both positive and negative) of the weight and normativity of the findings.

Legal truths emerging from various mechanisms are likely to flow into some kind of repository (archive); this can be structured or completely disjointed, accessible (or not) to the public in different ways, and curated and used by different actors for a variety of purposes. The notion and complexities of transitional

[129] S Szoke-Burke, 'Searching for the Right to Truth: The Impact of International Human Rights Law on National Transitional Justice Policies' (2015) 33(2) *Berkeley Journal of International Law* 526, 533.

[130] ibid.

[131] Buckley-Zistel (n 23) 144.

[132] ibid 145.

[133] ibid 148.

archives, some of which are informed substantially by the results of trials, truth commissions and other legalised truth-seeking initiatives, as well as other actors (such as civil society reporting in light of international human rights standards) merit further attention.[134] These patchwork collections of legal and historical records and other forms of documentation must be understood within the power structures and patterns of inclusion/exclusion of actors and narratives. As Julia Viebach argues, 'the transitional archive is never finished' and must be interrogated over time.[135] Inasmuch as transitional archives contain materials emerging from legal/legalised mechanisms, therefore, 'law can become a useful tool for censoring, rather than simply recording, the past', and a 'deliberately selective account of the violent past that serves powerful interests in the present is thus created and subsequently packaged as an apolitical "official" memory'.[136] As noted by Accatino and Collins concerning Chile:

> Cases, like truth commission investigations, produce voluminous written records. While investigations are ongoing, cases are still work in progress. They become files of a living history which is still being written, and much of their content therefore remains secret. The culmination of a case, however, writes the last page in the judicial file. While verdicts are univocal, the file preserves signs of internal dissent along the way. Thus, paradoxically, the file conserves all of the plurality that must be shed to arrive at the final decision. It is a cumulative, capacious repository from which no artefact is ever removed. Instead, each component is implicitly or explicitly judicially certified or rebutted. Certain putative truth claims are declared reliable, while others are discounted. In the process, the case file becomes a new 'meta archive', later open to new valuations.[137]

The packaging and conservation of legal truth, therefore, encapsulates contestation as much as it obscures it in an attempt to portray some sort of definitive truth, the chimera of transitional truth seeking. As Briony Jones and Ingrid Oliveira have argued, archives emanating from truth commissions – though the same can be said about trials and other forms of legalised truth seeking – could be conceived of as new democratic spaces; these are not simple 'depositories of the truth proclaimed in the final report' (or judgment), but 'rather as spaces where different actors can continue to reinterpret the past and re-imagine the future'.[138] This echoes literature in archive studies, such as Eric Ketelaar's claim (in relation to trials) that 'the court's verdict is final, but its reading of

[134] For a helpful definition, see J Viebach 'Transitional Archives: Towards a Conceptualisation of Archives in Transitional Justice' (2021) 25(3) *International Journal of Human Rights* 403, 404ff.

[135] ibid 25.

[136] Discussed in K Hearty, 'Truth Beyond the "Trigger Puller": Moral Accountability, Transitional (In)justice and the Limitations of the Legal Truth' (2021) *International Journal of Transitional Justice* (online version ahead of print).

[137] Accatino and Collins (n 15) 95.

[138] B Jones and I Oliveira, 'Truth Commission Archives as "New Democratic Spaces"' (2016) 8 *Journal of Human Rights Practice* 6, 20.

the historical event is not. Court records, therefore, don't have more value than other records.'[139] In this respect, archives are never finished, even after a trial is completed (or, by extension, a truth commission); the reactivation of a record through 'every interaction, intervention, interrogation, and interpretation by creator, user, and archivist' shape the 'archive's infinite meaning' over time.[140] Similarly, Joan M. Schwartz and Terry Cook explain how 'users of archives (historians and others) and shapers of archives (records creators, records managers, and archivists) add layers of meaning, layers which become naturalized, internalized, and unquestioned'.[141] Archives incorporating the findings of transitional truth seeking through legal/legalised mechanisms cannot, therefore, be taken as a 'face value' account of the truth; instead, their myriad uses require mindful engagement in light of the norms, actors and power dynamics at play in each context.

Truth seeking through legal/legalised mechanisms is informed by rich theoretical debates outside law.[142] Foucault's claim that 'truth isn't outside of power, or lacking in power: … Truth is a thing of this world: it is produced only by virtue of multiple forms of constraint' is apposite.[143] Moreover, 'truth is linked in a circular relation with systems of power which produce and sustain it, and to effects of power which it induces and which extend it. A "regime" of truth.'[144] The revelation, production and management of truth occurs within power dynamics; hence, it is both a tool of power and a tool to potentially disrupt power. It is capable of being contested within and outside the political space of transitions and thereafter. Teitel considers how TJ implies a 'displacement of one interpretative account or truth regime by another, even as the political regimes change, while preserving the narrative thread of the state'.[145] Law can be used to preserve new historical accounts but also to control competing accounts that reinterpret political events and may disrupt the fledgling new order.[146]

[139] E Ketelaar, 'Archives as Spaces of Memory' (2008) 29(1) *Journal of the Society of Archivists* 9, 12.

[140] ibid.

[141] JM Schwartz and T Cook, 'Archives, Records, and Power: The Making of Modern Memory' (2002) 2 *Archival Science* 1, 18.

[142] For background reading on this point, see EJ Lowe and A Rami (eds), *Truth and Truth-Making* (Stocksfield, Acumen, 2009).

[143] Naqvi (n 21) 252, citing M Foucault, *Power/Knowledge: Selected Interviews and Other Writings 1972–1977*, ed C Gordon (New York, Harvester Wheatsheaf, 1980) 114.

[144] ibid, again citing Foucault (n 143).

[145] Teitel (n 1) 115.

[146] ibid, 105ff. Examples of legal limitations of certain accounts and the barring of certain individuals from influencing public debates can be found in post-war constitutions and later court decisions. In Italy, Art XII of the 'Transitory and Final Provisions' of the 1948 constitution introduced a temporary political lustration of the Fascist cadres, limiting their voice in the political debate of the newly founded republic. In Germany, in the *Wunsiedel* case [Case No 1 BvR 2150/08, paras 1–110, 4 November 2009] the German Federal Constitutional Court (Bundesverfassungsgericht) held that the prohibition of neo-Nazi gatherings on symbolic days for the movement did not violate the constitutional right to freedom of expression. See M Payandeh, 'The Limits of Freedom of Expression in the Wunsiedel Decision of the German Federal Constitutional Court' (2010) 11(8) *German Law Journal* 929; Teitel (n 1) 103ff, and Roht-Arriaza (n 32) 13.

However, Teitel cautions against the 'attempt to entrench an identity based on a particular historical view'; this would be itself illiberal, clashing with freedom of expression norms.[147] To counteract this danger, therefore, ensuring a 'plurality of narratives, instability and political dialectic' is crucial.[148] It is precisely the dialogue between differing voices and competing accounts of the truth which must be reckoned with during and after the transition in order to avoid new or renewed illiberal regimes.

International trials, truth commissions and other truth-seeking initiatives can produce contrasting truths: competing accounts coexist and produce a mosaic impression of the past. Support for historical TJ that reckons with internal contradictions is offered in Drucilla Cornell's call to deconstruction to 'question [one's] own beliefs' and appreciate other perspectives.[149] There will always be multiple views and narratives about past harm: some accounts might be factually closer to historical events, but there is some value in engaging a range of competing truths and reckoning with them – even the most outlandish – in the interests not just of knowing more of the past, but of present and future coexistence. Given transitional truth seeking is inherently 'presentist', contradictions between truths (including legal truths) offer and juxtapose/synthesise a plurality of competing narratives that pave the way for political dialectics, as indicated by Teitel, that may shape other aspects of TJ, such as institutional reforms. Compared to other typologies of truth, the notion of 'legal truth' discussed in the following section lends itself more readily to closer critical scrutiny; while retaining its normative authority as a product of legal/legalised mechanisms, the legal truth may carry different political meanings and can be used over time in various ways.

III. INTERPRETING LEGAL TRUTH IN TRANSITIONAL JUSTICE

As discussed, truths produced by legal/legalised (or judicial/quasi-judicial) mechanisms can be understood in their broader political contexts and in light of power structures. This part of the chapter explores the notion of legal truth in greater detail, arguing that its specificities have been overlooked in identifying the practical, discrete object of transitional truth seeking, beyond the aspirational ideals behind general calls for 'the truth'. While some have indicated that the legal truth is 'merely a by-product of a dispute settlement mechanism',[150]

[147] Teitel (n 1) 108 and 117.

[148] ibid 117.

[149] D Cornell, *The Philosophy of the Limit* (London, Routledge, 1992), also discussed in JM Balkin, 'Deconstruction' in D Patterson (ed), *A Companion of Philosophy of Law and Legal Theory*, 2nd edn (Malden, MA, Blackwell, 2010) 367, 372.

[150] Naqvi (n 21) 246.

it can be argued that the legal truth is richer and more complex.[151] Constitutive theories of law suggest that 'law is not simply an instrument for enforcing a system of morality or justice but is also "part of a distinctive manner of imagining the real"'.[152] Robert Summers defines 'formal legal truths' as 'whatever is found by the legal fact-finder (judge or lay jurors or both), whether it accords with substantive truth or not', drawing on Hans Kelsen's identification of a created legal fact, which may exist in the sphere of law, even when it has not occurred in reality.[153] Considering the theoretical discussion in Chapter 2 on legal pluralism and comparative legal methods, legal truths are constituted by certain visible and invisible rules of the legal system (such as the procedures of trials and truth commissions), yet they are also playing a role in contributing to these rules. Despite law's 'relative impotence' compared to other social and political factors that inform transitional truth seeking, to borrow from Mark Osiel, 'one way the law might influence social norms is by shaping how certain events in society's history … are remembered'.[154]

The political power of the law affects the creation of narratives. Jack Balkin argues that 'law creates truth – it makes things true as a matter of law' and 'in the eyes of the law'.[155] He contends that 'law is continuously proliferating truth into the world'; by 'making things real', it has power in two ways: 'it can make things true or false in a way that matters to us' but also 'because it has power over us'.[156] Law 'creates legal knowledge', it is 'a form of cultural software that shapes the way we think about and apprehend the world', in a way 'compromis[ing] one's ability to understand what is true, because what is true from the standpoint of law is not really true'.[157] Judges, and similarly members of truth commissions, play a crucial role in constructing the legal truth about past abuse; consequently, their vision of society and politics is likely to trickle down into the official narratives of truth they construe.[158] Moreover, law is generally 'intertwined with, supports and is supported by the power

[151] For a theoretically engaging discussion of the legal truth, see MS Moore, 'The Plain Truth about Legal Truth' (2003) 26 *Harvard Journal of Law and Public Policy* 23.
[152] C Geertz, 'Local Knowledge: Fact and Law in Comparative Perspective' in *Local Knowledge: Further Essays in Interpretative Anthropology* (New York, Basic Books, 1983) 167, 184, cited in PS Berman, 'Telling a Less Suspicious Story' in A Sarat and J Simon (eds), *Cultural Analysis, Cultural Studies, and the Law: Moving Beyond Legal Realism* (Durham, NC, Duke University Press, 2003) 107.
[153] RS Summers, 'Formal Legal Truth and Substantive Truth in Judicial Fact-finding – Their Justified Divergence in Some Particular Cases' (1999) 18 *Law and Philosophy* 497, 498; quoting H Kelsen, 'Sovereign Equality of States' (1994) 53 *Yale Law Journal* 207, 218.
[154] Osiel (n 2) 209–10.
[155] JM Balkin, 'The Proliferation of Legal Truth' (2003) 26 *Harvard Journal of Law and Public Policy* 5, 6.
[156] ibid 7.
[157] ibid 7–10.
[158] For a critique of the role of the judiciary in transitions, see inter alia HO Yusuf, 'The Judiciary and Constitutionalism in Transitions: A Critique' (2007) 7(3) *Global Jurist*.

and authority of the state', or of equivalent political forces that dominate TJ experiences.[159] Given that in times of transition state authorities may be part of the bigger problem, finding the legal truth may occur outside the realm of state-sanctioned institutions.

In addition to legal truths emerging from judicial and quasi-judicial processes discussed previously, unofficial truth projects (UTPs), rooted in civil society organisations, may also contribute to uncovering the truth about past abuse.[160] Despite the absence of official law explicitly underpinning such projects, the comparative law method discussed in the previous chapter would indicate that they nonetheless carry normative qualities and as such they may produce forms of legal truth. One of the primary advantages of UTPs is the 'community level truth-telling' they entail.[161] Interesting examples are offered in the Colombian context, where the Catholic Church (and specifically, key local religious leaders) have spearheaded initiatives to construct social memory to challenge state-sponsored attempts to silence the past (and in other cases, they have participated in the silencing of truths).[162] Similarly, other traditional forms of truth telling can complement state prosecutions, as was the case in the Rwandan *gacaca*.[163] Indeed, as long as the truth-seeking processes are recognised in the society in which they operate, a degree of authority and formalism is met, regardless of the specific shape they take. This will be discussed in greater detail in the final chapter with reference to Islamic law. The 'from below' perspective led by a range of civil society actors can offer an alternative, or complementary, angle to state-led or international transitional truth-seeking initiatives.[164] Despite the usual caveats about local power structures and ambiguous roles of non-state actors in uncovering the truth about past harm,[165] they may enjoy a greater degree of respect and legitimacy at community level; this is especially the case when the state has been complicit in widespread abuse or the international community promoting the international mechanism is too distant from the realities on the ground. Nevertheless, it is fair to say that legal truths emerging from formalised judicial or quasi-judicial mechanisms continue to carry a certain weight and are easier to transpose across multiple legal/legalised sites.

[159] Balkin (n 155) 11.

[160] Bickford (n 89).

[161] ibid 995.

[162] See eg SMR Oyola 'Religion and the Social Reconstruction of Memory amid Violence in Bojayá, Chocó (Colombia): Creating Transitional Justice from Below' in SD Brunn (ed), *The Changing World Religion Map* (Heidelberg, Springer, 2015).

[163] P Clark, *The Gacaca Courts, Post-genocide Justice and Reconciliation in Rwanda* (Cambridge, Cambridge University Press, 2010) 186ff.

[164] See in general KMcEvoy and L McGregor (eds), *Transitional Justice from Below: Grassroots Activism and the Struggle for Change* (Oxford, Hart, 2008) 3.

[165] On this crucial point, regarding religious actors specifically, see I Cismas 'Reflections on the Presence and Absence of Religious Actors in Transitional Justice Processes: On Legitimacy and Accountability' in R Duthie and P Seils (eds), *Justice Mosaics: How Context Shapes Transitional Justice in Fractured Societies* (New York, ICTJ, 2017).

The legal truth is capable of reiteration across different forums and information about past abuse may be 'recycled' (as discussed again in the next chapter, in relation to the notion of the right to truth). A helpful example is provided in the uses of findings in the *Milošević* trial at the ICTY after the death of the defendant and the end of the proceedings.[166] Former prosecutor Carla Del Ponte indicated that:

> The lack of a judgment has not deprived the four-year trial from achieving some of its objectives, in particular that of satisfying to some extent the right to the truth or settling down a historical record.[167]

This suggests that despite the trial ending before a judgment was issued, trial documents provided a formal record of past harms and accountability. The general archival function as a living memory of the ICTY has been discussed elsewhere.[168] In the *Milošević* trial, the ICTY decided to lift the confidentiality of certain information after the death of the accused in order to facilitate related proceedings.[169] This possibility was discussed where there was 'a sufficient nexus' based on 'substantial geographical and temporal overlap' between cases,[170] or when individuals had been jointly accused.[171] Moreover, other truth-seeking projects in the Balkans (notably concerning Kosovo) have been able to use some of the legal truths emerging from the *Milošević* trial.[172] This illustrates the potential uses of legal truth across regions that share a history of past abuse, blurring the individual and social angles.

In the context of TJ, the legal truth is also connected to the production of 'an official statement about what happened' and the related right to know and the state obligation 'to disclose something'.[173] For Naqvi, the legal truth can

[166] *Milošević* case (Order Terminating the Proceedings) ICTY-02-54-T (14 March 2006).

[167] Naqvi (n 21) 247, citing press conference by ICTY prosecutor, Carla Del Ponte, The Hague, 12 March 2006.

[168] K Campbell, 'The Laws of Memory: The ICTY, the Archive, and Transitional Justice' (2013) 22(2) *Social & Legal Studies* 247.

[169] *Milošević* case (Order Lifting Confidentiality of Relevant Materials for Investigation Purposes) ICTY-02-54-T (16 March 2006). On the broader usefulness of the findings of the Milošević trials, see also J Armatta, 'Historical Revelations from the Milošević Trial' (2012) 36 *Southeastern Europe* 10; her abstract makes it clear: 'While there was no legal resolution, evidence revealed at trial provides a rich resource for historians to further examine some of the major controversies arising from the disintegration of Yugoslavia and the decade of wars that ensued.'

[170] *Karadzic* case (Decision on the accused's motion for access to ex parte filings in the Slobodan Milošević case (Srebrenica intercepts)) ICTY -95-5/18-T, ICTY-02-54-T (28 February 2011).

[171] *Hadzic* case (Decision on motion on behalf of Goran Hadzic seeking access to confidential material in prosecutor v Slobodan Milošević related to Croatia) ICTY-04-7S-PT, ICTY-02-S4-T (22 March 2012).

[172] Evidentiary material gathered in the Milošević trial has also found its way to the extraordinary Kosovo memory book, available at www.kosovskaknjigapamcenja.org/?page_id=29. See also G Visoka, 'Arrested Truth: Transitional Justice and the Politics of Remembrance in Kosovo' (2016) 8(1) *Journal of Human Rights Practice* 62.

[173] Naqvi (n 21) 250ff, discussing Derrida, *Prophets of Extremity* (n 127) and Derrida, *Of Grammatology* (n 127).

thus be understood as 'the legal conception of a right owed by the state to the individual',[174] which will be discussed in the following chapter as the right to truth. Through the production of legal truths, certain narratives resulting from recognition of past harm are elevated above others – by virtue of the procedures, actors and rituals that carry them. While this is problematic for the many different reasons discussed throughout this chapter, the formalities of legal truth offer something tangible for victims, survivors and societies to accept or contest through various means.

A. The Construction and Limits of Legal Truths

Competing narratives about the past coexist in the context of legal/legalised truth seeking: legal truths resulting from formal proceedings represent a temporary, context-specific compromise susceptible to repeated adjustments. They are never a final reading of the past, and their value is contextual. The law's limits in uncovering the truth are widely acknowledged, as summarised by Stanley Cohen: 'even a complete mosaic of the legal truths cannot create a full or shared knowledge of "what really happened", let alone *why* it happened'.[175] The legal truth can be understood as a social construct emerging from narratives, testimonies and witness accounts in given structures (eg trials and truth commissions).[176] It is an outcome of a judicial, or quasi-judicial, truth-seeking process, subject to the procedural rules of each specific mechanism, influencing how, and which, truths are revealed.[177] In this regard, the rules of evidence[178] and other formal requirements may in fact contribute to the gap between legal truth and historical truth.[179]

> Formal 'findings of fact' ... diverge from substantive truth not by design, but merely because this is the way the process happens to work, under the peculiar circumstances of the case.[180]

What the law is able to capture and see – and what it does not – indicates further ways in which legal truths discovered through formal proceedings can

[174] ibid 249ff.
[175] S Cohen, 'Unspeakable Memories and Commensurable Laws' in S Karstedt (ed), *Legal Institutions and Collective Memories* (Oxford, Hart, 2009) 28.
[176] Buckley-Zistel (n 23) 144.
[177] For a general discussion on the relationship between procedure and truth in the criminal trial, see T Weigend 'Should We Search for the Truth, and Who Should Do It' (2010) 36 *North Carolina Journal of International Law & Commercial Regulation* 389.
[178] On the limitations posed by rules of evidence, see inter alia: W Twining, *Rethinking Evidence, Exploratory Essays*, 2nd edn (Cambridge, Cambridge University Press, 2006); J Jackson and S Doran, 'Evidence' in D Patterson (ed), *A Companion of Philosophy of Law and Legal Theory* (Malden, MA, Blackwell, 1996) 172.
[179] Summers (n 153) 499.
[180] ibid.

be distorted.[181] This echoes some of the discussion on comparative legal methods presented in the previous chapter. From a postmodernist perspective, any type of legal truth may be devoid of objectivity and depart significantly from the factual truth about past abuse.[182] Through a positivist lens, the constructed legal truth emerging from those mechanisms should be approached with 'a healthy degree of scepticism about the justice and morality of the existing legal systems'.[183] Moreover, as established, legal truths exist within power dynamics and consequently reflect power in how narratives around past harm are formed and presented. Given it carries a forward-looking normative force, for example, with regards to institutional reforms and constitutional changes,[184] it cannot be divorced from its political context.

Among the possible misrepresentations of fact embedded in the legal truth in transition, Colm Campbell and Catherine Turner list the public/private divide, the marginalisation (or exclusion) of particular voices (including those of certain groups of victims) from the process, the rigidity of legal categories (namely, whether or not certain facts can be considered under the law), the exclusion from specific legal responsibilities under human rights law for non-state actors, and the hegemonic qualities of law.[185] An example of the public/private law divide that distorts the legal truth in TJ is highlighted by feminist critiques.[186] Notably, 'women's testimony, sexual violence, … [and] victim identity' are absent or marginalised in accounts of past harm outlined in TJ mechanisms.[187] Reasons for the relative marginalisation of gender issues in the legal truth produced in transitional truth seeking include the fact that 'women are silenced by shame,

[181] Campbell and Turner (n 60) 376ff.

[182] ibid 381.

[183] Balkin (n 155) 14ff, citing the seminal HLA Hart, 'Positivism and the Separation of Law and Morals' (1958) 71 *Harvard Law Review* 593.

[184] On the collective impact of transitional justice measures, such as transitional constitutionalism, see inter alia: RG Teitel, 'Post-Communist Constitutionalism: A Transitional Perspective' (1994) 26 *Columbia Human Rights Law Review* 167; KS Rosenn, 'Brazil's New Constitution: An Exercise in Transient Constitutionalism for a Transitional Society' (1990) *American Journal of Comparative Law* 773.

[185] Campbell and Turner (n 60) 376ff.

[186] See inter alia C Bell and C O'Rourke, 'Does Feminism Need a Theory of Transitional Justice? An Introductory Essay' (2007) 1(1) *International Journal of Transitional Justice* 23. Also, FN Aoláin and E Rooney, 'Underenforcement and Intersectionality: Gendered Aspects of Transition for Women' (2007) 1(3) *International Journal of Transitional Justice* 338; M O'Reilly, 'Peace and Justice through a Feminist Lens: Gender Justice and the Women's Court for the Former Yugoslavia' (2016) 10(3) *Journal of Intervention and Statebuilding* 419. There is a growing literature on gender in TJ: see inter alia S Buckley-Zistel and R Stanley (eds), *Gender in Transitional Justice* (London, Palgrave Macmillan, 2012); O Yacob-Haliso and O Omoigberale, 'Women and Transitional Justice in Africa and Latin America' in O Yacob-Haliso and T Falola (eds), *The Palgrave Handbook of African Women's Studies* (Cham, Palgrave Macmillan, 2020); A Björkdahl and J Mannergren Selimovic, 'Gender and Transitional Justice' in O Simić, *An Introduction to Transitional Justice*, 2nd edn (Abingdon, Routledge, 2020).

[187] V Nesiah, 'Discussion Lines on Gender and Transitional Justice: An Introductory Essay Reflecting on the ICTJ Bellagio Workshop on Gender and Transitional Justice' (2006) 15 *Columbia Journal of Gender and Law* 799, also discussed in Bell and O'Rourke (n 186).

choose silence to retain self-respect, use silence as a strategy of survival, or an agential act'.[188] Moreover, public violence tends to overshadow private violence in accounting for past abuse, ignoring the peculiarities of patterns of violence suffered by women and their long-term impact on societies.[189] As such, 'the institutional conditions and productive effects of the commissioning of truth' in TJ may conceal gendered private-sphere violence,[190] which may obscure the full factual truths about the extent of past harm and the total number of victims. Some truth commissions have explicitly incorporated gender violence.[191] And while in principle the issue of gender has been mainstreamed in transitional truth seeking, as evidenced in the recommendations set out by the International Center for Transitional Justice in relation to truth commissions,[192] and various UN instruments, its implementation remains inadequate.[193] Consequently, the marginalisation of gendered violence in transitional truth seeking flows into the limitations of the legal truth.

The legal truths uncovered in transitional truth seeking impose a partial vision of the past. The normative effects of official accounts of abuse may also carry hegemonic features. For example, the legal truth as a result of formal procedures of trials or truth commissions offers an interpretation of past violence through the lens of the state or other official apparatuses, limiting (or even suppressing) alternative or critical views. The vast literature on memory laws unpacks this issue in detail both doctrinally and with regard to a range of horrific chapters in recent history.[194] Again, power structures and fixed identity categories affect the

[188] E Porter, 'Gendered Narratives: Stories and Silences in Transitional Justice' (2016) 17 *Human Rights Review* 35.

[189] FN Aoláin, 'Women, Security, and the Patriarchy of Internationalized Transitional Justice' (2009) 31(4) *Human Rights Quarterly* 1055; and FN Aoláin and C Turner, 'Gender, Truth and Transition' (2007) 16 *UCLA Women's Law Journal* 229.

[190] A Orford, 'Commissioning the Truth' (2006) 15 *Columbia Journal of Gender and Law* 851, 883. Orford's critique offers a joint feminist and anticapitalist perspective.

[191] Notably, South Africa and Sierra Leone, as discussed in S Buckley-Zistel, 'Truth Commissions, Human Rights and Gender' in T Debiel, T Held and U Schneckener (eds), *Peacebuilding in Crisis: Rethinking Paradigms and Practices of Transnational Cooperation* (London, Routledge, 2016).

[192] V Nesiah et al for the International Center for Transitional Justice, *Truth Commissions and Gender: Principles, Policies, and Procedures* (2006) available at www.ictj.org/sites/default/files/ICTJ-Global-Commissions-Gender-2006-English_0.pdf.

[193] LL Langlois, 'Gender Perspective in UN Framework for Peace Processes and Transitional Justice: The Need for a Clearer and More Inclusive Notion of Gender' (2018) 12(1) *International Journal of Transitional Justice* 146.

[194] See inter alia: Gutman (n 2); Koposov (n 2); U Belavusau and A Gliszczyńska-Grabias (eds), *Law and Memory: Towards Legal Governance of History* (Cambridge, Cambridge University Press, 2017); Karstedt (n 2); I Markovits, 'Selective Memory: How the Law Affects What We Remember and Forget about the Past: The Case of East Germany' (2001) 35 *Law & Society Review* 513; A Sarat and T Kearns, 'Writing History and Registering Memory in Legal Decisions and Legal Practices: An Introduction' in A Sarat and T Kearns (eds), *History, Memory and the Law* (Michigan, University of Michigan Press, 2002); L Douglas, *The Memory of Judgment: Making Law and History in the Trials of the Holocaust* (New Haven, CT, Yale University Press, 2001).

performative process and restrict the validity of the truth derived from them.[195] Thus, drawing on Butler and Cover, formal words uttered in law courts (and by extension quasi-judicial forums, such as truth commissions that issue authoritative recommendations) may perpetuate violence including through the infliction of punishments.[196] Legal systems generally induce 'people to comply with a dominant set of practices and institutions' in an overarching manner because of a legal system's 'function as constitutive of social ontology'.[197] Even in non-transitional contexts the 'law is at the same time both repressive and constitutive', and its repressive features apparent 'from the presence of police, prisons, courtrooms with armed bailiffs, and the ever-ready national guard, which is called out to restore the status quo when a social disturbance arises'.[198] As such, the potentially violent and hegemonic properties of law, if ignored, may undermine the validity of the legal truth resulting from legal/legalised truth-seeking mechanisms and their uses.

During transitions, establishing certain narratives about the past through truth-seeking mechanisms may lead to the renegotiation of important aspects of the legal and constitutional framework.[199] The possible tensions between legal truths and other forms of knowledge revealed outside the confines of judicial or quasi-judicial truth seeking may impact a society emerging from a violent past.[200] When there is disagreement over past accounts, and different versions of the truth emerge, 'legal indeterminacy can actually proliferate law's power by spurring people to think, talk, contest, and argue using legal frameworks, legal concepts and legal terms'.[201] This momentum can feed into transitional constitutionalism. Highlighting the constructivist features of transitional constitution-making, Teitel describes two modalities of operation, one 'codifying' and expressing existing consensus, the other transformative, seeking to reconstruct the previous 'political order associated with injustice'.[202]

[195] For a general understanding of some of their critical approaches, see inter alia J Derrida, 'Force of Law' (1989–90) 11 *Cardozo Law Review* 920, and a commentary on this work, JP McCormick, 'Derrida on Law; Or, Poststructuralism Gets Serious' (2001) 29(3) *Political Theory* 395; J Butler, 'Performative Acts and Gender Constitution: An Essay in Phenomenology and Feminist Theory' (1988) 40(4) *Theatre Journal* 519; J Butler, 'Burning Acts: Injurious Speech' (1996) 3 *University of Chicago Law School Roundtable* 199, quoting R Cover, 'Violence and the Word' (1986) 95 *Yale Law Journal* 1601.

[196] See the joint reading of Cover (n 195) and Butler (n 195) 202.

[197] D Litowitz, 'Gramsci, Hegemony, and the Law' (2000) 2(1) *Brigham Young University Law Review* 515, 517 building on Gramsci's work.

[198] ibid 530.

[199] Teitel (n 1) 191ff. On transitional constitutionalism, see also C Turner and R Houghton, 'Constitution Making and Post-conflict Reconstruction' in M Saul and JA Sweeney (eds), *International Law and Post-conflict Reconstruction Policy* (London, Routledge 2015); and K McConnachie and J Morison, 'Constitution Making, Transition and the Reconstruction of Society' in K McEvoy and L McGregor (eds), *Transitional Justice from Below: Grassroots Activism and the Struggle for Change* (Oxford, Hart, 2008).

[200] Balkin (n 155) 12ff.

[201] ibid.

[202] Teitel (n 1) 196ff and 201.

As a result, 'the construction of constitutional constraints' responds to 'a state's political, historical and constitutional legacies'.[203] But 'the constructed truth is by no means hermetically sealed and eternal' as Suzanne Buckley-Zistel argues, 'for there are always counter-discourses, dissenting narratives, contingency and flux'.[204] In this context, despite its limitations as a vehicle for complete historical accuracy and inclusiveness, the legal truth participates in the renegotiation of the past through constitutive documents, which in turn can foster (or hinder) subsequent conversations and contestations. A range of actors shape this process: unsurprisingly, legal professionals play a special role.

B. Stakeholders of the Legal Truth

Truth seeking, whether through trials, truth commissions, or other TJ mechanisms, is a malleable concept and thus might carry different (even opposing) meanings for different actors.[205] Stakeholders involved in transitional truth-seeking efforts that produce legal truths play a variety of roles that may both benefit or hinder the processes.[206] In addition to victims and survivors, as well as perpetrators, truth entrepreneurs (including those within the UN system and large NGOs) play a special role in promoting transitional truth seeking, and they thus imbue the process with their own explicit or implicit agendas, political and social views and operate within their specific context.[207] Political forces, including state and non-state groups, as well as powerful elites within the political establishments (for instance, the judiciary or economic leaders) as well as external actors may also influence the process of formation of the legal truth. As part of the power adjustments between 'the forces of the past and the successor elites',[208] international organisations, NGOs and bilateral donors who fund, promote or support truth-seeking mechanisms, and endorse specific narratives,

[203] ibid 211.

[204] Buckley-Zistel (n 23) 159.

[205] See in general Rowen (n 87) 10ff.

[206] See eg T Madlingozi, 'On Transitional Justice Entrepreneurs and the Production of Victims' (2010) 2(2) *Journal of Human Rights Practice* 208, 225; C Ryngaert, 'Dealing with Organisations and Corporations' in P Malcontent (ed), *Facing the Past: Amending Historical Injustices Through Instruments of Transitional Justice* (Cambridge, Intersentia, 2016); P Gready and S Robins, 'Transitional Justice and Theories of Change: Towards Evaluation as Understanding' (2020) 14(2) *International Journal of Transitional Justice* 280, 296–97; S Rubli, 'Transitional Justice: Justice by Bureaucratic Means?' in Swiss Peace Working Paper Series (4/2012) available at www.files.ethz.ch/isn/154626/WP4_2012.pdf, 11; L Fletcher and HM Weinstein, 'How Power Dynamics Influence the "North–South" Gap in Transitional Justice' (2019) 36 *Berkeley Journal of International Law* 190, 191 and 204.

[207] On truth entrepreneurs in the UN system and the ICTJ, see in particular P Naftali, *La construction du "droit à la vérité" en droit international* (Bruxelles, Éditions Bruylant, 2017) 325–33.

[208] L Huyse, 'Justice after Transition: On the Choices Successor Elites Make in Dealing with the Past' (1995) 20(1) *Law & Social Inquiry* 51, 71.

all shape the formation of legal truths.[209] In mobilising the right to truth, argues Patricia Naftali, different actors pursue competing aims and exercises.[210] Those representing the memory of certain victims or the state might engage in different ideological battles.[211] Moreover, stakeholders in the quest and processes of uncovering the legal truth engage with their audiences in an attempt to garner the support of larger numbers. Jamie Rowen argues that proponents of TJ (as a transnational movement) 'must find frames that resonate with their audiences', including relevance to people's lives and credibility.[212] That is where invocations to specific local norms, including religious values, might be useful, as discussed in relation to Islamic law in the final chapter.

A special category of stakeholders in the processes that lead to articulations of legal truths is made up of lawyers, the judiciary and legal scholars – some of whom might work for the UN and large international or national NGOs. In truth-seeking initiatives, 'lawyers' arguments and judicial opinions are attempts to share truths of practical wisdom publicly, allowing that truth be experienced, seen and felt' in the guise of 'political or legal truth'.[213] On the other hand, lawyers can also be 'enemies of the truth' if they pursue 'truth-obscuring' and 'uncertainty' as a source of business – revealing 'a fundamental tension between lawyers and the public', who instead 'benefits from truth-eliciting rules'.[214] The role of different legal professionals can be ambiguous. Strategic legal activism in TJ can help uncover legal truths, as discussed earlier in relation to the creative circumvention of amnesty laws in Argentina. However, the 'culture of quietism' and the lack of engagement by lawyers may hinder transitional aims, as noted by Kieran McEvoy; likewise, an overly technical, legalistic approach divorced from political circumstances may also devalue those aims.[215] Thus, much like law itself, lawyers do not necessarily provide neutral technical input to transitional truth seeking, and the resulting legal truths can be shaped by their political orientation, job descriptions and many more factors.

[209] For example, see the set of recommendations directed at donors of the *gacaca* mechanisms in Rwanda: 'Justice Compromised: The Legacy of Rwanda's Community-based Gacaca Courts' [2011] *Human Rights Watch* 9, available at www.hrw.org/report/2011/05/31/justice-compromised/legacy-rwandas-community-based-gacaca-courts.

[210] P Naftali, 'Crafting a "Right to Truth" in International Law: Convergence Mobilizations, Divergent Agendas' (2016) XIII *Champ Penal/Penal Field* 1.

[211] B Rolston, 'Ambushed by Memory: Post-conflict Popular Memorialisation in Northern Ireland' (2020) 14 *International Journal of Transitional Justice* 320, 322–23.

[212] Rowen (n 87) 13.

[213] L Meyer, 'Between Reason and Power: Experiencing Legal Truth' (1998–99) 67 *University of Cincinnati Law Review* 727, 758.

[214] JO McGinnis, 'Lawyers as the Enemies of the Truth' (2003) 26 *Harvard Journal of Law and Public Policy* 231.

[215] K McEvoy (n 32); 'Beyond Legalism: Towards a Thicker Understanding of Transitional Justice' (2007) 24(4) *Journal of Law and Society* 411. In the latter article, McEvoy draws on the work of JN Shklar, *Legalism: Law, Morals, and Political Trials* (Cambridge, MA, Harvard University Press, 1964).

The ways in which judges interpret and apply law determine the formation of legal truths in trials.[216] There have been calls for a greater judicial proactivity in international criminal law in 'finding the material truth' about a certain chain of events' related to past harm.[217] However, the perceptions and relationships between domestic and international judges, and the previous and successor establishments affect how the legal truth is constructed. As human beings, judges cannot help but exercise discretion as informed by their personal and political beliefs. To the extent that a judge thinks of themselves as a 'loyal member of this society', they may 'import ... politics into legal processes' according to personal perceptions.[218] Robert Cover summarises this ambivalence: on the one hand, we 'hear the judge as a voice of reason [and] see her as the embodiment of principle', but on the other, there is a 'danger in forgetting the limits which are intrinsic to this activity of legal interpretation' and 'in exaggerating the extent to which any interpretation rendered as part of the act of state violence can ever constitute a common and coherent meaning'.[219] This 'institutional structure' allows for the transformation of a judge's understanding of a fact to be transformed into law, conferring 'meaning on the deeds which effect this transformation, thereby legitimating them as "lawful"' or somehow official.[220] Judges, however, may be reluctant to play a transformative role in TJ for a variety of contextual reasons. Consequently, this might result in the lack of effort by the judiciary to ensure 'justice for victims of gross human rights violations through an affirmation of the *right to truth*' for victims in TJ.[221] The conduct, actions and inaction of judges and legal professionals more generally, such as those involved in truth commissions, carry normative implications in the pursuit of legal truth through transitional truth seeking. As such, in light of the discussion in Chapter 2, the role of lawyers, in general, can become significant in the development of legal truths, which in turn informs the direction and developments of transitional truth seeking as a whole.

In addition to lawyers and judges, legal scholars may also contribute to the formation of the truth. Academic work may help 'reveal truth', and critical lawyers can contribute to 'reveal[ing] a world which is characterised more by conflict than by harmony, and by patterns of illegitimate hierarchy'.[222] Drawing

[216] For a critical overview of the role of the judiciary with reference to transitional Chile, see L Hilbink, *Judges Beyond Politics in Democracy and Dictatorship: Lessons from Chile* (Cambridge, Cambridge University Press, 2007).

[217] M Bohlander, 'Paradise Postponed? For a Judge-led Generic Model of International Criminal Procedure and an End to Draft-as-You-Go' (2014) *Netherlands Yearbook of International Law* 45.

[218] On this point, see eg Weyrauch (n 26) 708ff.

[219] Cover (n 195) 1628.

[220] ibid 1619.

[221] Yusuf (n 158) 3. By way of example of judicial behaviour, Yusuf reports how given an 'entrenched judicial tradition of plain-fact jurisprudence', in the *Oputa Panel* case, the court 'accorded primacy to protecting the federal character of the Nigerian polity over the rights of victims of gross violations of human rights' ibid 6, 13, also discussing the *Oputa Panel* case in Nigeria.

[222] AD Freeman, 'Truth and Mystification in Legal Scholarship' (1981) 90(5) *Yale Law Journal* 1229, 1230ff.

on Phil Scraton's work on the Hillsborough disaster (in a non-transitional context), academic research may be better placed to capture the 'alternative accounts' and the view from below (ie of the victims) 'contrasting the official discourse' of 'powerful institutions' (in the Hillsborough case, that of the state).[223] State institutions can 'engage in discourses of deceit, denial and neutralisation that protect and exonerate those in positions of power, those who stand highest in established hierarchies of credibility', subordinating and disqualifying the 'view from below'.[224] Independent academic voices are thus vital. Andrew Williams's account of the death of Baha Mousa during the British occupation of Iraq in 2003 is another pertinent example of how academic lawyers can help piece together the truth after serious violence.[225] As such, legal scholars may contribute to truth seeking through their specialist knowledge of the law and their research capacity. But not all legal academics are able and willing to speak truth to power. History is rife with examples of academics acting as mouthpieces of ruling elites before and after the transition, either through their own political convictions or external coercive pressure to follow a certain political orientation in order to continue public intellectual activities in universities.[226] Therefore, the role of legal scholars can be constructive or destructive of the legal truth, depending on a range of factors.

In sum, the notion of legal truth is separate from historical truth, but it plays an important role in setting down a record about past abuse and in legitimising it in official/legal language. This truth is capable of being reiterated and 'recycled' across different forums as well as constituting the foundation for radical institutional reforms based on an accepted set of sometimes competing narratives in the context of shifting politics and adjustments to power structures, potentially providing rules for the contestation of different accounts. In that regard, the legal truth is both an instrument of power as well as a constitutive force in itself, as it both codifies and transforms existing consensus and shapes narratives about past violence. The legal truth may misrepresent facts and conceal structural forms of violence that permeate transitional societies; distortions are determined by politics as well as by procedures of specific mechanisms. Moreover, the actors that shape the formation of the legal truth, including national elites (both pre and post-transition), international organisations involved in setting up truth-finding mechanisms and the lawyers that operate the process, all contribute to the contours of the resulting accounts of the past. Against this

[223] Scraton (n 72) 1.

[224] ibid 24.

[225] AT Williams, *A Very British Killing: The Death of Baha Mousa* (London, Vintage, 2013).

[226] On the relationship between scholars and the establishment during mass violence, see for instance the famous dispute between Italian professors Benedetto Croce (an antifascist who drafted the Manifesto of Antifascist Intellectuals of 1 May 1925) and Giovanni Gentile (pro-fascist). Croce (and many other antifascist intellectuals), however, notably signed the 1931 'Giuramento di fedeltà al fascismo', a formal endorsement of Mussolini's regime which enabled him to retain his academic post and thus contribute to public debates from a substantially antifascist perspective.

backdrop, some survivors may be marginalised from truth-seeking initiatives – which is why independent legal academia (as well as journalism, art and other forms of cultural production) is also an important part of the memorialisation process after mass violence. As the following section will discuss, truth-seeking initiatives and the resulting legal truths – while necessarily incomplete if taken individually – taken together contribute to the formation of collective memories and the long-term goals of transition.

IV. LEGAL TRUTHS BETWEEN COLLECTIVE MEMORIES AND PERFORMANCES OF TRANSITIONAL JUSTICE

The legal truth as a product of judicial and quasi-judicial mechanisms is not a static concept, nor can it ever deliver a final, universal and uncontested truth. Any legal truth must be juxtaposed with other legal truths emerging from parallel truth-seeking initiatives, as well as the entire extralegal dimension of truth seeking. Building on the previous discussion, this section situates the legal truth within the scope of collective memories as an outcome of transitional truth seeking, and considers the performative, ritualised and theatrical character of the processes involved. In light of the impulse in TJ to 'construct collective memory',[227] this process situates legal truths (which are themselves constructed, contextualised and contested) into a broader social and political tapestry, woven by different decision-makers and influencers.

Truth-seeking mechanisms such as trials and truth commissions can work towards 'establishing a particular and "politicised" common memory'.[228] Although memory is individual and unreproducible', as summarised by Susan Sontag, 'collective memory' builds a story 'of how [an event] happened, with pictures that lock the story in our minds'.[229] Legal truths contribute to the formation of collective memory within the context of how 'political elites, social groups and institutions reinterpret the past and the breakdown of civility and propagate new interpretative narratives about "what happened" to legitimate a new political dispensation and develop a new vision of the future'.[230] As such, argues Alexandra Barahona de Brito, this is a 'continuous process generating ongoing cycles of social memory-making'.[231]

[227] Teitel (n 1), 116. On the term 'collective memory', see inter alia: A Funkenstein, 'Collective Memory and Historical Consciousness' (1989) *History and Memory* 5; J Assmann and J Czaplicka 'Collective Memory and Cultural Identity' (1995) *New German Critique* 125.

[228] S Karstedt, 'Introduction: The Legacy of Maurice Halbwachs' in S Karstedt (ed), *Legal Institutions and Collective Memories* (Oxford, Hart, 2009) 8.

[229] S Sontag, *Regarding the Pain of Others* (New York, Picador, 2003) 86, cited (verbatim) in Scraton (n 72) 2.

[230] Barahona de Brito (n 14) 360.

[231] ibid 364.

According to Kennedy's theory of legal formality, decision-making includes two processes, 'rule application and decision according to purposes, or substantive rationality'.[232] As such, in addition to the normative principles contained in a given system, the route through which they are applied by an adjudicatory body is relevant. In any particular setting, therefore, there will be a spectrum on which different adjudicatory bodies enjoy differing degrees of acceptance in the community on the basis of both rule applications and substantive rationality. In relation to TJ settings, trials, truth commissions and other mechanisms may enjoy different legitimacy and authority based on multiple factors, which in turn will shape how the legal truths are woven into the collective memories of past harm. Discussing transitional historical justice, Teitel highlights the 'visible turn to the law, its processes, and framework … at a time when the social consensus is otherwise frayed' because the 'law offers a canonical language and established symbols and rituals of passage'.[233]

There is something artistic about the construction of narrative truth in legal and legalised truth-seeking mechanisms; Osiel (discussing trials, specifically) identifies the '"poetics" of legal storytelling', narrative devices employed by judges in the 'theatrical' genres of the courtroom, described as a 'theater of ideas'.[234] The rituals associated with the formality of law (rule application/procedure) and the validity of its aims (substantive rationality) contribute to discovering and sketching collective memories about past abuses.[235] There is a distinctive relationship between law and collective memory.[236] Osiel has argued that prosecutions influence public discussion, as well as serving traditional punitive aims: 'trials, when effective as public spectacle, stimulate public discussion' and 'indelibly influence collective memory of the events they judge'.[237] Legal storytelling and the 'public presentation of the truth' are 'much more dramatic when done through a trial'.[238] Examples such as the trial in Jerusalem of Nazi war criminal Eichmann,[239] the Rivonia trial of anti-apartheid leader Nelson Mandela,[240] Palestinian resistance leader Marwan Barghouti's trial in Tel Aviv[241]

[232] D Kennedy 'Legal Formality' (1973) *Journal of Legal Studies* 351, 355, 364.

[233] Teitel (n 1) 116.

[234] Osiel (n 2) 2–3.

[235] On the ritualised nature of transitional trials and truth commissions, see inter alia M Humphrey, 'From Victim to Victimhood: Truth Commissions and Trials as Rituals of Political Transition and Individual Healing' (2003) 14(2) *Australian Journal of Anthropology* 171.

[236] See inter alia JJ Savelsberg and RD King 'Law and Collective Memory' (2007) 3 *Annual Review of Law and Social Science* 189.

[237] Osiel (n 2) 1ff.

[238] Osiel (n 2) 3 and 15 citing CS Nino, *Radical Evil on Trial* (New Haven, CT, Yale University Press, 1996).

[239] H Arendt, *Eichmann in Jerusalem: A Report on the Banality of Evil* (New York, Viking Press, 1963).

[240] Inter alia A Allo, 'The Courtroom as a Space of Resistance: Reflections on the Legacy of the Rivonia Trial' in A Allo (ed), *The Courtroom as a Space of Resistance* (London, Routledge, 2016).

[241] A Allo 'Marwan Barghouti in Tel Aviv: Occupation, Terrorism, and Resistance in the Courtroom' (2017) 26(1) *Social & Legal Studies* 47.

and many other high-profile prosecutions of fundamental political significance illustrate the complex performative aspect of high-stakes prosecutions.[242] The presentation of narratives about a range of past abuses – and what is left out – emerging from such proceedings carry a profound social meaning. Osiel suggests that the outcomes of such processes are similar to founding myths, upon which societies are built or rebuilt; nevertheless, these myths may be deeply divisive for society and cause further fragmentation in the communities seeking to make sense of past violence.[243] As such, the stage upon which collective memories are formulated in legal terms – in the role-play of trials or truth commissions – cannot be overlooked.

A. Ritual Performances, Legal Masks and Truth Seeking

The political and social stage upon which truth-seeking initiatives operate and contrasting voices enter into dialogue brings to light the ritual and performative character of TJ, where actors (stakeholders) compete for central roles. A trial (and in many cases, a truth commission) can be understood as 'an arena of speakers and listeners' in which the 'search for truth always proceeds by way of competing attempts to shape and present narratives for particular audiences'.[244] As proposed by Paul Gewirtz:

> [T]hinking about the trial as narrative or story-telling can bring fresh attention to the communicative exchanges central to the trial, directing us to the fact that … the form of telling and the setting of listening affect everything, and that telling and listening are complex transactions that jointly create meaning and significance.[245]

Links between performance, theatricality, law and TJ have been found in truth commissions.[246] This highlights the performative role of truth-seeking activities beyond the mere production of the legal truth, where ritual performances of certain actions may contribute to the formation and narration of certain memories of past harms for collective purposes.

Transitional truth seeking can be understood as a performance going beyond questions of 'truth or falsity of the history produced'.[247] For Anne Orford, the 'language of truth' 'can be understood in terms of speech act theory – the idea that particular words or utterances accomplish an act'.[248] Historians working on

[242] Inter alia, A Allo, 'The Show in the Show Trial: Contextualising the Politicization of the Courtroom' (2010) 15 *Barry Law Review* 15.
[243] Osiel (n 2) 19.
[244] P Gewirtz, 'Victims and Voyeurs at the Criminal Trial' (1995–96) 90 *Northwestern University Law Review* 863, 865.
[245] ibid.
[246] See inter alia CM Cole, 'Performance, Transitional Justice, and the Law: South Africa's Truth and Reconciliation Commission' (2007) 59 *Theatre Journal* 167.
[247] Orford (n 190) 854ff. Orford draws on the work of Austin (n 24).
[248] ibid 855.

TJ have reached similar conclusions, finding that truth commissions in particular contribute to the 'politics of time', producing important sociopolitical effects in a performative, and not merely descriptive, fashion.[249] The effect, therefore, of the establishment of, and rituals associated with formal truth-seeking mechanisms – regardless of their ability ultimately to achieve their proposed aims within a reasonable timeframe – is in itself noteworthy and carries a complex social function in each context. The very fact that an individual is indicted – or not – before an international court for some of the most serious abuses contemplated in law sends a powerful visible message in the interim to those affected.[250]

The ritualistic nature of truth-seeking performances blurs the distinction between what is secular and transcendental in the invocation of law in transitions, with all the complexities that entails. The performative role of judicial and quasi-judicial truth-seeking processes – including trials and truth commissions – contributes to the understanding of formal justice mechanisms as rituals and of their outcomes (ie legal truths) as products of that ritual. As such, the ritual force of processes may be found in formal as well as in traditional mechanisms to uncover the truth – as will be discussed in greater detail in the final chapter of the book with reference to Muslim-majority societies. The fact that 'many norms and political/legal practices are produced by and grounded in ritualized activity'[251] illustrates the strength of formal truth-seeking procedures. Indeed, 'secular rituals' impact our society.[252] Andrew Cappel defines ritual as 'the performance of a more or less invariant sequence of formal acts and utterances not entirely encoded by the performer', and identifies eight typifying characteristics: formal, invariant, governed by rules, symbolic, sacred, traditional, performed and not encoded by the performer.[253] He notes how:

> Ritualization thus tends to insulate a normative order from the ordinary give and take of everyday life, by locating it instead in the realm of implicit, timeless reality. By doing so, ritual promotes the stability of these orders against too rapid change, and also against gradual deterioration as more and more people choose to violate a norm.[254]

He continues by linking formal (ie positive) law to the notion of secular rituals, which 'will become more stable and hence more unquestionable the closer they can be associated through ritualization with such an aura of sacredness',

[249] B Bevernage, *History, Memory and State-Sponsored Violence* (London, Routledge, 2012).
[250] A Whiting, 'In International Criminal Prosecutions, Justice Delayed Can Be Justice Delivered' (2009) 50(2) *Harvard International Law Journal* 323.
[251] AJ Cappel, 'Bridging Cultural Practice into Law: Ritual and Social Norms Jurisprudence' (2002–03) 43 *Santa Clara Law Review* 389, 390.
[252] ibid, citing SF Moore and BG Myerhoff (eds), *Secular Ritual* (Assen, Van Gorcum, 1977).
[253] ibid 408ff, citing RA Rappaport, *Ritual and Religion in the Making of Humanity* (Cambridge, Cambridge University Press, 1999).
[254] ibid 448.

gaining 'a transcendent legitimacy coming from outside human society itself'.[255] Similarly, Weyrauch points out that 'participants and observers of a legal system are less likely to criticize or even question decisions that appear to be based on an objective application of neutral laws', satisfying a 'quasi-religious faith' in the 'objectivity, neutrality and fairness' of the legal process.[256] In relation to finding the truth through formal procedures in the context of TJ, it may be argued that a truth originating from a recognised (and accepted) secular ritual – such as a judicial procedure – is of higher procedural 'pedigree' than an informal or unstructured attempt to discover and agree upon the truth. The 'Law' as an abstract concept carries the intrinsic potential of embodying the desirable substance and procedure of justice, regardless of its misuse by previous regimes. Thus, ritualisation preserves certain norms 'in a relatively immutable manner'.[257] Consequently, certain normative principles may acquire primacy through the rituals of transitional truth-seeking mechanisms such as trials and truth commissions, and become founding concepts of the post-transitional order. This echoes Weyrauch's idea that law involves 'rendering peace and to some extent ordering social interactions', a function which 'necessitates the development of legal rules, which inevitably become legal masks'.[258]

Secular rituals go beyond ordinary state-administered legal processes such as trials and truth commissions. Anthropologist Kimberly Theidon provides an interesting account of how 'communities also mobilize the ritual and symbolic elements of these transitional processes to deal with the deep cleavages left – or accentuated – by civil conflicts'.[259] In relation to the Peruvian transition, she notes that:

> A central tenet of transitional justice is that it includes important performative aspects; via the secular rituals embodied in transitional legal practices, collectives engage in 'ritual purification' and the reestablishment of group unity. From this perspective, law is not just a set of procedures but also a set of secular rituals that make a break with the past and mark the beginning of a new moral community.[260]

Local informal mechanisms presenting ritual characteristics must be handled with care, as argued by Lars Waldorf with reference to the *gacaca* in Rwanda.[261] There may even be a risk that appropriation of local mechanisms by state authorities may create 'state imposed "informalism" designed to expand the state's reach into local communities', which may consequently result in 'increased

[255] ibid 454.
[256] Weyrauch (n 26) 717ff.
[257] Cappel (n 251) 479.
[258] Weyrauch (n 26) 723ff.
[259] K Theidon, 'Justice in Transition: The Micropolitics of Reconciliation in Postwar Peru' (2006) 50 *Journal of Conflict Resolution* 433, 436.
[260] ibid.
[261] L Waldorf, 'Mass Justice for Mass Atrocity: Rethinking Local Justice as Transitional Justice' (2006) 79 *Temple Law Review* 1, 6.

formalism, decreased popular participation, and increased state coercion'.[262] Indeed, the ownership of the justice process – be it a formal trial or a local justice mechanism – may itself mask patterns of political domination of one group over another, sometimes confirming or reversing the power dynamics at the time of abuse. With reference to truth seeking, as noted in the previous section, power structures can distort the effects of rituals, reinforcing unfairness and violence. Ritualised legal procedures, as discussed again in the final chapter with reference to the invocation of Islamic law, may conceal more mundane political interests.

The analogy of law as a mask furthers our understanding of judicial rituals as social functions of the law – and the legal truths they might produce.[263] Weyrauch draws convincing parallels between 'the modern social functions of law and those of masks in earlier societies': official procedures carry the 'potential to dehumanize persons through the use of conceptual legal masks', camouflaging the 'human significance' and gravity of certain acts through the illusion that 'legal reasoning will remain on a level of neutral abstraction'.[264] In the theatrics of ritual performance, masks ensure that the show goes on as planned, but may hide the true human emotions behind the act. This is illustrated in the formal actions carried out in courtroom proceedings by the legal counsel of perpetrators of the worst crimes: when abuse and violence has been widely recognised and documented extrajudicially but not by a tribunal, the defendant (rightly) remains innocent until proven otherwise. Legal procedures and necessary fair trial guarantees, therefore, may mask true feelings by more formally containing expression of the horror even when society is faced with unfathomable evil.[265]

In addition to concealing human emotion, the stakeholders of a formal process will select and highlight certain elements or facts over others, reflecting 'the prevailing value judgments of the society in which they live[d]', giving prominence to certain issues in preference to others.[266] These considerations take on a deeper meaning in times of political flux and TJ when 'any attempt to introduce "irrelevant" matters into legal proceedings involves a challenge, sometimes subtly so, to the established values as protected by rules of law'.[267] Thus, the choice of facts to be included in judicial proceedings in the context of TJ highlights the power of discretion that stakeholders in the process have in determining ritualised truth-seeking activities (as discussed previously in this chapter concerning the limits of the process of formation of the legal truth).

[262] ibid 9.

[263] Weyrauch (n 26) discussing JT Noonan, *Persons and the Masks of the Law: Cardozo, Holmes, Jefferson and Wythe as Makers of the Masks* (Berkeley, University of California Press, 1976).

[264] Weyrauch (n 26) 699ff.

[265] In general, Arendt (n 239).

[266] Weyrauch (n 26) 708ff.

[267] ibid 710, fn 40, discussing Fidel Castro's assertions before the prevailing Cuban judiciary as quoted in J Berman, 'The Cuban Popular Tribunals' (1969) 69 *Columbia Law Review* 1317.

For example, the BICI report in Bahrain (discussed in more detail in Chapter 6), after an explosion of internal violence in 2011, set out a truth inquiry, nominally independent but invited by the authorities, to discover factual evidence and evaluate it under international law.[268] However, the failure at government level to implement the BICI recommendations[269] indicates the ritualistic, theatrical character of the whole procedure based on international law, which was not met by substantive responses by the authorities. Thus, by placing excessively high expectations on the law (in the Bahraini case, on the findings and existence of the BICI report, collated and analysed by eminent international jurists), a critical approach towards the legal process is lost, and with that comes the realisation that law masks politics.

In essence, truth-seeking initiatives of TJ contribute to the formation of collective memory of past abuse through the formalities of recognisable substantive and procedural rules. Indeed, in transitional settings, law provides a set of established rituals that communities recognise as authoritative in guiding historical TJ processes, laying the foundations for reconstructing the future social order. During the transitional phase as well as afterwards, opposing narratives coexist and shared rules help regulate these contradictions. The political and social context in which truth-seeking initiatives operate brings to light the ritual and performative character of TJ mechanisms such as trials and truth commissions. Against that backdrop, formal (ie positive) law assumes a sacred aura that strengthens its legitimacy in guiding truth-seeking rituals. The force of these secular rituals may also extend beyond ordinary state-administered processes, encompassing local informal mechanisms which display a comparable ritual character within a given community. However, it is important to note that law – and by extension, local norms – may mask the substance of truth seeking and distort the interpretation of past abuse. This shortcoming may be further exacerbated by the structural inequalities directly or indirectly promoted by powerful stakeholders of the process. To counter the risk of marginalising victims from truth-seeking ritual performances and to oppose the pitfalls of using the law as a mask, the developing right to truth (discussed in the next chapter) can help empower survivors to instigate investigations into past harm suffered.

V. CONCLUSIONS

This chapter considered the contested centrality of truth seeking in TJ, focusing on the distinctive notion of legal truth as emerging from legal/legalised

[268] For the text of the report and related documents, see www.bici.org.bh/.

[269] See, for instance, the reports by the Bahrain Center for Human Rights on how a recent Supreme Court of Appeal case presented serious inconsistencies with the findings and recommendations of the BICI report and put into question the independence of the judiciary from the government; available at www.bahrainrights.net/?p=5216.

mechanisms such as trials and truth commissions. It argues that the notion of legal truth is a helpful concept that encapsulates the possibilities and limitations of the 'truth' in relation to TJ; its legal underpinnings and normative function by virtue of the sacralisation of law across societies and the ritual characteristics of legal/legalised truth-seeking initiatives allow for a deeper critical evaluation of its role. As evident in the interdisciplinary literature on transitional truth seeking and memory studies, the truth may look to the past but is inherently presentist. In its backward-looking guise, truth seeking aims at discovering facts, though it is unlikely to represent a historical account of violence faithfully and fully. In its forward-looking intent, truth seeking interprets the past from the current standpoint, often linked (though not in an unproblematic manner) with other transitional aims. Legal truths, by nature, remain open to challenge and revisitation: narratives may clash, and accounts resulting from transitional truth-seeking mechanisms may take on different meanings if they flow from trials and truth commissions into archives and other repositories.

Cognisant of the shifting social meanings of legal truths produced in trials and truth commissions, this chapter highlights how the legal truth may both institutionalise and challenge dominant views on histories of past abuse, and how it may provide – or not – some scope to counter prevailing narratives within the existing power structures and legacies of inclusion/exclusion. Nevertheless, substantive and procedural rules may mask the substance of truth seeking and distort the interpretation of past abuse; likewise, powerful stakeholders of these processes may distort the process and its outcomes, and deliberately perpetuate structural inequalities through the laws selected to ground truth-seeking initiatives. As legal truth is the product of legal rituals, comparable to religious rituals, law assumes a sacred aura in guiding truth-seeking mechanisms – and the norms of local unofficial systems of justice may play a similar role. For these reasons, it is important for all types of truth-seeking initiatives in TJ to be understood holistically and contextually.

Structural, social, economic and political inequalities before, during and after violence tend to deform TJ processes and the resulting historical accounts and thereby risk marginalising the agency of survivors who have little chance of shaping policy. The exclusion of certain voices leaves two gaps: firstly, the truths uncovered about past abuses will be incomplete and inadequate, resulting in severely deficient historical accounts thus impacting related transitional aims (such as institutional and legal reforms); secondly, ex post, direct and indirect victims may suffer additional dispossession and violence due to their exclusion from debating the findings of truth-seeking initiatives (and related archives). For these reasons, the involvement of victims and survivors in TJ processes is crucial: but how can essentially top-down practices of TJ, likely to be dominated by former or new elites at local, national and international level, make room and hear survivors' voices as well as giving their accounts some form of legal effect?

To counter the risk of marginalising victims and survivors from truth-seeking initiatives, a bottom-up push for the legal truth may redress this unequal access to shaping the accounts of past abuse and facilitate reconciliation. The next chapter turns to the potential of the emerging right to truth as an actionable tool to empower survivors in instigating inquiries into past harm suffered at individual and collective level, as well as the related state obligation to investigate abuse. Given the ritualistic nature of truth seeking even in secular legal contexts, it should be possible for survivors to draw on comparable local justice (including religious norms) to pursue transitional truth-seeking goals, as will be discussed in relation to Islamic law in the final two chapters.

4

The Right to Truth in International Law

I. INTRODUCTION

THE LAW HAS a central role to play in the process of truth seeking and the construction, formalisation and contestation of collective and individual memories of past harm. As discussed in the previous chapter, the performative qualities of the legal truth, the ritualistic character of trials and other formalised procedures (such as truth commissions and inquiries), and the problem of legal concepts masking complex realities all contribute to problematising the very foundations of the right to truth. In analysing the establishment of the notion and content of the right to truth in international law, its holders and duty-bearers, and applicability in relation to harm inflicted during conflict and authoritarianism (and established democracies), the discussion of law cannot be divorced from the critical premises presented earlier. Nevertheless, the right to truth offers an opportunity to empower victims and society at large with a tool to demand to know details and responsibilities for past harm.

The right to truth is on an upward trajectory in international law, as evidenced in the literature.[1] Its modern origins can be found in the jurisprudence

[1] An earlier version of this chapter was published as A Panepinto, 'The Right to Truth in International Law: The Significance of Strasbourg's Contributions' (2017) 37 *Legal Studies* 739 – reproduced with permission. Since that article was accepted, the discussion of the right to truth has developed significantly, see in particular M Klinkner and H Davis, *The Right to the Truth in International Law* (Abingdon, Routledge, 2020); P Naftali, *La Construction du 'Droit à la Vérité' en Droit International* (Bruxelles, Bruylant, 2017); P Naftali, 'Crafting a "Right to Truth" in International Law: Convergence Mobilizations, Divergent Agendas' (2016) XIII *Champ Penal/Penal Field* 1; P Naftali, 'The "Right to Truth" in International Law: The "Last Utopia"?' in U Belavusau and A Gliszczyńska-Grabias (eds), *Law and Memory: Towards Legal Governance of History* (Cambridge, Cambridge University Press, 2017); A Oriolo, 'Right to the Truth and International Jurisprudence as the "Conscience" of Humanity. Comparative Insights from the European and Inter-American Courts of Human Rights' (2016) 16(2) *Global Jurist* 175; JA Sweeney, 'The Elusive Right to Truth in Transitional Human Rights Jurisprudence' (2018) 67(2) *ICLQ* 353; S Szoke-Burke, 'Searching for the Right to Truth: The Impact of International Human Rights Law on National Transitional Justice Policies' (2015) 33(2) *Berkeley Journal of International Law* 526. Earlier discussions of the topic include, inter alia, JE Méndez, 'Accountability for Past Abuses' (1997) 19 *Human Rights Quarterly* 255; PB Hayner, *Unspeakable Truths: Transitional Justice and the Challenge of Truth Commissions*, 2nd edn (London, Routledge, 2010).

of the Inter-American Human Rights system (IACHR) dealing with the legacy of violent regimes in Latin America.[2] In 2010 the UN General Assembly established the international day for the right to truth,[3] and two successive UN Special Rapporteurs on the promotion of truth, justice, reparation and guarantees of non-recurrence have been appointed.[4] More recently the ECtHR has taken steps towards acknowledging the right to truth (linked to the state obligation to investigate, through the procedural limb of Articles 2 and 3) in relation to authoritarianism and conflict (eg *Aslakhanova v Russia*,[5] *Association 21 December 1989 v Romania*[6] and *Mocanu v Romania*[7]), as well as in other contexts where state policies limit human rights, for instance as part of counterterror practices (eg Grand Chamber judgment of *El-Masri v FYRM*[8]).[9] Despite the multiple meanings of the right to truth in different fora as outlined by Patricia Naftali,[10] these developments at the ECtHR call for a reappraisal of the right to truth as an emerging norm in IHRL.

In the aftermath of widespread – and often symbolic – human rights abuses connected to conflict and authoritarianism, individual victims and society at

[2] Inter alia, EF Mac-Gregor, 'The Right to the Truth as an Autonomous Right under the Inter-American Human Rights System' (2016) 9(1) *Mexican Law Review* 121; B Galindo and J Passos de Castro, 'The Rights to Memory and Truth in the Inter-American Paradigms of Transitional Justice: The Cases of Brazil and Chile' (2018) 15(2) *Revista de Direito Internacional* 308; S Garibian, 'Ghosts also Die: Resisting Disappearance through the "Right to the Truth" and the Juicios por la Verdad in Argentina' (2014) 3 *Journal of International Criminal Justice* 515; K Dykmann, 'Impunity and the Right to Truth in the Inter-American System of Human Rights' (2007) 7(26) *Iberoamericana* 45; C de Campos Melo, 'Transitional Justice in South America: The Role of the Inter-American Court of Human Rights' (2009) IV(5) *Revista Cejil* 83; J Davis, *Seeking Human Rights Justice in Latin America. Truth, Extra-territorial Courts, and the Process of Justice* (Cambridge, Cambridge University Press, 2013). Earlier literature had already explored the concept: M Popkin and N Roht-Arriaza, 'Truth as Justice: Investigatory Commissions in Latin America' (1995) 20(1) *Law & Social Inquiry* 79; JM Pasqualucci, 'The Whole Truth and Nothing but the Truth: Truth Commissions, Impunity and the Inter-American Human Rights System' (1994) 12 *Boston University International Law Journal* 321; JE Méndez and J Mariezcurrena, 'Accountability for Past Human Rights Violations: Contributions of the Inter-American Organs of Protection' (1999) 26 *Social Justice* 84.

[3] UNGA Res 65/196, 'Proclamation of 24 March as the International Day for the Right to the Truth concerning Gross Human Rights Violations and for the Dignity of Victims' (21 December 2010) UN Doc A/RES/65/196.

[4] Human Rights Council Resolutions A/HRC/RES/18/7 of 29 September 2011 and A/HRC/RES/27/3 of 25 September 2014 setting out the mandate of the (first) Special Rapporteur, appointed 1 May 2012. After Pablo de Greiff's inaugural appointment, Fabian Salvioli was appointed in May 2018.

[5] *Aslakhanova and others v Russia*, Apps Nos 2944/06 and 8300/07, 50184/07, 332/08, 42509/10 (ECHR, 18 December 2012).

[6] *Association 21 Décembre 1989 v Romania*, App Nos 33810/07 and 18817/08 (ECHR, 24 May 2011).

[7] *Mocanu and others v Romania*, App Nos 10865/09, 45886/07 and 32431/08 (ECHR, 17 September 2014).

[8] *El-Masri v FYRM* [GC], App No 39630/09 (ECHR, 13 December 2012).

[9] F Fabbrini, 'The European Court of Human Rights, Extraordinary Renditions and the Right to the Truth: Ensuring Accountability for Gross Human Rights Violations Committed in the Fight Against Terrorism' (2014) 14(1) *Human Rights Law Reports* 85.

[10] See discussion in Naftali, 'Crafting a "Right to truth"' (n 1).

large reckon with the past in different ways, often (but not always[11]) attempting to acknowledge harm and identify those responsible. As discussed in Chapter 3, truth-seeking initiatives such as trials and truth commissions can contribute to the formation of collective memories, which can then become the object of further debates about the past.[12] Nevertheless, as discussed in previous chapters, top-down initiatives alone are likely to marginalise some victim accounts and disempower minority or counterestablishment views. The right to truth offers survivors a tool to instigate truth-seeking processes through an actionable right to hold authorities accountable for effective investigations. This right, however, remains elusive. Building on the literature on the right to truth,[13] this chapter analyses the comparative meaning of recent developments and iterations of this right and argues that for the right to truth to consolidate in international law it must be supported in as many sites of legal authority as possible – which includes Islamic law, discussed in the final chapter.

Specifically, this research presents a fresh analysis of the right to truth in light of new ECHR case law and examines its impact on its international formulation, suggesting that growing consistency around the invocation of the right to truth in different fora contributes to its evolution in PIL. The first part traces the evolution of the right to truth in global and regional sources, providing a comparative study of Inter-American and European human rights case law. Two distinct but intertwined themes are analysed: firstly, the connection between the state's duty to investigate and survivors' right to know the past through an actionable right; and secondly, the link between the individual and collective dimensions of the right to truth. The second part discusses what these developments mean in international law, and considers whether existing legal categories (customary international law (CIL) and general principles of law) are suited to the formalisation of the right to truth. The findings suggest that regardless of its formal characterisation, the repeated and varied uses of the right to truth demonstrate its importance and benefits. As such, the notion of the right to truth can evolve further to take stock of other regional and global developments, including the potential contributions of Islamic legal thinking as discussed in the final part of this book.

[11] See eg J Volpe Rotondi and N Eisikovits, 'Forgetting after War: A Qualified Defense' in C Corradetti, N Eisikovits, J Volpe Rotondi (eds), *Theorizing Transitional Justice* (London, Routledge, 2015).

[12] See discussion in ch 3, and in particular A Barahona de Brito, 'Transitional Justice and Memory: Exploring Perspectives' (2010) 15 *South European Society and Politics* 359; R López, 'Legalising Collective Remembrance after Mass Atrocities' in FM Ottanelli and SE Bird (eds), *The Performance of Memory as Transitional Justice* (Cambridge, Intersentia, 2014); E Daly, 'Truth Skepticism: An Inquiry into the Value of Truth in Times of Transition' (2008) 2 *International Journal of Transitional Justice* 23.

[13] In addition to the sources indicated above (n 1), see Y Naqvi, 'The Right to Truth in International Law, Fact or Fiction?' (2006) 88 *International Review of the Red Cross* 245 and TM Antkowiak, 'Truth as Right and Remedy in International Human Rights Experience' (2001–02) 23 *Michigan Journal of International Law* 977.

II. THE EMERGENCE OF THE RIGHT TO TRUTH

As discussed in the previous chapter, the discovery (and value) of truth about past harm through formal legal proceedings[14] is inherently permeable to uneven power structures that impact truth-seeking initiatives such as trials and truth commissions. Existing laws may (deliberately or not) include and privilege the accounts of some groups and marginalise others.[15] Through the applications of the right to truth, victims and survivors can attempt to challenge prevailing versions of history and compel authorities to investigate and make public contested accounts of the past. Framing the need to know as a right empowers individuals to instigate truth-seeking processes directly. This, in turn, may help broaden perspectives during truth-seeking processes and ensure greater inclusivity in building collective memories.

The slow recognition of the right to truth and its uneven application across the world calls for a study of its sources and development in order to understand its contours, normative status and value. In its 2013 resolution on 'The Right to the Truth', the UN General Assembly recalled that 'a specific right to the truth may be characterized differently in some legal systems as the right to know or the right to be informed or to freedom of information'.[16] As such, a comparative appraisal across different areas of international law and other jurisdictions is required. The origins of the right to truth have been traced in IHL:[17] Article 32 of the Additional Protocol I to the Geneva Conventions refers to the 'right of families to know the fate of their relatives', both with respect to the remains of the deceased (Article 34) and for missing persons (Article 33).[18] However, its application is limited to armed conflicts, excluding the full range of situations in which serious violations occur. Moreover, IHL lacks easily justiciable rights that individuals may action to uncover the truth about past harm, as well as appropriate tools to deal with non-state actors.

International criminal courts and tribunals 'are set up to with a view that ascertaining the truth is possible to a certain standard of probability'.[19] In

[14] The concept of the 'legal truth' is used here to describe information about past harm elicited as part of formal (legal) proceedings. On this topic, see inter alia JM Balkin, 'The Proliferation of Legal Truth' (2003) 26 *Harvard Journal of Law & Public Policy* 5; MS Moore, 'The Plain Truth about Legal Truth' (2003) 26 *Harvard Journal of Law & Public Policy* 23; RS Summers, 'Formal Legal Truth and Substantive Truth in Judicial Fact-Finding – Their Justified Divergence in some Particular Cases' (1999) *18 Law & Philosophy* 497.

[15] C Campbell and C Turner, 'Utopia and the Doubters: Truth, Transition and the Law' (2008) 28 *Legal Studies* 374, 376–77.

[16] UNGA Resolution 68/165 'Right to the Truth' (18 December 2013) UN Doc A/RES/68/165, 3.

[17] Naqvi (n 13) 248. See also analysis in International Commission of Jurists, *The Right to a Remedy and Reparation for Gross Human Rights Violations: A Practitioners' Guide* (2018) available at www.icj.org/wp-content/uploads/2018/11/Universal-Right-to-a-Remedy-Publications-Reports-Practitioners-Guides-2018-ENG.pdf, 117ff.

[18] Protocol Additional to the Geneva Conventions of 12 August 1949, and relating to the Protection of Victims of International Armed Conflicts (Protocol I) (adopted 8 June 1977) 1125 UNTS 3.

[19] Klinkner and Davis (n 1) 93.

international criminal law (ICL), the Rome Statute of the ICC provides only a 'limited realisation' of the right to truth, restricted to the 'context of enforced disappearances (Article 7(1)(i))'.[20] Although, in principle, it could accommodate this right, costly and largely ineffective victim participation schemes[21] suggest that ICL is not yet ripe for operationalising victims' right to truth. Moreover, the individual punitive nature of criminal law exacerbates tensions between justice served – ie convictions – and justice understood more broadly, in which accountability and punishment for past abuses could be uncoupled. Despite the limited direct truth-seeking function of the ICC, the right to truth was explicitly discussed in the *Katanga and Ngudijolo* case, in which the judge included the 'identification of responsible persons as a key element of the right to the truth'.[22] But essentially, the truth emerges as a 'by product of the criminal process', which is geared towards individual criminal responsibility and the narrow facts of a case, which can only incorporate a small section of the wider context (and degrees of cooperation) in which the crime was committed.[23]

Today, the right to truth – as presented in the language of rights – most closely relates to IHRL. It is framed as a right 'in relation to other fundamental human rights by human rights bodies and courts' and referred to as such in truth-seeking mechanisms.[24] Since the 1980s, the UN Human Rights Committee has considered cases about disappearances, death in police custody, prison torture and arbitrary detention in the contexts of authoritarianism and civil conflict in light of the International Covenant on Civil and Political Rights.[25] This right is now being channelled and developed through the work of the UN Special Rapporteur on the promotion of truth, justice, reparation and guarantees of non-recurrence, whose 2013 Report clearly states that the right to truth is 'enshrined in a number of international instruments'.[26]

[20] H Davis and M Klinkner, 'A Victim's Right to Truth and the ICC' (2013), available at eprints.bournemouth.ac.uk/21025/1/A%20victim%27s%20right%20to%20truth%20and%20the%20ICC%20-%20Summary%20report.pdf, 10; M Klinkner and E Smith, 'The Right to Truth, Appropriate Forum and the International Criminal Court' in N Szablewska and SD Bachmann (eds), *Current Issues in Transitional Justice: Towards a More Holistic Approach* (New York, Springer, 2015).

[21] Davis and Klinkner (n 20) citing C Van den Wyngaert, 'Victims Before International Criminal Courts: Some Views and Concerns of an ICC Trial Judge' (2012) 44 *Case Western Reserve Journal of International Law* 475.

[22] *Prosecutor v Katanga and Ngudijolo* (13 May 2008), discussed in Klinkner and Davis (n 1) 201.

[23] Klinkner and Davis (n 1) 97.

[24] Naqvi (n 13) 267.

[25] eg Human Rights Committee decisions *Dermit Barbato v Uruguay*, Comm No 84/1981 (1983); *Muteba v Zaire*, Comm No 124/1982 (1984); *Laureano v Peru* Comm No 540/1993 (1996); *Zelaya Blanco v Nicaragua*, Comm No 328/1988 (1994). For a more comprehensive discussion of the Human Rights Committee's approach to the right to truth, see inter alia Sweeney (n 1) 360–66.

[26] UNHRC, Twenty-fourth session, 'Report of the Special Rapporteur on the Promotion of Truth, Justice, Reparation and Guarantees of Non-recurrence, Pablo de Greiff' (28 August 2013) UN Doc A/HRC/24/42. These are: (1) International Convention for the Protection of All Persons from Enforced Disappearance (adopted 20 December 2006, entered into force 23 December 2010), 2715 UNTS (CED), Art 24(2) (in September 2013, 93 signatories and 40 ratifications); (2) Basic Principles

Building on existing sources, the 2013 Report by the Special Rapporteur on the promotion of truth frames the current UN understanding of the right to truth within the scope of human rights. The Report sets out a state requirement to 'establish institutions, mechanisms and procedures that are enabled to lead to the revelation of the truth', described as 'a process to seek information and facts about what has actually taken place, to contribute to the fight against impunity, to the reinstatement of the rule of law, and ultimately to reconciliation'.[27] This reflects the language of the 'Van Boven/Bassiouni Principles' adopted by the General Assembly in 2005, affirming that victims have the right to 'access to relevant information concerning violations and reparation mechanisms', and 'should be entitled' to 'learn the truth in regard to ... violations'.[28]

Among the sources listed in the 2013 Report, the only clear treaty provision enshrining the right to truth is Article 24(2) of the 2006 International Convention for the Protection of All Persons from Enforced Disappearance (CED):

> Each victim has the right to know the truth regarding the circumstances of the enforced disappearance, the progress and results of the investigation and the fate of the disappeared person.

The right to truth, however, extends beyond the specific instance of disappearance, as evidenced in Human Rights Commission and Human Rights Council resolutions.[29] The 2013 UN General Assembly resolution on 'The right to the truth' indicates a broad reach of this right, which includes 'to investigate

and Guidelines on the Right to a Remedy and Reparation for Victims of Gross Violations of International Human Rights Law and Serious Violations of International Humanitarian Law ('Van Boven/Bassiouni Principles'), UNGA Res 60/147 (16 December 2005) UN Doc A/RES/60/147; (3) Human Rights Council Resolutions 9/11 on the Right to the Truth, UNHRC Res 9/11 (24 September 2008) 'Right to the Truth', UN Doc A/HRC/9/L.12 para 1, and 12/12, UNHRC Res 12/12 (12 October 2009) UN Doc A/HRC/RES/12/12; (4) UN ECOSOC, Commission on Human Rights, Promotion and Protection of Human Rights, 'Study by the Office of the UN High Commissioner for Human Rights on the Right to Truth' (8 Feb 2006) UN Doc E/CN.4/2006/91; (5) UN Committee against Torture, 'Consideration of Reports Submitted by States Parties under Article 19 of the Convention, Concluding Observations: Colombia' (4 May 2010), UN Doc CAT/C/COL/CO/4, para 27; (6) UNHRC, 'Report of the Working Group on Enforced or Involuntary Disappearances' (26 Jan 2011) UN Doc A/HRC/16/48: 'The existence of the right to the truth as an autonomous right was acknowledged by the Working Group on Enforced or Involuntary Disappearances (WGEID) in its very first report (E/CN.4/1435, 22 Jan 1981, para 187)'; (7) UNHRC, 'Report of the Special Rapporteur on the Promotion and Protection of Human Rights and Fundamental Freedoms while Countering Terrorism' (1 Mar 2013) UN Doc A/HRC/22/52, para 23; (8) UNHRC, 'Report of the Special Rapporteur on Torture and other Cruel, Inhuman or Degrading Treatment or Punishment, Manfred Nowak, Mission to Paraguay' (1 Oct 2007) UN Doc A/HRC/7/3/Add.3, para 82; (9) UNHRC, 'Report of the Special Rapporteur on the Promotion and Protection of the Right to Freedom of Opinion and Expression' (20 Apr 2010) UN Doc A/HRC/14/23, para 34.

[27] ibid para 20.

[28] Basic Principles and Guidelines on the Right to a Remedy and Reparation for Victims of Gross Violations of International Human Rights Law and Serious Violations of International Humanitarian Law ('Van Boven/Bassiouni Principles') (n 26) Principle X.

[29] See UNCHR Res 2005/66 'Right to the Truth' (20 April 2005) UN Doc E/CN.4/RES/2005/66; UNHRC decision 2/105 (27 November 2006); UNHRC Res 9/11 and UNHRC Res 12/12.

violations of human rights and violations of international humanitarian law', so 'as to contribute to ending impunity and to promote and protect human rights'.[30] The 2005 UN Updated Set of Principles for the Protection and Promotion of Human Rights through Action to Combat Impunity ('Orentlicher Principles') had already acknowledged the broad scope of the right to truth:

> Every people has the inalienable right to know the truth about past events concerning the perpetration of heinous crimes and about the circumstances and reasons that led, through massive or systematic violations, to the perpetration of those crimes.[31]

Moreover, the 2006 Study on the Right to Truth of the Office of the UN High Commissioner for Human Rights confirmed the 'inalienable right to know the truth vis-à-vis gross human rights violations and serious crimes under the (sic) international law'.[32] This indicates its relevance across many instances of abuse, constituting a cross-cutting independent right that spans different contexts and types of harm inflicted during conflict and authoritarianism.

The 2005 Orentlicher Principles also outlined the link between the victims' right to know and the 'general obligations of states to take effective action to combat impunity'.[33] The state obligation to investigate is key to giving the right to truth a degree of justiciability, notwithstanding the difficulties of operationalising it in political contexts where human rights abuses are hushed up. In extending the right to truth to counterterrorism practices, the Special Rapporteur on the promotion and protection of human rights and fundamental freedoms while countering terrorism has stated that 'the legal right of the victim and of the public to know the truth' is matched by corresponding obligations on states which can be conveniently gathered together 'under the rubric of the international law principle of accountability', which extends to 'all three branches of government'.[34]

This is important for holding states to account when truth seeking is obstructed, or investigations are known from the start to be ineffective, as some of the regional case law has found (eg ECHR, *Association 21 Décembre v Romania*). So, by linking the right to truth to a corresponding state obligation, regardless of the successor regime's connection to past harms, survivors of abuse may in principle instigate inquiries into historic abuses, which in turn may contribute to shaping collective memories about past violence.

[30] UNGA (n 16) 4.

[31] ECOSOC, Commission on Human Rights, Promotion and Protection of Human Rights, 'Report of the Independent Expert to Update the Set of Principles to Combat Impunity, Diane Orentlicher' ('Orentlicher Principles') (8 Feb 2005) UN Doc E/CN.4/2005/102/Add.1, Principle 2.

[32] OHCHR 'Study on the Right to Truth' (8 February 2006) UN Doc E/CN.4/2006/91.

[33] Orentlicher Principles (n 31) Principles 1 and 4.

[34] Report of the Special Rapporteur on the Promotion and Protection of Human Rights and Fundamental Freedoms while Countering Terrorism (2013) (n 26) paras 23 and 27.

A. IACHR Contributions to the Right to Truth

The former Special Rapporteur on the promotion of truth, Pablo de Greiff, has stated that 'the Inter-American Commission on Human Rights and the Inter-American Court of Human Rights were at the forefront of developing jurisprudence on the right to truth of the victim, his or her next of kin, and the whole of society'.[35] Former President of the Inter-American Court of Human Rights (IACtHR) Antônio Augusto Cançado Trindade echoed this in relation to enforced disappearances.[36] IACtHR jurisprudence considers the truth as a fully justiciable right.[37] Two key intertwined principles emerge from its case law: firstly, the centrality of the state duty to investigate in order to satisfy the applicants' right to truth; secondly, the clear link between the individual and collective dimensions of the right to truth, recognising that society as a whole, in addition to direct victims, has an interest in knowing about the past.

The IACtHR has employed the right to truth to ensure states are held accountable for past institutional abuse and for refusing to investigate gross human rights abuses. This first principle can be invoked by direct victims as a corollary of enacted provisions (in particular, Articles 1, 8, 13 and 25),[38] but its effects are relevant more broadly. *Manuel Bolaños* was the first significant Inter-American Commission ('the Commission') case involving the right to truth about enforced disappearances and location of remains.[39] That decision found that the state's failure to 'use all means at its disposal to carry out a serious investigation of violations committed within its jurisdiction to identify those responsible' was a violation of the IACHR.[40] Specifically, the right to truth was linked to Article 25 (the Right to Judicial Protection), namely the right of the victim's family to know the fate of disappeared relatives. But as stated on the

[35] Report of the Special Rapporteur on the Promotion of Truth (2013) (n 26) para 19. For an overview of the evolution of the right to truth in the IACHR system, see Ferrer Mac-Gregor (n 2).

[36] AA Cançado Trindade, 'Enforced Disappearances of Persons as a Violation of Jus Cogens: The Contribution of the Jurisprudence of the Inter-American Court of Human Rights' (2012) 81 *Nordic Journal of International Law* 507.

[37] JE Mendez, 'An Emerging "Right to Truth": Latin-American Contributions', in S Karstedt (ed), *Legal Institutions and Collective Memories* (Oxford, Hart, 2009) 54–55. See also E González and H Varney (eds), *Truth Seeking: Elements of Creating an Effective Truth Commission* (Brasilia, Amnesty Commission of the Ministry of Justice of Brazil; New York, International Center for Transitional Justice, 2013) 5–6. Notably, the Special Rapporteur for Freedom of Expression of the Organization of American States (OAS) has placed the right to truth firmly on her agenda; see, for instance, the section on the 'Right to the Truth' on the OAS website: www.oas.org/en/iachr/expression/showarticle.asp?artID=156&lID=1.

[38] See eg *González Medina and family v Dominican Republic*, Judgment, Inter-American Court of Human Rights, Series C No 240 (27 February 2012), para 263 indicating Arts 8 and 25, and *Massacres of El Mozote and Nearby Places v El Salvador*, Judgment, Inter-American Court of Human Rights Series C No 252 (25 October 2012), para 298, indicating Arts 1(1), 8(1), 25 and 13.

[39] *Bolaños v Ecuador*, Case 10.580, Report No 10/95, Inter-American Commission on Human Rights (12 September 1995), as discussed by the OAS, 'Right to the Truth' (n 37).

[40] OAS, 'Right to the Truth' (n 37).

website of the Organization of American States, the right to truth also has a basis 'in Articles 1(1) (Obligation to Respect Rights), 8 (Right to a Fair Trial), and 13 (Freedom of Thought and Expression)'.[41] This suggests that while the right to truth is not listed in the IACHR, it is more than a procedural corollary to an existing right: it can be invoked in conjunction with an enumerated right, but it also carries a special weight of its own as a cross-cutting principle.

To counter attempts to simply forget about the past, the IACHR system has clarified that Article 13[42] is crucial to 'delivering' the right to truth to family members and society as a whole, as opposed to amnesties.[43] The IACtHR has stated that amnesty laws pose an obstacle to the right to truth,[44] because blanket policies to end investigations into past abuses cannot satisfy survivors' right to know the circumstances and responsibilities. This was reaffirmed in the landmark *Gomes Lund* case against Brazil (about the disappeared persons in the Guerrilha do Araguaia); that case also confirmed that the state duty to investigate is an obligation of means and not of results, and extended the time frame for investigating the most serious crimes.[45] In particular, 'once the State authorities are notified of the facts, they must initiate ex officio and without delay, a serious, impartial, and effective investigation'.[46] In that context, the IACtHR 'established the violation of the right to judicial guarantees and due judicial protection for the failure to investigate, prosecute, and eventually punish those responsible', 'in a reasonable period of time', emphasising the criminal justice expectation on those specific facts.[47]

There is an important emancipatory subtext for the victims (and their families) in the jurisprudence on the state duty to investigate in contexts where cover-ups and silencing about past abuse has become normalised. In *Vladimir*

[41] ibid.

[42] Art 13(1): 'Everyone has the right to freedom of thought and expression. This right includes *freedom to seek, receive, and impart information* and ideas of all kinds, regardless of frontiers, either orally, in writing, in print, in the form of art, or through any other medium of one's choice' (emphasis added).

[43] OAS, 'Right to the Truth' (n 37). A violation of Art 13 was found for the first time in *Ignacio Ellacuría v El Salvador*, Case 10.488, Report No 136/99, Inter-American Court of Human Rights (22 December 1999).

[44] *Alfonso René Chanfeau Orayce v Chile*, Cases 11.505 et al, Report No 25/98, Inter-American Court of Human Rights (7 April 1998); in relation to an amnesty law nullifying the recommendations of a Truth Commission, *Lucio Parada Cea, Héctor Joaquín Miranda Marroquín, et al v El Salvador*, Case 10.480, Report No 1/99, Inter-American Court of Human Rights (27 January 1999).

[45] *Gomes Lund et al v Brazil*, Judgment, Inter-American Court of Human Rights Series C No 219 59 (24 November 2010), para 325, declaring that 'the Brazilian Amnesty Law that prevent the investigation and punishment of serious human rights violations are not compatible with the American Convention, lack legal effect, and cannot continue as obstacles for the investigation of the facts of the present case, neither for the identification and punishment of those responsible, nor can they have equal or similar impact regarding other serious violations of human rights enshrined in the American Convention which occurred in Brazil', and para 138. The significance of this case is discussed inter alia in Oriolo (n 1) 23–25, and Naftali, 'The "Right to Truth" in International Law' (n 1).

[46] *Gomes Lund et al v Brazil* (n 45) para 138.

[47] ibid para 256.

Herzog v Brazil (about the state's cover up of fatal torture in 1975 by stating the cause of death as suicide), the IACtHR reaffirmed that

> judicial proceedings play a significant role in making reparation to the victims, who are no longer regarded as passive subjects in relation to the public authorities but 'become claimants of rights and participants in the processes by which the content, application and strength of the law are defined'.[48]

This requires 'substantive effort' and includes allowing 'judges, prosecutors and other independent investigation authorities to make on-site visits to the military and intelligence archives'.[49] Invoking Articles 8 (fair trial) and 25 (judicial protection) of the Convention, the Court found that the state had 'violated the victims' right to know the truth, because it has failed to clarify judicially the violations in this case and has not identified the corresponding individual responsibilities'.[50]

The second principle that emerges in the IACHR jurisprudence is the overlap between individual and collective functions of the right to truth, understood as serving interests beyond the parties to a case. *Lucio Parada Cea et al v El Salvador* describes the right to truth as a:

> Collective right which allows a society to gain access to information essential to the development of democratic systems, and also an individual right for the relatives of the victims, allowing for a form of reparation.[51]

The notorious *Villagran-Morales et al v Guatemala* (street children case) case also provides a pertinent example of the importance for society at large to uncover the truth about the state's role in abuse.[52] The inextricable connection between the individual and collective right to know became apparent in the high-profile case of the political assassination of Monsignor Óscar Romero, Archbishop of El Salvador. The Commission found that the state's failure to investigate the circumstances of extrajudicial killing constituted a violation of its duty to reveal the truth to both the victim's family as well as to society at large.[53] It specified that an investigation:

> Must be undertaken in good faith and must be diligent, exhaustive and impartial and geared to exploring all possible lines of investigation that make it possible to identify the perpetrators of the crime, so that they can be tried and punished.[54]

[48] *Vladimir Herzog v Brazil*, Judgment, Inter-American Court of Human Rights Series C No 353 (15 March 2018), para 375.

[49] ibid para 337.

[50] ibid para 338.

[51] *Lucio Parada Cea et al v El Salvador.*

[52] *Villagran-Morales et al v Guatemala* (Street Children case), Judgment, Inter-American Court of Human Rights Series C No 63 (19 November 1999) para 190.

[53] *Monsignor Oscar Arnulfo Romero y Galdámez v El Salvador*, Case 11.481, Report No 37/00, Inter-American Court of Human Rights (13 April 2000).

[54] ibid para 80.

The IACtHR had already outlined the requirements of investigations in *Velásquez Rodríguez*:

> [Investigations] must be undertaken in a serious manner and not as a mere formality preordained to be ineffective. An investigation must have an objective and be assumed by the State as its own legal duty, not as a step taken by private interests that depends upon the initiative of the victim or his family or upon their offer of proof, without an effective search for the truth by the government.[55]

This case notably established the state's positive obligation to investigate violations alongside its (preceding) duty to prevent them.[56] The IACtHR upheld this position in the more recent *Contreras*, linking the 'violation of the right to truth, understood as a violation of the rights contained in Articles 8, 13 and 25 of the Convention' to the state obligation to 'demonstrat[e] that they have taken all the measures at their disposal to prove that the requested information does not exist'.[57] The case also highlighted the importance of the state's positive obligation to investigate in 'democratic societies', in which 'every individual, including the next of kin of the victims of grave human rights violations' has 'the right to know the truth, so that they and society as a whole must be informed on what happened'.[58] Similarly, in *Vladimir Herzog*, the IACtHR reaffirmed that 'right to truth entitles the victim, his or her relatives and the public at large to seek and obtain all relevant information concerning the commission of the alleged violation'.[59] This sample of cases illustrates how the IACtHR has continued, over time, to consider serious investigations in light of the right to truth, understood as an individual and a collective matter.

So while there is a direct, actionable right to truth held by individuals affected by the violation, and the corresponding state duty to uncover the past through investigations, trials and other truth-seeking mechanisms, the state must also respond to the need for the general public and society at large to know what happened. IACtHR jurisprudence thus establishes that the state obligation to investigate is relevant beyond the parties to individual cases, because truths uncovered contribute to constructing collective memories and inform political debates. That Court's vision of the right to truth – in light of Latin American experiences of transitional truth seeking – have arguably shaped the understanding of the UN Special Rapporteur on this right, given the first two mandate-holders have been prominent jurists from Colombia and Argentina.[60]

[55] ibid para 79, quoting *Velásquez Rodríguez v Honduras*, Judgment, Inter-American Court of Human Rights Series C No 4 (29 July 1988) para 177.

[56] On the significance of the state obligations set out in *Velásquez Rodríguez*, see inter alia N Roht-Arriaza, 'State Responsibility to Investigate and Prosecute Grave Human Rights Violations in International Law', (1990) 78 *California Law Review* 449, 467–468.

[57] *Contreras et al v El Salvador*, Judgment, Inter-American Court of Human Rights Series C No 232 (31 August 2011) paras 5 and 166.

[58] ibid 170 and 173, linking the right to the truth to Arts 1(1), 8(1), 25 and, under certain circumstances, Art 13.

[59] *Vladimir Herzog v Brazil*, para 377.

[60] Pablo de Greiff and Fábian Salvioli, respectively.

But given the evolution of the right to truth at the ECtHR and elsewhere, the notion of the right to truth can evolve further to take stock of other regional and global developments, including the potential contributions of Islamic legal thinking as discussed in the final part of this book.

B. ECHR Contributions to the Right to Truth

In contrast to the Inter-American human rights instruments, 'the right to truth has been comparatively slow to develop' in the Council of Europe system.[61] Over the past few years there has been a growing interest in the ECtHR's relationship to TJ, including in relation to truth seeking and the right to truth.[62] An initial acknowledgement came in 2005 when a series of resolutions of the Parliamentary Assembly of the Council of Europe recognised families of disappeared persons as 'independent victims', to be granted a 'right to be informed of the fate of their disappeared relatives'.[63] However, it was only in the *El-Masri* judgment of December 2012 that the Grand Chamber made its first explicit reference to the right to truth.[64] This case, which emerged in the context of extraordinary renditions (and not transitions), brought to light the question of the right to truth in relation to the procedural limb of Article 3 of the ECHR (prohibition of torture), dealing with the enforced disappearance and ill-treatment of the applicant, as well as the subsequent lack of effective state investigations.

The *El-Masri* judgment and concurring opinions 'cautiously expand the function of the state duty to undertake a credible investigation', setting 'a novel standard to secure accountability of human rights violations committed in other national security cases and beyond'.[65] Yet all the judgment says about the right to truth is that 'inadequate investigations' had an 'impact on the right to the truth'.[66] For the substantive discussion on the right to truth, the concurring opinions offer valuable insights into the debate between judges about this right

[61] JA Sweeney, *The European Court of Human Rights in the Post-Cold War Era: Universality in Transition* (London, Routledge, 2012) 72. See also Antkowiak (n 13) 982. For further discussion of the ECHR jurisprudence on the right to truth, see Sweeney, 'The Elusive Right to Truth' (n 1) 372–83; and Klinkner and Davis (n 1) 130–55.

[62] Inter alia, J Gallen, 'The European Court of Human Rights, Transitional Justice and Historical Abuse in Consolidated Democracies' (2019) 19(4) *Human Rights Law Rev* 675, 681–82; ICJ, *The Right to a Remedy and Reparation for Gross Human Rights Violation* (n 17) 129ff; F Ní Aoláin, 'Transitional Justice and the European Convention on Human Rights' (2017) Academy Briefing No 10: Geneva Academy of International Humanitarian Law and Human Rights, 28 available at www.geneva-academy.ch/joomlatools-files/docman-files/Transitional%20Justice%20and%20the%20European%20Convention%20on%20Human%20Rights.pdf.

[63] Parliamentary Assembly of the Council of Europe (PACE), 'Resolution 1463 on Enforced Disappearances' (2005).

[64] *El-Masri v FYRM*, para 191.

[65] Fabbrini (n 9) 102.

[66] *El-Masri v FYRM*, para 191.

in relation to the ECHR and international law more generally. The key questions explored the status of the right to truth within the scope of the ECHR, whether it constitutes a new right, its relationship to the duty to investigate, and who holds it.

In the separate opinion[67] of Judges Tulkens, Spielmann, Sicilianos and Keller, the right to truth is described as a 'well-established reality' which is 'far from being either innovative or superfluous'.[68] They argue that it is neither 'a novel concept' in the Court's jurisprudence, 'nor is it a new right'. To support their claim, they relied on the Court's case law, global IHRL instruments,[69] IACHR jurisprudence,[70] EU[71] and Council of Europe statements,[72] as well as evidence provided by third-party interveners.[73] So by referring to the right to truth as an established reality, these judges seem to pre-empt opposition to the introduction of unenumerated rights. Moreover, this indicates a conscious contextualisation of the ECHR within broader human rights developments.

The second concurring opinion in *El-Masri* took the opposite stance. Judges Casadevall and Lopez Guerra asserted that judges have no place in introducing a right 'different from, or additional to' the provisions set out in the ECHR and the Court's case law,[74] dismissing the idea that the right to truth merits attention either as an extension of Convention provisions or as a novel human right. Contrary to Tulkens et al, Casadevall and Lopez Guerra argued that it was not necessary to address the right to truth 'as something different from, or additional to, the requisites already established in such matters' in previous case law,[75] concluding that 'a separate analysis of the right to the truth becomes redundant'. Yet this reductionist approach seems disconnected from the evolution of the right to truth elsewhere. A closer analysis of the Court's case law suggests that the substance of the right to truth, which includes the state duty to investigate and the collective dimension of knowing about past abuse, is nothing

[67] On separate opinions, see inter alia R White and I Boussiakou, 'Separate Opinions in the European Court of Human Rights' (2009) 9 *Human Rights Law Review* 37. See also FJ Bruinsma and M de Blots, 'Rules of Law from Westport to Wladiwostok: Separate Opinions in the European Court of Human Rights' (1997) 15 *Netherlands Quarterly of Human Rights* 175; FJ Bruinsma 'The Room at the Top: Separate Opinions in the Grand Chambers of the ECHR (1998–2006)' (2007) 2 *Recht der Werkelijkheid* 7.

[68] *El-Masri v FYRM*, Joint Concurring Opinion of Judges Tulkens et al.

[69] Specifically, 'Convention on Enforced Disappearances', Art 24, para 2; 'Updated Set of Principles for the Protection and Promotion of Human Rights'; UNHRC Res 9/11 and UNHRC Res 12/12.

[70] *Velásquez Rodríguez v Honduras* and *Contreras v El Salvador*.

[71] European Union, 'Council Framework Decision on the Standing of Victims in Criminal Proceedings' (15 March 2001) 2001/220/JHA.

[72] Council of Europe, 'Guidelines of the Committee of Ministers of the Council of Europe on Eradicating Impunity for Serious Human Rights Violations', adopted by the Committee of Ministers (30 March 2011) 1110th meeting of the Ministers' Deputies.

[73] Including UNHCHR, Redress, Amnesty International and the International Commission of Jurists; see *El-Masri v FYRM*, paras 175–79.

[74] *El-Masri v FYRM*, Joint Concurring Opinion of Judges Casadevall and Lopez Guerra.

[75] ibid.

new in Strasbourg. However, the ECtHR is yet to formulate a coherent analysis of the right to truth: its jurisprudence and separate opinions on the issue reveal the Court's interest and ambiguity towards this emerging principle. Reflecting on the largely symbolic use of the right to truth in the ECHR jurisprudence, which has led to no substantial change in the case law, Patricia Naftali considers that the 'ECtHR's hesitance to give a distinct meaning to the "right to truth" is likely to frustrate truth activists'.[76] Nonetheless, a comparative analysis cannot ignore this invocation even if it has limited value as positive enforceable law: its utterance is significant inasmuch as it contributes to the circulation of the concept despite its contested and ambiguous content and uses. In line with the previous analysis of the right to truth in the IACHR system, the two key aspects to consider in assessing the Court's position on the right to truth are its relationship to the state duty to investigate and its individual and collective dimensions.

i. The Right to Truth and the State Duty to Investigate

The right to truth is connected to the 'right to know what happened'.[77] ECtHR jurisprudence has long consolidated the state duty to investigate violations,[78] echoing the substance of the positive obligation to investigate set out by in IACHR jurisprudence concerning the right to truth. In *El-Masri*, the Grand Chamber traced a link between the lack of an effective investigation and the right to truth, noting in relation to the procedural limb of Article 3:

> Another aspect of the inadequate character of the investigation in the present case, namely its impact on the right to the truth regarding the relevant circumstances of the case.[79]

This landmark reference to right to truth requires analysing in conjunction with the state duty to investigate, which the Court has invoked in various contexts.

Addressing widespread violence during authoritarian regimes, the Court has considered investigations in light of Article 2 (and 3). In *Association 21 Décembre 1989* (on the violent repression of anti-government demonstrations in Romania)[80] the Third Section drew on previous case law to restate that in

[76] Naftali, 'The "Right to Truth" in International Law' (n 1) 81–83.

[77] *El-Masri v FYRM*, para 191.

[78] Notably *McCann and others v UK*, App No 18984/91 (ECHR, 27 September 1995). With reference to confirmed killings, see in J Chevalier-Watts, 'Effective Investigations under Article 2 of the European Convention on Human Rights: Securing the Right to Life or an Onerous Burden on a State?' (2010) 21(3) *European Journal of International Law* 701.

[79] *El-Masri v FYRM*, para 191.

[80] The context of this case is described as 'dans le cas de l'usage massif de la force meurtrière à l'encontre de la population civile lors de manifestations antigouvernementales précédant la transition d'un régime totalitaire vers un régime plus démocratique', *Association 21 Décembre 1989 v Romania*, para 144 concerning 'la mort ou les blessures par balles et les mauvais traitements et privations de liberté infligés à plusieurs milliers de personnes, dans plusieurs villes du pays', para 9.

order to be effective, investigations must be 'prompt, complete, impartial and thorough' in order to 'identify and punish those responsible'.[81] This is an 'obligation of means and not of results': authorities must demonstrate the adoption of reasonable measures, promptly and with reasonable diligence, to obtain evidence and allow public scrutiny of results, ensuring that investigations are conducted by independent persons not implicated in the events.

The ECtHR has also considered the state obligation to investigate enforced disappearances during conflict. In the unanimous judgment of *Aslakhanova* (pertaining to hostilities between Russia and Chechen groups), the First Section listed the regional and international instruments applicable to investigating enforced disappearances, explicitly acknowledging the right to truth.[82] With reference to Article 2 and in light of the Court's 'settled case-law' (including *Association 21 Décembre 1989*), this judgment listed the guiding principles 'for an investigation to comply with the Convention's requirements', characterised as an obligation of means, and not of results.[83] In order to be effective, investigations must be carried out by persons independent from those implicated in the events, and be 'capable of ascertaining the circumstances' and determining whether the force used was justified, and identifying and punishing those responsible. This requires 'promptness and reasonable expedition', accessibility to family members and some public scrutiny. With regard to Article 3, investigations into alleged ill-treatment should be thorough and prompt and 'in principle be capable of leading to the establishment of the facts of the case' and identifying and punishing those responsible.[84] Moreover, there must be 'a sufficient element of public scrutiny of the investigation or its results',[85] suggesting that investigations matter to the parties to the case and also to society at large.

The criteria to assess the effectiveness of investigations were listed again in the Grand Chamber judgment, *Mocanu* (in the context of violent crackdown on anti-government demonstrations in Romania in 1990).[86] While the Court did not address the right to truth explicitly, it built on previous jurisprudence and on Articles 2, 3 and 6(1) to restate the requirements of effective investigations: independence, expedition and adequacy of the investigation, as well as the participation of the victim's next of kin in the process. This judgment also

[81] *Association 21 Décembre 1989 v Romania*, paras 133–45.

[82] *Aslakhanova v Russia*, paras 60–61, quoting 'PACE Resolution 1463' (n 63); 'Convention on Enforced Disappearances' (CED); also noting that Art 5 CED and Art 7 Rome Statute of the International Criminal Court (17 July 1998, entered into force on 1 July 2002) A/CONF.183/9, both describe widespread or systematic practice of enforced disappearance as a crime against humanity.

[83] *Aslakhanova v Russia*, para 121.

[84] ibid paras 144–45.

[85] ibid para 145.

[86] *Mocanu v Romania*, paras 332–51; upheld in *Bouyid v Belgium* [GC], App No 23380/09 (ECHR, 28 September 2015) para 114; and *Jeronovičs v Latvia* [GC], App No 44898/10 (ECHR, 5 July 2016) para 103.

considered the importance of investigations in the presence of numerous other similar cases:

> The number of violations found in cases similar to the present case is a matter of particular concern and casts serious doubt on the objectivity and impartiality of the investigations.[87]

With regards to the passage of time leading to statutory limitations, in *Mocanu v Romania* the Court noted that high 'political and societal stakes' for Romanian society 'should have led the authorities to deal with the case promptly and without delay in order to avoid any appearance of collusion in or tolerance of unlawful acts'.[88] This echoes IACtHR jurisprudence on the duty to conduct serious investigations, especially when violence affects the entire society.

The Court's jurisprudence on the state duty to investigate suggests that this is a key principle in the Convention. In conjunction with Article 1, an effective investigation in relation to the right to life (Article 2) requires, as recalled in *Mustafa Tunç and Fecire Tunç v Turkey*, 'that there should be some form of effective official investigation when individuals have been killed as a result of the use of force' and how the investigation 'must be, inter alia, thorough, impartial and careful'.[89] The type of investigation 'varies according to the nature of the infringement of life: although a criminal investigation is generally necessary where death is caused intentionally, civil or even disciplinary proceedings may satisfy this requirement where death occurs as a result of negligence'.[90] In some instances, such as *Janowiec and others v Russia* (relating to the historic inquiry into the Katyn massacre of Polish prisoners by Soviet forces in 1940), the Court has found that

> the work of parliamentary commissions and other bodies tasked with establishing 'historical truths' cannot be viewed as procedural acts able to satisfy the requirements of Articles 2 and 3 of the Convention, being incapable of leading to the identification and punishment of those responsible or to an award of compensation to the injured party.[91]

In others, such as *Tagayeva and Others v Russia* (on the Beslan school siege by armed Chechen fighters in South Ossetia), it found that parliamentary commissions 'ensured important advances in securing, collecting and publicising information about the aspects of the terrorist attack and the authorities'

[87] *Mocanu v Romania*, para 334.
[88] ibid paras 338 and 288.
[89] *Mustafa Tunç and Fecire Tunç v Turkey* [GC], App No 24014/05 (14 April 2015) para 169 (concerning the death of a man during his military service while assigned to a site belonging to a private oil company).
[90] ibid para 170.
[91] *Janowiec and others v Russia*, App Nos 55508/07 and 29520/09 (ECHR, 21 October 2013) para 143, cited in *Tagayeva and Others v Russia*, App No 26562/07 (18 September 2017) para 630.

response that were overlooked or insufficiently examined by the investigation'.[92] As such, that work 'could be regarded as an aspect of effective remedies aimed at establishing the knowledge necessary to elucidate the facts, distinct from the State's procedural obligations under Articles 2 and 3 of the Convention'.[93] This, affirmed the Court, 'ensured access by the applicants, and the public in general, to knowledge about the aspects of the serious human rights violations that would have otherwise remained inaccessible'.[94] Moreover, in some (rare) cases, the effectiveness of domestic investigations might depend on international cooperation: in *Güzelyurtlu v Turkey and Cyprus* the Court found that the effectiveness of the investigations concerning the procedural limb of Article 2 depended on the duty to cooperate between the Cypriot and Turkish authorities, including the authorities of the Turkish Republic of Northern Cyprus (TRNC).[95] Taken together, these cases illustrate how the Court has interpreted what is meant by effective investigations in light of each context. Thus, the type of truth-seeking mechanism required to satisfy the requirements of the procedural limb of Articles 2 and 3, in conjunction with other provisions (such as Article 13), is informed by the facts and circumstances of each case.

Notwithstanding the attention the Court affords to the state obligation to investigate, its interconnectedness to the right to truth has not been clearly established. In the first *El-Masri* concurring opinion, Judges Tulkens et al regretted the judgment's 'over-cautiousness' in making a 'somewhat timid allusion to the right to the truth in the context of Article 3 and the lack of an explicit acknowledgment of this right in relation to Article 13' (effective remedy), and to procedural obligations under Articles 3, 5 and 8.[96] Tulkens et al drew on *Association 21 Décembre 1989* to argue that 'in the absence of any effective remedies … the applicant was denied the "right to the truth"', explaining that this right encompasses 'an accurate account of the suffering endured and the role of those responsible'. They also suggested that if the right to truth includes the 'right to ascertain and establish the true facts', it would be better situated in relation to Article 13, given the 'scale and seriousness' of violations and the political context of widespread impunity. As such,

> The search for the truth is the objective purpose of the obligation to carry out an investigation and the *raison d'être* of the related quality requirements (transparency, diligence, independence, access, disclosure of results and scrutiny).

In the contrasting *El-Masri* concurring opinion Judges Casadevall and Lopez Guerra contended that the right to truth was equivalent to the right to a serious investigation understood procedurally as a 'serious attempt' to 'finding out

[92] *Tagayeva and Others v Russia*, paras 630–31.
[93] ibid.
[94] ibid.
[95] *Güzelyurtlu v Turkey and Cyprus*, App No 36925/07 (29 January 2019).
[96] *El-Masri v FYRM*, Joint Concurring Opinion of Judges Tulkens et al, paras 10–11.

the truth of the matter'.[97] For them, investigations must establish the facts of the case, the cause of harm suffered, and the identity of those responsible, as a procedural obligation linked to the deprivation of life (Article 2) and torture, inhuman or degrading treatment (Article 3), actionable only by direct victims. So by characterising the right to truth as equivalent to the procedural limb of Articles 2 and 3 and the state duty to investigate, they argue it does not merit consideration as a separate issue. Yet Casadevall and Lopez Guerra's approach seems unnecessarily cautious in light of the Court's jurisprudence on the state duty to investigate, which indicates recognition of the broader significance of knowing the truth about past abuse. By discounting the development of the right to truth about widespread violations as a principle that transcends individuality and affects society as a whole, this position ignores the ECtHR's own gradual contributions and the established position of the UN and IACHR jurisprudence.

ii. The Individual and Collective Dimensions of the Right to Truth

As noted earlier, and in relation to the IACHR jurisprudence, the right to truth carries a collective element as well as an individual one. An acknowledgement of this has appeared also in the jurisprudence of the ECtHR. Intervening as a third party in *Al Nashiri v Poland* (subsequent to *El-Masri*), the UN Special Rapporteur on the promotion and protection of human rights and fundamental freedoms while countering terrorism clarified the UN understanding of the right to truth as having 'two dimensions – a private dimension and a public dimension'.[98] Indeed, 'where gross or systematic human rights violations were alleged to have occurred, the right to know the truth was not one that belonged solely to the immediate victim but also to society'. Importantly, he outlined that recognising a 'free standing right to truth belonging to society at large' gave 'any individual with a legitimate interest in the truth' the entitlement to invoke that right.[99] If, instead:

> the right to truth were to be confined to the individual who had suffered the violation or his representatives, then the exposure of grave and systematic international crimes would necessarily be dependent on the chance occurrence of there being an individual victim or relative who was able and willing to bring proceedings.[100]

The Special Rapporteur's words, reported in the *Al Nashiri* judgment, indicate the Court's awareness of the collective dimension of the right to truth, besides its importance for direct victims and relatives. According to the Grand Chamber in *El-Masri*, the 'right to know what happened', as linked to the right to truth, is

[97] *El-Masri v FYRM*, Joint Concurring Opinion of Judges Casadevall and Lopez Guerra.
[98] *Al Nashiri v Poland*, App No 28761/11 (ECHR, 24 July 2014) paras 482–83.
[99] ibid.
[100] ibid.

relevant to the victim (applicant), whose Convention rights are allegedly violated and who has standing before the Court; his (or her) family; 'other victims of similar crimes'; and the 'general public'.[101] The broader understanding of the category of victims echoes established IACHR jurisprudence. So, in *El-Masri*, the ECtHR stated:

> The great importance of the present case not only for the applicant and his family, but also for other victims of similar crimes and the general public, who had the right to know what had happened.[102]

The importance for the victim's family to know about the past through an enquiry is established in the Court's jurisprudence: there is a continuing violation of Article 3 found when a state persistently fails to account for missing persons.[103] In *Association 21 Décembre*,[104] the Court found that the ongoing failure of the state to provide families of the victims with adequate and prompt access to an independent judicial enquiry into brutal repression contributed to the violation of Article 2.[105] Thus, relatives directly enjoy independent victim status when state investigations are inadequate, not vicariously through the violation of a loved one's rights. Regarding disappearances, in *Aslakhanova* the Court stated that the 'essence of such a violation does not lie mainly in the fact of the "disappearance" of the family member but rather concerns the authorities' reactions and attitudes to the situation when it is brought to their attention' (linking to Articles 2, 3 and 5).[106] A disappearance is 'a distinct phenomenon, characterised by an ongoing situation of uncertainty and unaccountability in which there is a lack of information or even a deliberate concealment and obfuscation of what has occurred', which 'over time, prolong[s] the torment of the victim's relatives'.[107] So for as long as 'the person is unaccounted for',

[101] *El-Masri v FYRM*, para 191.

[102] ibid.

[103] eg *Cyprus v Turkey*, App No 25781/94 (ECHR, 10 May 2001); see also D Groome, 'Identifying Synergies between the Right to the Truth and International/Domestic Criminal Law in Combating Impunity' (2011) 29 *Berkeley Journal of International Law* 175, 179–80. However, in older cases, eg *Çakici v Turkey*, App No 23657/94 (ECHR, 8 July 1999), paras 98–99, the Court refused to recognise an automatic 'general principle that a family member of a "disappeared person" is thereby a victim of treatment contrary to Article 3', suggesting that affording victim status to relatives depends on 'special factors' which give 'the suffering of the applicant a dimension and character distinct from the emotional distress', based on the proximity of familial ties, the circumstances of the relationship and whether the harm was directly witnessed.

[104] *Association 21 Décembre* also discussed in Sweeney, *The European Court of Human Rights in the Post-Cold War Era* (n 61) 74–75. Also, JA Sweeney, 'Restorative Justice and Transitional Justice at the ECHR' (2012) 12 *International Criminal Law Review* 313, 322.

[105] *Association 21 Décembre* paras 142–45; in particular para 143: Or, 'l'obligation procédurale découlant de l'article 2 de la Convention peut difficilement être considérée comme accomplie lorsque les familles des victimes ou leurs héritiers n'ont pas pu avoir accès à une procédure devant un tribunal indépendant appelé à connaître des faits'.

[106] *Aslakhanova v Russia*, para 131.

[107] ibid 122.

> The investigation must be accessible to the victim's family to the extent necessary to safeguard their legitimate interests.[108]

In the high-profile case of *Tagayeva*, the Court relied on Article 13 in consideration of the importance of 'access to information and thus the establishment of truth for the victims of the violations alleged, as well as ensuring justice and preventing impunity for the perpetrators'.[109] It considered that 'access to information and the effectiveness of any ensuing remedies are interlinked' under Article 13, given that 'the knowledge necessary to elucidate facts … is often in the sole hands of State officials or authorities'.[110] Similarly to what emerged from some of the IACtHR jurisprudence, affording victims access to knowledge about the violations seeks to rebalance the structural imbalance between the individual and the state, whereby the authorities are the only ones in possession of relevant information and do not make it accessible to the affected persons.

The collective dimension of the right to truth expands the purpose of the state's obligation to investigate. While it is established that victims and close relatives are entitled to make a legal claim, the general public's interest in knowing the truth about widespread abuse that affects large portions of society contributes an additional, distinct dimension to the right to truth. This interest can take a variety of forms. In *Association 21 Décembre* the judges considered that 'the public must have a sufficient right to examine (*droit de regard*) the investigation or its findings, in order to challenge (*mise en cause*)' it both in practice and in theory, depending on each case.[111] Moreover, the general public may also want to know what emerged from those investigations through a related 'right to access relevant information about alleged violations', as noted by Tulkens et al in their concurring opinion in *El-Masri*.[112] This connects the right to truth to the right to access information of public interest, also emerging in the Court's jurisprudence.[113]

In essence, when harm has affected society collectively, the right to truth acquires significance for groups beyond persons directly affected. Since *El-Masri*, the Court has reaffirmed that in cases of serious human rights violations

> the right to the truth regarding the relevant circumstances of the case does not belong solely to the victim of the crime and his or her family but also to other victims of

[108] ibid 121.

[109] *Tagayeva and Others v Russia*, paras 627, 630.

[110] ibid citing *Öneryildiz v Turkey* [GC], App No 48939/99 (30 November 2004).

[111] *Association 21 Décembre*, para 133.

[112] *El-Masri v FYRM*, Joint Concurring Opinion of Judges Tulkens et al, para 4.

[113] The emerging right to access information of public interest by members of the general public supports the existence of a collective dimension and social relevance of the right to the truth in relation to the state duty to investigate. The ECtHR has begun to outline its understanding of this in relation to Art 10, most recently in cases involving NGOs seeking information of public interest, such as *Youth Initiative for Human Rights v Serbia*, App No 48135/06 (ECHR, 25 June 2013) and very recently in the Grand Chamber decision of *Magyar Helsinki Bizottság v Hungary* [GC], App No 18030/11 (ECHR, 8 November 2016).

> similar violations and the general public, who have the right to know what has happened.[114]

The Court has also found that if authorities fail to conduct serious investigations, they may appear tolerant of human rights violations and undermine the rule of law. In *El-Masri* the Grand Chamber stated that an adequate response and investigation is 'essential in maintaining public confidence in their adherence to the rule of law and in preventing any appearance of collusion in or tolerance of unlawful acts'.[115] Subsequent case law upholds this,[116] evidencing the Court's view that failure to conduct serious investigations undermines respect for the rule of law in general. To support this, Tulkens et al drew on IACHR cases (*Contreras* and *Velásquez Rodríguez*) to illustrate that victims and relatives, as well as society as a whole, had 'the right to know the truth'.[117] Citing from *Contreras*, they recalled that in democratic societies, there must be knowledge 'about the facts of grave human rights violations',[118] which is especially important after conflict or authoritarianism.

However, recognising the collective dimension of the right to truth does not clearly identify rights-holders and, accordingly, subjects entitled to claim its violation. In order for human rights to be given legal effect and rendered justiciable, a degree of certainty around the rights-holders is needed. In older cases the Court has accepted applications from family members as indirect victims,[119] and in relation to enforced disappearances, this includes spouses,[120] parents,[121] a nephew with close ties to the direct victim and the violation,[122] but not an adult sibling living in a different city.[123] This limited understanding of who may claim a violation clashes with the broad societal significance of the right to truth articulated recently in *El-Masri* and *Association 21 Décembre*. This discrepancy can be interpreted as part of the Court's gradual recognition of the *significance*

[114] Also, in finding a violation of the procedural limb of Art 3, in *Al Nashiri v Poland*, App No 28761/11 (ECHR, 24 July 2014), para 495, and (verbatim) in *Husayn (Abu Zubaydah) v Poland*, App No 7511/13 (ECHR, 24 July 2014), para 489.

[115] *El-Masri v FYRM*, para 192, restated in the Joint Concurring Opinion of Judges Tulkens et al, para 6: 'The desire to ascertain the truth plays a part in strengthening confidence in public institutions and hence the rule of law.' And previously, *Association 21 Décembre*, paras 134, 144 and 194 with reference to the importance of society to know what happened to victims of violent transition in the context of structural and widespread harm.

[116] In particular, *Al Nashiri v Poland*, para 495; *Aslakhanova v Russia*, para 231, noting that addressing 'conditions of guaranteed impunity' for abuses committed by state agents is especially important in establishing of the rule of law and building public confidence.

[117] *El-Masri v FYRM*, Joint Concurring Opinion of Judges Tulkens et al.

[118] *Contreras v El Salvador* 173; 170. This echoes the Court's own understanding of the ECHR as 'an instrument designed to maintain and promote the ideals and values of a democratic society', as discussed inter alia in *Soering v UK*.

[119] 'Where there is a personal and specific link between the direct victim and the applicant', Council of Europe/ECHR, 'Practical Guide on Admissibility Criteria' (2014) para 30.

[120] *McCann and Others v UK*, App No 18984/91 (ECHR, 27 September 1995).

[121] *Kurt v Turkey*, App No 15/1997/799/1002 (ECHR, 25 May 1998) paras 130–34.

[122] *Yaşa v Turkey*, App No 63/1997/847/1054 (ECHR, 2 September 1998) para 66.

[123] *Çakici v Turkey*, App No 23657/94 (ECHR, 8 July 1999) paras 98–99.

of the collective dimension of the right to truth: in certain instances, knowing the past is clearly relevant to society at large in principle, but in practice, only a small number of claimants may be entitled to take legal action. As such, the right to truth as a collective matter strengthens the right to know held by specific individuals and groups, but the Court is yet to afford a clear, actionable right to truth to satisfy that collective dimension.

The second concurring opinion in *El-Masri* adopted this more conservative position, arguing that it is 'the victim and not the general public' who is entitled to know, regardless of the general public's interest (and curiosity) towards the case.[124] So while not completely dismissing the fact that certain cases are significant beyond the parties to the dispute, Judges Casadevall and Lopez Guerra considered the interest of society at large as irrelevant under the law. But this more conservative approach seems to completely miss the distinctive collective aspect of the right to truth, especially when the outcome of a case is likely to affect large sections of society. The right to truth is more than the state obligation to investigate: in some cases, finding out about past abuses is a public concern, in addition to being a specific entitlement of persons who enjoy victim status.

A narrow legal analysis is unable to appreciate the important extralegal implications of uncovering the truth about the past, which may carry individual and collective healing functions. Studies in criminology and sociolegal studies have explored the emotional repair of truth finding.[125] Some suggest that 'the restorative nature of truth is as much remedial as it is reparative, as much procedural as substantive, and as much immediate as enduring'.[126] In *El-Masri* Tulkens et al acknowledged the importance of knowing the truth because:

> Establishing the true facts and securing an acknowledgment of serious breaches of human rights and humanitarian law constitute forms of redress that are just as important as compensation, and sometimes even more so.[127]

These considerations give the right to truth an additional meaning that cannot be understood – or characterised – through law alone. But the Court may not (yet) have the tools to formalise this meaning. And while the ECtHR has reflected on similar issues emerging from IACHR case law, the development of the right to truth through the ECHR does not match IACHR jurisprudence. Nevertheless, the Court is not oblivious to the potential of the right to truth.

Since *El-Masri*, and *Association 21 December 1989* before it, the Grand Chamber has faced the question of the collective significance of the right to

[124] *El-Masri v FYRM*, Joint Concurring Opinion of Judges Casadevall and Lopez Guerra.

[125] eg J Doak, 'The Therapeutic Dimension of Transitional Justice: Emotional Repair and Victim Satisfaction in International Trials and Truth Commissions' (2011) 11 *International Criminal Law Review* 263.

[126] Antkowiak (n 13) 101.

[127] *El-Masri v FYRM*, Joint Concurring Opinion of Judges Tulkens *et al*, para 6.

truth in relation to widespread past abuses of a number of ECHR provisions (including Articles 7, 10 and 38). In *Janowiec v Russia* the ECtHR found a failure to comply with the obligations under Article 38 and recognised both

> the public interest in a transparent investigation into the crimes of the previous totalitarian regime and the private interest of the victims' relatives in uncovering the circumstances of their death.[128]

Taking this further in their separate opinion, Judges Ziemele, De Gaetano, Laffranque and Keller pointed to a 'clear trend towards recognising a right to the truth in cases of gross human rights violations', reiterating that

> the obligation to investigate and prosecute those responsible for grave human rights and serious humanitarian law violations serves fundamental public interests by allowing a nation to learn from its history and by combating impunity.[129]

Citing from the UN Updated Set of Principles for the Protection and Promotion of Human Rights through Action to Combat Impunity, Ziemele et al argued that the right to truth 'protects the collective memory of the affected people',[130] again indicating a willingness of some judges to acknowledge more directly its collective significance.

Judge Ziemele's separate opinion in *Vasiliauskas v Lithuania* (another historic case on the retroactive conviction for genocide of a former KGB official for killing partisans in the 1950s) also highlights the broader social importance of certain cases:

> the Court is not only dealing yet again with the rights of the applicant, but also finds itself at the centre of a complex social process in a society seeking to establish the truth about the past and its painful events.[131]

Judge Ziemele, again, cited the UN Updated Set of Principles for the Protection and Promotion of Human Rights in arguing that while maintaining the rule of law standards contained in Article 7, the Court is also guided by the 'broader principles regarding the right to truth and prohibition of impunity'.[132] This suggests that some judges have developed an understanding of investigations and accountability within the scope of the Convention that appreciates the collective and social significance of certain cases in addition to the importance for individual claimants. Their position clearly affects the work of the Court, but the fact that the collective significance of investigations is being discussed in separate opinions suggests that the judges are not unanimous on this issue.

[128] *Janowiec and others v Russia*, para 214.

[129] *Janowiec and others v Russia*, Joint Partly Dissenting Opinion of Judges Ziemele, De Gaetano, Laffranque and Keller, paras 9 and 24.

[130] ibid.

[131] *Vasiliauskas v Lithuania* [GC], App No 35343/05 (ECHR, 20 October 2015), Dissenting Opinion of Judge Ziemele, para 27.

[132] ibid.

Consequently, the Court's jurisprudence on the collective dimension of the right to truth remains fragmented.

The Grand Chamber has also been presented with missed opportunities to consider the collective significance of the right to truth when fraught histories are debated. For example, in *Perinçek v Switzerland* the majority found that the criminal prosecution of a Turkish man denying the 1915 Armenian genocide in Switzerland (and not Turkey) constituted a violation of Article 10.[133] Yet seven of the seventeen judges dissented, accepting the possibility for states instead 'to make it a criminal offence to insult the memory of a people that has suffered genocide'.[134] Perhaps this case would have been more interesting for the elucidation of the Court's position on the collective significance of the right to know and debate the past had the respondent state been Turkey, where the Armenian massacre is yet to be politically accounted for and included in institutional memory.

When confronted with 'historically and legally' complex cases,[135] the Court has exercised its discretion to tackle disputes about more general historical truths emerging incidentally from the facts of a specific case. And while the Court is not mandated to settle disputes about the past, in establishing a violation of a Convention right it cannot ignore the wider political context and possible collective significance of a specific case. The jurisprudence illustrates the judges' fragmented approach in engaging the right to truth incidentally, by attaching it to different substantive articles depending on the facts, the applicant's submissions, the state's responses and often the persuasiveness of third-party interventions, and at times referring to it as an overarching principle not appended to a listed right. Yet the Court's incidental consideration of the right to truth in relation to historical abuses remains difficult to conceptualise coherently: perhaps its role, as noted by Judge Ziemele, permits only the following:

> While maintaining the rule-of-law standard that Article 7 provides, it is particularly important that this Court, at the level of the presentation of facts and the choice of methodology and issues, is guided by these broader principles regarding the right to truth and prohibition of impunity.[136]

How exactly the presentation of facts and methodological choices would operate in practice, however, remains open to further scrutiny.

The differences of opinion around the right to truth within the Court evidenced in its jurisprudence are reflected in the limited degree of justiciability of the right to truth. Existing case law does indeed recognise the significance of

[133] *Perinçek v Switzerland* [GC], App No 27510/08 (ECHR, 15 October 2015) paras 213ff.
[134] *Perinçek v Switzerland*, Joint Dissenting Opinion of Judges Spielmann, Casadevall, Berro, De Gaetano, Sicilianos, Silvis and Kuris, para 2.
[135] To borrow from the language used in *Vasiliauskas v Lithuania* [GC], App No 35343/05 (ECHR, 20 October 2015), Dissenting Opinion of Judge Ziemele, para 27.
[136] ibid.

the collective dimension of the right to truth. However, no tangible legal effect has been given to that recognition, placing the ECtHR behind the pioneering decisions of the IACHR instruments. The explanation for this gap is likely to be informed by the political histories of the two regions, and the extent to which dealing with legacies of widespread violence of dictatorships has been a central or peripheral preoccupation for each Court. Yet the ECtHR is facing a wider range of contexts in which the right to truth can be of use to victims and societies as a whole, which include postauthoritarian transitions, counterterror practices, international and non-international armed conflicts as well as illiberal policies of established democracies. This variety may expand the uses of the right to truth within the scope of the ECHR, as future research may observe.

Nevertheless, in connection with the right to truth emerging in the ECHR system, victims are able to hold states accountable for conducting inquiries into the circumstances and responsibilities for past abuse and instigate inquiries themselves. This serves the interests of the rule of law and human rights in general, as well as public confidence in state institutions, which affects the whole of society. At the same time, the outcomes of formal truth seeking informs the dynamic process of building, undoing and contesting the formation of collective memories in contexts of competing narratives. As such, identifying the contours of the right to truth and its status in global IHRL, and making it justiciable, may help empower survivors of abuse and rebuild political communities recovering from violent histories. The ECtHR's gradual process of recognition of the right to truth seems encouraging for its further consolidation and actionability. Moreover, the position of the European human rights system is significant beyond its jurisdictional boundaries, strengthening the development of the right to truth internationally.

III. THE STATUS OF THE RIGHT TO TRUTH IN INTERNATIONAL LAW

The question of whether the right to truth constitutes a *lex lata* norm of international law, or is instead *lex ferenda*, is moot. For some, it is a legally binding norm beyond the narrow treaty provisions found in the 2006 International Convention for the Protection of All Persons from Enforced Disappearance and the 1977 Additional Protocol I to the 1949 Geneva Conventions.[137] For others, it remains conceptually and legally elusive, despite its value and prevalence in soft law.[138] More than a decade ago, Yasmin Naqvi considered whether the right to truth is emerging as 'something approaching a customary right' or a general principle of law, concluding that it stood 'somewhere on the threshold of a legal

[137] eg Szoke-Burke (n 1) 535.
[138] Sweeney, (n 1) 357–58.

norm and a narrative device'.[139] Today, these claims can be reassessed in light of new developments in ECHR jurisprudence on the right to truth – and other developments elsewhere in law and extralegal contexts. This right has emerged in a 'diffuse manner' that goes beyond 'landmark legal cases and documents' and includes contributions from non-legal academics and activists.[140] As such, two features of its emergence and gradual consolidation emerge: firstly, the comparative value of cross-referencing of the concept of the right to truth in different fora, legal and extralegal. The references to UN and IACHR developments in the Strasbourg court illustrate the possibilities of transjudicial dialogue, or at least a degree of borrowing useful concepts (even if their validity and uses are nebulous). Secondly, the extralegal contributions to the emergence of this right, evidenced in the work of civil society organisations, practitioners and academics in specific local contexts, illustrates that the notion of the right to truth 'speaks' to different contexts, and as such can be related to different social and cultural realities – echoing the discussion in Chapters 1 and 2. In the absence of clear treaty status in PIL, does the right to truth reach the threshold of CIL or general principles? The significance of the ECHR jurisprudence in the global debates suggests that cross-referencing this right and promoting it in different fora contributes to the discursive evolution and formalisation of the right to truth internationally.

A. The Right to Truth and Customary International Law

In 2006 Naqvi explored the customary status of the right to truth based on 'repeated inferences' as related 'to other fundamental human rights by human rights bodies and courts' and the proliferation of truth-seeking mechanisms.[141] She relied on Meron's seminal work on human rights and custom to discuss how the right to truth could reflect a CIL norm,[142] concluding that it struggled to meet the requirements. The question, therefore, is whether the fact that the ECtHR has referred to the right to truth, joining the IACtHR and the UN, demonstrates its emerging customary status.

Establishing the customary status of a norm under PIL remains a notoriously arduous and contested task as evidenced in current literature.[143] The work

[139] Naqvi (n 13) 267 and 273.

[140] YG Park, 'Truth as Justice: Legal and Extralegal Development of the Right to Truth' (2010) 31(4) *Harvard International Review* 24.

[141] Naqvi (n 13) 267.

[142] ibid 10, 254, discussing T Meron, *Human Rights and Humanitarian Norms as Customary Law*, 3rd edn (Oxford, Clarendon Press, 1989), and in particular the description of the 'dynamic relationship between custom and treaty', in which the latter may generate 'new rules of customary law and may eventually acquire probative value for establishing the customary character of the new rules', 89–90.

[143] See eg B Chimni, 'Customary International Law: A Third World Perspective' (2018) 112(1) *American Journal of International Law* 1; H Thirlway, 'Human Rights in Customary Law: An

of the International Law Commission on CIL and the wealth of (often critical) academic writing on this topic demonstrate the enduring complexity of identifying custom.[144] Defining international custom 'as evidence of a general practice accepted as law', Article 38(1)(b) of the ICJ Statute is understood by the ILC[145] (and scholars) as setting out two constituent elements of CIL: general practice and acceptance as law (*opinio juris*). The 2018 ILC Draft Conclusions indicate that the practice of states, and in some cases international organisations, 'contributes to the formation, or expression, of rules of customary international law'[146] (Draft Conclusion 4) and may take a variety of forms (Draft Conclusion 6).[147] The earlier 2014 International Law Commission 'Report on identification of customary international law' had already reaffirmed that acts of the executive branch in international contexts are to be understood as state practice.[148] With regards to *opinio juris*, 'the practice in question must be undertaken with a sense of legal right or obligation'[149] (Draft Conclusion 9) and may take a variety of forms (Draft Conclusion 10).[150] The 2014 Report had already stressed that 'accepted as law' is a better term for understanding the 'subjective element' of CIL, acknowledging the paradoxes of *opinio juris* evidenced in academic debates.[151] The Draft Conclusions (16) also envisage rules of particular CIL at regional, local or other levels – applicable among a limited number of states.[152]

One aspect of the right to truth – the state obligation to investigate serious human rights violations – has been addressed in the context of the state practice requirement of CIL.[153] Naomi Roht-Arriaza acknowledged that 'although

Attempt to Define Some of the Issues' (2015) 28(3) *Leiden Journal of International Law* 495; R Crootof, 'Change Without Consent: How Customary International Law Modifies Treaties' (2016) 41 *Yale Journal of International Law* 238; OC Tassinis, 'Customary International Law: Interpretation from Beginning to End' (2020) 31(1) *European Journal of International Law* 235.

[144] See ILC, 'Draft Conclusions on Identification of Customary International Law, with Commentaries', Report of the International Law Commission (2018) UN Doc A/73/10 (ILC 'Draft Conclusions' 2018). https://legal.un.org/ilc/texts/instruments/english/commentaries/1_13_2018.pdf. See also previously, in that mandate, ILC, 'Idenfication of Customary International Law: Text of the Draft Conclusions Adopted by the Committee' (2 May–10 June and 4 July–12 August 2016) UN Doc A/CN.4/L.872. And inter alia: JL Kunz, 'The Nature of Customary International Law' (1953) 47 *American Journal of International Law* 662; A D'Amato, 'Trashing Customary International Law' (1987) 81 *American Journal of International Law* 101; JP Kelly, 'The Twilight of Customary International Law' (1999–2000) 40 *Virginia Journal of International Law* 449; A Roberts, 'Traditional and Modern Approaches to Customary International Law: A Reconciliation' (2001) 95 *American Journal of International Law* 757; N Arajarvi, 'Between Lex Lata and Lex Ferenda? Customary International (Criminal) Law and the Principle of Legality' (2011) 15 *Tilburg Law Review: Journal of International & European Law* 163.

[145] ILC 'Draft Conclusions' (2018) (n 144).

[146] ibid 130.

[147] ibid 133.

[148] ILC, 'Second Report on Identification of Customary International Law' (66th session, 5 May–6 June 2014), UN Doc A/CN.4/672, para 41.

[149] ILC 'Draft Conclusions' (2018) (n 144) 138.

[150] ibid 140.

[151] ILC (n 148) para 68.

[152] ILC 'Draft Conclusions' (2018) (n 144) 154.

[153] Roht-Arriaza (n 56) 489.

state-sponsored grave violations of human rights persist' and states often fail to investigate them, 'other aspects of state practice show that states do recognise these failures as breaches of international norms'.[154] She points to verbal statements of governmental representatives in international organisations as 'recognition of an international obligation to investigate and prosecute'.[155] But this does not directly address the *opinio juris* requirement of CIL, or consider the collective dimensions of the right to truth emerging from regional case law.

The recent developments in ECHR jurisprudence adding to IACHR and UN advancements call for an overall reassessment of the right to truth in relation to CIL through its two constitutive elements. For the purpose of this analysis, and in the absence of state statements against the right to truth elaborating on *opinio juris*, the role of the ECtHR will be interpreted as relevant to regional CIL and significant for international custom more generally.

With regards to the significance of Strasbourg's jurisprudence in relation to IHRL (and PIL more broadly), the ECHR operates in the context of the rest of IHRL. Consequently, it is permeable to global human rights trends and ECtHR case law feeds back into those developments.[156] The separate opinion of Judges Tulkens et al in *El-Masri*, citing UN developments[157] and IACHR case law, evidences the judges' attention to global human rights debates. Established jurisprudence describes the ECHR as a 'living instrument' to be 'interpreted in the light of present-day conditions';[158] while this is primarily understood in relation to the Court's internal hermeneutics,[159] in practice, it provides ways for the Court to read global human rights developments into its mandate and through the ECHR. The progressive development of new rights through evolutive interpretation[160] may help the Court respond to new challenges – looking to other human rights actors and leading to forms of cross-fertilisation across jurisdictions. References to the right to truth developments through the UN and IACHR, as occurred in *El-Masri* and related judgments, illustrate this.

[154] ibid 492.

[155] ibid 493.

[156] JG Merrills, *The Development of International Law by the European Court of Human Rights*, 2nd edn (Manchester, Manchester University Press, 1993) discussing *Soering v UK* and *Cruz Varas and others v Sweden*, App No 15576/89 (ECHR, 20 March 1991).

[157] Notably, 'Report of the Working Group on Enforced or Involuntary Disappearances' (n 26), 13.

[158] *Tyrer v UK*, App No 5856/72 (ECHR, 25 April 1978), para 31. This should ensure rights that are 'practical and effective', not just 'theoretical or illusory', as notably stated in *Airey v Ireland*, App No 6289/73 (ECHR, 9 October 1979) para 24; *Tyrer v UK*, *Klass v Germany* and *Goodwin v UK*, App No 28957/95 (ECHR, 11 July 2002) discussed in L Wildhaber, 'The European Convention on Human Rights and International Law' (2007) 56 *ICLQ* 217, 221–23. See also A Mowbray, 'The Creativity of the European Court of Human Rights' (2005) 5 *Human Rights Law Review* 57, 60 and I Ziemele, 'Customary International Law in the Case Law of the European Court of Human Rights – The Method' (2013) 12 *Law & Practice of International Courts & Tribunals* 243.

[159] In light of the Vienna Convention on the Law of Treaties (23 May 1969), Art 31(3)(b) on taking into account 'any subsequent practice in the application of the treaty'.

[160] Wildhaber (n 158) 223. For a discussion of evolutive interpretation, see also G Letsas, *A Theory of Interpretation of the European Convention on Human Rights* (Oxford, Oxford University Press, 2007) 74.

ECHR jurisprudence carries normative value both within its regional jurisdiction and beyond,[161] and contributes to 'international legal culture' by providing important 'elucidation and development of international law' as well as developing 'principles of general applicability'.[162] Jointly with the IACHR, the ECtHR gives regional effect to general IHRL principles that may otherwise remain non-justiciable for rights-bearers. Thus, dialogue between regional human rights courts informs global human rights developments, including the right to truth.

References to international law in the Court's jurisprudence denote an interactive, reciprocal correlation. Former President of the Court Luzius Wildhaber highlighted the 'dynamic and evolutive' relationship between the ECHR and PIL, 'checking and building on each other'.[163] As 'part of the legal background' of the ECHR (a treaty under PIL[164]), international law is a 'vital reference point' for the Court.[165] By drawing on other international law instruments, the Court in effect develops a reading of the Convention mindful of other areas of IHRL.[166] Thus, the ECHR plays a 'key role' in IHRL and PIL, which is desirable, argues Wildhaber, 'if it contributes to the evolution of international law at large' and furthers human rights.[167]

The Court has relied on international law to determine 'the effect of some substantive provisions of the Convention' and looked at global developments to interpret and apply it.[168] Yet 'unlike international treaties of the classic kind', it creates 'more than mere reciprocal engagements between contracting States'

[161] eg extraterritorially, see *Al-Skeini v UK*, App No 55721/07 (ECHR, 7 July 2011).

[162] Merrills (n 156) 252 and 17.

[163] Wildhaber (n 158) 230.

[164] Thus, the 1969 Vienna Convention on the Law of Treaties applies to its interpretation, as confirmed in *Loizidou v Turkey*, App No 15318/89 (ECHR, 18 December 1996) para 43, discussing, inter alia, *Golder v the United Kingdom*, para 29.

[165] Merrills (n 156) 203–05. The ECHR explicitly mentions international law in Art 7, Art 15, Art 35 and Art 1 Protocol I, and the Court's case law has clarified that 'the Convention should so far as possible be interpreted in harmony with other rules of international law of which it forms part', as noted in *Al-Adsani v UK* [GC], App No 35763/97 (ECHR, 21 November 2001) para 55, discussed in Wildhaber (n 160) 220. The same phrase is repeated elsewhere, eg *M and Others v Italy and Bulgaria*, App No 40020/03 (ECHR, 31 July 2012); *Catan and Others v Moldova and Russia*, App Nos 43370/04, 8252/05 and 18454/06 (ECHR, 19 October 2012). The Court routinely considers PIL within the applicable legal framework in deciding cases, under the heading 'Relevant International Law' (eg *Sørensen and Rasmussen v Denmark*, App Nos 52562/99 and 52620/99 (ECHR, 11 January 2006)), or jointly under the heading of 'Relevant Comparative and International Law' (eg *Othman (Abu Qatada) v UK*, App No 8139/09 (ECHR, 17 January 2012)) and references ICJ jurisprudence (eg *Cyprus v Turkey*, 85–86). The ECtHR has also considered customary law provisions as part of applicable PIL, eg *Cudak v Lithuania*, App No 15869/02 (ECHR, 23 March 2010) para 66.

[166] Merrills (n 156) 203 and 218–26.

[167] Wildhaber (n 158) 220 and 231. See also, broadly, M Forowicz, *The Reception of International Law in the European Court of Human Rights* (Oxford, Oxford University Press, 2010), discussed in S McInerney-Lankford, 'Fragmentation of International Law Redux: The Case of Strasbourg' (2012) 32(3) *OJLS* 609.

[168] *Al-Adsani v UK* in Wildhaber (n 158) 225.

and establishes obligations that benefit from 'collective enforcement'.[169] The ECHR's special character as a treaty for the collective enforcement of human rights and fundamental freedoms[170] (and related democratic intent[171]) makes it permeable to global IHRL developments in other treaties, fora, practices and debates. As such, the Court may reflect or give effect to IHRL trends even when these are not squarely set out in the Convention, and thus has been able to recognise the significance of the right to truth within the scope of the ECHR. At the same time, ECHR judgments feed into global human rights developments and may be constitutive of PIL. ECHR jurisprudence, especially in Grand Chamber formation (eg *El-Masri*), contributes to the consolidation of new norms, such as the right to truth.

Could ECtHR general developments around the right to truth provide a form of authoritative interpretation in relation to human rights in CIL,[172] similar to UN human rights bodies? Bruno Simma and Philip Alston have examined the notion of authoritative interpretation by the UN in relation to CIL, arguing that UN Member States, 'having in good faith undertaken treaty obligations to respect "human rights"' are bound by 'the definition of "human rights" which has evolved over time' through the 'virtually unanimous practice' of UN organs.[173] Yet this reading is far from unanimous.[174] Another indicator for tracing the establishment of CIL norms proposed by Meron is the 'degree to which a statement of a particular right in one human rights instrument, especially a human rights treaty, has been repeated in other human rights instruments',

[169] *Ireland v UK*, App No 5310/71 (ECHR, 18 January 1978), para 239.

[170] Evidenced in case law, eg *Mamatkulov and Askarov v Turkey* [GC], App Nos 46827/99 and 46951/99 (ECHR, 4 February 2005) para 100; *Loizidou v Turkey*; *Al-Adsani v UK*, para 55; *Fogarty v UK*; *Cudak v Lithuania*; *Sabeh El Leyl v France*, App No 34869/05 (ECHR, 29 June 2011). The Court has questioned 'the fact that at the heart of any treaty-based agreement there could only be an agreement', as 'the integrity and unity of the Convention system' go 'beyond the consent- and sovereignty-oriented rules of general international law', as noted in Wildhaber (n 158) 229, discussing *Belilos v Switzerland*, App No 10328/83 (ECHR, 29 April 1988) and *Loizidou v Turkey*.

[171] Previous case law has indicated that interpretations must be consistent with 'the general spirit of the Convention, an instrument designed to maintain and promote the ideals and values of a democratic society'. See eg *Mamatkulov and Askarov v Turkey* para 101, citing *Soering v UK*, para 87, and, mutatis mutandis, *Klass v Germany*, para 34.

[172] In general on CIL and human rights through the UN, see inter alia RB Lillich, 'The Growing Importance of Customary International Human Rights Law' (1995) 25 *Georgia Journal of International & Comparative Law* 1; IR Gunning, 'Modernizing Customary International Law: The Challenge of Human Rights' (1990) 31 *Virginia Journal of International Law* 211.

[173] B Simma and P Alston, 'The Sources of Human Rights: Custom, Jus Cogens and General Principles' (1988–89) 12 *Autralian Yearbook of International Law* 82, 100.

[174] Notably, Meron (n 142) 87, expresses scepticism towards the 'attempt to endow customary law status instantly upon norms approved by consensus or near-consensus at international law conferences' (such as UN human rights conferences); and more recently, warnings against 'a vague and easily manipulable consensus criterion' have been highlighted by JL Goldsmith and EA Posner, 'A Theory of Customary International Law' (1998) Chicago Working Paper Series in Law and Economics (Second Series), 73 available at www.law.uchicago.edu/Lawecon/workingpapers.html; and also JL Goldsmith and EA Posner, *The Limits of International Law* (Oxford, Oxford University Press, 2005).

countered by 'the degree to which a particular right is subject to limitations'.[175] Meron (and others[176]) posit that regional human rights courts may also contribute to the customary formation and interpretation of IHRL, especially through the 'cumulative weight of their case-law' in influencing and consolidating developments of customary human rights law.[177] Moreover, the jurisprudence of regional human rights bodies is 'frequently and increasingly invoked outside the context of their constitutive instruments and cited as authoritative statements of human rights law'; taken cumulatively, this 'has a significant role in generating customary rules'.[178] The notion of the right to truth has indeed been repeated across different fora, including the ECtHR.

But the extent to which new developments around the right to truth at ECHR level and the cross-referencing consolidate this right in relation to CIL remains unclear – primarily because the understanding of regional courts' contribution to the formation of CIL remains under-theorised in light of the two constituent elements. As such, and despite recent ECHR developments, qualifying the right to truth as CIL would be imprecise. Moreover, it would be problematic for dialogue and developments in two regional human rights courts to become determinative of international custom worldwide, in the absence of sufficient support in other legal traditions outside the realm of the ECtHR and IACHR system. As such, it is worth considering whether the right to truth might constitute a general principle.

B. The Right to Truth and General Principles

It is tempting to interpret the increasing references to the right to truth across different fora (judicial and extrajudicial) as indicating an emerging general principle of law 'as recognised by civilised nations'.[179] This concept is another nebulous area of international law that continues to fascinate scholars.[180] Naqvi

[175] Meron (n 142) 93.
[176] Arajarvi (n 144) 182.
[177] Meron (n 142) 80, 89.
[178] ibid 100.
[179] See Art 38(1)(c) of the ICJ Statute.
[180] See eg I Saunders, *General Principles as a Source of International Law* (Oxford, Hart, 2021); M Andenas et al (eds), *General Principles and the Coherence of International Law* (Leiden, Brill, 2019); RP Mazzeschi and A Viviani, 'General Principles of International Law: From Rules to Values?' in R Pisillo Mazzeschi and P De Sena (eds) *Global Justice, Human Rights and the Modernization of International Law* (Cham, Springer, 2018); J d'Aspremont, 'What Was Not Meant to Be: General Principles of Law as a Source of International Law' in R Pisillo Mazzeschi and P De Sena (eds), *Global Justice, Human Rights and the Modernization of International Law* (Cham, Springer, 2018); and earlier, RB Schlesinger, 'Research on the General Principles of Law Recognized by Civilized Nations' (1957) 51 *American Journal of International Law* 734; FTF Jalet, 'The Quest for the General Principles of Law Recognized by Civilized Nations – A Study' (1962) 10 *UCLA Law Review* 1041; W Friedmann, 'The Uses of "General Principles" in the Development of International Law' (1963) 57 *American Journal of International Law* 279; B Cheng, *General Principles of Law as Applied by International Courts and Tribunals* (Cambridge, Cambridge University Press, 1994).

suggested that jurisprudence of human rights courts may indicate a nascent general principle; more specifically, procedural obligations that address violations of fundamental rights are emerging as 'an expected response by a state to a violation'.[181] Despite their colonial heritage,[182] and contested meaning,[183] general principles of international law may offer 'a means to resolve a variety of issues which neither conventional nor customary international law' are able to address, for example in developing human rights.[184] For Simma and Alston, the notion of general principles admits a situation in which a '[human rights] norm invested with strong inherent authority is widely accepted even though widely violated'.[185] In the absence of treaty provisions, this offers 'a more plausible explanation of how substantive human rights obligations may be established in general international law, than that offered by a strained, or even denatured "new" theory of custom'.[186]

Considering both national and international sources of general principles, Cherif Bassiouni posited that 'comparative legal technique' offers an 'objective test to measure breadth and depth of recognition and applicability of a given principle in national legal systems'[187] – and by extension, in international (including regional) contexts. Therefore, the more a principle (to a degree of sameness) 'is reiterated in national and international sources, the more it deserves deference'.[188] Despite (and due to) the lack of 'the precise wording of particular treaties', the convergence in meaning noted by Sweeney suggests that 'in slightly different but functionally equivalent ways, the HRC, IACHR and ECtHR have upheld the substance of the right to truth'.[189] A comparative analysis of the right to truth across the UN, IACHR and ECHR mechanisms, teamed with the explosion of truth commissions and commissions of enquiry worldwide, and the writings of commentators in different traditions may signal a timid emergence of a right under general principles. The existence (or acceptance) of this norm would have to be evidenced across jurisdictions to indicate its status: it is simply not sufficient to rely on two regional human rights instruments and the UN sources to establish this right as a general principle. For this reason, the final two chapters of this book will turn to the legal systems of Muslim-majority societies to evaluate whether the right to truth and the broader

[181] Naqvi (n 13) 268.

[182] Credited to Belgian law professor and colonial apologist Descamps at the 1899 Hague Peace Conference, reported in M Koskenniemi, *The Gentle Civilizer of Nations: The Rise and Fall of International Law 1870–1960* (Cambridge, Cambridge University Press, 2001) 161.

[183] Discussed inter alia in the literature cited at n 174, and also GJH van Hoof, *Rethinking the Sources of International Law* (Deventer, Kluwer Law, 1983) 131–51.

[184] MC Bassiouni, 'A Functional Approach to "General Principles of International Law"' (1990) 11 *Michigan Journal of International Law* 768, 769.

[185] Simma and Alston (n 173) 102.

[186] ibid 100–02 and 104.

[187] Bassiouni (n 184) 772–73.

[188] ibid 811 and 813–14.

[189] Sweeney (n 1) 383–84.

aims of truth seeking after serious harm are supported in Islamic law, jurisprudence and practices. If the principle of the right to truth exists, even indirectly, in the legal systems of Muslim-majority societies, as well as in Islamic law and jurisprudence, then this norm will gain further ground towards becoming a general principle of law. Future research directions might expand this further, testing the extent to which other legal traditions might also support the notion of the right to truth.

The lack of clarity as to the formal contours of the right to truth does not detract from that fact it is being referred to and used to provide an actionable tool for (some) victims and survivors, with an important function for societies at large. Perhaps in the future, gradual repeated references to the right to truth will be (borrowing from Koskenniemi) 'formulated in non-controversial language' giving the principle 'good chance' of acceptance 'as part of the discursive stuff out of which international law is made'.[190] The role of normative principles expressed outside of 'black-letter' international law – a legal system in its own right – echoes some of the discussion in Chapter 2 on the combined value of the theory of legal pluralism and Sacco's comparative legal method as an interpretative lens. In particular, the emergence of the right to truth discursively, organically, through the work of legal practitioners as well as academics and civil society actors indicates that this principle must be understood contextually.[191] The multidisciplinary foundations of the right to truth in different truth-seeking mechanisms can support its applicability in different cultural settings and thus can help connect the international law elements to the local contexts.[192] That discursiveness and the iterability of the notion of the right to truth across different settings (as will be discussed in Chapter 6 in relation to Islamic law) is part of its strength as an idea that travels – regardless of its formal status in international law.

C. The Right to Truth as a Reiterated 'Performative Utterance' in International Law

Despite the difficulties of qualifying the right to truth as a CIL norm or general principle of law, it is far from irrelevant. Indeed, its reiterations across different fora cannot be overlooked.[193] Through Austin's theory of

[190] M Koskenniemi, 'General Principles: Reflexions on Constructivist Thinking in International Law' in M Koskenniemi (ed), *Sources of International Law* (Dartmouth, Ashgate, 2000) 398.

[191] See Park (n 142) 26.

[192] ibid 27.

[193] For a helpful discussion of performativity in relation to human rights, see K McNeilly, *Human Rights and Radical Social Transformation: Futurity, Alterity, Power* (London, Routledge, 2017) ch 3 – exploring performativity also in relation to making rights claims; for a critical discussion on iterability, see FB Farrell, 'Iterability and Meaning: The Searle–Derrida debate' (1988) 19(1) *Metaphilosophy* 53. And discussing iterability in relation to law, see inter alia JM Balkin, 'Deconstructive Practice and Legal Theory' (1986) 96 *Yale Law Journal* 743, 749ff – drawing on Derrida's

performativity,[194] the right to truth can be interpreted as being constituted in international law through repeated utterances in different fora, which cumulatively elevate this right's global significance and standing. Furthermore, recognising that the right to truth is already performed in two regional human rights courts (albeit to differing degrees, and with a slightly different focus and content so far) and within the UN system might also contribute to the formal process of formation of general international law over time. This supports the theses of human rights developments through general principles of law put forward by Bassiouni – as evidence of the comparative legal technique (discussed at length in Chapter 2) – and by Simma and Alston as a new norm invested with strong inherent authority. The ultimate test for the status of the right to truth in international law, however, is whether it will continue to be used (performed) for practical purposes in different settings to allow victims and societies to find out about past violence and ensure accountability of those responsible.

This evidence points to the fact that while falling short of a formal status under PIL, the right to truth is being used productively across different international contexts and fora. An innovative way of interpreting these increasing – and cumulative – references could be as 'performative utterances' that do not merely describe an existing legal principle but actually constitute it.[195] In light of Austin's theory of performativity, the repetition of the expression 'right to truth' by different actors, at different times, in different contexts indicates a statement that is not true or false (accurate or inaccurate) as such.[196] Instead, this succession of performative utterances is constitutive of the right to truth in international law, regardless of whether it meets the formal criteria of a CIL norm or a general principle of law. Uttering the words 'right to truth' does not only describe a norm but actually contributes to the creation of a new norm even if its parameters remain unclear.

In this context, there are two aspects to consider in analysing the emergence of a new human right: first, the use of the phrase itself, and second, the repetition by the various systemic agents across different sites of authority in IHRL. The enunciations, repetitions and relative success of the wording 'right to truth' in different languages and fora provide strong empirical evidence. Given the absence of a clear and universal treaty provision on the right to truth as discussed earlier, its invocation in different sites of norm production of IHRL (regional human rights courts, UN, local initiatives) reveals an intention by those bodies – as well as 'truth entrepreneurs'[197] – to find ways to establish this right and put it to good

reading of Austin – and 779ff and J Butler, *Excitable Speech: A Politics of the Performative* (Abingdon, Routledge, 1997).

[194] JL Austin, *How to Do Things with Words* (Oxford, Oxford University Press, 1962).

[195] ibid.

[196] ibid 12.

[197] Borrowing this term from Naftali, 'Crafting a "Right to Truth" in International Law' (n 1).

use. The extent to which a new right emerging from performative utterances is enshrined in formal international law through established procedures is thus subsidiary to the empirical fact of the phrase itself being used by key systemic agents in international law and given some form of legal effect (although the role of these actors is not without problems, as discussed by Naftali[198]). As such, performance is constitutive of this principle and contributes to its legal authority in international law and local settings. Despite its uneven applications and contested meaning, there is significant convergence in the ritualised practice of invoking the right to truth across the fora discussed in this chapter; moreover, through repetition and (cross) citation the force of its authority is accumulated and endorsed by civil society groups and the bottom-up human rights community, as well as by the UN and two regional courts. Given the aims of the right to truth and the seriousness of the abuse it seeks to investigate, it would be paradoxic for this right to be beholden to the traditional theory of sources and formalism. As a performative utterance, capable of iterability, the right to truth is a fascinating example of how a new norm can emerge organically in international law – even if it takes time to become a fully fledged actionable right.

Some ECtHR judges have argued that 'in international law there is a clear trend towards recognising a right to the truth in cases of gross human rights violations'.[199] And in his 2013 annual report, the (then) UN Special Rapporteur on the promotion of truth listed *El-Masri* among the regional sources that consolidate the right to truth globally, alongside the rich IACHR jurisprudence and the African Commission on Human and Peoples' Rights work.[200] Previously the UN-HRC and the IACHR judges drew on ECHR jurisprudence to elucidate laws applicable within their jurisdictions,[201] suggesting that this could happen again in relation to understandings and invocations of the right to truth in different contexts. The emergence of truth-seeking efforts in Muslim-majority societies, such as Morocco, Tunisia and Bahrain (discussed in the final chapter), can also contribute to this trend. As such, the establishment of the

[198] Naftali, *La Donstruction du 'Droit à la Vérité' en Droit International* (n 1).

[199] Joint Partly Dissenting Opinion of Judges Ziemele, De Gaetano, Laffranque and Keller, *Janowiec and others v Russia* [GC] App Nos 55508/07 and 29520/09 (ECHR, 21 October 2013) para 9; *Husayn (Abu Zubaydah) v Poland*, App No 7511/13 (ECHR, 24 July 2014 – application to the Grand Chamber pending) para 489.

[200] Report of the Special Rapporteur on the promotion of truth (2013) (n 26) 19. In relation to the African Commission, the right to the truth is an aspect of the right to an effective remedy to a violation of the African Charter.

[201] ibid 18, citing as a sample: UNGA, 'Report of the Human Rights Committee', 34th session (1979) Doc A/33/40, paras 246, 345. On the IACHR references to the ECHR jurisprudence: *Velásquez Rodríguez v Honduras*, para 28; *Proposed Amendments to the Naturalization Provisions of the Constitution of Costa Rica*, Advisory Opinion OC-4/84, Inter-American Court of Human Rights Series A No 4 (19 January 1984), para 56. See also GL Neuman, 'Import, Export, and Regional Consent in the Inter-American Court of Human Rights' (2008) 19(1) *European Journal of International Law* 101, 106–07. Also, Merrills (n 158) 20.

right to truth in international law depends on its progressive identification in different contexts and on the basis of different legal traditions.

There is a further consideration about the reiterations of the right to truth that cannot be ignored: the expansion of its applicability. Moving beyond the narrow confines of IHL and disappearances, the right to truth is now also attached to torture and inhuman treatment (in principle also including rape, in light of parallel developments in international law that have recognised sexual violence as a form of torture[202]), and extrajudicial executions.[203] The breadth of contexts in which this norm has been invoked is also expanding. In addition to the postauthoritarian transitions of Latin America and Central and Eastern Europe considered by the IACHR and ECHR instruments, the ECtHR has also referred to the right to truth in relation to institutional patterns of human rights abuse in the context of counterterror measures and extraordinary renditions (*El-Masri*, *Al-Nashiri*), historic mass violence (*Janowiec*, *Vasiliauskas*), more recent conflicts (*Aslakhanova*) and current debates about past abuses (*Perinçek*) concerning a range of substantive rights.

The turn to an extralegal theoretical framework to understand the value of the right to truth in international law can help illustrate its importance in practice, without forcing a premature characterisation through formal sources of PIL. It also opens up more critical conversations about how 'right to truth entrepreneurs' shape the process of formulation and diffusion of this principle across jurisdictions.[204] This will be a fundamental premise of the discussion (introduced in Chapter 1, and expanded in Chapter 6) of how Islamic law principles can be invoked to promote truth seeking after serious violence.

IV. CONCLUSION

Analysing the emergence of the right to truth in international law, this chapter considered the significance of the developments and cross-fertilisation between the IACHR, ECHR and UN systems. As such, it argued that despite differences

[202] On rape as a form of torture in international law, see *Delalić et al* (IT-96-21-T), Judgment, Trial Chamber, 16 November 1998, at 487, discussed in O de Frouville, 'The Influence of the European Court of Human Rights' Case Law on International Criminal Law of Torture and Inhuman or Degrading Treatment' (2011) 9(3) *Journal of International Criminal Justice* 633, quoting verbatim: 'it is difficult to envisage circumstances in which rape by, or at the instigation of a public official, or with the consent or acquiescence of an official, could be considered as occurring for a purpose that does not, in some way, involve punishment, coercion, discrimination or intimidation. … Accordingly, whenever rape and other forms of sexual violence meet the aforementioned criteria, then they shall constitute torture, in the same manner as any other acts that meet [these] criteria.' See inter alia discussion in PV Sellers, 'Sexual Torture as a Crime Under International Criminal and Humanitarian Law' (2007) 11 *NY City Law Review* 339; and WA Schabas, 'The Crime of Torture and the International Criminal Tribunals' (2005) 37 *Case Western Reserve Journal of International Law* 349, 362–63.

[203] As discussed in Kilinkner and Davis (n 1) 20–28.

[204] Naftali, 'Crafting a "Right to Truth" in International Law' (n 1). See more extensive discussion in Naftali, *La Construction du 'Droit à la Vérité'* (n 1).

in how the regional jurisdictions and UN have invoked the right to truth and its uncertain legal formalisation in international law, this norm is significant because it is being used (to different degrees and in different ways) by victims and societies at large to hold perpetrators of serious violence to account.

Much like in the IACHR jurisprudence, the ECtHR has considered the right to truth through two distinct, yet related, issues: the link between the right to truth and the state duty to investigate, and the individual and collective dimensions of the right to know about the past in the context of widespread violations that affect society as a whole. In that regard, a more clearly defined right to truth is desirable inasmuch as it helps strengthen the rule of law and promotes confidence in public institutions, as well as contributing to the formation of narratives that feed into broader debates about legacies of violence and abuse at domestic, regional and international levels.

In the quest for a more formal recognition of the right to truth, it may be tempting to characterise it as a CIL norm or a general principle of law to give it greater authority and justiciability. However, it seems premature to qualify the right to truth formally as a source set out in Article 38 of the ICJ Statute. Nevertheless, this does not detract from the substance and usefulness of the right to truth: its repeated uses across different fora can be interpreted as performative utterances that contribute to its practical existence in international law. Regardless of its formal status under PIL, its uses indicate its growing significance regionally as well as internationally – with great domestic potential as well. As such, the upward trajectory of the right to truth and the role of its promoters ('truth entrepreneurs'[205]) should continue to be closely monitored; and, most importantly, there should be no hesitation in invoking this right by those seeking the truth about widespread abuse, in order to hold authorities to account.

This analysis reveals that the expressions of the right to truth in both the IACHR and ECHR systems, as well as the UN, rely on a degree of legal pluralism and comparative law as an interpretative lens. Building on these findings, and in light of the considerations in previous chapters, the next two chapters will turn to the legal systems of Muslim-majority societies where the right to truth requires further conceptualisation for two reasons. First, in light of the comparative approach, it would evidence that there is a broader geographic and cultural appreciation of the right to truth, which in turn will help consolidate the international law foundations of the norm. Indeed, a norm of IHRL cannot be truly 'international' if it does not resonate across different contexts worldwide. Second, demonstrating that the right to truth is conceptualised in both international law and in legal systems informed by Islamic law will increase the chances of its applications in those contexts, offering an additional tool for victims and societies to hold perpetrators of serious violence to account.

[205] On this see in general Naftali, *La Construction du 'Droit à la Vérité'* (n 1) 325 and elsewhere.

5

Islamic Law in the Legal Systems of Muslim-Majority Societies

I. INTRODUCTION

DUE TO RECENT political events and old and new conflicts and forms of authoritarianism affecting Muslim-majority societies, the juxtaposition between the framework of TJ and Islamic law principles merits further analysis. Just as the international normative underpinnings of TJ – described as a 'mess' in Chapter 1[1] – are characterised by legal pluralism, the legal systems of Muslim-majority societies are also made up of a range of normative influences, including formal and informal, official and unofficial, local and transnational, secular and sacred law. As such, the comparative law approach outlined in Chapter 2 can assist in identifying and navigating different normative elements that coexist in a given legal space, including the formants of a legal system, and cryptotypes that shape it.[2]

The distinctive normative force of the *shari'ah* in certain contexts, even when absent in formal law, has been recognised by law-in-context scholars.[3] As a formant – to greater or lesser degrees, depending on context – of the legal systems of Muslim-majority societies, Islamic law principles can inform official lawmaking as well as everyday attitudes, behaviours and narratives around the law and the understandings of justice. For believers who seek to live by the principles of divine revelation, the *shari'ah* is normatively significant because it is morally mandated, regardless of whether the state in which they live identifies as Muslim or not.[4] Nonetheless, as Lama Abu Odeh cautions, the presumption that

[1] In ch 1, C Bell, 'The "New Law" of Transitional Justice' in K Ambos et al (eds), *Building a Future on Peace and Justice: Studies on Transitional Justice, Peace and Development* (Berlin, Springer-Verlag, 2009).

[2] In ch 2, R Sacco, 'Legal Formants: A Dynamic Approach to Comparative Law' (1991) *American Journal of Comparative Law* 1.

[3] On the normative force of *shari'ah*, see B Dupret, 'La sharî'a comme référent législatif: Du droit positif à l'anthropologie du droit' (1996) 25 *Égypte/Monde arabe* 121.

[4] See on this point: JND Anderson, 'The Significance of Islamic Law in the World Today' (1960) 9(2) *American Journal of Comparative Law* 187. On the meanings of 'Islamic law', see inter alia MA Baderin (ed), *Islamic Legal Theory*, vol 1 (Farnham, Ashgate, 2014) xiii, distinguishing between the entire legal system and jurisprudence (*shari'ah*), Islamic jurisprudence only (*fiqh*), and applied law derived from the *shari'ah*.

Islamic law is all-encompassing in the legal systems of Muslim-majority societies is far from reality.[5] Moreover, Islamic law is not a monolithic set of inflexible uniform rules but a rich, doctrinally diverse and dynamic legal tradition with many manifestations.[6] Any legal system, sums up Nahed Samour, 'regardless of the nature of its origin, is to be understood as the reflection of the society of which it is a creation': as such, Islamic law and the international legal order 'must be understood both as powerful systems of rules and norms of reference, but also as legal narratives rooted in, and consequently shaped by, the historical, political, economic, and cultural environment in which they were constituted'.[7] These premises are the starting point for the discussion throughout this chapter.

This chapter provides a general overview of Islamic law and jurisprudence as it may (but not necessarily does) manifest itself within the legal systems of Muslim-majority societies. Drawing primarily on English-language sources, the first part introduces the normative role, sources and methods of Islamic law. The second part considers the human endeavours of jurists in developing Islamic law historically, setting the foundations for today. The third part addresses the relationship between international law and Islamic law, through the substantive and procedural synergies and tensions in the areas of criminal justice and human rights that underpin truth seeking. Taken as a whole, this chapter illustrates how Islamic law can be taken as a fascinating comparator for the pluralistic international framework of TJ. This sets the scene for Chapter 6, which explores how Islamic law might support the right to truth in more detail.

II. ISLAMIC LAW IN CONTEXT: DIVINE NORMATIVITY IN THIS WORLD

In pluralistic legal systems, where state law coexists with other customary and religious beliefs at individual and collective level, comparative law tools informed by anthropology and sociology reveal a multitude of explicit and implicit normative factors that shape society.[8] An example of how religious principles exercise direct and indirect normative influence in society is provided by the varied, and contested, assessments of Christian thought in European legal systems – even when they are formally secular.[9] The normative force of Islamic

[5] L Abu-Odeh, 'The Politics of (Mis)recognition: Islamic Law Pedagogy in American Academia' (2004) 52 *American Journal of Comparative Law* 789.

[6] For a useful account of early differences in Islamic law, see eg R Meshal, 'Antagonistic Sharīʿas and the Construction of Orthodoxy in Sixteenth-Century Ottoman Cairo' (2010) 21(2) *Journal of Islamic Studies* 183.

[7] N Samour, 'Modernized Islamic International Law Concepts as a Third World Approach to International Law' (2012) 72 *Zeitschrift für ausländisches öffentliches Recht und Völkerrecht* 543, 544.

[8] Sacco, 'Legal Formants' (n 2).

[9] European examples of religious invocations in support of constitutions include the Preamble of the Irish Constitution that reads 'In the Name of the Most Holy Trinity, from Whom is all authority and to Whom, as our final end, all actions both of men and States must be referred'

thought in the legal systems of Muslim-majority societies today is comparable. As such, the influence and role of (divine) Islamic law (*shari'ah*) and (human) jurisprudence (*fiqh*) in Muslim-majority contexts (and states) requires careful scrutiny.

The quasi-totality of law in Muslim-majority societies emanates from states (explicitly Islamic, or not), and most of that law is secular and political in nature; the *shari'ah* therefore does not exist in splendid isolation in any context apart from in scholarly work. As such, in its earthly manifestations, Islamic law principles coexist alongside other law, and might be more or less visible or prominent depending on a myriad of factors. Therefore, as Lama Abu Odeh cautions, presuming the primacy of the *shari'ah* in the legal systems of Muslim-majority societies would create a 'fantasy effect' failing to account for non-Islamic law in those settings, including Western legal transplants, and products of colonialism.[10] From its beginnings, Islamic law was intimately connected to local Arab customs.[11] It deals with both religious duties (*'ibadat*) as well as human transactions (*mu'amilat*): some scholars have described the latter as 'a man-made law' with 'no pretense to being a religious law except that it may be said to lay more emphasis on moral considerations than is usually the case with other legal systems'.[12] Moreover, as Fatima Mernissi explains in relation to the invocation of tradition in Muslim societies, which could include invocations to the *shari'ah*, there is a fundamental difference between 'what people actually do, the decisions they make, the aspirations they secretly entertain or display', and 'the discourses they develop about themselves' used 'to articulate their political claims'.[13] As Abu Odeh explains, 'giving Islamic law an overarching status analytically in our approach to law in the Islamic world, distorts our understanding of legal phenomena'.[14] Instead, it is vital to consider how the uses and discourses around the *shari'ah* carry a social and political meaning, as well as a religious one. This chapter, as well as the entire project, is premised on this contextual understanding.

and 'Humbly acknowledging all our obligations to our Divine Lord, Jesus Christ', available at www.irishstatutebook.ie/en/constitution/. Even at regional EU level there has been a heated debate around the (non) inclusion of a formal reference to the Christian heritage of Europe; see inter alia JHH Weiler, *Un'Europa cristiana: un saggio esplorativo* (Milan, BUR, 2003); R McCrea, 'Religion as a Basis of Law in the Public Order of the European Union' (2009) 16 *Columbia Journal of European Law* 81. From a regional human rights perspective on the role of religion in the jurisdiction of the ECHR, see inter alia I Leigh and R Ahdar, 'Post-secularism and the European Court of Human Rights: Or How God Never Really Went Away' (2012) 75(6) *MLR* 1064.

[10] Abu-Odeh (n 5) 823.

[11] On this point, see inter alia M Khadduri, 'Nature and Sources of Islamic Law (1953) 22 *George Washington Law Review* 3.

[12] On this distinction in relation to the (non)religious nature of Islamic law, see GM Badr, 'Islamic Law: Its Relation to Other Legal Systems' (1977–78) 26 *American Journal of Comparative Law* 187, 188–89.

[13] F Mernissi, *Beyond the Veil: Male–Female Dynamics in Modern Muslim Society* (Bloomington, Indiana University Press, 1987) viii.

[14] Abu-Odeh (n 5) 823.

Notwithstanding these warnings, a sociolegal analysis cannot, equally, ignore Islamic law. Building on Bourdieu's sociology of the juridical field and Marie-Françoise Rigaux's theory of *réticularité des ordres normatifs*, Baudouin Dupret explores the relationship between the *shari'ah* and state law (specifically, Egypt), whereby autonomy and compenetration of religious and secular norms coexist.[15] In the context of ideological sedimentation (*sédimentation idéologique*), the pull of (presumably) traditional culture, such as the *shari'ah*, offers an important set of normative values for individuals as well as legal systems.[16] Thus, the potential significance of the *shari'ah* as a *référent législatif* in Muslim-majority societies cannot be overlooked.

The moral pull of Islamic law allows even ostensibly non-Islamic, neutral formal laws to be interpreted through a religious lens by religious individuals among elected representatives, civil society and citizens of secular states.[17] For religious citizens living outside a 'religiously homogeneous population within a religiously legitimated state', as is the case of many contemporary societies, the 'certainties of faith' coexist with the 'fallible beliefs of a secular nature'.[18] A joint reading of An-Na'im and Habermas suggests that when citizens of a state (or, more broadly, society) are Muslim and participate in the public sphere, their religious convictions are capable of seeping into a secular political and legal system. A historical example can be found in the relationship between *shari'ah* and *qanun* (religious law and secular law) throughout the Ottoman Empire.[19] Today, Islamic law holds a special position in the legal systems of Islamic states – those twenty-six countries whose constitutions 'proclaim an Islamic state or Islam as the state religion', as indicated by Paul McDonough.[20] However, regardless of the formal Islamic designation of official state laws, secular legal systems of Muslim-majority societies and societies where there is a sizeable Muslim community may be influenced by Islamic law.[21] The degree of permeability of the legal systems of Muslim-majority societies to normative religious principles is context-dependent and is not the object of this study. Suffice it to

[15] Dupret (n 3) 130–31.

[16] ibid 144.

[17] AA An-Na'im, *Islam and the Secular State: Negotiating the Future of Shari'a* (Cambridge, MA, Harvard University Press, 2009).

[18] J Habermas, 'Religion in the Public Sphere' (2006) 14(1) *European Journal of Philosophy* 1, 9, also drawing from J Rawls, 'The Idea of Public Reason Revisited' (1997) 64(3) *University of Chicago Law Review* 765.

[19] On this point, see eg C Imber, *Ebu's-su'ud: The Islamic Legal Tradition* (Edinburgh, Edinburgh University Press, 1997) 24ff. On the Ottoman Empire, see inter alia H Inalcik, *The Ottoman Empire: The Classical Age 1300–1600* (London, Phoenix, 1973); D Quataert, *The Ottoman Empire, 1700–1922* (Cambridge, Cambridge University Press, 2008).

[20] P McDonough, *Human Rights Commitments of Islamic States* (Oxford, Hart, 2020) 2.

[21] A fascinating example is the emergence of British-Muslim law; see eg RC Akhtar, 'Plural Approaches to Faith-based Dispute Resolution by Britain's Muslim Communities' (2019) 31(3) *Child & Family Law Quarterly* 189; L Pilgram, 'British-Muslim Family Law and Citizenship' (2012) 16(5) *Citizenship Studies* 769; SS Ali, 'Authority and Authenticity: Sharia Councils, Muslim Women's Rights, and the English Courts' (2013) 25 *Child & Family Law Quarterly* 113.

say that when secular and religious norms meet, synergies and tensions can be approached through a sociolegal lens, informed by theories of legal pluralism and comparative methods (discussed in Chapter 2), and in light of the autonomy–compenetration thesis espoused by Dupret.[22]

The normative force of Islamic law, jurisprudence and legal traditions in Muslim-majority societies is based on the revealed sacred nature of the *shari'ah*.[23] The core normative corpus draws on the Qur'an and the Sunna/Hadith (traditions of the prophet Mohammad), which are uncontested in their primacy,[24] and the supplementary sources, *ijma'* (juristic consensus) and *qiyas* (legal analogy).[25] Islamic law also includes subsidiary sources/legal methods that influence the normative corpus to varying degrees, such as *ijtihad* (legal reasoning), *istihsan* (juristic preference), *istislah* or *maslaha* (welfare/common good/public interest), *urf* (custom) and *darurah* (necessity).[26] The supplementary sources – which tend to overlap with methodological approaches – and the subsidiary legal methods are 'products of human reasoning' through which the revealed sources 'could be extended to cover new developments of life'.[27] Therefore, the phrase 'Islamic legal tradition' denotes a multilayered Islamic normative *acquis* (borrowing, mutatis mutandis, from EU law), capturing the rich discourse around law based on, and inspired by, the *shari'ah* and its legal methods.

[22] Dupret (n 3) 130–31.

[23] The term 'Islamic law' has been widely discussed in the English language academic literature; see eg R Peters and P Bearman, 'Introduction: The Nature of the Sharia' in P Bearman and R Peters (eds), *The Ashgate Research Companion to Islamic Law* (Aldershot, Ashgate, 2014): 'it denotes at least two different concepts. On the one hand it can stand for Islamic normativity in the fields of ritual, morality and law – in other words, Sharia in its totality. … On the other hand, Islamic law can refer only to the legal normativity of Sharia – Sharia in a narrow sense.'

[24] For an overview of different academic approaches on the Qur'an and Sunna as the primary sources, see H Berg, 'The Divine Sources' in P Bearman and R Peters (eds), *The Ashgate Research Companion to Islamic Law* (Aldershot, Ashgate, 2014).

[25] There is a rich literature on Islamic law in English, including inter alia, recent handbooks: A Emon and R Ahmed, *The Oxford Handbook of Islamic Law* (Oxford, Oxford University Press, 2018); K Abou El Fadl, AA Ahmad and SF Hassan (eds), *Routledge Handbook of Islamic Law* (London, Routledge, 2019); P Bearman and R Peters (eds), *The Ashgate Research Companion to Islamic Law* (Aldershot, Ashgate, 2014); and other authoritative works, such as MH Kamali, *Principles of Islamic Jurisprudence*, 3rd edn (Cambridge, The Islamic Texts Society, 2003), and *Shari'ah Law: An Introduction* (Oxford, Oneworld, 2008); WB Hallaq, *An Introduction to Islamic Law* (Cambridge, Cambridge University Press, 2009) and *Shari'a* (Cambridge, Cambridge University Press, 2009); M Rohe, *Islamic Law in Past and Present* (Leiden, Brill, 2015); as well as earlier 'Orientalist' and Western studies of Islamic law, including I Goldziher, *Muslim Studies* (Albany, SUNY Press, 1967) (German version 1889–90) and *Introduction to Islamic Theology and Law* (Princeton, NJ, Princeton University Press, 1981) (German version 1910); J Schacht, *The Origins of Muhammadan Jurisprudence* (Oxford, Oxford University Press, 1950) and *Introduction to Islamic Law* (Oxford, Clarendon Press, 1966); B Weiss, *The Spirit of Islamic Law* (Athens, University of Georgia Press, 1998).

[26] For a comprehensive overview and analysis of the sources and methods of Islamic law, see literature cited at n 25.

[27] MA Baderin, *International Human Rights and Islamic Law* (Oxford, Oxford University Press, 2003) 37.

Straddling positivism and natural law theory, Islamic law has been described as 'the process of a practiced discipline of deliberative and purposeful practical reasoning in which rulings are developed primarily through analogical dynamics'.[28] While the *shari'ah* is 'immutable, unchangeable, objectively perfect Divine truth', *fiqh*, the human understanding of *shari'ah*, is 'subjective, partial, subject to error and change', explaining the 'number of competing schools of thought of *fiqh*'.[29] *Fiqh* has been described as the 'practical jurisprudence' concerned with 'the articulation of actual rules of law', whereas *usul al-fiqh* is the 'theoretical jurisprudence', addressing 'the theory of law and the methodological principles governing the formulations of rules of law'.[30] For Kamali, *usul al-fiqh* is 'the science of the sources and methodology of the law', whereby 'the Qur'an and *Sunnah* constitute the sources and the subject-matter to which the methodology of *usul al-fiqh* is applied' – combining theoretical and pragmatic aspects.[31] This illustrates how intertwined positive norms and theoretical jurisprudence are in the conceptualisation, applications and development of Islamic law.

The discussion so far illustrates the centrality of human effort in developing Islamic law. Wael Hallaq identifies four stages: (1) 'the evolution of a complete judiciary with a fully-fledged court system and law of evidence and procedure'; (2) 'the full elaboration of a positive legal doctrine'; (3) 'the full emergence of a science of legal methodology and interpretation' reflecting 'hermeneutical, intellectual and juristic self-consciousness'; and (4) 'the full emergence of the doctrinal legal schools'.[32] The endeavours of judges, lawmakers, scholars and teachers have shaped Islamic law both theoretically and practically, alongside the compenetration with non-religious norms (discussed earlier, referencing Dupret); the centrality of human efforts in developing Islamic law emerges as a theme throughout this chapter.

As a legal tradition based on human effort as well as divine revelation, 'Islamic law unfolded through the robust activity of legal specialists who established a process of continuous use, interpretation, exposition and expansion, and a technical linguistic practice that became the heart and soul of the legal system.'[33] Khaled Abou El Fadl highlights the 'markedly pluralistic, discursive and exploratory ethos that became the very heart of [the Islamic legal tradition's]

[28] K Abou El Fadl, 'What Type of Law Is Islamic Law?' in K Abou El Fadl, AA Ahmad and SF Hassan (eds), *Routledge Handbook of Islamic Law* (London, Routledge, 2019).

[29] ibid. On the schools of Islamic law (*madhab*), see inter alia LA Bsoul, 'The Emergence of the Major Schools of Islamic Law' in K Abou El Fadl, AA Ahmad and SF Hassan (eds) *Routledge Handbook of Islamic Law* (London, Routledge, 2019) and PR Powers, 'The Schools of Law' in P Bearman and R Peters (eds) *The Ashgate Research Companion to Islamic Law* (Aldershot, Ashgate, 2014).

[30] Weiss (n 25) xi.

[31] Kamali, *Principles of Islamic Jurisprudence* (n 25) 1ff, 9ff.

[32] WB Hallaq, *The Origins and Evolution of Islamic Law* (Cambridge, Cambridge University Press, 2004) 3ff.

[33] Abou El Fadl (n 28).

distinctive character'.[34] But the term 'tradition' fails to capture the variations within Islamic law.[35] Also, Islamic law as 'tradition' may be invoked instrumentally to bestow a divine, untouchable aura on law as a tool of control within social power relations.[36] Moreover, the impact of colonialism and indigenous elitism has narrowed down the structural and epistemological understanding of *shari'ah* by 'imposing a positivist model'.[37] As such, Islamic law cannot be reduced to a single, discrete, positive legal system, neither of a self-declared Muslim state, nor of an idealised abstract *shari'ah* divorced from *fiqh* and social context. These premises help situate the following analysis of the sources of Islamic law.

A. Sources of Islamic Law

As discussed previously, the sources of Islamic law are understood through both sacred and secular lenses. The classical jurist-theologians agreed that the infallible Qur'anic revelations were an unquestionable source of law, but, as Khadduri reports, 'here agreement ended, since the Koran provided no clear guidance for further legislation'.[38] For scholars today, the challenge remains the same. The paragraphs that follow offer a summary overview of the main sources, drawing primarily on Kamali's *Principles of Islamic Jurisprudence* and other key texts in English, as well as more critical approaches by An-Na'im. This review indicates that the two main sources of Islamic law are open to a range of textual interpretations that are, essentially, a product of human endeavours.

i. Qur'an

It is generally uncontested that the Qur'an, divinely revealed to the prophet Mohammed through the angel Gabriel, is the primary and most important source of Islamic law.[39] Hinting at the human agency in giving effect to its normative primacy, Fazur Rahman suggests that the Qur'an 'must be made the primary and indeed the sole director of human life and the source of law',

[34] ibid.

[35] On the variations within Islamic law, see eg TP Daniels, 'Introduction: Sharia Dynamics and the Anthropology of Islam' in T Daniels (ed), *Sharia Dynamics: Contemporary Anthropology of Religion* (Cham, Palgrave Macmillan, 2017).

[36] On tradition, E Hobsbawm and T Ranger (eds), *The Invention of Tradition* (Cambridge, Cambridge University Press, 1983), in conjunction with law and social power in P Bourdieu, 'The Force of Law: Toward a Sociology of the Juridical Field' (1986) 38 *Hastings Law Journal* 805.

[37] Abou El Fadl (n 28).

[38] M Khadduri, *War and Peace in the Law of Islam* (Baltimore, MD, Johns Hopkins University Press, 1955) 54. And also M Khadduri, 'Islam and the Modern Law of Nations' (1956) 50(2) *American Journal of International Law* 358.

[39] See inter alia Kamali (n 25) 18.

regardless of its relatively small portion of 'strictly legislative' verses.[40] Kamali identifies roughly 350 legal *ayat* (verses) out of around 6,200, generally revealed in response to practical problems faced by the community.[41] More conservative estimates indicate 190 legal verses (3 per cent of the total).[42] But the content of the provisions is not always crystal clear.

To deal with textual uncertainties, Kamali distinguishes between definitive text, which is clear, specific and not open to interpretation, and speculative text open to interpretation and *ijtihad*, informed by the overall meaning and purpose of the holy book and the Sunna (traditions of the Prophet).[43] More radical approaches to textual uncertainties distinguish between verses revealed in Mecca (a time of peace) or Medina (during conflict), as proposed by Taha and An-Na'im.[44] According to their (controversial) position, the 'earlier message of Mecca is in fact the eternal and fundamental message of Islam, emphasizing the inherent dignity of all human beings, regardless of gender, religious belief, race, and so forth'.[45] In particular, An-Na'im considers the Meccan verses more in line with the principles of international human rights.[46] He proposes therefore a 'new principle of interpretation that would permit applying some verses of [the] Qur'an and accompanying Sunna instead of others, … breaking the deadlock between the objectives of reform and the limitations of the conception and techniques of historical Shari'a'.[47] In practice, this approach can contribute (and has contributed) to deepening the conversation on the synergies between Islamic law and human rights, but it has not been received with universal enthusiasm. For example, Kamali rejects the possibility of critical textual analysis because:

> The Qur'an is an indivisible whole, and a guide for belief and action that must be accepted and followed in its entirety. Hence, any attempt to follow some parts of the Qur'an and abandon others will be totally invalid.[48]

The tensions, however, might be more about how the interpretative process is framed than about substantive outcomes. It is clear that uncertainty is approached and resolved through human efforts.

Other contentious issues surrounding Qur'anic interpretation include the distinction between literal and metaphorical meanings of the text and the relationship between general principles and specific applications.[49] Kamali argues

[40] Fazur Rahman, *Islam*, 2nd rev edn (Chicago, IL, University of Chicago Press, 1979) 68ff.
[41] Kamali, *Principles of Islamic Jurisprudence* (n 25) 26.
[42] Badr (n 12) 188.
[43] Kamali, *Principles of Islamic Jurisprudence* (n 25) 27ff, 35ff.
[44] MM Taha, *The Second Message of Islam* (Syracuse, NY, Syracuse University Press, 1987), and AA An-Na'im, *Toward an Islamic Reformation: Civil Liberties, Human rights, and International Law* (Syracuse, NY, Syracuse University Press, 1996).
[45] An-Na'im (n 44) 52, quoting Taha (n 44).
[46] ibid 52–68.
[47] ibid 34ff.
[48] Kamali, *Principles of Islamic Jurisprudence* (n 25) 18.
[49] ibid 35ff.

that 'the Qur'an is specific on matters that are deemed to be unchangeable, but in matters that are liable to change, it merely lays down general guidelines'.[50] He argues that 'the general in the Qur'an has a value of its own' and provides guidance, validity and 'substance for an ever-continuing series of commentaries and interpretations'.[51] Thus, 'commentators throughout the centuries have attempted to derive a fresh message, a new lesson or a new principle from the Qur'an that was more suitable to the realities of their times and the different phases of development in the life of their community' – attesting to the adaptability of the Qur'an across time and place.[52] Kamali warns against rigidity, as 'the Qur'an itself warns the believers against seeking the regulation of everything by the express terms of divine revelation'.[53] He argues that the purpose of an injunction 'gives the *mujtahid* [ie the scholar performing ijtihad/independent legal reasoning] the green light to enquire into the causes and reasons behind its injunctions, or whether it exists simply to facilitate a better understanding of the text'.[54] As such, the importance of human analysis is reaffirmed:

> Since the realisation of the objectives (maqasid) of the Shari'ah necessitates identification of the cause/rationale of the *ahkam*, it becomes our duty to discover these in order to be able to pursue the general objectives of the Lawgiver.[55]

This analysis suggests that the general principles in the Qur'an are sufficiently dynamic to accommodate an exploration of whether transitional truth seeking might be supported. Moreover, according to the proposition that 'what the Qur'an has left unregulated is meant to be devised, in accordance with the general objectives of the Lawgiver, through mutual consultation and *ijtihad*',[56] there would be ample scope to explore the right to truth in the absence of clear textual injunctions to the contrary (which are absent). Thus, it is possible to explore whether the Qur'an might support transitional truth seeking and the right to truth. This becomes evident in the *ayat* cited in support of the right to truth in Islamic law, selected by the esteemed Islamic scholars interviewed for this project and reported in Chapter 6.

ii. Hadith

The second most important source in Islamic law is the *hadith* (Sunna), the collection of 'the Prophet's lifetime sayings, deeds and tacit approvals on

[50] ibid 39.
[51] ibid 44.
[52] ibid.
[53] ibid 42, citing 'O you believers, do not keep asking about things which, if they were expounded to you, would become troublesome for you' (5:101).
[54] ibid 46ff.
[55] ibid 49–50.
[56] ibid. On *ijtihad*, see inter alia WB. Hallaq, 'Was the Gate of Ijtihad Closed?' (1984) 16(1) *International Journal of Middle East Studies* 3.

different issues, both spiritual and temporal'.[57] Unlike the Qur'an, the 'redaction and canonization of the Sunna of the Prophet' in major collections of *hadith* has been less linear.[58] As a result, ascertaining *hadith* accuracy and authenticity is complex and contested.[59] Reports of sayings or practice of the prophet witnessed directly or indirectly by contemporary followers (male and female) were transmitted to subsequent generations of Muslims and codified over time.[60] It is worth noting in this context the centrality of women in transmitting the *hadith*: Leila Ahmed reports that over 2,210 *hadith* are attributed to Aisha (Mohammed's widow), of which around 300 are contained in the most highly regarded collections (Al Bukhari and Muslim), known for their stringent standards.[61] She aptly points out that 'to accept women's testimony on the words and deeds of the prophet was to accept their authority on matters intended to have a prescriptive, regulatory relation to mores and laws'.[62] As such, the second most important source of the *shari'ah* does not discriminate between the gender of the transmitter, which offers a strong argument for gender equality in the study and promotion of Islamic law.

iii. Additional Sources

Additional sources are essentially man-made rules based on applications through *ijtihad* of normative principles based on the Qur'an and *hadith* in a given spatial and temporal context.[63] The exact number of these additional sources varies between scholars; for example, Cherif Bassiouni lists twelve supplemental sources of Islamic law, which build on analogy and consensus:

1. Ijma, consensus of opinion of learned scholars and judges
2. Qiyas, analogy
3. 'Urf, custom and usage
4. Istislah or Maslahah, consideration of the public good

[57] Baderin (n 27) 35.

[58] Berg (n 24) 4ff. The six main Sunni collections of *hadith* are: al-Bukhari, Muslim, Abu Dawud, al-Tirmidhi, al-Nasa'i and Ibn Majah. Berg reports that the Shia collections of *hadith* are broader and include the (Shia) imams.

[59] For a comprehensive overview of the *hadith*, see MH Kamali, *A Textbook of Hadith Studies: Authenticity, Compilation, Classification and Criticism of Hadith* (Markfield, The Islamic Foundation, 2005). See also JAC Brown, *Hadith: Muhammad's Legacy in the Medieval and Modern World* (New York, Oneworld, 2009); H Motzki (ed), *Hadith: Origins and developments* (London, Routledge, 2016).

[60] The most authoritative collection of *hadith* was compiled by al-Bukhari, about 300 years after the time of Mohammed, as discussed in Kamali (n 59) 31ff.

[61] L Ahmed, *Women and Gender in Islam: Historical Roots of a Modern Debate* (New Haven, CT, Yale University Press, 1992) 73. See also A Sayeed, *Women and the Transmission of Religious Knowledge in Islam* (Cambridge, Cambridge University Press, 2013) 26; and NH Barazanghi, *Women's Identity and Rethinking the Hadith* (Abingdon, Routledge, 2016).

[62] Ahmed (n 61) 72–75.

[63] On this, see inter alia Kamali, *Shari'ah law: An Introduction* (n 25) 19ff.

5. Istihsan, reasoning based on the best outcome, or equity
6. The practices of the four first 'wise Khulafa', a form of authoritative precedent
7. The decisions of learned judges
8. Treaties and pacts
9. Contracts
10. The edicts of the Khulafa and local rulers which are in conformity with the Shari'ah
11. Fatawa (plural of fatwa) of the most learned scholars
12. Ijtihad.[64]

Supplementary sources allow a degree of flexibility for derogation as they are not in principle immutable like divine revelations. For instance, the practice of a medieval *khalifa* may contrast present-day human rights treaties;[65] or Ottoman judgments on commercial transactions may contradict business practices today.[66] Among other examples, the death penalty has been challenged because it does not guarantee the best outcome (*istihsan*),[67] and gender inequality can be opposed on the grounds of public good (*maslaha*).[68] This flexibility, and the *maslaha* in particular, provides helpful interpretative tools to pursue transitional truth seeking in the legal systems of Muslim-majority contexts.

B. Objectives of Islamic Law (*Maqasid as-Shari'ah*) and *Maslaha*

The main literary sources of Islamic law discussed earlier do not account for many contemporary legal challenges – including those emerging from conflict or authoritarianism. To fill these gaps, normative principles that underpin the entire system of Islamic law and jurisprudence can help. The objectives of *shari'ah* – *maqasid as-shari'ah* – provide an illustration of the core principles of Islamic law while at the same time illustrating the deeper meaning of the *shari'ah* beyond literal aspects, the 'higher intents of Islamic law'.[69] The *maqasid as-shari'ah* are intimately linked to the notion of *maslaha*, described as 'a cause or source of something good and beneficial', understood as public interest and

[64] MC Bassiouni, *The Shari'ah, Islamic Law and Post-conflict Justice* (distributed at the 11th Specialization Course in International Criminal Law, International Institute of Higher Studies in Criminal Sciences (ISISC) Siracusa, 2011) 26 (subsequently published as MC Bassiouni, *The Shari'a and Islamic Criminal Justice in Time of War and Peace* (Cambridge, Cambridge University Press, 2014).

[65] See inter alia An-Na'im (n 44).

[66] For background reading, see F Akaddaf, 'Application of the United Nations Convention on Contracts for the International Sale of Goods (CISG) to Arab Islamic Countries: Is the CISG Compatible with Islamic Law Principles' (2001) 13 *Pace International Law Review* 1.

[67] For instance WA Schabas, 'Islam and the Death Penalty' (2000) 9 *William & Mary Bill of Rights Journal* 223; Baderin (n 27) 66ff.

[68] See eg M Fadel, 'Two Women, One Man: Knowledge, Power, and Gender in Medieval Sunni Legal Thought' (1997) 29(2) *International Journal of Middle East Studies* 185.

[69] M Bohlander, 'Sisters in Law – Using Maqāṣid al-Shariʿah to Advance the Conversation between Islamic and Secular Legal Thinking' (2014) 28(3) *Arab Law Quarterly* 257, 259.

more broadly as well-being or welfare.[70] These close ties between the objectives of the *shari'ah* and *maslaha* suggest the two, while distinct, cannot be treated separately.[71] The connection between *maqasid* and *maslaha* is highlighted by 'the purposive nature of Islamic law' aimed at 'promoting the social welfare of the people'.[72] This perspective reflects the 'shift [of] one's hermeneutical emphasis from the letter of the text to its purpose, and thus, to the ethical direction behind it'.[73] There is also a special relationship also between *maqasid* and *ijtihad*: Kamali suggests that the former is essential to the latter, because literal textual examinations would be insufficient without a broader understanding of the general aims of Islamic law.[74] As such, the objectives of the *shari'ah* and *maslaha* provide a valuable moral and ethical compass in understanding and interpreting Islamic law, as well as conceptualising how the *shari'ah* may regulate issues not explicitly dealt with in the primary sources.

The conventional list of *maqasid as-shari'ah* by twelfth-century scholar al-Ghazali and reported across numerous sources comprises five necessities: the protection of religion, life, intellect, offspring and property.[75] These also reflect the 'criminology' of the Qur'an.[76] Over time, this list has evolved, with some commentators including justice, freedom and equality, and offering novel interpretations of the purposes of law in light of *maslaha*.[77] For instance, Kamali

[70] F Opwis, 'Maslaha in Contemporary Islamic Legal Theory' (2005) 12 *Islamic Law & Society* 182, 182–83. In footnote 4, Opwis considers that *maslaha* 'should be translated as "public interest" only when it refers to the permissibility of the political authorities to issue rulings that concur with the public good within the sphere of *siyasa*. When, however, a mufti gives a legal opinion on grounds of maslaha, this has little to do with "public" well-being but is usually based on considerations of a single, private case.' See also F Opwis, *Maṣlaḥa and the Purpose of the Law: Islamic Discourse on Legal Change from the 4th/10th to 8th/14th Century* (Leiden, Brill, 2010).

[71] The phrase '*maqasid cum maslaha*' is reported in F Opwis, 'New Trends in Islamic Legal Theory: *Maqāṣid al-Sharī'a as a New Source of Law?*' (2017) 75 *Die Welt des Islams* 7, 17, and on the distinctions between them, 13–14.

[72] A Duderija, 'Contemporary Muslim Reformist Thought and Maqāṣid cum Maṣlaḥa Approaches to Islamic Law: An Introduction' in A Duderija (ed), *Maqasid al-Shari'a and Contemporary Reformist Muslim Thought: An Examination* (New York, Palgrave Macmillan, 2014) 3.

[73] D Johnston, 'Maqasid al-Shari'a: Epistemology and Hermeneutics of Muslim Theologies of Human Rights' (2007) 47(2) *Die Welt des Islams* 149, 186.

[74] MH Kamali, '*Maqasid al-Shari'ah*: The Objectives of Islamic Law' (1999) 38(2) *Islamic Studies* 193, 204ff referencing M Tahir ibn 'Ashur, *Maqasid al-Shari'ah al'Islamiyyah* (Tunis, Matba'at al-Istiqamah, 1996).

[75] A Ḥāmid Muḥammad b. Muḥammad al-Ghazāli, *al-Mustaṣfā min 'ilm al-uṣūl*, cited in Opwis (n 71) 10 (at footnote 8), and discussed widely in the literature on the *maqasid as-shari'ah*, including inter alia Kamali (n 74) 199; GE Attia, *Towards Realization of the Higher Intents of Islamic Law: Maqasid Al-shari'ah: a Functional Approach* (London, International Institute of Islamic Thought, 2007); Johnston (n 73); J Auda, *Maqasid al-Shariah: A Beginner's Guide* (London, International Institute of Islamic Thought, 2008); I Nassery et al (eds), *The Objectives of Islamic Law: The Promises and Challenges of the Maqāṣid Al-sharī'a* (Lanham, MD, Lexington Books, 2018); A Duderija (ed), *Maqasid al-Shari'a and Contemporary Reformist Muslim Thought: An Examination* (New York, Palgrave Macmillan, 2014); F Opwis, 'Maqaṣid al-Shari'ah' in K Abou El Fadl, AA Ahmad and SF Hassan (eds), *Routledge Handbook of Islamic Law* (London, Routledge, 2019).

[76] Kamali (n 74) 200.

[77] Opwis, 'Maslaha in Contemporary Islamic Legal Theory' (n 70) 182–83.

reports that classical jurist ibn Taymiyyah departed from the notion of a finite number of *maqasid*, expanding to 'an open-ended list of values' generally accepted by his contemporaries.[78] Among those, Yusuf al-Qaradawi included social welfare, freedom, human dignity and fraternity.[79] Kamali himself adds economic development and research in technology and science.[80] This open-ended list of values echoes human rights debates around what aims are worthy of protection (such as the emerging right to truth).

As aptly summarised by Felicitas Opwis, 'the attainment of *maṣlaḥa* is God's intention in revealing His law to humankind. A ruling that brings about *maṣlaḥa* thus accords with the objectives of the divine law.'[81] According to Kamali (and other contemporary scholars), *maslaha* is indeed 'the summa' of the objectives of Islamic law, and justice (and education) are corollaries of it.[82] The shift from individual values of the *maqasid as-shari'ah* of the classic al-Ghazali approach, towards societal and collective values espoused more recently illustrates the dynamism of the aims of *shari'ah* and *maslaha*.[83] Indeed, the 'commitment to universal social values can be regarded as the strength of modern interpretations of the purposes of the law'.[84] As such, the *maslaha* contributes to the gradual renewal and formalisation of normative principles of collective value.

The 'usefulness of *maqāṣid al-sharīʿa* as a philosophic-legal cum hermeneutical tool' in what Adis Duderija terms the 'the contemporary Muslim reformist project' is apparent.[85] The notion of *maslaha* can serve as 'a vehicle of legal change' to regulate situations not addressed in scriptural sources.[86] The constructive encounter between *shari'ah* and human rights (discussed again later) provides an example.[87] But 'the lack of agreement on how to define maṣlaḥa in concrete terms and its relationship to the textually explicit rulings of the Qurʾan and Sunna leave it open to much controversy and misuse in the name of the divine intent'.[88] More generally, the definition of *maqasid as-shari'ah* risks being subsumed by states and 'state ideology' as expressed through law-making, policy-making and institutions.[89] Claims to govern 'in accordance to the divine law'

[78] Kamali (n 74) citing T al-Din ibn Taymiyyah, *Majmu' Fatawa Shaykh al-Islam Ibn Taymiyyah*, comp A al-Rahman ibn Qasim (Beirut, Muassasat al-Risalah, 1398) 200–01.

[79] ibid, citing Y al-Qaradawi, *al-Madkhal li Dirasat al-Shari'ah al-Islamiyyah* (Cairo, Maktabah Wahnah, 1411/1990).

[80] ibid 201.

[81] Opwis. 'New Trends in Islamic Legal Theory' (n 71) 10.

[82] Kamali (n 74) 194.

[83] For a discussion of modern scholars, see Opwis (n 71) 29.

[84] ibid 30.

[85] Duderija, 'Contemporary Muslim Reformist Thought' (n 72). Similar points are made by Baderin (n 27) 42–44.

[86] Opwis, 'Maslaha in Contemporary Islamic Legal Theory' (n 71) 182–183 and 188.

[87] Johnston (n 73). And generally, Baderin (n 27). For an overview of the various approaches to Islamic law and human rights, see S Dunn, 'Islamic Law and Human Rights' in AM Emon and R Ahmed (eds) *Oxford Handbook of Islamic Law* (Oxford, Oxford University Press, 2015).

[88] Opwis, 'New Trends in Islamic Legal Theory' (n 71) 31.

[89] ibid.

(*siyasa shari'ah*) helps 'ensur[e] that Islamic law does not become obsolete in the modern state', and 'bestows legitimacy to the state by rendering its laws and policies authentically Islamic'.[90] But the risks of politicisation, and indeed political abuse, of the *maqasid as-shari'ah* and *maslaha* cannot be overlooked. In relation to human rights, there could be manipulations by governments and those in power, as well as 'by western powers to achieve greater control in the Mideast, and by opposition groups in those same countries in order to resist their governments' attempt to curtail their activism'.[91] Thus, while the *maqasid as-shari'ah* and *maslaha* operate within a specific social and political context, with the consequences that may entail, they can still make an important contribution in developing laws that meet the requirements of Islamic law as well as international human rights standards, including for transitional truth seeking, as discussed in the final chapter.

III. THE MANIFESTATIONS AND JURISPRUDENTIAL EVOLUTIONS OF ISLAMIC LAW: HUMAN EFFORTS

The discussion so far offered a glimpse into the role of Islamic law in the legal systems of Muslim-majority societies, in which *shari'ah* and Islamic jurisprudence operate as formants, bridging sacred and secular normative dimensions. Despite the manifestly divine character of the core sources of Islamic law, its jurisprudence and supplementary sources owe their development to human endeavours. Moreover, as a considerable portion of Islamic law regulates human relations, its interpretations and applications are informed by context. In light of the purposive nature of Islamic law, the objectives of *shari'ah* and the principle of *maslaha* illustrate the dynamism and flexibility in responding to contemporary challenges and surviving the test of time thanks to two key factors: firstly, its normativity (discussed earlier); secondly, the skill of its interpreters and proponents.

The survival of Islamic law despite the consolidation of the state-centric shift in Ottoman Turkey and nineteenth-century Egypt, teamed with legal borrowing and colonial influences, illustrates its continued significance in Muslim-majority societies.[92] Today, the discourse of Islamic law is employed for many purposes. In the context of contemporary modernism, as noted by Suha Taji-Farouki, 'tradition is recruited either to legitimise change, or to defend against perceived innovation and to preserve threatened values'.[93] It can therefore operate as a double-edged sword. Proponents of progressive Muslim thought, as described

[90] ibid.
[91] Johnston (n 73) 181.
[92] O Arabi, *Studies in Modern Islamic Law and Jurisprudence* (The Hague, Kluwer Law International, 2001) 1 and elsewhere.
[93] S Taji-Farouki, *Modern Muslim Intellectuals and the Qur'an* (Oxford, Oxford University Press, 2004) 1.

by Adis Duderija, challenge 'both (neo)traditional and puritan Islamic hegemonic discourses on many issues' and 'their Western-centric conceptualisations and interpretations'.[94] For these actors, many of whom are women, 'religious knowledge can act as the basis for social transformation, revolution, and collective political activism'.[95] Of course, this camp is far from homogeneous. And, as proposed by Duderija, progressive Muslim thought should be understood of as a critical approach embracing social and gender justice, and retaining scepticism towards the hegemonies of the global North, the patriarchal and 'ethically ossified interpretations' of the Islamic legal tradition, and some of the core tenets of the Enlightenment.[96] This approach offers the full range of critical tools against all potentially hegemonic discourses; as such, it supports the investigation into how truth-seeking elements of the international framework of TJ can be localised in the legal systems of Muslim-majority societies.

It has long been recognised that 'the Shari'a can be adapted to support the social upheavals and progress of modern times', embedding Islamic law in its social contexts (and human interpretations).[97] Kamali acknowledges 'a measure of flexibility in *usul al-fiqh* [*the methodology of law*] which allows for necessary adjustments in the law to accommodate social change' alongside the core sources of *shari'ah* which 'may not be overruled on grounds of either rationality or the requirements of social conditions'.[98] Despite the fallibility of human endeavours, contemporary interpretations can offer pragmatic answers to new questions, and as the previous paragraph illustrates, potential emancipatory uses of Islamic law against all forms of oppression. Historically, Hallaq describes early debates in Islamic jurisprudence between traditionalists (*ahl al-hadith*) and rationalists (*ahl al-ra'y*) in which (traditional) textualists attempted to discredit the 'rational, pragmatic and practical considerations' of rationalists.[99] In support of independent reasoning to address contemporary challenges, rationalists relied on good examples of predecessors (*sunan*), presenting the *ra'y* as 'an extension of, and based upon' *'ilm* (knowledge of precedent).[100] By incorporating the authority of the *sunan* (which includes the *hadith*, the traditions of the Prophet's companions and potentially pre-Islamic traditions not repealed) Islamic jurisprudence reflects an 'established, continuous practice' that became 'a model to follow' beyond textual sources.[101] Historically, and today, human interpretations still define applications of Islamic law. Moreover, as McDonough describes, the 'distinction between primary and secondary sources

[94] A Duderija, *The Imperatives of Progressive Islam* (New York, Routledge, 2017) 1–2.
[95] ibid.
[96] ibid 4–5.
[97] NJ Coulson, *History of Islamic Law* (Edinburgh, Edinburgh University Press, 1964) 6.
[98] Kamali, *Principles of Islamic Jurisprudence* (n 25) 7ff.
[99] Hallaq (n 32) 74–76.
[100] ibid 199ff.
[101] ibid.

can blur': some early (and, arguably, some more modern) commentators 'have gained such respect' that their work is viewed as 'unassailably correct restatements of law'.[102]

A. The Role of Jurists (Judiciary, the Juristic Schools and the Jurisprudents)

Jurists have played an enormous role in shaping Islamic law. Among Western scholars, Schacht famously referred to Islamic law as an 'extreme case of a jurist's law'.[103] Likewise, for Sacco 'the revealed texts are only the historical starting point of the *shari'a* which is a scholarly creation', given the lack of a central authority defining an official theology grounding Islamic law, and the absence of 'a cult of judicial precedent'.[104] Muslim scholars have also described Islamic law as 'lawyer's law', highlighting 'the teachings of the authoritative jurists'.[105] An-Na'im's suggests that *shari'ah* as is it known today 'was in fact *constructed* by Muslim jurists over the first three centuries of Islam' through human interpretation.[106] Discussing the power of legal authority, Hallaq explains the primacy of lawyers in Islamic law 'because the jurists are the carriers of the authority that sustained it for over a millennium'.[107] The following paragraphs explore three types of jurists that have shaped Islamic law: the judiciary, the juristic schools and the muftis whose independent legal reasoning fills normative gaps. Just as their classical predecessors, jurists today can advance Islamic law for practical needs of Muslim-majority societies, including in TJ.

i. *Judiciary*

Historically, alongside secular courts, the 'Islamic judge' emerged as a professional category in relation to (and constitutive of) the legal system.[108] In early Islamic societies, 'the judge represents the authority of the Imam (head of the state) and exercises power in the capacity of his *wakil* (representative)'.[109] By the mid-eighth century, it is reported that the judiciary had become

[102] McDonough (n 20) 5.
[103] Schacht, *Introduction to Islamic Law* (n 25) discussed also in Weiss (n 25) 113.
[104] Sacco (n 2) 348.
[105] Inter alia, Badr (n 12) 189.
[106] An-Na'im (n 44) 185ff.
[107] WB Hallaq, 'Juristic Authority vs State Power: The Legal Crises of Modern Islam' (2003) *Journal of Law and Religion* 243, 245. For a complementary analysis of the judiciary in relation to MENA legal systems, see C Mallat, 'From Islamic to Middle Eastern Law: A Restatement of the Field (Part II)' (2004) *American Journal of Comparative Law* 209.
[108] MK Masud, R Peters and DS Powers (eds), *Dispensing Justice in Islam: Qadis and Their Judgements* (Leiden, Brill, 2006).
[109] MH Kamali, 'Appellate Review and Judicial Independence in Islamic Law' (1990) 29(3) *Islamic Studies* 215, 225.

professionalised and separate from administrative, policing and fiscal bodies.[110] For Hallaq, the consolidation of judicial independence is a milestone in the Islamic legal tradition.[111] In early Islam, the composition of the *qadi*'s (judge's) court evidences the judiciary's role and contribution to the developing Islamic law. Hallaq lists various court staff supporting the needs and function of the bench, including scribes, assistants such as the court chamberlain to ensure order and supervise litigants, court interpreters and witness examiners (*ashab al-masa'il*), whose job it was to 'enquire about the integrity of character witnesses whose function it was in turn to attest to legal records, contracts and all sorts of transactions passing through the court'.[112]

The (relative) binding force of a judgment[113] and the possibility to appeal or reverse a decision exemplifies the possibility of error – even by the prophet Muhammad himself.[114] Thus, if a judge has exerted sound legal reasoning in good faith, that decision is enforceable and cannot be reviewed by another judge, only by the original one.[115] But if there was a 'gross error of judgment' not based on 'sound *ijtihad* and lead[ing] to a manifest miscarriage of justice', then the decision was reviewable.[116] This suggests that in its adjudicatory function the judiciary was expected to exercise sound legal reasoning, and if necessary reflect on the potential shortcomings of one's own or someone else's conclusions. This classic approach can have important contemporary applications in relation to truth-seeking endeavours in transitional contexts.

ii. Juristic Schools

Scholarly writings are central to Islamic law.[117] Around the eleventh century, four Sunni schools of Islamic law were 'recognized as orthodox': Hanafi, Maliki, Shafi'i and Hanbali.[118] At the same time, independent legal reasoning (*ijtihad*), described as 'the maximum effort expended by the jurist to master and apply the principles and rules of *usul al-fiqh* (legal theory) for the purposes of discovering God's law', was limited.[119]

> The door of *ijtihad* was closed and the efforts of the jurists were reduced to *taqlid* (literally, 'imitation') or submission to the canons of the four schools. The writings

[110] Hallaq (n 32) 97ff.
[111] ibid 83ff.
[112] ibid 85ff.
[113] On Islamic case law, see inter alia L Rosen, 'Islamic "Case Law" and the Logic of Consequence' in J Starr and JF Collier (eds), *History and Power in the Study of Law: New Directions in Legal Anthropology* (Ithaca, NY, Cornell University Press, 1989) 302; and also J Makdisi, 'Legal Logic and Equity in Islamic Law' (1985) 33(1) *American Journal of Comparative Law* 63.
[114] Described in Kamali (n 109) 228.
[115] ibid 229.
[116] ibid.
[117] As discussed in the previous chapter and in Sacco (n 2) 347ff.
[118] Khadduri (n 11) 19.
[119] On this controversial issue, see inter alia Hallaq (n 56) 3.

of the founders of these schools (or their disciples) became the standard textbooks for all students of law and any effort to depart from them was denounced as *bid'a* (innovation).[120]

The four schools 'were not formal educational institutions or officially-sanctioned law-making bodies'; instead, 'they were rather groups of jurists each following a certain doctrine that can be traced back to a prominent pioneer of the second century of the Muslim era whose name the school carries'.[121] The eventual formalisation of legal schools marks 'one of the most defining characteristics of Islamic law'.[122] Their doctrinal influence emerged alongside their institutional capacity.[123]

Jurists possess what Weiss calls 'interpretative or declaratory authority', which has the actual force of influencing positive law as opposed to legislative authority, which instead belongs to God.[124] The *mujtahids* (performers of *ijtihad*) derived law from the sacred texts, whereas non-*mujtahids* interpreted secondary sources.[125] These jurists reportedly employed all the techniques of legal reasoning, the principles of text criticism and intentionalist hermeneutics.[126] Their knowledge included 'legal theory, Quranic exegesis, *hadith* and its criticism, legal language, the theory of abrogation, substantive law, arithmetic, and the all-important science of juristic disagreement'.[127] Hallaq stresses the 'dynamic and vibrant nature' of *taqlid* (authority) emanating from the doctrinal schools,[128] indicating a diverse and active community of legal scholars. The rich scholarly debate on Islamic law today outside the confines of the juristic schools (ie in university settings) suggests that the field remains dynamic and vibrant.

iii. Jurisconsults (Muftis)

As a third category, the *mufti* is a 'jurisprudent who issues fatwas', formally non-binding legal opinions, which judges may adhere to.[129] 'The fatwa represented a legal opinion stated in universal terms, reflecting both the most authoritative law in the school as well as legitimised legal practice.'[130]

[120] Khadduri (n 11).
[121] Badr (n 12) 89.
[122] Hallaq (n 32) 150ff.
[123] B Weiss, 'The Madhhab in Islamic Legal Theory' in PJ Bearman, R Peters and FE Vogel (eds), *The Islamic School of Law: Evolution, Devolution, and Progress* (Cambridge. MA, Islamic Legal Studies Program, Harvard Law School Harvard University Press, 2005). See also W Hallaq, 'Can the Sharia Be Restored?' in YY Haddad and BF Stowasser (eds), *Islamic Law and the Challenges of Modernity* (Walnut Creek, CA, Altamira Press, 2004) for a discussion of the *madhab.*
[124] Weiss (n 25) 114.
[125] ibid 115ff, 135.
[126] ibid.
[127] Hallaq (n 32) 156ff.
[128] WB Hallaq, *Authority, Continuity and Change in Islamic Law* (Cambridge, Cambridge University Press, 2001) 120.
[129] These definitions are taken from the glossary in Hallaq (n 32).
[130] Hallaq (n 107) 248.

Messick has situated *muftis* in the 'interpretative interface of theory and practice of Islamic law', filling the 'niche between the jurist as teacher and the jurist as judge'.[131] This describes:

> The tension between the dictates of textual theory and the circumstances of actual cases results, in a fatwa, in a 'reading' of a textual theory, while in a judgment it leads to a 'reading' of a practical fact.[132]

The synergy between theory and practice is important historically and today. In a detailed historical examination of the role of *fatwa* in developing substantive law, Hallaq refutes the claim that 'after the formative period Islamic substantive law became increasingly rigid, eventually losing touch with the political, social, and economic developments',[133] suggested by scholars such as Coulson and Schacht.[134] Instead, he defends the 'important role that the *fatwas* played in the development of legal doctrine as embodied in the *furu'* (substantive law) works', connecting '*fatwa* as a legal discourse and *fatwa* as a social instrument'.[135]

To describe how *fatwa* developed in connection to society, Hallaq suggests they 'were the outcome of a concrete and particular reality that originated outside the jurists' minds', revolving 'around … persons in highly particular circumstances'[136] Later Ottoman manuals on *fatwa* were 'highly practical and pragmatic', and a dictum linked to fatwas recites that 'no *fatwa* should be issued with regard to a problem that has not yet occurred in the real world', and as such they 'emanated from a particular social reality involving real people with real problems'.[137] Only a *fatwa* 'that added new material to the current body of legal doctrines' was incorporated into substantive law.[138]

On the basis of this, Hallaq argues that it was the *mufti*, and not the *qadi*, 'who was responsible for the development of the legal doctrine embodied in the *furu'* works' after the second century of Islam (the eighth century), breaking from the function of the early judges in developing substantive Islamic law.[139] The relationship between the *mufti* (issuing *fatwa*) and the *qadi* (issuing a judgment in relation to judicial disputes) 'is explained by the fact that the judge depended heavily upon the mufti's opinions' – to the

[131] B Messick, 'The Mufti, the Text and the World: Legal Interpretation in Yemen' (1986) 21(1) *Man* 102, 103ff.
[132] ibid.
[133] WB Hallaq, 'From Fatwas to Furu': Growth and Change in Islamic Substantive Law' (1994) 1 *Islamic Law and Society* 1, 29.
[134] ibid, referencing NJ Coulson, 'The State and the Individual in Islamic Law' (1957) 6 *ICLQ* 57; and Schacht, *The Origins of Muhammadan Jurisprudence* (n 25).
[135] Hallaq (n 133) 30ff.
[136] ibid 32ff.
[137] ibid 37ff.
[138] ibid 50.
[139] ibid.

extent to which often muftis were attached to a court and their *fatwas* became binding.[140] Thus:

> The stipulation that the judge must resort to the *mufti* for legal advice underscores the fact that it is the *mufti*, not the *qadi*, who is the ultimate expert on the law.[141]

Muftis enjoyed numerous advantages over *qadis*: they performed *ijtihad*; they were independent from government authorities, and possibly less susceptible to corruption; and a *mufti*'s *fatwa* could question or reverse a *qadi*'s judgment, honouring the *mufti*'s duty to 'discover and apply the law'.[142] In relation to the prominent role of *muftis* in developing Islamic law through *fatwa*, Hallaq concludes that 'our current perception of Islamic law as a jurists' law [as argued by Schacht] must now be further defined as a mufti's law'.[143] Today, this proposition is still valid, although the relationship between *muftis* and authorities has become more fluid, which includes the more recent phenomenon of state *muftis*.[144] Nevertheless, new media offers new ways for *muftis* to operate more independently, as attested by the appearance (and success) of internet *fatawa*.[145]

This historic role of jurists illustrates, again, the significant human contribution to the development of Islamic law. Today, jurists still have scope to shape the understanding and applications of Islamic law in light of the *maqasid* and *maslaha*; moreover, they could develop appropriate tools to further the truth-seeking objectives of TJ, as discussed in the opinions provided by esteemed contemporary Islamic law scholars cited in the final chapter.

IV. ISLAMIC LAW AND INTERNATIONAL LAW: FOUNDATIONS FOR TRANSITIONAL JUSTICE TRUTH SEEKING

The juxtaposition (and interaction) between elements of Islamic law and international law is a reality in all Muslim-majority societies: the two normative frameworks coexist as formants in the legal systems. There is a rich and nuanced literature in English on this encounter.[146] Nevertheless, widespread misconceptions about Islamic law as well as international law remain. Conservative

[140] ibid 56.

[141] ibid.

[142] ibid. Hallaq reports a prophetical saying 'on the Day of Resurrection the judges will join the Sultans, but the "*ulama*" (=*muftis*) will join the Prophets', indicating the muftis' proximity to the essence of Islamic law.

[143] ibid 65.

[144] J Skovgaard-Petersen, 'A Typology of State Muftis' in YY Haddad and BF Stowasser (eds), *Islamic Law and the Challenges of Modernity* (Walnut Creek, CA, Altamira Press, 2004).

[145] On this topic, see SS Ali, *Modern Challenges to Islamic Law* (Cambridge, Cambridge University Press, 2017) ch 8.

[146] Writings on international law and Islamic law include D Westbrook, 'Islamic International Law and Public International Law: Separate Expressions of World Order' (1992–93) 33 *Virginia Journal of International Law* 819; SW al-Zuhili, 'Islam and International Law' (2005) 87(858) *International Review of the Red Cross* 269; M Frick and AT Müller (eds), *Islam and International Law: Engaging Self-centrism from a Plurality of Perspectives* (Leiden, Brill, 2013); N Samour,

scholars and politicians in both camps have been guided by prejudice.[147] In many Western circles the demonisation of Muslims and *shari'ah* culminated after 9/11.[148] Regrettably, even the European Court of Human Rights has suggested that 'sharia is incompatible with the fundamental principles of democracy' of Europe.[149] Moreover, there is a subtext (often overtly expressed) of antagonism between human rights principles set out in international law instruments, and Islam. As Samuel Moyn has posited, 'mainstream secular observers are generally unaware of … the Christian incarnation of human rights',[150] but this might also explain the undercurrents of mutual suspicion between international human rights law and Islamic law. These stereotypes have been around for a long time, as attested by the negative trope of the Islamic judge portrayed as *Kadijustiz*.[151] Such polarised views are rebutted by a growing literature on the substantive overlap of methods and objectives of international law and *shari'ah* despite tensions between religious and secular sources.[152] This approach has uncovered fascinating exchanges between the two normative systems, reflecting the complexities and pluralisms of today's legal orders.[153] A constructive conversation on the convergence and tensions between truth seeking in the international legal framework of TJ and Islamic law and jurisprudence is not only possible, but auspicious.

In broad terms, the aims of *shari'ah* converge with the substance of public international law, in particular for human rights, criminal justice and

'Is there a Role for Islamic International Law in the History of International Law?' (2014) 25(1) *European Journal of International Law* 313; MA Baderin (ed), *International Law and Islamic Law* (Abingdon, Routledge, 2017); I De La Rasilla and A Shahid (eds), *International Law and Islam: Historical Explorations* (Leiden, Brill 2018).

[147] eg J Rehman, 'Islamophobia after 9/11: International Terrorism, Sharia and Muslim Minorities in Europe – The Case of the United Kingdom' (2003) 3(1) *European Yearbook of Minority Issues Online* 217.

[148] On the purposeful exclusion of Muslims from the idea of law and rights in the west, see inter alia S Razack, *Casting Out: The Eviction of Muslims From Western Law and Politics* (Toronto, University of Toronto Press, 2008); and WB Hallaq, 'Muslim Rage and Islamic law' (2002) 54 *Hastings Law Journal* 1705. And from a feminist angle S Maira, '"Good" and "Bad" Muslim Citizens: Feminists, Terrorists, and US Orientalisms' (2009) 35(3) *Feminist Studies* 631.

[149] Notably, in *Refah Partisi and others v Turkey* (Applications Nos 41340/98, 41342/98, 41343/98 and 41344/98) 13 February 2003, para 123.

[150] S Moyn, 'Christian Human Rights: An Introduction' (2017) 28(1) *King's Law Journal* 1, 2.

[151] Cited in IA Rabb, 'Against Kadijustiz: On the Negative Citation of Foreign Law' (2015) 48 *Suffolk University Law Review* 343.

[152] eg A Maged, 'Arab and Islamic Shari'a Perspectives on the Current System of International Criminal Justice' (2008) 8(3) *International Criminal Law Review* 477; M Bohlander and MM Hedayati-Khakhi, 'Criminal Justice under Shari'ah in the 21st Century – An Inter-cultural View' (2009) 23 *Arab Law Quarterly* 417.

[153] For examples of fruitful analyses of both directions of legal borrowing, see M Fadl, 'International Law, Regional Developments: Islam', *Max Planck Encyclopedia of International Law* (2008) available at www.opil.ouplaw.com/view/10.1093/law:epil/9780199231690/law-9780199231690-e711?prd=OPIL on importing the tenets and instruments of PIL inclusive of ICL within the realm of Islamic law; and ME Badar, 'Islamic Law (*Shari'a*) and the Jurisdiction of the International Criminal Court' (2011) 24 *Leiden Journal of International Law* 407 on the inclusion of the Islamic legal system among those considered by the international criminal judge.

international humanitarian law. Islamic states have human rights commitments through the ordinary instruments of international law as well as the moral imperatives set out in the *shari'ah*.[154] Drawing on classical principles, the adoption of valid international treaties through diplomatic relations channels international law through Islamic international law (*siyar*).[155] Islamic international law does not directly provide a framework for relations between states, but offers Muslims 'a code of conduct' through 'a compilation of rules that allow for binding international agreements'.[156] The notion of *siyar* emerges from Mohammad Al-Shaybani's eighth-century book *Al-Siyar Al-Kabir*, described by Bashir as a 'comprehensive treatise regulating international relations from the Islamic perspective'.[157] *Siyar* is based on the *shari'ah*, and enables Muslims (ie Muslim states) to enter into relations with non-Muslims through international treaties.[158] Given the international framework for TJ truth seeking hinges on international law, *siyar* can foster the integration of Islamic and international norms for those aims.

Islamic international law articulates the classic doctrinal distinction between *dar al-islam* (the territory of Islam – ruled by Muslims under *shari'ah* for the benefit and security of the faithful); *dar al-harb* (the territory of war, when Muslims were under non-Muslim domination or threat); and *dar al-suhl* (also referred to as *dar al-ahd*, a non-Muslim territory which had a peace treaty with the Muslims).[159] Under *dar al-islam* and *dar al-suhl* valid international treaties can comply with *shari'ah*. This tripartite distinction has limited textual foundation in the Qur'an or Sunna.[160] Nonetheless, it is supported by the fact that the prophet Mohammed himself entered into diplomatic agreements with many non-Muslim rulers, and there were treaties between Muslims and Christians throughout the Middle Ages and early Modernity.[161]

For contemporary scholars, the category of *dar al-harb* became obsolete with the rise of international law and the United Nations, where friendly relations between nations aim to eradicate war and military conquest.[162] This is despite the legacies of colonialism and imperialist connotations inherited by

[154] McDonough (n 20).

[155] Fadl (n 153) 5ff. For an overview of Islamic international law, see M Khadduri, *The Islamic Law of Nations: Shaybani's Siyar* (Baltimore, MD, Johns Hopkins University Press, 1966).

[156] Samour (n 7) 546.

[157] KR Bashir, *Islamic International Law: Historical Foundations and al-Shaybani's* Siyar (Cheltenham, Edward Elgar, 2018) Preface.

[158] M Munir, 'Islamic International Law (Siyar): An Introduction' (2012) 40(4) *Hamdard Islamicus* 37.

[159] Fadl (n 153) 2ff.

[160] Samour (n 7) 547.

[161] Fadl (n 153) 2ff. For more examples of the development of this type of law during the Ottoman Empire, see M Khadduri, 'Islam and the Modern Law of Nations' (n 38) 360ff, and GM Badr, 'A Survey of Islamic International Law' (1982) 76 *American Society of International Law Proceedings* 56. See similar discussion in Samour (n 7) 553–54.

[162] Fadl (n 153) 9, listing prominent Islamic jurists that support the view that the category of *dar al-harb* became obsolete.

international law.[163] Over time, as Nahed Samour notes, Islamic international law has responded 'to changing perceptions of threat' and moved away from having 'a strong imperial character' itself.[164] As such, Muslims and Muslim states have participated in international affairs throughout the twentieth century, including in 'international conferences, in the League of Nations, and the United Nations and its agencies'.[165] Among Islamic contributions to the field, Corri Zoli lists 'the shared history of public international law, modern Muslim leadership in IHL, and the too-rarely-treated role of Muslim states in the early Geneva and Hague diplomatic conferences'.[166] As such, individually, and through membership of the Organization of Islamic Cooperation (OIC), Muslim states and states with a sizeable Muslim population continue to be part of the UN system. That organisation's international peace and security agenda supports the current global existence of *dar al-sulh*.[167] In principle, therefore, 'any State that committed itself to providing Muslims freedom of religion and permitted Islam to be taught freely could not be considered part of *dar al-harb*';[168] based on this, it would appear that all countries have the chance of being considered part of the *dar al-sulh* unless they pursue or endorse racist and Islamophobic policies and practices that limit Muslim freedom of religion.

The general rule is that Islamic law protects international agreements, provided they are consistent with the principles of *shari'ah*; at the same time, Islamic international law (*siyar*) contributes to developing general PIL too.[169] The sources of PIL, established in Article 38 of the ICJ Statute, include customary international law, general principles of law, case law and scholarly writings in addition to international treaties.[170] According to Munir, given international

[163] For example, regarding general principles, MC Bassiouni, 'Functional Approach to General Principles of International Law' (1989) 11 *Michigan Journal of International Law* 768, 782ff. In general, see inter alia A Anghie, 'Finding the Peripheries: Sovereignty and Colonialism in Nineteenth-century International Law' (1999) 40 *Harvard International Law Journal* 1.

[164] Samour (n 7) 544.

[165] M Khadduri, 'Islam and the Modern Law of Nations' (n 38) 370–71; also referring in footnote 42 to the work of AW Dejany, 'Competence of the General Assembly in the Tunisian–Moroccan Questions' (1953) *Proceedings of the American Society of International Law* 53–59, on the competence of the UNGA to deal with Muslim countries. See also McDonough (n 20) 93. It is important, however, to note that the concentration of international power still rests largely with the West. On this see inter alia M Müftüler-Bac, 'Through the Looking Glass: Turkey in Europe' (2000) 1(1) *Turkish Studies* 21; K Culcasi, 'Constructing and Naturalizing the Middle East' (2010) 100(4) *Geographical Review* 583; L Struckman and T Sturm, 'Introduction: Interrogating Conventional Geopolitics of the Middle East' (2012) 16(1) *The Arab World Geographer* 3. And, of course, E Said, *Orientalism* (New York, Vintage Books, 1979).

[166] C Zoli, 'Islamic Contributions to International Humanitarian Law: Recalibrating TWAIL Approaches for Existing Contributions and Legacies' (2015), 109 *AJIL Unbound* 271, 272.

[167] SS Ali and J Rehman, 'The Concept of Jihad in International Islamic Law' (2005) 10(3) *Journal of Conflict & Security Law* 321, 333ff.

[168] Fadl (n 153) 9.

[169] J Rehman, *Islamic State Practices, International Law and the Threat from Terrorism: A Critique of the 'Clash of Civilizations' in the New World Order* (Oxford, Hart, 2005) 45ff.

[170] Art 38 lists: 'a. international conventions, whether general or particular, establishing rules expressly recognized by the contesting states; b. international custom, as evidence of a general

law is neutral, it may draw on the *shari'ah* within the range of norms it considers within the sources set out in Article 38.[171] Muslim-majority states have recognised the jurisdiction of the ICJ;[172] the OIC and some of its members have presented written statements to the ICJ when an OIC member was affected.[173] This has influenced the operation of PIL. It is certainly the case that more references to the *shari'ah* would lead to greater inclusivity in the international community, as Badar argues in relation to the ICC.[174] More generally, 'modernized Islamic international law concepts' might offer an important critical and constructive tool to analyse the contemporary international legal order; as Samour suggests, there is more to these concepts 'than a religious take on international law' as a response to foreign domination.[175] This pragmatism is reflected in the 2004 UN report on *The Rule of Law and Transitional Justice*, which includes Islamic law among the legal systems to consider in the international legal framework of TJ.[176] Therefore, the comparative analysis of Islamic law and the international framework of TJ is more than a static (and hierarchical) comparison, in which one accommodates the other: principles of Islamic law not only endorse TJ, but can also become an integral part of its international framework, as other localised and religious elements have done in the past.

A recurring challenge for comparative analyses is identifying what to compare. The somewhat amorphous international framework of TJ discussed in Chapter 1 includes PIL and aspects of human rights (IHRL) and international criminal law (ICL). In the absence of anything resembling an Islamic law of TJ, and indeed a corpus of Islamic law equivalent to IHRL and ICL, the methodological approach described in Chapter 2 requires a holistic understanding of Islamic law and jurisprudence to identify relevant norms, not only positive law of self-styled Muslim states, classic accounts of *shari'ah*, or statements

practice accepted as law; c. the general principles of law recognized by civilized nations; d. subject to the provisions of Article 59, judicial decisions and the teachings of the most highly qualified publicists of the various nations, as subsidiary means for the determination of rules of law.'

[171] Munir (n 158) at footnote 80 in particular.

[172] For example, Egypt, Pakistan, Somalia and Sudan have issued 'Declarations Recognizing as Compulsory the Jurisdiction of the Court', available at www.icj-cij.org/en/declarations; this is in addition to all the ipso facto parties to the ICJ Statute by virtue of Art 93(1) UN Charter.

[173] *Legal Consequences of the Construction of a Wall, Advisory Opinion* [9 July 2004] ICJ Rep 136, Written Statement of the Organisation of the Islamic Conference (30 January 2004) and also statements of Saudi Arabia, Egypt, Jordan, Kuwait, Lebanon, Syria, Yemen, Morocco, Indonesia, Sudan, Pakistan and Malaysia, available at www.icj-cij.org/en/case/131/written-proceedings.

[174] With reference to the work of the ICC, see Badar (n 153).

[175] Samour (n 7) 565.

[176] United Nations Security Council, *The Rule of Law and Transitional Justice in Conflict and Post-conflict Situations: Report of the Secretary General*, S/2004/616, 23 August 2004, para 61: 'A mix of expertise that includes knowledge of United Nations norms and standards for the administration of justice, experience in post-conflict settings, an understanding of the host country's legal system (inter alia, common law, civil law, Islamic law), familiarity with the host-country culture, an approach that is inclusive of local counterparts, an ability to work in the language of the host country and familiarity with a variety of legal areas.'

from international organisations with Islamic character (such as the OIC Cairo Declaration on Human Rights in Islam[177]). As discussed in Chapter 4, the IHRL framework broadly sustains the emerging right to truth, which is supported by a range of other principles and practices; moreover, the aims of ICL also feed into truth seeking when they include 'the telling of the history of a conflict, ... reconciling societies and capacity building in domestic judicial systems'.[178] A second issue to consider is the political and social context in which law emerges and operates, including Islamic law principles invoked today. Human rights law in general focuses on 'political and legal justice' so they 'cannot compete with cultural and religious traditions'.[179] Similarly, Muslim human rights documents such as the OIC Cairo Declaration are informed more by politics than divinity.[180] Nonetheless, borrowing from Rawls's doctrine of 'overlapping consensus' (ie focusing on end results despite contrasting theoretical justifications[181]), similarities can emerge.[182] The following sections discuss substantive and procedural convergence between Islamic law and some of the key norms of ICL and IHRL of the international legal framework underpinning truth seeking in TJ.

A. The Overlap of Substantive Justice Aims of Islamic Law and ICL/IHRL

The truth-seeking aims of TJ discussed in Chapters 3 and 4 draw on IHRL and ICL. There is a rich scholarship exploring the meeting between Islamic law and IHRL,[183] and Islamic criminal law and ICL, indicating substantive

[177] Organization of the Islamic Conference (OIC), Cairo Declaration on Human Rights in Islam, 5 August 1990, available at www.refworld.org/docid/3ae6b3822c.html, and academic commentary including A Al-Ahsan, 'Law, Religion and Human Dignity in the Muslim World Today: An Examination of OIC's Cairo Declaration of Human Rights' (2008) 24(2) *Journal of Law and Religion* 569; T Kayaoglu, 'A Rights Agenda for the Muslim World: the Organization of Islamic Cooperation's Evolving Human Rights Framework' (2013) APSA 2013 Annual Meeting Paper; and R Carle, 'Revealing and Concealing: Islamist Discourse on Human Rights' (2005) 6(3) *Human Rights Review* 122.

[178] R Cryer et al, *An Introduction to International Criminal Law and Procedure* (Cambridge, Cambridge University Press, 2007) 17, citing A Cassese, 'Reflections on International Criminal Justice' (1998) *MLR* 1, 6–7.

[179] H Bielefeldt, '"Western" versus "Islamic" Human Rights Conceptions? A Critique of Cultural Essentialism in. the Discussion on Human Rights' (2000) *Political Theory* 90, 116.

[180] AE Mayer, 'Universal versus Islamic Human Rights: A Clash of Cultures or a Clash with a Construct? (1994) 15 *Michigan Journal of International Law* 307, 402.

[181] J Rawls, 'The Idea of an Overlapping Consensus' (1987) 7(1) *OJLS* 1.

[182] Bielefeldt (n 179) 114ff.

[183] Inter alia: Baderin (n 27); An-Na'im (n 44); AE Mayer, *Islam and Human Rights: Tradition and Politics* (Boulder, CO, Westview Press, 1991); AA An-Na'im, 'Islam and Human Rights: Beyond the Universality Debate', in American Society of International Law, Proceedings of the 94th Annual Meeting (2000); B Tibi, 'Islamic Law/Shari'a, Human Rights, Universal Morality and International Relations' (1994) 16 *Human Rights Quarterly* 277; MH Kamali, 'Fundamental Rights of the Individual: An Analysis of Haqq (Right) in Islamic Law' (1993) 10(3) *American Journal of Islamic Social Sciences* 340; and more recently McDonough (n 20). Beyond the English-language academic setting, see inter alia H Elliesie (ed), *Beiträge zum Islamischen Recht VII: Islam und Menschenrechte/Islam and Human Rights* (Frankfurt, Peter Lang, 2010).

convergence overall.[184] Well-known tensions between international standards and Islamic principles remain, such as barbaric punishments for *hudud* crimes, and the unequal status of women in testimony, but can be addressed through careful and constructive analysis. For instance, the punishment for *hudud* crimes requires unattainably high standards of proof, suggesting that there is no Islamic imperative to impose inhumane punishments or the death penalty.[185] Furthermore, the practice of granting female testimony lesser value than male witnesses can be reassessed via renewed textual exegesis and interpretive choices taking stock of human rights standards.[186] By exploring the *shari'ah* equivalents of the IHRL and ICL provisions that help guide the right to truth and the state duty to investigate, this analysis acknowledges the inclusion of Islamic law among the legal systems to consider in the international legal framework of TJ in the 2004 UN report on *The Rule of Law and Transitional Justice*.[187]

The Islamic *shari'ah* and international criminal law share key objectives,[188] summarised by Adel Maged:

- To prevent the commission of serious crimes and acts of aggression;
- To bring to justice persons allegedly responsible for committing such grave crimes;
- To protect the civilians and other protected groups;
- To render justice to the victims;
- To deter criminals from committing crimes;
- To contribute to the restoration of peace by achieving justice and promoting reconciliation.[189]

These objectives feed into the individual truth-seeking elements of TJ, specifically through the 'rendering justice to the victims' aim, and the collective element, specifically through 'the restoration of peace' aim. Islamic law translates its broad criminal justice objectives into practice through three categories of offences.

First, *hudud* crimes, prescribed in the Qur'an and Sunna, are crimes against God and constitute the backbone of the Islamic criminal order.[190] This group includes six/seven specific crimes (notwithstanding differences of opinion

[184] Inter alia MC Bassiouni, *The Islamic Criminal Justice System* (London and Rome, Oceana Publications, 1982); M Lippman, 'Islamic Criminal Law and Procedure: Religious Fundamentalism v Modern Law' (1989) 12 *Boston College International and Comparative Law Review* 29.

[185] See inter alia MH Kamali, 'Punishment in Islamic Law: A Critique of the Hudud Bill of Kelantan, Malaysia' (1998) 13(3) *Arab Law Quarterly* 203; and also RHA Alsoufi, 'Strategies for the Justifications of Ḥudūd Allah and their Punishments in the Islamic Tradition' (PhD Thesis, University of Edinburgh, 2012) available at www.era.lib.ed.ac.uk/handle/1842/7989.

[186] eg A Barlas, *Believing Women in Islam: Unreading Patriarchal Interpretations of the Qur'an* (Austin, University of Texas Press, 2009).

[187] UN Security Council, *The Rule of Law and Transitional Justice in Conflict and Post-conflict Situations* (n 176) para 61.

[188] For an overview of the aims of ICL, see inter alia Cryer (n 178) 17–36.

[189] Maged (n 152) 484.

[190] For an overview of the *hudud* crimes, see MC Bassiouni, 'Crimes and the Criminal Process' (1997) 12(3) *Arab Law Quarterly*, 269; M Lippman, S McConville, and M Yerushalmi, *Islamic Criminal Law and Procedure: An Introduction* (New York, Praeger, 1988); Kamali (n 185) 218ff.

among different juristic schools): apostasy, transgression (*baghi*),[191] theft, highway robbery, adultery (*zina*), slander and drinking alcohol. Penalties include corporal and capital punishments, which generally clash with international law provisions, as illustrated in the contexts where such crimes have been reintroduced.[192] If applied, the *hudud* penalties are likely to violate the prohibition of torture (Article 1 CAT and Article 7 ICCPR).[193] However, the almost unattainably high standard of proof required suggests that punishment cannot be inflicted lightly.[194] Moreover, the Qur'an emphasises repentance (and reform) for those who have committed a *hudud* offence, and the *hadith* indicates the suspension of punishment when there is doubt.[195]

The *hudud* offences may be relevant to TJ truth seeking in different ways according to context. For the purposes of this study, a brief consideration of *zina* and *baghi* can offer examples of the interaction between *hudud* crimes and the truth-seeking element of the international legal framework for TJ. *Zina*,[196] extramarital sexual relations (between a man and a woman), has been understood by some conservatives as encompassing instances of rape and gender-based violence (GBV) – resulting even in punishment for victims.[197] This completely inappropriate position may result in a rape victim's report of violence being taken as a confession of *zina* then followed by punishment, instead of considering the violent act itself as an abominable violation of IHRL, as well as a crime under ICL (and IHL) requiring investigation (and punishment) of the perpetrator and compassion for the victim.[198] The growing feminist literature on TJ also

[191] *Baghi* in Arabic language and Islamic *Shari'ah* is the transgression or rebellion against the legitimate leader by the use of force. For a detailed discussion of this topic, see K Abou El Fadl, *Rebellion and Violence in Islamic Law* (Cambridge, Cambridge University Press, 2001) 8ff.

[192] With reference to Malaysia, see Kamali (n 185); ML Seda-Poulin, 'Islamization and Legal Reform in Malaysia: The Hudud Controversy of 1992' (1993) *Southeast Asian Affairs* 224. And for Nigeria: VO Orlu Nmehielle, 'Sharia Law in the Northern states of Nigeria: To Implement or Not to Implement, the Constitutionality is the Question' (2004) 26(3) *Human Rights Quarterly* 730; OE Anyanwu, 'Crime and justice in Postcolonial Nigeria: The justifications and Challenges of Islamic Law of Shari'ah' (2006) *Journal of Law and Religion* 315.

[193] International Covenant on Civil and Political Rights, United Nations General Assembly resolution 2200A (XXI) (16 December 1966). Convention against Torture and Other Cruel, Inhuman or Degrading Treatment or Punishment, General Assembly resolution 39/46 (10 December 1984).

[194] On the harshness of punishments for the *hudud* crimes, and high standards of proof, see Baderin (n 27) 75ff.

[195] Reported in Kamali (n 185) 221 and 231.

[196] For a critical overview of *zina*, see inter alia Z Mir-Hosseini, 'Criminalizing Sexuality: Zina Laws as Violence Against Women in Muslim Contexts' (2011) 15 *SUR-International Journal on Human Rights* 7; H Azari, *Protection of Women Victim of Rape: Islamic and International Legal Perspectives* (PhD Thesis, Tilburg University, 2014) 55 ff.

[197] See discussion, for instance, in R Mehdi, 'The Offence of Rape in the Islamic Law of Pakistan' (1997) 18 *Women Living under Muslim Laws: Dossier* 98; A Quraishi, 'Her Honor: An Islamic Critique of the Rape Laws of Pakistan from a Woman-Sensitive Perspective' (1997) 18 *Michigan Journal of International Law* 287; H Azam, 'Rape as a Variant of Fornication (Zina) in Islamic Law: An Examination of the Early Legal Reports' (2012) 28 *Journal of Law & Religion* 441.

[198] See inter alia T Meron, 'Rape as a Crime Under International Humanitarian Law' (1993) *American Journal of International Law* 424; CA MacKinnon, 'Rape, Genocide, and Women's

points to the urgency of taking GBV seriously.[199] As such, if a woman reports rape or other GBV, the authorities have a duty to investigate the perpetrator, not punish the victim. A closer reading of the Islamic sources, as proposed by Hajar Azari, indicates that despite contemporary conservative approaches and victim-blaming, the true *shari'ah* conception of *zina* makes a distinction between consensual and coercive *zina*;[200] the latter would include the crime of rape, thus can be used to bring perpetrators to justice and uphold victims' rights.

The second example is *baghi*, transgression, or revolt against the righteous leader, described by Al-Azhar as:

> transgression or rebellion against the legitimate leader by the use of force. The crime of baghi includes for example the outset of the ruler by the use of force and violence and acts of destruction of public property.[201]

Baghi was reassessed from within the Islamic establishment after the Arab Spring uprisings.[202] In 2011, after the ousting of Mubarak, Al-Azhar scholars responded publicly to exonerate protestors from accusations of *baghi*, which may have resulted in religiously motivated public condemnation and the imposition of *hudud* punishments. The Al-Azhar Declaration in Support of the Arab Revolutions of 31 October 2011 uses *shari'ah* and IHRL to reaffirm that an uprising against an unjust ruler is not *baghi*:

> When the voice of national popular opposition and peaceful protest arises, this is the inherent right of people to correct and guide their rulers when they … ignore legitimate demands which call for freedom, justice and equity. Those patriotic protestors are not considered as committing baghi; … national peaceful movements constitute the core of human rights in Islam, as confirmed by all international conventions. Furthermore, it is the people's duty to reform their society and correct their rulers.[203]

The second category of crimes in Islamic law, *qisas*, regulates murder, manslaughter, battery and other crimes against the person.[204] The Qur'an and Sunna do not set out specific or mandatory penalties, but the harm is regulated

Human Rights' (1994) 17 *Harvard Women's Law Journal* 5; CN Niarchos, 'Women, War, and Rape: Challenges Facing the International Tribunal for the Former Yugoslavia' (1995) 17(4) *Human Rights Quarterly* 649. RJ Goldstone, 'Prosecuting Rape as a War Crime' (2002) 34 *Case Western Reserve Journal of International Law* 277; TL Tompkins, 'Prosecuting Rape as a War Crime: Speaking the Unspeakable' (1994) 70 *Notre Dame Law Review* 845.

[199] *Inter alia* C Bell, and C O'Rourke, 'Does Feminism Need a Theory of Transitional Justice? An Introductory Essay' (2007) 1(1) *International Journal of Transitional Justice* 23.

[200] Azari (n 196) 55ff.

[201] The Al-Azhar Declaration in Support for the Arab Revolutions, 31 October 2011, tr A Maged and A Panepinto, available at www.dur.ac.uk/ilm/newsarchive/?itemno=13661.

[202] ibid and also The Al-Azhar Document on the Future of Egypt (Al-Azhar and a group of Egyptian Educated elite), 21 June 2011, translation on file with the author. For an insightful commentary on the Document's significance and a video of Grand Imam Al-Azhar, shaykh Ahmad al-Tayyib reading it on television, see M Zeghal, 'The "al-Azhar Document": Further Thoughts on al-Azhar in the Revolution', *On Islam and Politics* (1 September 2011) available at onislamandpolitics.wordpress.com/2011/09/01/the-al-azhar-document-further-thoughts-on-al-azhar-in-the-revolution.

[203] Al-Azhar Declaration in Support for the Arab Revolutions (n 201).

[204] Bassiouni (n 190) 269ff.

at individual level, either through the 'talion law' (eye for an eye) or *diyya*, victim compensation.[205] Unlike *hudud* crimes against god, *qisas* 'infringe upon the claims of human beings'.[206] Therefore, victims and families may pardon perpetrators, as well as requesting blood money or other compensation. The peculiarity of *qisas* is the discretion left to the victim and family in determining penalties. This classic category of crime can assist truth-seeking aims and even restorative justice, providing a path to discover the truth about past abuse.[207] As such, through the flexibility of *qisas*, victims and families may request an effective investigation to uncover the truth about harm suffered, in a manner that is compatible with IHRL and ICL standards.

The third category of Islamic crimes, *ta'azir*, describes residual – potentially infinite – offences against community interests or public order 'punishable by penalties left to the discretion of the ruler or the judge'.[208] These include certain criminal acts related to the *hudud* but not amounting to *hudud*, or falling below the standard-of-proof test, as well as 'all acts under the provisions of law, which are not punished by *hudud*'.[209] Most statutory criminal provisions in Muslim countries today fall under this category. As these provisions emanate from ordinary legislation and adjudication, and not divine injunctions, they can be created and implemented to be fully compatible with international legal standards to pursue truth-seeking initiatives.

This summary overview of the three classic categories of offences illustrates the overall convergence of the substantive justice aims of Islamic law and the standards set out in IHRL and ICL that underpin transitional truth seeking. In particular, the flexibility of the *qisas* and *ta'azir*, combined with the possibilities of more progressive interpretations of *hudud*, indicates that the *shari'ah* does not hinder the truth-seeking element of TJ, and would, in fact, be well-equipped to support it.

B. The Convergence of Procedural Standards of Islamic Law and ICL/IHRL

Procedural rules informed by IHRL and ICL standards are relevant to truth seeking, as illustrated in Chapter 4. The right to a fair hearing and due process set out in Article 14 ICCPR, and Articles 6, 7, 8, 9, 10, 11 UDHR have been

[205] ibid.

[206] S Tellenbach, 'Islamic Criminal Law' in MD Dubber and T Hörnle (eds), *The Oxford Handbook of Criminal Law* (Oxford, Oxford University Press, 2014).

[207] On the role of restorative justice and *qisas*, see SC Hascall, 'Restorative Justice in Islam: Should Qisas Be Considered a Form of Restorative Justice' (2011) 4 *Berkeley Journal of Middle East & Islamic Law* 35; and R Abdulkadir and C Ackley, 'The Role of Shari'a-based Restorative Justice in the Transition from Armed Conflict to Peacebuilding: Do Somalis Hold the View that the Restorative Justice Aspects Within Qisas Offer a Solution?' (2014) 14(2) *Northeast African Studies* 111.

[208] Badar (n 153) 414. See also Lippman (n 184) 44.

[209] Badar (n 153) 414.

deemed generally compatible with the principles of Islamic law by comparative scholars, including Sunni[210] and Shia perspectives.[211] Mohamed Elewa Badar identifies three principles and two defences in ICL which echo *shari'ah* rules: the principle of legality and non-retroactivity, the presumption of innocence, and equality before the law; the defence of superior orders and official capacity immunity.[212]

The principle of *nullum crimen sine lege* enshrined in Article 22 of the Rome Statute[213] echoes the Qur'anic verses 17:15,[214] 28:59,[215] 4:165,[216] 6:19[217] and 5:98,[218] and a number of *hadith*, as noted by Cherif Bassiouni.[219] Both *hudud* crimes and *qisas* must respect the principle of legality, providing fixed procedures and punishments.[220] Conversely, the *ta'azir* crimes leave ample discretion to rulers (and lawmakers) and judges, but the principle of legality can be ensured through the standard legislative processes (with no religious barriers).[221] The convergence of the principle of legality and *shari'ah* is enshrined in Article 19 (d) of the OIC Cairo Declaration on Human Rights in Islam, providing that 'There shall be no crime or punishment except as provided for in the Shari'a.'[222]

The presumption of innocence until proven guilty is set out in Article 66 of the Rome Statute.[223] The *shari'ah* echoes this principle, as illustrated in

[210] Baderin (n 27) 97ff (Sunni angle).

[211] see eg S Tabandeh, *A Muslim Commentary on the Universal Declaration of Human Rights* (Guildford, FJ Goulding, 1970) (Shia angle).

[212] Badar (n 153) 419ff; Bassiouni (n 64) 42ff.

[213] Art 22 Rome Statute (*nullum crimen sine lege)* must be read in conjunction with Art 23 (*nulla poena sine lege*) and Art 24 (*non-retroactivity ratione personae*) of the Rome Statute, components and corollaries of the principle of legality.

[214] Qur'an in *sūrat al-Isrā'*: (Allāh) said: 'Be thou among those who have respite' (17:15) [Ali translation], cited in Bassiouni (n 64) 42, explaining that 'the accused must first be given the opportunity to know the law, and thus no punishment can be imposed without prior law'.

[215] Qur'an in *sūrat al-Qasas*: 'Nor was thy Lord the one to destroy a population until He had sent to its centre a messenger, rehearsing to them Our Signs; nor are We going to destroy a population except when its members practice iniquity' (28:59) [Ali translation], cited in Bassiouni (n 64) 42, explaining that 'establishment of the law and its divulgation (notice) must precede its application'.

[216] Qur'an in *sūrat al-Nisā'*: 'Messengers who gave good news as well as warning, that mankind, after (the coming) of the messengers, should have no plea against *Allāh*: For *Allāh* is Exalted in Power, Wise' (4:165) [Ali translation], cited in Bassiouni (n 64) 42.

[217] Qur'an in *sūrat al-An'am*: 'Say: "What thing is most weighty in evidence?" Say: "*Allāh* is witness between me and you; This Qur'an hath been revealed to me by inspiration, that I may warn you and all whom it reaches. Can ye possibly bear witness that besides *Allāh* there is another *Allāh*?" Say: "Nay! I cannot bear witness!" Say: "But in truth He is the one *Allāh*, and I truly am innocent of (your blasphemy of) joining others with Him" (6:19)' [Ali translation], cited in Bassiouni (n 64) 42.

[218] Qur'an in *sūrat al-Mā'idah*: "Know ye that *Allāh* is strict in punishment and that *Allāh* is Oft-forgiving, Most Merciful" (5:98) [Ali translation], cited in Bassiouni (n 64) 42.

[219] As cited by Badar (n 153) 419. See also Bassiouni (n 64) 41ff.

[220] Badar (n 153) 420.

[221] ibid.

[222] OIC, *Cairo Declaration on Human Rights in Islam* (n 177).

[223] Art 66 (*presumption of innocence*) encompasses the principle of 'innocent until proven guilty' (66.1), placing the onus on the prosecution (66.2) and setting the standard of proof sought by the court 'beyond reasonable doubt' (66.3).

Article 19(e) of the Cairo Declaration. Under Islamic law, Badar reports, 'no one is guilty of a crime unless his guilt is proved through lawful evidence'.[224] With specific reference to the *hudud*, the presumption of innocence is upheld in a *hadith* transmitted by Aisha.[225] Consistently, 'it is also a well-established principle in *qisas* crimes … that circumstantial evidence favorable to the accused is to be relied upon, while if unfavorable to him it is to be disregarded'.[226] The same is also applicable to the *ta'azir*.[227] Bassiouni reports that in the Farewell Sermon, the Prophet said: 'Your lives, your property, and your honor are a sacred trust upon you until you meet your Lord on the Day of Resurrection', which can be interpreted as evidence of a requirement for 'positive proof of crime' to interfere with an individual's interests and freedoms.[228] According Baderin, the *hadith* 'everyone is born inherently pure', teamed with the legal principle of *istishab* (presumption of continuity), indicates that 'an accused person is considered innocent until the contrary is proved'.[229] Intisar Rabb puts forward similar points.[230] Moreover, the presumption of innocence in Islamic law is corroborated by the 'right to compensation of a person who suffers injury or is punished through judicial error or miscarriage of justice'.[231] This suggests that under Islamic law, judges must not only follow correct procedures, but must also acknowledge mistakes and make amends.

Equality before the law is enshrined in the UDHR,[232] in the ICCPR[233] and in numerous subsequent international law documents, and thus underpins the truth-seeking efforts within the international paradigm of TJ. The principle is enshrined in Article 19(a) of the Cairo Declaration, which includes an explicit reference to the equality before the law between the ruler and the ruled. In the Qur'an, crimes, punishments and criminal proceedings must apply equally, in order to limit the judge's discretionary power.[234] Moreover, as noted by Baderin,

[224] Badar (n 153) 421, 427, the reported legal maxims: 'certainty is not overruled by doubt'; 'the norm of [Shari'a] is that of non-liability'.

[225] 'Avoid condemning the Muslim to *Hudud* whenever you can, and when you can find a way out for the Muslim then release him for it. If the Imam errs it is better that he errs in favour of innocence [pardon] than in favour of guilt [punishment]' cited in Bassiouni (n 64) 43.

[226] Bassiouni (n 64) 43, and Badar (n 153) 421, citing IA Rabb, 'Islamic Legal Maxims as Substantive Canons of Construction: Hudud – Avoidance in Cases of Doubt' (2010) 17 *Arab Law Quarterly* 63, 64–65.

[227] Bassiouni (n 64) 43.

[228] ibid.

[229] Baderin (n 27) 110.

[230] IA Rabb, *Doubt in Islamic Law: A History of Legal Maxims, Interpretation, and Islamic Criminal Law* (Cambridge, Cambridge University Press, 2014).

[231] Baderin (n 27) 110.

[232] Art 7.

[233] Art 14.

[234] Bassiouni (n 64) 44ff, citing Qur'an in *sūrat al-Nisā*': 'O mankind! Reverence your Guardian-Lord, who created you from a single person, created, of like nature, His mate, and from them twain scattered [like seeds] countless men and women; – reverence Allāh, through whom ye demand your mutual [rights], and [reverence] the wombs [That bore you]: for Allāh ever watches over you' (4:1) [Ali translation]. Qur'an in *sūrat al-Hujurāt*: 'O mankind! We created you from a single [pair] of a

'the Prophet himself and the righteous Caliphs after him demonstrated the principle of equality before the courts and tribunals both in words and in deeds'; for instance, Caliph Umar reprimanded a judge for treating him more favourably due to his status and political power.[235] So in principle, like international law, Islamic law places powerful authorities and ordinary individuals on equal footing before the institutions of justice.

The principle of equality before the courts, however, clashes with the famous Qur'anic verse indicating that a man's testimony is equal to that of two women.[236] Contemporary Islamic law scholars have reassessed the scope of this provision, limiting it to commercial transactions in light of the historic context of its revelation (women had limited access to trade).[237] Baderin also suggests that the rationale behind this rule seeks to serve the interests of substantive justice in a particular context, and as such can be retuned to meet the needs of contemporary society.[238] Furthermore, drawing on Ahmed,[239] it would be paradoxic to bestow upon women the responsibility to transmit *hadith* authoritatively, shaping the very essence of *shari'ah*, but bar women from testifying in court. As such, the provision in Qur'an 2:282 should be understood in its limited context, without prejudicing full equality of testimony.

Moving to the list of defences, Article 33 of the Rome Statute excludes the 'possibility of the plea of superior orders for the most odious and egregious international crimes, ie genocide and crimes against humanity, offences which normally involve widespread attack on innocent civilians'.[240] Under *shari'ah*, 'Islam confers on every citizen the right to refuse to commit a crime, should any government or administrator order him to do so.'[241] As such, there seems to be no Islamic justification for admitting the defence of superior orders, which in turn would bolster the ability to seek justice for the most serious crimes and know the truth about orders and the chain of command.

male and a female, and made you into nations and tribes, that ye may know each other [not that ye may despise each other]. Verily the most honoured of you in the sight of Allāh is [he who is] the most righteous of you. And Allāh has full knowledge and is well acquainted [with all things]' (49:13) [Ali translation].

[235] Reported in Baderin (n 27) 100.

[236] ibid, 101 citing Qur'an: 2:282. This verse has been discussed at length, including Fadel (n 68) 185; K Bauer, 'Debates on Women's Status as Judges and Witnesses in Post-formative Islamic Law' (2010) 130(1) *Journal of the American Oriental Society* 1.

[237] Including Baderin (n 27) and NH Barazangi, 'Why Muslim Women are Re-interpreting the Quran and Hadith: A Transformative Scholarship-Activism' in M Failinger et al (eds), *Feminism, Law and Religion* (London, Routledge, 2016) 266.

[238] Baderin, (n 27) 102.

[239] Ahmed (n 61).

[240] P Gaeta, 'The Defence of Superior Orders: The Statute of the International Criminal Court versus Customary International Law' (1999) 10 *European Journal of International Law* 172, 190.

[241] AA Maududi, *Human Rights in Islam* (Lahore, Islamic Publications 1977), cited in Badar (n 153) 426.

The second defence considered by Badar is official capacity immunity, enshrined in Nuremberg Principle III[242] and Article 27 of the Rome Statute. This provision informs the international paradigm of TJ and can be used to bring to justice state officials responsible for grave abuse. Badar recalls that 'in Islamic law, there is no recognition of special privileges for anyone and rulers are not above the law'.[243] This is supported in the *hadith*: Caliph Umar reports that the Prophet himself did not expect any special treatment that would place him above the law.[244] Therefore, even for this aspect the ICL and Islamic law would converge in a TJ context dealing with accountability of state officials for serious violations.

To sum up, the substance of Islamic law and the procedural standards set out in the international legal framework underpinning TJ broadly converge. Truth-seeking efforts, therefore, are not hindered by substantive or procedural provisions of Islamic law. On the contrary, victims seeking the truth about past harm through judicial means might find ample support in the *shari'ah* as discussed in the final chapter.

V. CONCLUSION

Adopting the comparative law lens presented in Chapter 2, this chapter addresses the normative force of Islamic law in the legal systems of Muslim-majority societies through an analysis of its sources and methods, the centrality of human endeavours throughout time, and the relationship between the *shari'ah* and the international legal framework underpinning the truth-seeking element of TJ. This enables a frank and constructive examination of Islamic norms in their social context, without the risk of entering theology or the fiction of 'unseeing' – or overstating – the role of religious normative principles. This sets the scene for the final chapter, which will explore the encounter between Islamic law and the international framework of TJ for truth seeking in more detail.

The discussion of the objectives of Islamic law, and in particular the role of *maslaha* (public benefit), sheds light on the dynamic purposive nature of the *shari'ah*, as well as its inherent ability to respond effectively to new challenges posed by social and political realities. As such, when societies emerge from conflict or authoritarianism and deal with legacies of abuse, the *maqasid* and

[242] Nuremberg Principle III reads: 'The fact that a person who committed an act which constitutes a crime under international law acted as Head of State or responsible government official does not relieve him from responsibility under international law.'

[243] Badar (n 153) 426ff, drawing on Kamali, *Shari'a Law: An Introduction* (n 25) as well as Maududi (n 241).

[244] This is reported in relation to unjustly striking a soldier at the battle of Badr; reported by Badar (n 153) 427, citing Maududi (n 241).

the *maslaha* can offer a vital *référent legislatif* (to borrow from Dupret[245]) alongside the international legal framework. Far from being a static, immutable set of traditional laws, the *shari'ah* and *fiqh* allow a degree of creativity in the spirit of the objectives of Islamic law to support accountability, justice and reconciliation for Muslim societies facing a violent past. The sources of Islamic law, as well as the Islamic law conception of international law, support the substantive and procedural norms that enable truth-seeking processes premised on IHRL and ICL. As such, nobody – not even state authorities – is immune from scrutiny if they have been involved in inflicting harm. The *maqasid* require the protection of religion, life, intellect, family and property – as a minimum core, expanded by subsequent jurists. The right to know details of past harm against those values must be understood in this context. Moreover, the *maslaha*, much like IHRL, compels leaders to consider the public interest in ensuring justice to victims and survivors, as well as providing answers to the community as a whole about widespread past harm. Upholding the common good is an integral part of Islamic law, and there seems to be ample scope to include truth-seeking initiatives in contexts where this is beneficial to individuals and society.

Building on these considerations, it would seem that in principle nothing in Islamic law creates an obstacle to the right to truth regarding forced disappearances, unlawful killings and torture, in line with the international legal framework. Based on the sources and scholarship, it would be fundamentally incorrect to claim that Islamic law does not uphold the right of victims and their families to know the truth about harm suffered; moreover, there is no specific barrier to making the truth about the past publicly available for society at large in appropriate forms (such as archives), to satisfy the dual collective and individual dimensions of the right to truth. Therefore, when states (Islamic or not) fall short of their duty to carry out effective investigations into past harm the reason is purely political: the *shari'ah* is never an obstacle to rendering justice to victims and their families through truth seeking. Developing these arguments further, the final chapter will look at the convergence of the right to truth as emerging in international law and the principles of Islamic law emanating from the sources, *maqasid* and *maslaha*, and supplemented by some authoritative voices of contemporary Islamic jurists.

[245] Dupret (n 3).

6

Transitional Truth Seeking and the Right to Truth in Muslim-Majority Legal Systems

I. INTRODUCTION

PAST AND PRESENT violence in the Middle East and other Muslim-majority societies raises urgent questions about how to hold perpetrators to account and satisfy the need of victims and society to know the truth about harm inflicted upon them. As the previous chapter illustrated, Islamic law offers a holistic approach to justice understood as a core aim of *shari'ah*.[1] Doctrinally, this understanding of justice supports the right of victims and their families to know the truth about harm suffered, and places a corresponding duty on the authorities to investigate, even when the state itself is implicated.

The lack of direct references to truth seeking and the right to truth in the two core sources of Islamic law is not an obstacle to their pursuit through human efforts in the spirit of *shari'ah*. Qur'anic provisions support the right to truth by analogy (*qiyas*) in light of the purpose and aims of Islamic law (*maqasid as-shariah* – the objectives of the *shari'ah*); moreover, the overarching principle of *maslaha* can orient contemporary jurists' understanding and development of the right to truth that fits the requirements of the *shari'ah* as well as the standards of international law and human rights.

Turning to Islamic law to revisit the intertwined themes of truth seeking in transition and the partial view offered by legal truths emerging from legalised truth-seeking initiatives enables a further reflection of the complex and contested nature of these central concepts.[2] Relatedly, by considering the Islamic

[1] See eg MC Bassiouni, *The Shari'a and Islamic Criminal Justice in Time of War and Peace* (Cambridge, Cambridge University Press, 2014); MH Kamali, '*Maqasid al-Shari'ah*: The Objectives of Islamic Law' (1999) 38(2) *Islamic Studies* 193; F Opwis, 'Maslaha in Contemporary Islamic Legal Theory' (2005) 12 *Islamic Law & Society* 182.

[2] See eg A Barahona de Brito, 'Transitional Justice and Memory: Exploring Perspectives' (2010) 15 *South European Society and Politics* 359; M Osiel, *Mass Atrocity: Collective Memory, and the Law* (New Brunswick, NJ, Transaction, 1997); L David, *The Past Can't Heal Us: The Dangers of Mandating Memory in the Name of Human Rights* (Cambridge, Cambridge University Press, 2020) and others.

law support for the emerging right to truth for victims and societies,[3] the discussion furthers the exploration of this principle not only in Muslim-majority contexts, but also as part of a more inclusive global framework of reference for TJ. This chapter, therefore, draws together the different parts of this project by combining notions of transitional truth seeking and the right to truth outlined in Chapters 3 and 4 with the aims of Islamic law and jurisprudence presented in Chapter 5, in light of the methodological considerations of comparative law illustrated in Chapter 2.[4]

The discussion is based on a largely doctrinal study of relevant aspects of *shari'ah* and *fiqh* and secular experiences of truth seeking in Muslim-majority contexts. Moreover, this chapter is supported by interviews with three prominent contemporary Islamic law thinkers from the Arab world asked to elaborate on the Islamic foundations of truth seeking and the right to truth. Two interviewees are from the Sunni tradition, one of whom is a Sheikh and teacher of the Hanafi school of jurisprudence in a prestigious centre of Islamic learning ('Hanafi Sheikh'), the other is a senior jurist in a secular profession whose education and experience blends Islamic and state law ('secular jurist (Sunni tradition)'); the third interviewee is from the Shia tradition ('Shia Seyyed'), and has held a high-profile religious role in his home country and continues to be a spiritual leader. This chapter is divided into three substantive sections. The first part analyses the convergence between the international framework of TJ and *shari'ah* to support truth seeking and the role of both judicial and extra judicial mechanisms, including through creative uses of *fatwas* and *sulh*. The second part turns to the historic uses of legal archives in Islamic court practices, which by analogy, can support transitional truth seeking. This part also discusses the spiritual imperative of synergy between legal truths and historic/factual truths, and considers recent experiences of truth seeking in Muslim-majority societies. The third and final part addresses the right to truth in Islamic law and jurisprudence, illustrating synergy with the developing international norm in relation to torture, extrajudicial killings and forced disappearance, the dual individual and collective function of this right, and the corresponding state duty to investigate.

The findings demonstrate ample scope for supporting transitional truth seeking and the right to truth within the parameters of *shari'ah* and *fiqh*; indeed, a correct understanding of the *maqasid as-shari'ah* and *maslaha* in Muslim-majority societies emerging from conflict or authoritarianism indicates that accountability for serious harm inflicted must be pursued to satisfy the

[3] As outlined in M Klinkner and H Davis, *The Right to the Truth in International Law: Victims' Rights in Human Rights and International Criminal Law* (Abingdon, Routledge, 2020); P Naftali, *La construction du "droit à la vérité" en droit international* (Bruxelles, Éditions Bruylant, 2017) and others.

[4] In particular, the comparative law concepts outlined in R Sacco, 'Legal Formants: A Dynamic Approach to Comparative Law', Instalments I and II (1991) 39 *American Journal of Comparative Law* 1 and 343.

victims, their families and society as a whole. Accountability need not be conflated with criminal punishment: uncovering the truth about past violence may take different forms, and there are no apparent barriers to establishing truth commissions, inquiries and other fact-finding activities that satisfy the requirements of *shari'ah* and *fiqh*. This is an important *doctrinal* finding for international and comparative lawyers seeking to localise transitional truth seeking in the legal systems of Muslim-majority societies; it will be up to others, and especially scholars in sister disciplines and practitioners, to draw on contemporary empirical developments and develop practical applications to ensure past violence in Muslim-majority contexts is accounted for, for the sake of victims and societies as a whole.

II. TRUTH SEEKING: FROM INTERNATIONAL LAW TO ISLAMIC LAW

In light of the broad compatibility between the aims of Islamic law and public international law, in particular IHRL and ICL as discussed in the previous chapter, this section illustrates the convergence between the international framework of TJ and *shari'ah* in supporting truth seeking, and specifically the support for this principle within Islamic law and jurisprudence independently of international law. As such, the first level of synergy between the right to truth as understood in the international law framework of TJ and as conceptualised in Islamic law is quite straightforward, because it requires respect for international treaties entered into that do not contradict the *shari'ah*. As noted by one interviewee,

> We must also always bear in mind that Islamic law requires Muslims to respect the implementation of treaties concluded by the Muslim rulers, as long as they do not contradict the principles of Islamic law. Among those are international treaties that establish 'the right to truth' and 'the right to reparation and compensation'.[5]

Recognising Islamic law support for this principle contributes to the consolidation of the right to truth under international law, based on wider acceptance across jurisdictions and legal systems (as discussed in Chapter 4). The distinctiveness of *shari'ah* discussed in the previous chapter is its divine and thus immutable character as a system of justice, on the one hand, and its adaptability to take into account contextual factors, on the other. Thus, it lends itself well to transitional truth seeking: the higher justice aims of Islamic law are doctrinally fixed, but its applications allow for a degree of flexibility to respond to the specificities of each political, social and cultural context.

The second level of synergy does not require any triangulation with international law: Islamic *shari'ah* itself champions knowing the truth about

[5] Secular jurist-scholar (from Sunni tradition) interview ('secular jurist (Sunni tradition)'), translation on file with the author.

harm suffered. Drawing on the teachings of classical scholars Ibn Rushd and Al Ghazali, Adel Maged argues that discovering the truth is mandated both intellectually (ie based on human efforts) and religiously.[6] Everyone should be able to know what happens in their nation, especially regarding matters of public interest.[7] This echoes the foundations of the right to truth in international law: victims and survivors possess this right individually, but also society at large has an interest in knowing the truth on matters of shared concern (despite dissonant views, discussed in Chapter 3). Truth seeking as a principle, therefore, is anchored firmly in the *shari'ah* inasmuch as it pursues justice and knowledge about past violence.

Despite the absence of a clearly defined and labelled right to truth in Islamic law, its foundation in the *shari'ah* with a broadly comparable content can be deduced through analogy (*qiyas*) in light of the purpose and aims of Islamic law (*maqasid as-shari'ah* – the objectives of the *shari'ah*) and the overarching principle of *maslaha*. The interviewees in this project, both Sunni and Shia, situated truth seeking within the broader notion of justice in Islam. In the words of one interviewee, the Qur'an and *hadith* 'establish that the right to truth in Islamic *Shari'ah* is a necessary goal and method for reaching the truth, in other words to achieve justice'.[8] The right to know the truth is understood as part of a comprehensive legal framework (the Islamic *shari'ah*) set out to guarantee human dignity, which includes accountability for harm inflicted. Examples taken from Islamic criminal law can therefore be applied through *qiyas* (analogy) to situations of wars, conflicts or revolutions against oppressive rulers. As such, the right to truth and the value placed upon truth seeking is situated within the broad justice aims guiding the *shari'ah*, which apply in all situations.[9]

The interviewees converge on the fact that truth seeking and the right to truth find a basis in the *shari'ah*. What emerges from the responses to the questionnaire is a blend of the aims of truth and justice that cannot be easily taken apart in the *shari'ah*. The Hanafi Sheikh stated that 'right to truth is an established concept in Islamic *shari'ah*' as a 'right for all, without distinction between people and nations', 'established with certainty, without concealment, fraud, equivocation or dishonesty'. In essence, it 'is the right of every person and every nation (ie society) to know the truth of the things (that concern them), and the things they are unaware of or they seek to know'. As a right, he continued, it is related to the 'public good' (*maslaha*) and is not exclusive to any individual person. Similarly, the secular jurist (Sunni tradition) described the right to truth in Islamic *shari'ah* as a 'requirement to seek, explore, and trace the truth, and

[6] A Maged, العدالة الانتقالية في الشريعة الإسلامية / *Transitional Justice in Islamic Sharia* (IRZ, German Foundation for International Legal Cooperation, 2013) 58–61, translation on file with the author.
[7] ibid.
[8] Secular jurist (Sunni tradition) interview.
[9] ibid.

make sure of it'; it is 'the right of a person or society at large to know the truth of certain events in a definite and conclusive manner'. The Shia Seyyed took a more specific criminal law view of the concept: 'where a criminal act is committed against someone, the victim, their family and the public have a right to know the truth about what happened. This right exists in order to preserve justice and is upheld through criminal trials', clarifying that the right to truth 'enables the public to watch (ie have oversight of) the judicial system' and does 'not depend on whether the criminal act happened in the past or more recently'.

These findings echo the value placed on knowing the truth and, by analogical extension, truth seeking, as elaborated in various sources of Islamic law. The Hanafi Sheikh clarified that 'not only does Islamic heritage offer many examples of this concept but Islamic *Shari'ah* is overflowing with texts on the concept of "truth" and a person's "right to truth"'. He offered a selection of verses in the Qur'an that support the right to truth. Surat Al Tawbah 'suggests two important things: the first is the necessity of informing and presenting the whole truth to a person as this is their established right, and the second is ensuring the safety of this person and not letting them become subjected to harm'.[10] Surat Al Israa 'stipulates that no person or *ummah* can be punished without a reason and that every person must know what is required of them and not be judged based on what they are ignorant of'.[11] Surat Al Nisaa offers further 'evidence that Islam sanctifies the truth, even if the one departing from the truth (unintentionally) is the Prophet Muhammed himself', demonstrating 'reverence for the truth, and the importance of judging among people fairly, in a manner that follows God's words'.[12] The context of the *sura* is significant, because it illustrates that truth seeking based on Islamic law does not discriminate in favour of Muslims over non-Muslims:

> A man stole a shield from another person's house. When they said that so-and-so is the thief, the thief took the shield and planted it in a Jewish man's house, so the family of the thief went to the Prophet and said that the Jewish man had stolen the shield. The Prophet almost believed them but God Almighty immediately assisted his Prophet and guided him to the truth. In this incident, the words of God Almighty were sent down to the Prophet to reveal the truth and to absolve the Jew.[13]

There is further support for the right to truth in two more verses of Surat Al Nisaa, which taken together 'provide that one should not support or argue

[10] Surat Al Tawba, verse 6: 'And if any of the polytheists asks you for protection, grant him protection so that he may hear the Word of Allah; then escort him to his place of safety', cited in Hanafi Sheikh interview, translation on file with the author.

[11] Surat Al Israa, verse 15: 'nor do We ever punish until We have sent a messenger' in Hanafi Sheikh interview.

[12] Surat Al Nisaa verse 105: 'We have revealed to you the Scripture, with the truth, so that you judge between people in accordance with what Allah has shown you. And do not be an advocate for the traitors' in Hanafi Sheikh interview.

[13] ibid.

for the benefit of traitors, as they betrayed God'.[14] Moreover, this *sura* contains an important admonishment for offenders who escape accountability in this life: God will judge them on the Day of Resurrection.[15] As the Hanafi Sheikh sums up, 'if a person does not obtain the truth in this life, he will in the afterlife, because we all know how many offenders escaped their offences and how many criminals escaped from their crimes': Allah is omniscient, and will hold them accountable for their actions. This establishes a duty for Muslims to seek the truth, because 'if the truth is concealed in this world, it will not be concealed on the Day of Resurrection'. Therefore, concludes the Hanafi Sheikh, 'the aim of these noble verses is to explain the extent to which Islam seeks to inform people of the truth, and not merely to define the truth but to hold those who conceal the truth accountable'.

A similar principle emerges in another passage of the Qur'an cited by the secular jurist (Sunni tradition), in which Allah says to (biblical) David (a prophet and messenger in Islam):

> O David, verily we have placed you as a successor on Earth, so judge between people in truth and do not follow your own desires lest they mislead you from the path of Allah. Verily, those who wander astray from the path of Allah, shall surely face severe punishment for forgetting the Day of Reckoning.[16]

Taken together, these Qur'anic provisions suggest that the right to truth is afforded to both Muslims and non-Muslims, and that accordingly there is a corresponding duty of those in power: in Surat Al Nisaa, for instance, this was the Prophet, but by analogy this could be extended to the judiciary and all relevant state institutions that might participate in truth-seeking initiatives.

The Sunna (*hadith*) provides similar support for the principle of truth seeking and the right to truth for Muslims and non-Muslims. The Hanafi Sheikh narrated a *hadith* in which Muhammad came to know that a Muslim had killed a *dhimmi* (non-Muslim living in a Muslim-majority community): the Prophet ordered that *qisas* (retribution) be implemented, and that the Muslim killer be handed over to the relatives of the non-Muslim person murdered.[17] Therefore, 'as long as the true facts emerge' there is 'no distinction between Muslims and non-Muslims', although there can be exceptions to this rule in the context of war between Muslims and non-Muslims.[18] Furthermore, the Hanafi Sheikh

[14] Surat Al Nisaa verses 106–07: 'And ask Allah for forgiveness. Allah is Forgiving and Merciful' and 'And do not argue on behalf of those who deceive themselves. Allah does not love the deceitful sinner' in Hanafi Sheikh interview.

[15] Surat Al Nisaa verses 108–09: 'They hide from the people, but they cannot hide from Allah. He is with them, as they plot by night with words He does not approve. Allah comprehends what they do' and 'Here you are! advocating for them in this life, but who will dare to advocate for them before Allah on the Day of Judgment? Or who will come to their defense?' in Hanafi Sheikh interview.

[16] Surat Sad, Q:38:26, cited in Secular jurist (Sunni tradition) interview.

[17] Reported in Hanafi Sheikh interview as narrated by Abdelrahman Al Yamamy: 'I am the keenest to honour my pledges to the *dhimmis*.'

[18] ibid.

indicated that the practices of Caliphs Omar Ibn Khattab and Ali reaffirmed the equality principle regarding access to justice; by interpretative analogy, therefore, the equality principle can be extended to the right to truth inasmuch as it is a corollary of access to justice.

A. Adjudication as Truth Seeking

The process of adjudication and the role (and good faith) of the judge emerge as central themes in the Islamic conceptualisation of the right to truth in both Sunni and Shia traditions. A *hadith* reported by the Secular jurist (Sunni tradition) illustrates a comparable norm emerging from the Traditions of the Prophet:

> Judges are three – two in hell, one in heaven: a man who judges by other than truth, knowingly, is in hell, a man who did not know the truth and ruled according to his ignorance is in hell, and a man who recognised the truth and ruled accordingly, is in heaven.[19]

Similar scrutiny of a judge's investigation into a matter is found in the Shia tradition. As an example of the right to truth as a principle in Islamic law and jurisprudence, the Shia Seyyed reported an event during Imam Ali's caliphate about a boy seeking to know the truth about his father's death and recover stolen funds through a judge:[20]

> There was a wealthy man (hereinafter the 'victim') who had a young boy. The victim travelled with a group of men (hereinafter the 'suspects') for business. After a while the suspects returned without the victim. The boy asked the suspects where his father was. 'He died', the suspects said. 'Where is his money?' The boy asked. The suspects replied 'he did not have any money'.
>
> The boy complained to Shuraih Alqadhi (a prominent local judge)[21] who consequently interrogated the suspects. He decided they were innocent: there was no evidence, and the suspects took an oath swearing that they did not kill the victim.
>
> Imam Ali saw the boy crying in a mosque in Al-Kufa and asked him what was wrong. 'Shuraih Alqadhi, the judge, made an unfair decision' the boy said. 'What is your standing in this case?' Imam Ali asked. The boy replied: 'these people – gesturing towards a man in the mosque – they travelled with my father and came back without him, and when I asked them where he was, they said he died. I asked about his money, and they said they did not know that he had money. Shuraih (the judge) demanded that the suspects swear their statements were true, and they did, so the judge asked me to leave them alone.'

[19] Reference in Sunan Al- Tirmidhi, *ḥadith* no 1322, cited in Secular jurist (Sunni tradition) interview.

[20] Shia Seyyed interview, translation on file with the author.

[21] Shuraih Ibn Al-Harith Ibn Qais Ibn Al-jahm Al-Kandi (590–698 AD) was known as 'Shuraih Alqadhi'. *Alqadhi* means 'the judge'. Shuraih was a jurist, poet and a fine judge in Al-Kufa for almost sixty years (translator's note).

So, Imam Ali said to Qanbar (his servant): 'bring the four suspects to me, and also call *Shurtat Al-Khamis*'.[22] The suspects and the boy sat before Imam Ali, who asked the boy to repeat what he had said to him earlier about the case. The boy cried and explained what happened again: 'I am accusing these men of taking advantage of my father; they made him travel with them and stole his money.'

Imam Ali asked the suspects if this was true. But they repeated exactly what they had said to Shuraih the judge: 'the victim died, and we do not know anything about his money'. Then, Imam Ali looked them in the face and said: 'what do you think? Do you think I do not know what you did to this boy's father? You think I am ignorant?'

So, Imam Ali asked the suspects to disperse in the mosque, each man standing in front of a pillar. He called for his scribe Obaid Ibn Abi Rafe'a and asked him to sit down. Imam Ali then called only one of the suspects, and asked: 'tell me as quietly as possible, what day did you leave your houses with the boy's father?' The suspect answered which day it was. Imam Ali told his scribe: 'write it down'. 'What month?' The suspect answered which month it was. Imam Ali told his scribe: 'write it down'. 'Which year?' Imam Ali asked. The suspect answered which year it was. The scribe wrote all the answers down. 'What was the victim's illness?' Imam Ali asked. The suspect answered what the victim's illness was. 'In which house did the victim die?' Imam Ali asked. The suspect answered. 'Who washed and wrapped the body?' Imam Ali asked. The suspect answered. 'What burial shroud was used?' Imam Ali asked. The suspect answered. Imam Ali asked: 'who handled the funeral prayer?' The suspect answered who it was. Imam Ali asked the suspect who buried the body and the suspect answered. The scribe wrote everything down.

When the interrogation was over, Imam Ali said '*Allahu Akbar*'[23] loud enough that everyone in the mosque could hear him. He then asked the first suspect to go back to where he was standing. Imam Ali then called the second suspect and asked him the same questions that he had asked the first suspect. But the second suspect's answers were different from the first suspect's answers. The scribe wrote all the answers down. When Imam Ali finished questioning the second suspect, again he said '*Allahu Akbar*' loud enough for everyone in the mosque to hear. Imam Ali then asked the two men he had interrogated to leave the mosque and to wait in front of the prison gates.

Imam Ali questioned the third suspect. That suspect answered differently from the first two suspects. Imam Ali said '*Allahu Akbar*' and asked the third suspect to wait with his co-suspects in front of the prison gates. Then Imam Ali called the last suspect who was stuttering. Imam Ali was staring at him in an intimidating fashion. The man confessed that he and the other men had killed the victim, taken his money and buried him near Al-Kufa. Imam Ali said '*Allahu Akbar*' and sent the perpetrators to jail. He then called one of the perpetrators and said: 'you said the victim died naturally but the truth is that you killed him – you better admit it'. The suspect confessed that he killed the victim. Imam Ali called the other suspects, they showed remorse and admitted that they had killed the man. So, Imam Ali ordered the group of men to return the victim's money to the boy.

[22] *Shurtat Al-Khamis* (Elite Guards, in English) was a sizeable military force established by Imam Ali. It consisted of warriors who preserved safety, law enforcement and who generally accompanied Imam Ali (translator's note).

[23] *Allahu Akbar* (God is the greatest) (translator's note).

> Imam Ali asked the boy: 'now you know who the perpetrators are, what do you want me to do with them?' The boy said: 'I want justice between me and them to be handed down by Allah, but I forgive them in this life'. Imam Ali did not execute them, but applied another sentence.[24]

This account is fascinating for a number of reasons. First, it illustrates the Islamic support, including in the Shia tradition, of the value of truth seeking and the revelation of factual truths surrounding a criminal act. While this story pertains to non-transitional criminal justice, the underpinning truth-seeking norm can be extended by analogy to other contexts, including transitions from conflict and authoritarianism. Second, the narrative lends itself to the extrapolation of a norm in support of truth seeking that can be applied at different stages of an investigation to ensure it is effective, and scrutinised by a different arbiter if necessary. Third, the lenient penalty applied (prison, as well as returning the stolen money), despite the concurrent crimes of murder (regulated through *qisas*, and thus *diyya*, victim compensation) and robbery (regulated through *hudud*, and thus usually meriting a harsh punishment), suggests that the purpose of the investigation was not retributive justice, but uncovering the truth and ensuring justice for the victim and their family were aims in their own right. Once the truth emerged, and the money was returned, the boy chose to forgive the perpetrators, and leave the final judgment to God. Imam Ali's intervention to overrule the first judge's findings is motivated by the boy's quest for an effective investigation; this suggests that the victim and family have an important role in initiating proceedings (in this case, an 'appeal' as well). In a historical context where political and judicial authorities overlapped significantly, this account can be interpreted as illustrating support for effective (criminal) investigation and scrutiny of proceedings where the outcome remains unsatisfactory for the victim and family. The normative principle emerging from this, therefore, is that

[24] The rest of the answer provided by the interviewee offers the 'rationale' behind Imam Ali's leniency, through an earlier account:

> Shuraih Alqadhi, the judge, asked Imam Ali bewilderedly: what made you make that decision?
>
> Imam Ali replied: once upon a time Prophet Dawud walked past two boys, one of them was calling the other 'dead religion'. Dawud called the latter and asked about his name. My name is 'dead religion', the boy answered. Who named you that? Dawud asked. My mother, the boy said. Where is your mother? Dawud asked. In her house, the boy answered.
>
> Dawud asked the boy to lead him to his mother. Dawud then asked the mother: what is your son's name? His name is 'dead religion'. Dawud asked: who named him that? His father, the mother said. What was the reason behind this name? Dawud asked. The mother said: his father travelled with a group of men, I was pregnant, the group of men came back without my husband. I asked them where he was, they said he is dead. I asked them about his money, and they said he did not have any money with him. I said: did he leave a letter for me? They said: yes, he said you are pregnant, and if you have a boy then name him 'dead religion' so I did.
>
> Dawud asked the mother if she knew where these men are. She said that she did. He asked her to bring them to him, and it was proved that they killed her husband, but he only asked for the victim's money without executing them. Then Dawud told the mother: re-name your son 'alive religion'.

authorities have a duty to investigate harm inflicted, and victims and their families not only have a right to petition the judge, but they may also seek further investigations to uncover the truth if unsatisfied. Its potential relevance to transitional truth seeking after conflict and authoritarianism is apparent: by analogy, the victim (and family's) right to truth and the related state duty to investigate can be deduced.

B. Extrajudicial Mechanisms for Truth Seeking

In addition to judicial mechanisms (trials) and other formal inquiries led by state authorities, uncovering the truth about past harm can emerge from lawful extra-judicial mechanisms outside the scope of the state (as discussed earlier in this book). In that flexible context, Islamic law can offer a foundation for actioning truth seeking about serious harm inflicted in relation to conflict or authoritarianism. The truth can be both the direct aim of a particular mechanism, but also the necessary collateral outcome of processes contingent on truth seeking. The examples of *fatwa* and *sulh* that follow illustrate these possibilities.

The first example, *fatwa*, already discussed in Chapter 5, is a non-binding legal opinion emanating from an established scholar, which may (or may not) be relied upon in the adjudication of a dispute.[25] In its historical function, a *fatwa*, argues Amalia Zomeño, was 'constructed as a legal story', in which the question and the answer to a legal question 'were considered legal precedents and compiled as such, so that the social and legal stories were transformed into pieces of jurisprudence'.[26] She recalls, however, Mohamed Fadel's admonishment that 'a fatwa falls somewhere between the ideal and the real', as it constitutes 'the empirical manifestation of his [the mufti's] opinion and it emerges from a unique set of empirical facts'.[27] Moreover, the formulation of the response by the mufti – a legal scholar himself – is imbued with the complex persona of his role which includes the administration of justice, teaching and debating the law, advising the judge in court (based on his independence, actual or purported).[28] *Fatwa* compilations were meant to last throughout history: after the answer by the mufti was compiled, a *fatwa* went through a process to establish the 'official' version.[29] Zomeño summises:

> The only access we have to knowing what really happened in society comes from a text constructed by a jurist. Our access to this record happens only after the mustafi, who is in most cases a judge, makes a selection of the relevant events in the legal

[25] See, in general, WB Hallaq, 'From Fatwas to Furu': Growth and Change in Islamic Substantive Law' (1994) 1(1) *Islamic Law and Society* 29.

[26] A Zomeño, 'The Stories in the Fatwas and the Fatwas in History', in B Dupret, B Drieskens and A Moors (eds), *Narratives of Truth in Islamic Law* (London, IB Tauris 2008) 25ff.

[27] ibid, citing M Fadel, 'Fatwas and Social History' (1996) 8(2) *al-'Usur al-Wusta* 32–34.

[28] Zomeño (n 26) 32.

[29] ibid 47.

> sphere. Historians depend on the job of the mustafi, who, in principle, should be objective and provide the mufti with accurate information on the story.[30]

Building on the historical significance of *fatwa* – but mindful of the human fallibility of muftis – a legal opinion emerging from a qualified, independent individual, office or committee able to investigate grievances seems in principle able to synthesise an account of the truth resembling legal truth, with the set of caveats discussed in Chapter 3 applicable in this instance as well.

The second example of extrajudicial processes uncovering the legal truth is found in the *sulh* mechanism, roughly translated as 'amicable settlement', an alternative dispute settlement mechanism under Islamic law 'grounded upon compromise negotiated by the disputants themselves or with the help of a third party'.[31] As an alternative to trials, it encompasses the concepts of 'conciliation' and 'peacemaking',[32] resonating with transitional aims. Its applications include both civil and criminal justice contexts.[33] In conjunction with trials, *sulh* provides the procedural option to 'defer disputants to mediation before trying their case or at any stage of trial'.[34] As such, it can become a flexible and personalised tool to reach a shared position on past injustices.

The merits of uncovering and reconciling contrasting accounts of the past through *sulh* after conflict and violence have been explored in detail by Rashda Diab.[35] As a 'relational and moral good' *sulh* is 'rendered meaningful by its relation to the values of '*adl*, *ihsan* and *hikmah*' (justice, beneficence and wisdom), and the Islamic 'obligation to rightfully testify and pursue justice'.[36] It offers a 'cultural reservoir' as a means to build collective memory 'unlike forensic memory' which instead pursues retributive justice.[37] Many voices are engaged dialogically in *sulh*, including 'transgressors, victims, their families, mediators, … and community members at large who sometimes weigh in as silent but often as vociferous participants'.[38] *Sulh* is a good example of how truth seeking and restorative aims interact. Unlike trials 'that give primacy to the distant role of

[30] ibid.

[31] For an historical overview of amicable settlements as an alternative to trial in the Islamic tradition, see A Othman, '"And Amicable Settlement is Best": Sulh and Dispute Resolution in Islamic Law' (2007) 21 *Arab Law Quarterly* 64, 65ff.

[32] A Al-Ramahi, '*Sulh*: A Crucial Part of Islamic Arbitration', LSE Law, Society and Economy Working Papers 12/2008 (2008) available at ssrn.com/abstract=1153659.

[33] MS Hossain, 'Arbitration in Islamic Law for the Treatment of Civil and Criminal Cases: An Analytical Overview' (2013) 1 *Journal of Philosophy, Culture and Religion* 1.

[34] Othman (n 31) 65.

[35] R Diab, *Shades of Sulh: The Rhetorics of Arab–Islamic Reconciliation* (Pittsburgh, PA, University of Pittsburgh Press, 2016).

[36] ibid 44, citing the Qu'ranic verse al Nisa' 136: 'O you who have believed, be persistently standing firm in in justice, witness for Allah, even if it be against yourselves or parents and relatives. Whether one is rich or poor, Allah is more worthy of both. So follow not [personal] inclination, lest you not be just. And if you distort [your testimony] or refuse [to give it], then indeed Allah is ever, with what you do, acquainted.'

[37] ibid 49.

[38] ibid 62.

the judge who seeks only factual or forensic truth', *sulh* offers a space to tell and listen to 'excess narratives',[39] going far beyond the procedural constraints imposed upon the legal truths emerging from ordinary judicial proceedings. Historic examples presented by Diab include the Charter of Medina in the early days of Islam, in which the Prophet Mohammed sought to reconcile different groups after a period of violent conflict and establish a unified political community, despite deep differences and a legacy of violence. The malleability of *sulh* and its potential in piecing together competing accounts of past wrongs remains an important tool to deal with more recent episodes of violence.

And although the primary aim of *sulh* is reconciliation, it also builds a narrative and collates factual evidence in order for the dispute to be solved. Indeed, just like in proceedings before a judge, the 'third party' of *sulh* must be satisfied with the narrative and evidence in order to adjudicate. Aida Othman argues that under Islamic law 'the trial process is not regarded as an ultimate truth-finding mechanism that will lead to substantive justice'.[40] Therefore, a *sulh* settlement can synthesise the competing narratives, demands and positions as accepted by the adjudicator – resulting in the formation of legal truths of sorts.

The scope of potential applications of *sulh* extends to 'conflicts between members of society' when such application 'is in the public's interest (*al-maslahah al-mursalah*)'.[41] It appears in medieval and modern penal codes.[42] Today, *sulh* is notably used in commercial arbitration.[43] The favour afforded to *sulh* in the Islamic legal tradition is based on the Qur'anic encouragement to solve disputes amicably,[44] preferring forgiveness and reconciliation:

> The recompense for an injury is an injury equal thereto (in degree): but if a person forgives and makes reconciliation, his reward is due from Allah, for (Allah) loveth not those who do wrong.[45]

The *hadith* supports this. A tradition attributed to Caliph Umar indicates that adjudication without an amicable settlement leads to bitterness.[46] Othman recalls

[39] ibid 75.

[40] Othman (n 31) 69, citing Qur'an 4:128: 'If a wife fears cruelty or desertion on her husband's part, there is no blame on them if they arrange an amicable settlement between themselves; and such settlement (*sulh*) is best. And Qur'an 4:35: If ye fear a breach between them [the spouses], appoint (two) arbiters, one from his family and the other from hers; if they wish for peace, Allah will cause their reconciliation: For Allah hath full knowledge, and is acquainted with all things.'

[41] ibid and EA Alsheikh, 'Distinction Between the Concepts Mediation, Conciliation, Sulh and Arbitration in Shari'ah Law' (2011) 25 *Arab Law Quarterly* 367, 369 and fn 8, citing Qur'an 3:35: 'And if you fear a breach between the two [spouses], then appoint a judge from his people and a judge from her people; if they both desire agreement, Allah will effect harmony between them, surely Allah is knowing, aware.'

[42] Othman (n 31) 72, citing the Dulkadir in Anatolia and the Ottoman Mejelle (1885).

[43] Al-Ramahi (n 32).

[44] ibid 12.

[45] Qur'an 42:40 cited in Othman (n 31).

[46] Othman (n 31) 69, citing Raddū-l-khusūm hattā yastalahū, fa-inna-l-qadā yūrith al-daghā'in', 8 (15304): 303–04; Ibn Abī Shayba, al-Musannaf 7 (2938): 213–14: 'Dispel the disputants until they settle amicably with one another (yastalatu); for truly adjudication leads to rancour.'

that 'the Prophet was said to have encouraged compromise and to have mediated both public disputes, such as those between fighting clan members, and private ones, including those between his Companions and their creditors'.[47] This is especially interesting for truth seeking after conflict or authoritarianism because it confirms the applicability of *sulh* both for private and for public affairs. In a similar manner to other forms of local, informal dispute settlement discussed previously in this study, *sulh* allows greater flexibility and wider scope than ordinary court proceedings, potentially uncovering a greater range of truths.

On the basis of this description, *sulh* may have a role in uncovering the truth about past violence and in giving formal recognition to the accounts of disputing parties. Although the resulting legal truth is unable to offer a comprehensive account of factual truths, given the focus on a specific dispute, it nevertheless is able to contribute to uncovering some truth about past harm. Firstly, much like trials, *sulh* uncovers truths as part of a legal ritual, setting down a record of sorts about a past dispute (or abuse) and legitimising and formalising its discovery in official/legal language. Secondly, its findings provide a synthesis of competing narratives mediated by a third party, combining potentially competing versions of the past. Unlike trials, however, it is mostly a voluntary instrument based on choice.

The legal truths that emerge through *sulh* depend heavily on the actors that shape the process – as in any truth-seeking initiative. Thus, unless there is a further mechanism to appeal the resulting truths, *sulh* may favour more powerful accounts, try to put a premature and summary end to a discussion about the past, or enable (or perpetuate) other forms of violence. If truths uncovered through *sulh* mechanisms are given public effect through archiving or publication, depending on how they are conserved in practice, they can not only help reconstruct and challenge dominant historical accounts, but also feed into contested and evolving narratives of the past. Moreover, *sulh* could be linked in two ways to the formal judicial system (domestic or international): first, parties in trials could be offered a joint procedural right to access *sulh*, allowing victims to instigate this mechanism to uncover truth and apportion responsibilities about past abuse beyond the formalism of courts. Second, *sulh* could be used as a non-criminal procedure with the possibility to refer more serious cases to the criminal courts. In general, *sulh* could operate analogically to some truth commissions – a mechanism already tested in Muslim-majority contexts.[48] Therefore, *sulh* is an interesting option available to policymakers seeking to

[47] ibid.

[48] Notably, the Moroccan Equity and Reconciliation Commission (ERC). See inter alia F Loudiy, *Transitional Justice in Morocco: Negotiating the Years of Lead* (Abingdon, Routledge, 2014); L Wilcox, 'Reshaping Civil Society Through a Truth Commission: Human Rights in Morocco's Process of Political Reform' (2009) 3(1) *International Journal of Transitional Justice* 49, 58; and B Dennerlein, 'Remembering Violence, Negotiating Change: The Moroccan Equity and Reconciliation Commission and the Politics of Gender' (2012) 8(1) *Journal of Middle East Women's Studies* 10, 13.

develop TJ initiatives to uncover the truth which also resonate with Islamic law, given the favour afforded to *sulh*.

III. THE PRODUCTION OF LEGAL TRUTHS IN MUSLIM-MAJORITY SOCIETIES: HISTORIC PRACTICE, MORAL IMPERATIVES, AND CONTEMPORARY APPLICATIONS

Analysing the right to truth in Islamic law and jurisprudence must be contextualised in the broader discussion of the complexities of truth seeking and the formation of legal truths discussed in Chapter 3. What emerges is a gap between the potential offered in historic Islamic legal practice and the moral imperatives derived from a religious understanding of truth and justice, on the one hand, and the relatively limited invocation of religious language and principles when Muslim-majority societies have attempted to address legacies of violence. This part, first, considers historic practice and spiritual imperatives that underpin the production of legal truths, then, secondly, reviews a sample of recent situations in which Muslim-majority societies have engaged in transitional truth seeking. In the third, and final, section the discussion reveals the very limited uses of Islamic law so far: but this should not deter future initiatives from embracing the potential of *shari'ah* in the context of truth seeking.

A. Compiling Legal Truths in Historic Islamic Legal Practice

Legal truths emerge from legal rituals – in TJ, these include trials, truth commissions and public inquiries – which present similarities to religious rituals (discussed in Chapter 3). These processes are shaped by key actors and procedural binds, which may play an ambiguous role in uncovering as well as masking the truth about past harm. Historically, written documentation of legally relevant facts has played an important role in the legal systems of Muslim-majority societies, inasmuch as documents help prove a legal title, right or interest *inter partes* as well as *erga omnes*. In Islamic law there is 'a remarkable interest in recording … the outcomes and effects of wars, invasions and conflicts, and documenting the facts related to them, with a strong focus on remembering victims, whether these victims are Muslims or non-Muslims'.[49] Moreover, Islamic law permits the documentation of crimes of unjust rulers, in order to hold them accountable in different ways. The documentary and archival function of written material in the Islamic legal tradition chimes with the understanding of archives emerging in the TJ literature, whereby transitional archives contribute 'to a new social contract following massive human rights abuses which have put

[49] Secular jurist (Sunni tradition) interview.

to question trust in the state and in fellow citizens'.[50] As argued by Julia Viebach, transitional archives 'are created through these different types of records and materials' and 'captured, (re)assembled, (re)purposed and (re)contextualised for an institutionalised state-led or bottom-up transitional justice process'; their societal, political and historical significance is broad, and as such they possess a 'multi-layered afterlife'.[51] The richness of historic archival material in the Islamic legal tradition supports contemporary compilations and uses of written materials documenting violence, which can be woven into the transitional truth-seeking processes as required – and contested in democratic debates.

In the early *shari'ah* courts, the judge's scribe 'recorded the statements, rebuttals and dispositions of the litigants, and, moreover, drew up legal documents on the basis of the court records for those who needed the attestation of the judge'.[52] Outside the court, private notaries (*shuruti*) drafted legal documents for individuals entering into contracts.[53] These documents could be referred to beyond an individual case or transaction. With reference to truth seeking in transitional contexts, written records of private and public matters (including criminal matters) contribute to uncovering the truth about past abuse and archiving information.[54]

Early Islamic legal practice sought to systematise and retain information for future access. Alongside court scribes and private notaries, by the eighth century there are reports of established *diwan* and collections of court records (*sijillat*).[55] These included judges' decisions on claims made by the parties, as well as registers including prisoners' names and terms of imprisonment.[56] Hallaq has described the *diwan* as embodying 'the complete record of the judge's work in the court, and the chief tool by which judicial practice preserved its continuity', passing to successive judges, allowing protracted cases to continue in new hands, and the work of predecessor judges to be scrutinised.[57] Keeping written evidence of legal matters in a formal, established repository meant creating a record of the facts (or perceived facts) for future consultation.

As illustrated in the previous chapter there is no single legal system or court that represents the *shari'ah* that can be drawn upon to ascertain how the legal truth is understood in Islamic law. Instead, in order to identify relevant practices,

[50] B Jones and I Oliveira, 'Truth Commission Archives as "New Democratic Spaces"' (2016) 8(1) *Journal of Human Rights Practice* 6, 7.

[51] J Viebach 'Transitional Archives: Towards a Conceptualisation of Archives in Transitional Justice' (2021) 25(3) *International Journal of Human Rights* 403, 404ff.

[52] WB Hallaq, *The Origins and Evolution of Islamic Law* (Cambridge, Cambridge University Press, 2004) 92ff.

[53] ibid.

[54] On archives and transitional justice, see UNHRC, Twenty-fourth session, 'Report of the Special Rapporteur on the Promotion of Truth, Justice, Reparation and Guarantees of Non-recurrence, P de Greiff' (28 August 2013) UN Doc A/HRC/24/42, para 81.

[55] Hallaq (n 52) 92ff.

[56] ibid.

[57] ibid 95ff.

it is necessary to look holistically at Islamic law and its practices across time and place. For the purposes of this discussion, the production and preservation of documents by Ottoman *shari'ah* courts offers a historic example of records, statements and judgments that respond to certain procedural rules and authoritativeness. Two key caveats are necessary: first, historic examples should be approached contextually, and second, they do not reflect the whole scope of possible legal truths that could emerge from judicial, quasijudicial and formalised extrajudicial mechanisms invoking Islamic law.[58] Nevertheless, they offer a helpful set of comparative materials and indicate a historic tradition elevating formal written records of legally relevant facts.

The *sijillat* are a widely studied body of formal written records produced in Ottoman courts (explicitly based on *shari'ah*) since the 1300s.[59] These documents, and the legislation that regulated their production and preservation, demonstrate the importance afforded to record-keeping in relation to justice and administration and offer fascinating insights into social and political matters across the Ottoman Empire. Ahmed Akgunduz reports over 20,000 *shari'ah* record books (*sijillat*) from the Istanbul courts alone, and quotes a detailed decree by a fourteenth-century sultan on procedural rules for writing and preserving such documents.[60] The information contained in such documents varied, but essentially it enabled the parties to the dispute as well as third parties to consult an authoritative account of facts, any witness/expert statements and the judge's decision. These shared archival practices, reports Guy Burak, 'broke the connection between a specific diwān and a specific judge' and 'contributed to the preservation of both court records and registers'.[61] This feature, namely the recognition that written records have both *inter partes* significance and more general uses for posterity, is distinctive of the legal truth, which has both an individual and public/collective dimension. It also echoes the Sunni–Hanafi discourse of the 'use of the written word as legal evidence'.[62] This reflects the potential reiteration of legal truths emerging from the Ottoman courts across other settings.[63] Once a narrative was enshrined in legal language and sealed with the formal approval of the judge, it became much more than a simple written summary of a case. Ottoman court records were more than just a by-product of a dispute-settlement mechanism: they contributed to the creation of legal facts, regardless of their exact correspondence to reality, like any legal truth.

[58] There are many more reasons to be cautious, including selection bias, analysed in MM Coşgel and BA Ergene, 'The Selection Bias in Court Records: Settlement and Trial in Eighteenth Century Ottoman Kastamon' (2013) 67(2) *Economic History Review* 517.

[59] For an overview, A Akgunduz, 'Shari'ah Courts and Shari'ah Records: The Application of Islamic Law in the Ottoman State' (2009) 16 *Islamic Law & Society* 202.

[60] ibid 205.

[61] G Burak 'Evidentiary Truth Claims, Imperial Registers, and the Ottoman Archive: Contending Legal Views of Archival and Record-Keeping Practices in Ottoman Greater Syria (Seventeenth–Nineteenth Centuries)' (2016) 79(2) *Bulletin of SOAS* 233, 253.

[62] ibid 254.

[63] See discussion in ch 3 with examples drawing from ICTY trials.

The general considerations and critiques outlined in Chapter 3 with regards to the factual, political and social limits of legal truths[64] hold true also in relation to the narratives contained in the *sijillat* as an example of the legal truth in the Ottoman Islamic legal tradition. Ottoman judicial records were not immune from political influence. Guy Burak reconstructs the debate in the seventeenth–nineteenth centuries over the validity and evidentiary authority of the imperial registers (*defter*) alongside and on a par with judicial records (*sijillat*), which illustrates not only the different scholarly positions of Ottoman jurists at that time, but also the way in which politics could influence the legal sphere.[65] The gap between the descriptive historical content of the *sijillat* and reality suggests that

> the sijills are carefully constructed narratives in which the legal aspect, although invisible to the reader, is still the essence of the record. In other words, the record discusses the case not as it actually unfolded but rather in terms consistent with legal doctrine and practice.[66]

Dror Ze'evi lists contradictory narratives, power relations and the influence of the authorities, as well as the relatively narrow scope of what is reported, the possible interference of translators and scribes, and the linguistic choices of formal legal language as key challenges to the validity of the *sijillat* as an authoritative historical document – and thus the emerging legal truths at the time of writing and for the future.

As discussed previously, legal truths contribute to the development of narratives which in turn feed into historical TJ processes in building collective memories. With reference to legal truths in Muslim-majority legal systems, Baudouin Dupret and Barbara Drieskens separate 'the law as a topic of inquiry in its own right and legal texts and stories as a resource for social history'.[67] The centrality of understanding legal stories in their context is described as 'the many cultural, institutional, substantive and procedural practicalities, relevancies and

[64] See eg K Hearty, 'Truth Beyond the "Trigger Puller": Moral Accountability, Transitional (In)justice and the Limitations of the Legal Truth' (2021) *International Journal of Transitional Justice* (online version ahead of print); O Bakiner, 'One Truth Among Others? Truth Commissions' Struggle for Truth and Memory' (2015) 8(3) *Memory Studies* 345; S Buckley-Zistel, 'Narrative Truths: On the Construction of the Past in Truth Commissions' in S Buckley-Zistel, TK Beck, C Braun and F Mieth (eds), *Transitional Justice Theories* (London, Routledge, 2014). For a helpful overview of the judicial truth specifically, see D Accatino and C Collins, 'Truth, Evidence, Truth: The Deployment of Testimony, Archives and Technical Data in Domestic Human Rights Trials' (2016) 8(1) *Journal of Human Rights Practice* 81.

[65] Burak (n 61) 252.

[66] D Ze'evi, 'The Use of Ottoman Sharīʿa Court Records as a Source for Middle Eastern Social History: A Reappraisal' (1998) 5(1) *Islamic Law and Society* 35, 38.

[67] B Dupret, B Drieskens and A Moors (eds), *Narratives of Truth in Islamic Law* (London, IB Tauris 2008) 8ff, 12ff. For an interesting analysis of the language games of truth formation in courts, see B Dupret, *Practices of Truth: An Ethnomethodological Inquiry into Arab Contexts* (Amsterdam, John Benjamins, 2011) 59ff.

technicalities that concurred to constraining the specific course of action'.[68] They explain how legal texts 'are both contextualizing and contextualized',[69] supporting the claim that legal material is both a product of a certain context but can also be constitutive of it. Actors (religious and secular) who contribute to the initiatives constructing legal truths as well as their intended present and future 'audiences' have a role in uncovering past truths.

Regarding the formation of legal narratives in *shari'ah* courts, Brinkley Messick recalls that 'all lawsuits are built of conflicting narratives' and at the conclusion of the litigation, 'the judge's ruling selectively evaluates these conflicting narratives and either finds for one or imposes his own final narrative'.[70] For example, the mid-twentieth-century Yemeni *hukm* (final judgment records) included a number of components:

> The opening claim and response texts, any later responses (by either party), primary evidentiary texts (including, as sub-varieties, both oral testimony and a range of written documents, including notarial instruments), and the judge's concluding ruling itself (*hukm* in the narrow sense), all of which were quoted in the terminal judgment record.[71]

Courts make strategic decisions on what to include in the official narrative of the records, which carries legal weight.[72] Records can be very detailed and include lengthy passages from statements by the parties.[73] But the 'dictates and emphases of specific archival cultures', the 'forms imposed by legal genres' and the 'dialogic developments between opposing narratives in the course of a given trial' must be approached critically.[74] A final ruling, therefore, might be based on only 'one of the narratives, or at least a relevant part of it', which does not capture the full picture.[75] As discussed previously, the formation of the legal truth and related collective memories pertaining to past violence based on narrow rulings might ignore wider implications. This could be countered by ensuring judicial records are collected and made accessible to a wider public (as supported by Islamic legal practice) when it is in the public good (*maslaha*) to do so.

When courts are set up to protect the interests of those in power, legal truths uncovered as part of the truth-seeking efforts can be skewed.[76] This emerges in the interview with the Hanafi Sheikh, who identified this as a major problem today, also referring to the partial justice delivered by international courts

[68] Dupret, Drieskens and Moors (n 67) 13.
[69] ibid.
[70] B Messick, 'Legal Narratives from Shari'a Courts' in Dupret et al (eds), *Narratives of Truth in Islamic Law* (n 67) 52.
[71] ibid 53.
[72] ibid 58.
[73] ibid 66.
[74] ibid 67.
[75] ibid 68.
[76] See discussion in ch 3, including eg JM Balkin, 'The Proliferation of Legal truth' (2003) 26 *Harvard Journal of Law and Public Policy* 5.

in the context of the legacies of North–South colonialism.[77] He provocatively asked whether one party to the case will be a judge, leading to 'those oppressed [being] portrayed as the oppressor and those who oppress being portrayed as the oppressed' to highlight the ongoing challenge of fair and impartial proceedings – which may in turn pollute the veracity of the account as well as the justice of the judgment itself.

Islamic law, in principle, has a tool to deal with the absurdity of those in power presiding over trials against them. Historically, alongside the ordinary judiciary, a new set of tribunals standing at the margins of *shari'ah* courts appeared, known as *mazalim* tribunals (ie boards of grievances), for the purpose of 'correcting wrongs committed by state officials'.[78] The *mazalim* were also mentioned by one of the interviewees for this project in relation to the right to truth about human rights violations committed by the authorities.[79] Hallaq describes these courts as supplementary, more limited and sporadic, compared to the jurisdiction of ordinary courts. The *mazalim* (or *Dar al Mazalim*) are:

> Courts that served as tribunals of administrative law where the public directly appealed to the ruler or his deputies against the abuse of or failure to exercise power by other authorities, as well as against decisions made by judges.[80]

Reports and interpretations of the *mazalim* illustrate the ambiguities of their nature and purpose, given they were often placed under the direct control of the political ruler and separate from *qadi* courts.[81] The *mazalim*, operating alongside *qadi* courts, illustrate a changing division of legal labour.[82] A distinguishing feature of the *mazalim* courts highlighted by Mawardi (and reported in Shahar) is the different degree of freedom accorded to the litigant according to the type of claim involved.[83]

> In criminal cases involving the 'rights of man' (*huquq adami*), plaintiffs are free to choose whether to apply to the *qadi* court or the governor in his capacity as *mazalim* judge. However, cases involving violations of the 'rights of God' (*huquq Allah*), which belong to the sphere of public interest, fall under the jurisdiction of the governor (and the not *qadi*).[84]

[77] Hanafi Sheikh interview.

[78] Hallaq (n 52) 99.

[79] Secular jurist (Sunni tradition) interview: '[T]he early Islamic State had established *Diwan Al-Mazalem* (Ombudsman's Office) to look into all types of grievances submitted before it, including human rights violations. This mandate relies on principles of Islamic law which necessitate administering justice and repelling injustice with regards to the violations committed by the governors and rulers who have authority and influence over their subjects.'

[80] 'Mazalim Courts' in JL Esposito (ed), *The Oxford Dictionary of Islam* (Oxford, Oxford University Press, 2003) www.oxfordislamicstudies.com/article/opr/t125/e1487.

[81] M Tillier, 'The Mazalim in Historiography' in A Emon and R Ahmed (eds), *The Oxford Handbook of Islamic Law* (Oxford, Oxford University Press, 2019) 358–59.

[82] I Shahar, 'Legal Pluralism and the Study of Shari'a Courts' (2008) 15 *Islamic Law and Society* 112, 126ff.

[83] ibid 126ff, citing ABM Mawardi, 'Al-Ahkham al-Sultaniyya wa'l-Wilayat al-Diniyya'.

[84] ibid.

This suggests that the *mazalim* courts exercised jurisdiction upon claimants' action where their interest had been interfered with, as opposed to the automatic jurisdiction exercised by the ordinary courts involving *huquq Allah* violations (ie *hudud* crimes). Hallaq identifies four main areas in which the *mazalim* tribunals operated:

(1) They prosecuted injustices committed in the performance of public services, such as unfair or oppressive collection of taxes, or non-payment of salaries by government agencies;
(2) They dealt with claims against government employees who transgressed the boundaries of their duties and who committed wrongs against the public, such as unlawful appropriation of private property;
(3) They heard complaints against Shari'a judges that dealt mainly with questions of conduct, including abuses of office and corruption;
(4) They enforced Shari'a court decisions that the *qadi* was unable to carry out.[85]

In terms of the relationship between courts, Hallaq reports an Egyptian instance of the ninth century, in which a *mazalim* court was established due to a lack of qualified men to serve as *shari'ah* judges, and subsequent *shari'ah* courts overturned the *mazalim* decisions.[86] The value of these courts seems to be their flexibility compared to ordinary courts, which, if not managed correctly, might challenge today's fair trial and due process standards. For the purposes of this study, however, the historic existence of the *mazalim* can open a discussion about the role of successor regimes in establishing new forums to address past abuse when the ordinary judicial system is implicated with the former regime. The precise nature of the new forum would necessarily flow from the context in which a 'special' forum for grievances about past injustices carried out by the (previous) authorities emerges; it could also include quasijudicial mechanisms such as truth commissions or other public inquiries geared to hear individual grievances.

B. Bridging the Tension between Legal Truths and Historical/Factual Truths in Islamic Law: The Spiritual Imperatives of Convergence

The tension between legal truth and historical/factual truth in transitional truth-seeking efforts[87] is echoed in the Islamic legal tradition. The dichotomy

[85] Hallaq (n 52) 100.
[86] ibid 101.
[87] On this point, see the discussion in ch 3, including Deborah Posel's 'rainbow of truths' metaphor, drawing on the South African TRC's four notions of truth: factual/forensic; personal/narrative; social/dialogue; and healing/restorative, in D Posel, 'The TRC Report: What Kind of History? What Kind of Truth?' (1999) 10; and also R Aldana summary of the potential importance, for victims, of forensic truth/hard facts; emotional truth; general truth emerging from criminal trials and truth commissions in R Aldana, 'A Victim-centered Reflection on Truth Commissions and Prosecutions as a Response to Mass Atrocities' (2006) 5(1) *Journal of Human Rights* 107, 109.

between legal truth and historical/factual truth reflects the gap between legal validity based on judicial-procedural formality, and the ethical dimension of the truth understood in relation to holistic justice, discussed earlier with reference to the interviews. Some of the challenges of truth finding (and more broadly adjudication) through trials and other formal mechanisms are summarised in the following *hadith*:

> You bring me lawsuits to decide, and perhaps one of you is more skilled in presenting his plea than the other and so I judge in his favour according to what I hear. He to whom I give in judgment something that is his brother's right, let him not take it, for I but give him a piece of the Fire.[88]

In Islamic law, explained the secular jurist (from the Sunni tradition) interviewed for this project,

> whoever commits a sin (in its modern version of human rights violations) cannot escape punishment. Punishment could be during a person's life time, in the form of *hadd* (punishment prescribed in the Qur'an), *qisas, ta'zír (*judicial discretionary punishment), or in the afterlife, or both. In all cases, these violations must be documented, and perpetrators should be held accountable.[89]

As such, internal religious convictions bestow a sacredness on these responsibilities, giving accountability for harm inflicted a divine meaning as well.

In practice, legal truth emerging from any initiative in this life is the product of mere human effort. However well-intentioned, it risks reasserting unequal social structures in the course of trials and other truth-seeking initiatives. Under Islamic law, a *qadi*'s decision based on incorrect facts is problematic: 'the execution of the title or the obligation is licit only if the judgment concurs with the truth of the facts' because 'even if the qadi ignores this truth the parties' memory preserves it'.[90] This becomes a spiritual issue as much as a legal and political one – but nevertheless, one marred by human fallibility.

In reviewing the positions of (Sunni) classical jurists on 'legally and procedurally impeccable judgment[s] which [are] blatantly wrong in [their] appreciation of the facts' Baber Johansen found a gradual shift.[91] For instance, in the Hanafi and Hanbali traditions there seems to be a tendency towards 'the sacred character of the judiciary's verdict: the judge's decision is God's norm as revealed by his deputy and the believers have to abide by it'.[92] Conversely, on the basis of Qur'anic provisions and *hadith*, later Hanafi scholars objected to the doctrine of the 'ethically binding character of the judge's verdict which is based on error

[88] M ibn Anas (d 179/795), al-Muwattā (Beirut: Dār al-Gharb al-Islāmī, 1996) vol 2 under Kitāb al-Aqḍiya [Book of Judgments] (2103), cited in Othman (n 31) 69.

[89] Secular jurist (Sunni tradition) interview.

[90] B Johansen, 'Truth and Validity of the Qadi's Judgment: A Legal Debate Among Muslim Sunnite Jurists from the 9th to the 13th centuries' (1997) 14 *Recht van de Islam* 1, 18.

[91] ibid 9.

[92] ibid 12ff.

in fact', upholding the 'believer's ethical and religious duty to behave according to his knowledge of the truth of the facts'.[93] As such, an important distinction is introduced between internal and external forums (ie conscience and expression) of knowledge of factual truths, providing a new perspective on how legal truth can be understood in Islamic legal settings. According to Johansen:

> In the relation 'between the individual and God' the 'forum internum' is governed by the knowledge which the parties have of the truth of the facts. Only in referring to his or her knowledge of the facts can the individual person define his or her responsibilities before God. If the judge's decision does not correspond to the truth of the facts it cannot, before the forum internum, determine the individual's ethical responsibility.[94]

For the Shafii doctrine (and Maliki[95]), there is no dividing line between legal and ethical validity, and an erroneous judgment 'may even lose its legal validity in face of ethical opposition', as the *forum internum* rules over the *forum externum*.[96] Thus, the *qadi* must 'do justice to both dimensions, the legal and the ethical one'.[97] This approach consolidates the religious significance of the truth, which may (and religiously, should) influence the formation of the legal truth and its subsequent uses.

In general, Johansen indicates that the vast majority of Sunni scholars concur in that the 'qadi's judgment constitutes a legal title, the confirmation of a legal claim'.[98] However, parties to a case must act according to 'ethical considerations', as a 'religious duty to act according to the truth of the facts', based on the significance of *forum internum* religious considerations that guide Muslims:

> The truth of the facts as preserved by the parties' memory is recognized by the jurists as the decisive criterion of the forum internum for the legitimacy of the verdict's implementation by the parties. It is on the level of its implementation by the parties that the qadi's judgment remains related to and dependent upon the truth of the facts. Before the forum internum the qadi's decision is valid only if it is based on true assumptions as far as the facts of the case are concerned.[99]

Accordingly, 'legal and the ethical dimension of religious normativity have to co-exist' for Islamic law.[100] Nonetheless, there is a difference between 'the authority of the judicial verdict which is based on correct procedure and independent legal reasoning' and 'the truth of the facts which remain hidden to

[93] ibid, referencing A Yusuf and ash-Shaybani; and Qur'an 2:188: 'And do not consume one another's wealth unjustly or send it [in bribery] to the rulers in order that [they might aid] you [to] consume a portion of the wealth of the people in sin, while you know [it is unlawful].'
[94] ibid.
[95] ibid 17.
[96] ibid 15.
[97] ibid 16.
[98] ibid 18ff.
[99] ibid.
[100] ibid.

the qadi'.[101] As such, uncovering the legal truth is a procedural question, whereas revealing the factual truth is one of ethics and faith, as well as a substantive one.

Commenting on the difference between Islamic and secular (ie IHRL-based) requirements to uncover the factual truth about past violence, one of the interviewees considered that:

> The main difference between Islamic *shari'ah* and man-made laws in this regard, is that in Islamic *shari'ah*, the primary motive for admitting guilt and disclosing the truth is based on an ethical and divine basis, while in man-made laws it is purely based on one's own benefit.[102]

Taking stock of this analysis, two main conclusions can be drawn with regards to the relationship between legal and factual truth in Islamic law: (1) *how to find the truth* – a *qadi*-led trial set out to uncover the truth (legal and factual) is supplemented by a spiritual imperative. A *mazalim* hearing, *sulh* procedure and potentially a *fatwa* could be equally acceptable depending on context. And (2) *why to find the truth* – on the basis of the religious ethics that underpin the distinction between *forum internum* and *forum externum*, factual truth is valued more highly than the legal truth, which is why truth-seeking efforts must be genuine and effective (much like what is required in IHRL – as discussed in Chapter 4). Ideally, of course, they would converge.

Truth-seeking initiatives that uncover legal truth that departs from factual truth (verifiable or not through other means), therefore, are met with an ethical-religious higher level of justice in the *forum internum*, whereby believing perpetrators will face the creator on the day of judgment. As such, while there seems to be a religious imperative to ensure truth seeking in this life reflects the factual truth as closely as possible, Islamic law acknowledges that this is not always possible, but that is rectified by the fact that ultimately divine justice will be served. In this vein, the secular jurist (Sunni tradition) interviewed for this project recalled the moral imperatives of human rights that underpin the requirement to uncover the facts about human rights violations – inviting 'the West' to engage more deeply with the *shari'ah* justifications for the right to truth:

> Human rights in Islamic law is not a granted by a king or ruler, or a decision issued by an international authority or organization. Rather they are binding rights by virtue of their divine nature and source, these rights are not to be erased, abrogated, obstructed, or waived, and no infringement of these rights is permitted. Therefore, the endorsement of these rights is the correct approach to establishing a true Islamic society.
>
> Some researchers in Islamic law have – rightly – categorized human rights as 'sanctities/inviolabilities' that are sacred, and shouldn't be subject to violations, as

[101] ibid 19.
[102] Secular jurist (Sunni tradition) interview.

> God granted them to humans. Accordingly, the preservation of those rights should be considered as a devotion to Allah, as all rights of Allah's worshippers are fortified by Allah. Thus, the protection and preservation of human rights should be considered as a sort of piety to Allah.[103]

Given the absolute primacy of the internal, moral and religiously mandated dimension in Islamic legal thinking, a primacy that should constitute the benchmark for truth seeking in this world as well, there seems to be no overarching obligation under Islamic law to override factual truth with procedurally sound legal truth; indeed, this would contradict the holistic justice aims of the *shari'ah*. Moreover, there is no obligation to establish truth through trials alone, especially if courts have been unable to deliver legal truths to match factual (and ethically sound) truths. As such, transitional truth-seeking mechanisms can, in light of the Islamic legal tradition, depart from ordinary justice (which in the Islamic legal tradition can be ascribed to *qadi*-led justice) in uncovering legal truths more closely linked to factual truth. This confirms that truth commissions and other non-judicial enquiries do not contravene Islamic law; instead, experimenting with *fatwa* and exploring the possibilities of *sulh* and *mazalim* may inspire more effective ways to pursue transitional truth seeking after past abuse.

The discussion confirms that, for believers, a fallible trial conducted by humans comes second to accountability before God. This may have important ramifications for deeply religious perpetrators of crimes, for whom divine judgment (and condemnation for harm inflicted) could become a significant factor in encouraging participation in truth-seeking initiatives (as discussed earlier in relation to religion and TJ more generally). When a trial delivers legal truths that depart from factual truths, Islamic law's holistic conception of justice offers ample opportunity for the perpetrator to give an account of harm inflicted in alternative mechanisms designed ad hoc, based on the *sulh* or *mazalim* model adapted to contemporary realities and IHRL standards. The Qur'an itself provides incentives for believers to participate in (and promote) truth-seeking initiatives by establishing religious rewards:

> O you who believe! Be maintainers of justice, bearers of witness for God's sake, even if though it be against your own selves, you parents, or your near relatives, and whether it be against [the] rich or [the] poor.
>
> O you who believe! Be upright to God, bearers of witness with justice.[104]

More broadly, giving truth-seeking initiatives a religious grounding might increase local ownership at societal level in light of the value of Islamic law. For the reasons outlined earlier in this chapter, pursuing factual truth through legal and extralegal (but lawful) avenues gains a spiritual meaning for believing third parties in Muslim-majority societies. And despite the distortions of the usual

[103] Secular jurist (Sunni tradition) interview.

[104] Qur'an 4:135 and 5:8 cited in MA Baderin, *International Human Rights and Islamic Law* (Oxford, Oxford University Press, 2003) 99.

political and personal power structures that permeate any given setting, truth-seeking initiatives through multiple mechanisms can – and should – be couched in a broadly inclusive way, which in some contexts might encompass the secular and spiritual benefits of uncovering the truth about past harm and apportioning responsibility accordingly.

C. Contested Truths and Collective Memories: Recent Examples in Muslim-Majority States

There are no specific examples of clearly defined Islamic truth-seeking mechanisms – both explicitly Islamic and explicitly truth seeking – in recent history. However, some initiatives in Muslim-majority countries facing legacies of violence reveal how religion has been deployed – or not – by key actors to address contested truths and help build collective memories. The approaches taken in Morocco and Tunisia – both adopting a truth commission of sorts – and to an extent Bahrain, offer some interesting perspectives on how religion may be used (or not used) to further truth-seeking efforts, while Egypt illustrates how key religious actors may wield their social and political weight in transitions. The broader context in which religion and religious discourse is used in TJ, including truth seeking, has been addressed in earlier chapters. The examples discussed in this section illustrate, firstly, how the full meeting between the truth-seeking aims of TJ and Islamic law to address legacies of violence is yet to occur in Muslim-majority societies. Secondly, they support the thesis presented by Elham Kazemi:[105] despite the calls to incorporate Islamic principles in TJ to ensure greater local legitimacy, using religious principles and actors in the localisation process is itself deeply political and should be approached mindfully.

i. Morocco

The Equity and Reconciliation Commission (Instance Equité et Réconciliation, IER) was set up in Morocco in 2004 to

> establish the truth about the violations that occurred during the Years of Lead, compensate victims, initiate a process of national reconciliation, and most importantly, promote a culture of human rights and respect for human dignity and life to contribute to the associated project of democratic transition.[106]

[105] E Kazemi, 'Transitional Justice in Tunisia: When Religion Meets State' (2019) 13 *International Journal of Transitional Justice* 590.

[106] Loudiy (n 48) 5–7. The state violence, including torture, kidnapping, arbitrary arrests and murders perpetrated by officials acting on behalf of the monarchy between the 1960s and 1990s are well documented in the academic literature and civil society reports on the Years of Lead. The final Report of the IER available at www.cndh.ma/an/rubriques/documentation/publications/report-equity-and-reconciliation-commission-ier.

Despite the range of shortcomings of the IER described in numerous NGO reports, Fadoua Loudiy identifies the accounts presented by victims and their families in 'public hearings, commemorations, books, testimonies, interviews' as the 'nations' collective memory of the recent past, the consciousness of that people, and … reminders of what happened, so that it does not happen again'.[107] The IER's contribution to building collective memories of painful and contested truths is the first such example in a Muslim-majority Arab country.

Religion did not feature explicitly in the Moroccan IER experience, but the role of Islam as the majority faith in a distinctive political context cannot be overlooked. According to the Moroccan constitution, Islam is the state religion, despite recognising that its citizens profess different faiths (or none).[108] The monarch, descended from the Alaoui dynasty descended from the Prophet Mohammed, is largely 'an uncontested symbol of religious and political power, continuity and stability' (even in light of the legacy of French colonialism).[109] Loudiy explains how the religious credentials of the Moroccan monarchy and the psychological deference of the country's subjects-citizens towards the descendants of the Prophet have bestowed legitimacy upon the kings, but also shielded violent actions of the state from political criticism, resulting in the absolute power (and semi-authoritarianism) of Hassan II. The infusion of religious authority in the person of the monarch (to this day, with Mohammed IV) and the fact that Islam is the state religion and majority faith would suggest that despite the secular nature and aims of the IER, which did not engage openly with the *shari'ah*, religion cannot be engineered out of the truth-seeking process. The Islamic milieu of Morocco was (and remains) present even in the absence of explicit references. What this suggests for the purposes of this study is that the IER could not have been proposed, developed and implemented if it had been in stark opposition to Islamic law and principles.

ii. Tunisia

A more recent example of truth seeking in a Muslim-majority country is the Tunisian Truth and Dignity Commission (Instance Vérité et Dignité, IVD) set up by the Transitional Justice Law in 2013 for 'discovering the truth about human rights violations, but also holding perpetrators accountable, providing reparations for victims, and preserving and documenting the collective memory' about the dictatorship period, from 1955 to 2013.[110] This chimes with the emergence

[107] ibid 6.
[108] ibid 68–69.
[109] ibid 62–63.
[110] Kazemi (n 105) 602–03. Truth and Dignity Commission, *The Final Comprehensive Report*, May 2019 can be accessed (in English) here: www.ivd.tn/rapport/doc/TDC_executive_summary_report.pdf. For some international civil society reporting on the IVD, see inter alia 'Tunisia: Truth Commission Outlines Decades of Abuse' (*Human Rights Watch*, 5 April 2019) available at www.hrw.org/news/2019/04/05/tunisia-truth-commission-outlines-decades-abuse and, 'Tunisia: Truth Commission

of guarantees of non-repetition in TJ discourse, discussed in earlier chapters. The truth-seeking aims of the IVD are foregrounded in the law that established it. Article 1 of the Organic Law on Establishing and Organizing Transitional Justice describes TJ as:

> An integrated process of mechanisms and methods used to understand and deal with past human rights violations by revealing their truths, and holding those responsible accountable, providing reparations for the victims and restituting them in order to achieve national reconciliation, preserve and document the collective memory, guarantee the non- recurrence of such violations and transition from an authoritarian state to a democratic system which contributes to consolidating the system of human rights.[111]

The centrality of the truth is reaffirmed throughout that law. Article 2 states that 'Revealing the truth about the violations is a right guaranteed by law to every citizen taking into consideration the respect of the victims' interest and dignity and the protection of private information', and Article 4 explains further:

> Revealing the truth shall consist of a series of methods, procedures and research used to dismantle the authoritarian system by identifying and determining all the violations as well as determining their causes, conditions, sources, surrounding circumstances, and repercussions. In cases of death, missing persons, and enforced disappearance, it shall uncover the fate and whereabouts of the victims as well as the identity of the perpetrators and those responsible for such acts.
>
> The particularity of the violations' impact on the elderly, women, children, those with special needs and vulnerable groups of society, and the sick shall be taken into account when revealing the truth.[112]

Much like the Moroccan IER, the Tunisian IVD did not engage directly with religion, although Article 20 of the Organic Law indicates that (among other members) the commission should include a specialist in religious sciences, and Article 27 describes an oath to God for members taking office. Elham Kazemi elaborates on the contested relationship between Islam and the state since Tunisia's independence from France, which contextualises Tunisia's recent truth-seeking efforts as well as its renewed constitutional profile (civil nature of the state, with references to Islam) as a consensus between secular and Islamist political actors.[113] Her distinction between Islam as a religion and Islamists as a political group (embodied in the Ennahda party) is fundamental in understanding the contextual uses and invocations to Islam before and after Ben Ali's

Findings Must Lead to Justice for Thousands of Victims of Human Rights Violations' (*Amnesty International*, 25 March 2019) www.amnesty.org/en/latest/news/2019/03/tunisia-truth-commission-findings-must-lead-to-justice-for-thousands-of-victims-of-human-rights-violations/.

[111] Tunisia, Organic Law on Establishing and Organizing Transitional Justice, Unofficial translation of the ICTJ available at www.ohchr.org/Documents/Countries/TN/TransitionalJusticeTunisia.pdf.

[112] ibid.

[113] Kazemi (n 105) 603–06.

fall. Given that 'religion is more likely to play a role as a marker of political and collective identity',[114] any references to Islam in the Tunisian IVD process cannot be disentangled from that context. What the IVD experience reveals as a whole (despite its shortcomings and the tensions between secular and religious political forces) for the purposes of this project is that its truth-seeking mandate, scope and activities are broadly compatible with Islamic law principles, given its endorsement by Islamist as well as secular groups.

iii. Bahrain

A further example to consider is the Bahrain Independent Commission of Inquiry (BICI) established in 2011 by a royal order to investigate human rights violations during a period of civil unrest resulting in serious violence earlier that year.[115] Its purpose was:

> to investigate and report on the events occurring in Bahrain in February/March 2011, and any subsequent consequences arising out of the aforementioned events, and to make such recommendations as it may deem appropriate.[116]

The Commission's final report set out to contain the following aims:

> a. A complete narrative of the events that occurred during February and March 2011;
> b. The context for these events;
> c. Whether during these events there have been violations of international human rights norms by any participants during the events or in the interaction between the public and the government;
> d. A description of any acts of violence that have occurred including the nature of the acts, how they occurred, who the actors were and what consequences derived therefrom …;
> e. Instances of alleged police brutality and alleged violence by protestors and/or demonstrators against police and others, including foreigners;
> f. The circumstances and appropriateness of arrests and detentions;
> g. Examination of allegations of disappearances or torture;
> h. Ascertain whether there was any media harassment, whether audiovisual or written, against participants in demonstrations and public protests;
> i. Examination of alleged unlawful demolition of religious structures; and
> j. Ascertain any involvement of foreign forces and foreign actors in the events.[117]

Despite the lack of a clear political transition in Bahrain, the purpose and scope of the inquiry resemble truth-seeking efforts after authoritarianism.

[114] ibid 606.
[115] MS Helal, 'Two Seas Apart: An Account of the Establishment, Operation and Impact of the Bahrain Independent Commission of Inquiry (BICI)' (2019) 30(3) *European Journal of International Law* 903.
[116] Report of the Bahrain Independent Commission of Inquiry (BICI) (23 November 2011) ('BICI Report') available at www.bici.org.bh/BICIreportEN.pdf, 1.
[117] ibid.

As such, its significance is worth investigating for this study on Islamic support for truth seeking after violence and abuse. The Bahraini legal system is a hybrid of various traditions, with Article 2 of the constitution indicating the Islamic *shari'ah* as the principal source of legislation.[118] Moreover, the composition of the BICI took stock of the religious make-up of the country with sizeable Sunni and Shia communities alongside non-Muslim groups.[119] It was chaired by esteemed Egyptian-American legal scholar M. Cherif Bassiouni, and included Dr Mahnoush H. Arsanjani and Dr Badria A. Al-Awadhi whose legal education in Iran and Egypt, respectively, offered complementary Sunni and Shia doctrinal knowledge, as well as international non-Muslim experts.[120] The role of Islam in Bahrain and the majority Muslim-heritage commissioners in the BICI suggest that the purpose and scope of the report are compatible with the principles and aims of Islamic law.

It is worth noting that aim (a) of the list provided above sets the bar extremely high, given that no single complete narrative is capable of capturing the divergent perspectives of past violence, memories of which remain contested in transitioning societies (as discussed in Chapter 3). The issues investigated included the lack of accountability and culture of impunity for excessive use of force by state actors, including torture.[121] As summed up by Mohamed Helal:

> BICI made 27 recommendations, most of which related to accountability for human rights abuses. The commission recommended the establishment of a 'national independent and impartial mechanism to determine the accountability' of officials, 'including those in the chain of command', who committed 'unlawful or negligent acts' that led to human rights violations.[122]

In the aftermath of the BICI report, the Bahraini government established various bodies to implement the recommendations.[123] The push for accountability for torture, deaths and other forms of mistreatment, and the holding of those responsible to account, has however been limited to a handful of prosecutions and resulted in inadequate sentences for the crimes committed.[124] Despite the political realities hindering the intended effects of the BICI, the report itself offers a valuable resource for all human rights work in the country, contributing to the formation of a narrative about the past for various actors to digest and build upon. As such, the BICI experience offers another a helpful example of how a truth-seeking mechanism addressing contested truths and building collective memories can be used to address contested memories and attempt to uncover the truth about past abuses in a mixed Sunni–Shia Muslim-majority society.

[118] ibid 37.
[119] For figures, see ibid 13.
[120] See biographies of the BICI Commissioners at www.bici.org.bh/index0d2a.html?page_id=20.
[121] BICI Report 418.
[122] Helal (n 115) 917.
[123] ibid 917–18.
[124] ibid 920–22.

iv. Egypt

Another instance where the truth-seeking aims of TJ have been indirectly engaged by an institution presenting itself as a guardian of Islam is the response of Al Azhar to the events that occurred in 2011 in Egypt. Islam's centrality in Egypt is undisputed: the principles of Islamic *shari'ah* were the main source of legislation in the 1971 constitution, and remained so in its 2014 iteration (Article 2).[125] Al-Azhar enjoys a special role in the country and beyond. Founded in the 900s as a centre of Islamic learning, Al-Azhar has been described by Malika Zeghal as providing:

> 'the humanly devised constraints' that shape the interaction between men and God, or to be more precise, a structure of mediation between the divine and the human that offers interpretation of scripture to the faithful, manages religious ritual and transmits religious knowledge.[126]

Throughout history the relationship between Al-Azhar and (Egyptian) politics has been complex and marked by attempts by the authorities to control the religious sphere.[127] In the late 1900s Egyptian authorities championed Al-Azhar as the voice of moderate Islam, approved by politicians and theologians alike; this has helped distance national Islam from the Muslim Brotherhood and other Islamist groups, as well as secular forces.[128] Its leaders enjoy the prerogative to 'speak for religion in public life' as recognised learned scholars, and are separate from the state-run *dar al-ifta*, the *fatwa*-issuing body (also) consulted by the institutions.[129] Since the fall of Mubarak, Al-Azhar's religious authority has been deployed in a highly charged political context under Morsi and General al-Sisi.[130]

Shortly after Mubarak's deposition, Al-Azhar demonstrated its religious and political support of transition by issuing two fascinating statements in 2011: the Al-Azhar Declaration on Support of the Arab Revolutions[131] and the Al-Azhar

[125] Egypt's Constitution of 2014, available in English at www.constituteproject.org/constitution/Egypt_2014.pdf. See also discussion in C Lombardi and N Brown, 'Islam in Egypt's new Constitution' *Foreign Policy* (13 December 2020) available at foreignpolicy.com/2012/12/13/islam-in-egypts-new-constitution/.

[126] M Zeghal, 'The "Recentering" of Religious Knowledge and Discourse: The Case of al-Azhar in Twentieth Century Egypt' in R Heffner and MO Zaman (eds), *Schooling Islam: The Culture and Politics of Modern Muslim Education* (Princeton, NJ, Princeton University Press, 2007) 107ff.

[127] For a historical analysis, see inter alia D Crecelius, 'Al-Azhar in the Revolution' (1966) 20(1) *The Middle East Journal* 31; and M Zeghal, 'Religion and Politics in Egypt: The Ulema of al-Azhar, Radical Islam, and the State (1952–94)' (1999) 31(3) *International Journal of Middle East Studies* 371.

[128] Zeghal (n 126) 109. See also S Barraclough, 'Al-Azhar: Between the Government and the Islamists' (1998) 52 *The Middle East Journal* 236.

[129] NJ Brown, 'Post-Revolutionary Al-Azhar', The Carnegie Papers, Middle East (2011) 5ff.

[130] This is described by M Bano and H Benadi, 'Regulating Religious Authority for Political Gains: al-Sisi's Manipulation of al-Azhar in Egypt' (2018) 39(8) *Third World Quarterly* 1604.

[131] The Al-Azhar Declaration in Support for the Arab Revolutions, 31 October 2011, tr A Maged and A Panepinto, available at www.dur.ac.uk/ilm/newsarchive/?itemno=13661.

Document on the Future of Egypt.[132] Neither document tackles truth seeking directly, but they offer important evidence of how religious institutions participate in a transitional context in Egypt and across the Muslim world. Al-Azhar's early engagement in the Arab uprisings has been described as a 'good example' of its 'latent reform potential ... for the development of Islamic principles',[133] which may help further TJ goals. Egyptian commentators welcomed these developments:

> Both documents should have an influence on the constitutional structure of the emerging Egyptian regime and the legal rules governing the right to protest and revolt against authoritarian regimes throughout the Arab world.[134]

The text of the Al-Azhar Document on the Future of Egypt refers to the general principles of *shari'ah*, leaving 'considerable room for a modern interpretation of Islamic concepts and values rather than citing specific provisions in the traditional Islamic rules'.[135] In the Preamble, the institution presents itself as 'guiding toward right moderate Islamic thinking'. Broadly speaking, this modern (functionalist) interpretation seems consistent with the principle of *maslaha*. Offering its support to anti-Mubarak revolutionaries, the Document calls for the establishment of 'a modern and democratic state' supported by 'Islamic precepts' that 'include pluralism, rotation of power, determining specializations, monitoring performance, seeking people's public interests in all legislations and decisions, ruling the state in accordance with its laws, tracking corruptions and ensuring the accountability of all people' (Articles 1 and 2). The references to accountability and democratic principles in this 2011 document suggest that there would be ample scope within this religious institution's approach to pursue the right of victims and society to know the truth about past abuse.

The Al-Azhar Declaration in Support of the Arab Revolutions has a similar purpose. It amplifies Al-Azhar's influence beyond Egypt (listing Tunisia, Libya, Syria and Yemen expressly) recalling the 'spirit of freedom in Islam and the Islamic rules on the legitimacy of authority and reform, and the achievement of the objectives and the supreme interests of the nation' (Preamble). This declaration engages directly and critically with literal Qur'anic provisions, informing its audience of correct or spurious interpretations of specific verses

[132] The Al-Azhar Document on the Future of Egypt (Al-Azhar and a Group of Egyptian Educated elite), 21 June 2011, translation on file with the author. For an insightful commentary on the Document's significance and a video of Grand Imam Al-Azhar, shaykh Ahmad al-Tayyib reading it on television, see M Zeghal, 'The "al-Azhar Document": Further Thoughts on al-Azhar in the Revolution', *On Islam and Politics* (1 September 2011) available at onislamandpolitics.wordpress.com/2011/09/01/the-al-azhar-document-further-thoughts-on-al-azhar-in-the-revolution.

[133] M Bohlander, 'Political Islam and Non-Muslim Religions – A Lesson from Lessing for the Arab Transition', (2014) 25(1) *Islam and Christian–Muslim Relations* 27, 29.

[134] A Maged, 'Commentary on the Al-Azhar Declaration in Support of the Arab Revolutions' (2012) 4(3) *Amsterdam Law Forum* 69ff.

[135] ibid 70.

on obedience towards rulers (Article 1). The Declaration notably absolves peaceful demonstrators (termed 'patriotic protesters' in the text) against unjust rulers from accusations of *baghi* (the armed rebellion against the legitimate leader) (Article 2). It highlights the synergies between Islamic law and IHRL in guaranteeing freedom of assembly and peaceful political protest (Article 2). Article 3 then divests power from authorities who violently oppress civilians, by citing a Qur'anic verse.[136] This Declaration, much like the Document on the Future of Egypt, does not engage directly with the right to truth, but by referring to accountability (Article 1) there would be ample scope to pursue that right.

These statements must be evaluated in light of Elham Kazemi's cautionary note (above) that the use of religion in TJ is deeply political. Early commentators (in 2013) considered that Al-Azhar presented itself a certain way:

> Unlike the Islamists, al-Azhar was scholarly and not mired in politics. Unlike the Salafists, its approach to religion could be presented as more consistent with the needs of a twenty-first-century society. And unlike both, Ahmed el-Tayeb [the Grand Imam of Al-Azhar] posed as a promoter of consensus, leading national dialogues and issuing widely supported statements and documents to guide the tumultuous political process.[137]

More recent analysis of Al-Azhar's role as the pre-eminent religious actor in Egypt in the post-Mubarak era seems to support Kazemi's thesis in full: its institutional role blends spiritual ideals and political realities.[138] For the purpose of this project, the Egyptian experience highlights the significance of religious actors in transitional contexts (echoing some of the discussion in Chapter 1 pertaining to religious actors and transitions drawing on Ioana Cismas's work[139]), but also their limitations in light of specific political contexts. While transitional truth seeking has not been the focus of these two documents issued by Al-Azhar, there seems to be no religious barrier preventing this Islamic institution from issuing its strong support to such initiatives and the right to truth on Islamic grounds.

What these examples illustrate, taken together, is firstly, that the meeting between transitional truth seeking and Islamic principles and actors has, to date, been tentative and often indirect, and secondly, that the invocation of religion cannot be untangled from the complexities of the political context. Nevertheless, the fact that Muslim-majority countries have engaged with violent pasts in an attempt to address contested truths and build collective memories supports the thesis that truth seeking is not incompatible with Islamic law, but instead can be

[136] If anyone killed a human being – unless it be [in punishment] for murder or for spreading corruption on earth –, it shall be as though he had killed all humankind; whereas, if anyone saves a life, it shall be as though he had saved the lives of all humankind (Qur'an, Surah Al-Mâ'idah: 5:32).

[137] A Morsy and NJ Brown, 'Egypt's al-Azhar Steps Forward' (Carnegie Endowment for Global Peace, 7 November 2013), available at carnegieendowment.org/2013/11/07/egypt-s-al-azhar-steps-forward#.

[138] Bano and Benadi (n 130).

[139] I Cismas, 'Reflections on the Presence and Absence of Religious Actors in Transitional Justice Processes: On Legitimacy and Accountability' in R Duthie and P Seils (eds), *Justice Mosaics: How Context Shapes Transitional Justice in Fractured Societies* (New York, ICTJ, 2017).

grounded in it. The following section will unpack this claim further by looking at the support to the right to truth in Islamic law and jurisprudence.

IV. RIGHT TO TRUTH IN ISLAMIC LAW AND JURISPRUDENCE

Support for the right to truth in Islamic law and jurisprudence can be deduced from Islam's holistic understanding of justice, based on the *maqasid as-shari'ah* and the principle of *maslaha*, as well as the historic practices of courts and other forms of judicial and extrajudicial mechanisms to pursue justice and thus provide an account of the truth. The interviews with the Sunni and Shia scholars point to the same conclusions, namely that the notion of the right to truth as emerging in IHRL can be accommodated and also enhanced by the *shari'ah* – as demonstrated in the first part of this chapter discussing the Islamic support for truth seeking (which is closely entwined with the right to truth). The secular jurist (Sunni tradition) interviewed provided a very succinct answer to the question of how the right to truth may be understood in Islamic law:

> The translation of the 'right to truth' in Islamic Jurisprudence and Shari'ah is similar to the original meaning of the concept in English.[140]

In essence, this statement reveals the ample scope for the right to truth as conceptualised in international law to be situated within Islamic law as well. The Shia position points to the same findings. Asked to consider the equivalent to the right to truth in *shari'ah* and *fiqh*, the Shia Seyyed, offered the following reflections:

> Since the gist of the right to truth is to prevent unfairness and spread justice, the closest translation in Islamic *Shariah* and *Fiqh* is the concept of 'bringing justice to the unjustly treated'[141] and those who bring justice to the 'unjustly treated' would be called 'guardians of rights'. The translation can be found in some Islamic resources. For instance, God said in the Qur'an: 'Let not the hatred of a certain people prevent you from acting justly.'[142] and: 'when you judge between people, judge with justice'[143] and 'the greatest justice is this which protects the unjustly treated'.[144] Additionally, *Imam Ali* said, in a letter to his sons *Al-Hassan* and *Al-Hussain*: 'speak the truth, work for God's rewards, be an enemy to the person who commits the injustice, and a supporter of the unjustly treated.'[145]

[140] Secular jurist (Sunni tradition) interview.
[141] Shia Seyyed interview. Note that the word 'weak' is used several times and is the proposed translation of '*Mazloum* مظلوم' which indicates generally a person who suffers from all kinds of injustice (translator's note). This author uses 'unjustly treated' and 'oppressed' in some of the translation of the same term.
[142] Qur'an, 5:8.
[143] Qur'an 4:58.
[144] Said by Imam Ali Ibn Abli Talib (translator's note).
[145] Shia Seyyed interview.

A list of Qur'anic provisions that support the right to truth as articulated by the Hanafi Sheikh is reported in the first part of this chapter. Additional examples offered by that interviewee include an account from the time of Caliph Ali:

> Ali found his shield in the hands of a Jewish man, so he said to him 'this is my shield' and the Jewish man replied 'this is not your shield … it is mine', and so Caliph Ali replied, 'do you have proof? … let us go to a judge'. Caliph Ali and the Jewish man went to Judge Shuraih (Appointed by Caliph Ali), one of the most well-known judges in Islam, who previously adjudicated for Abu Bakr, Omar, Othman and Ali. Judge Shuraih seated them and Caliph Ali stated 'I found my shield in the hands of this Jewish man' and so judge Shuraih asked the Jewish man 'does this shield belong to *Ameer Al-Mu'mineen* (Commander of the believers) Ali?'; the Jewish man replied 'no it is my shield' and so judge Shuraih asked Ali 'what evidence do you have that this shield is yours?' (this is the evidence for the right to truth). Ali replied 'Al Hassan Ibn Ali and Kanbar are my witnesses' (Al Hassan was Ali's son and Kanbar was Ali's friend), and so judge Shuraih replied 'I will not accept Al Hassan's statement' … 'I will not take his statement as the statement of a son about his father is not accepted'. And so judge Shuriah's final judgment was for the benefit of the Jewish man. … It was then said that the Jewish man returned the shield to *Ameer Al-Mu'mineen* and told Caliph Ali '*Ameer Al-Mu'mineen's* Judge found against the Caliph (Ali) and decided for my benefit. Indeed, the shield fell from you during the battle of Safeen and so I took it.'[146]

This account illustrates that in the Islamic legal tradition the archetypal good judge, Shuriah, was willing to rule against the powerful Caliph (who had assigned him to the role), indicating that there is no *shari'ah*-based justification for the courts to favour Muslim leaders over others in ensuring the proper rules of evidence that underpin investigations. Among the historic examples provided by the Hanafi Sheikh is an interesting account from the rule of Amr Ibn El Aas (who led the Arab conquest of Egypt in 639 AD):

> When Amr Ibn El Aas ruled Egypt, he offered Egyptians security and safety. At that time, the head of the Egyptian church went missing, after he contravened the Roman church and the Romans discriminated against the Egyptian Christians. Thus, he ran away and went into hiding because the Romans had killed his brother brutally and thrown him in the Nile. So the Egyptians went to Amr Ibn El Aas and said to him that Benyameen, the head of the church, had run away from the Romans and that they were unable to find him. Amr Ibn El Aas immediately sent the 'callers' to search for him in every part of Egypt, until he came out of hiding as a result of Amr Ibn El Aas's command, and Amr Ibn El Aas asserted the covenant, and reappointed him as the head of the church.

This account illustrates how a Muslim ruler offered protection to a persecuted individual from another faith. While this is not directly an example of the right to truth, it implies that Amr Ibn El Aas was made aware of the violent death

[146] Hanafi Sheikh interview.

of Benyameen's brother and thus acknowledged the risk for the head of the Egyptian Christians as well, and took the necessary steps to act upon that information to avoid repetition of the injustice.

More explicitly linking the right to truth to the prevention of future violence, the responses from the Shia Seyyed situate it in relation to conflict and authoritarianism:

> War is the cause of a lot of hidden violations of communities' as well as individuals' human rights. The concept of the 'right to truth' can stop these violations, and it assists courts to protect people's rights. It also reduces the possibility of war: it makes unjust rulers who have participated in wars think twice before starting a new one, because they are scared of being tracked down and held criminally liable.
>
> The concept of the 'right to truth' spreads awareness amongst the public to reject war and conflict, and it is a way to protest against unjust rulers. This is a way to achieve a peaceful jehad that aims for change and justice. It resonates with what prophet *Mohammad* said: 'the best jehad is to say the truth in the face of an unjust ruler.'[147]

The same interviewee also elaborated on the temporal scope of the right to truth, suggesting there is no statute of limitations to knowing the truth about past injustice, and making amends:

> There is no difference in *shari'ah* between a right that existed in the past or continues to exist in the present: the kind of justice that *shari'ah* demands includes both rights. There was a man who was a governor for quite a long time (as rulers changed and he still remained a governor). He said to *Mohammad ibn Baqir*:[148] 'I have been a governor since Al-Hajjaj's times,[149] is there a way to repent for that? Ibn *Baqir* remained silent. The governor repeated his question. Ibn *Baqir* said: no, there isn't, until you give everyone their due.'
>
> When *Imam Ali* became the ruler, he was told to avoid investigating misappropriations of public funds that happened during the time of the previous ruler. *Imam Ali* said: a 'right never vanishes, and if I found out that the funds were used for marriage purposes, or that they caused battles between states, I would still bring them back to where they should be, though it might be challenging, but it is even more challenging to not do something about it.' And *Imam Ali* said to one of the governors who stole the money of the orphans, widows and others: 'fear God and return their money, and if you do not, you will be punished.'
>
> From the above references we can conclude that there should be no difference in priority based on whether the right existed in the past or present, but rights will be prioritised if victims demand them. Imam Ali used to say to workers who were harmed from armies passing their lands: 'complain to me when you cannot protect yourselves, I will do what should be done.'[150]

[147] Shia Seyyed interview.
[148] Mohammad Albaqir (677–733 A.D.), the fifth shia Imam (translator's note).
[149] Abu Mohammad Alhajjaj (660–714 A.D.), a leader during the Umayyad Caliphate (translator's note).
[150] Shia Seyyed interview.

The insights provided by the scholars interviewed illustrate the key thesis of this chapter: the Islamic *shari'ah* is capable of embracing the right to truth as emerging in IHRL, and even independently of it. Moreover, based on the substantial convergence, the Islamic sources can (and should) be used to support the comparative appreciation of the right to truth across different jurisdictions, legal traditions and conceptions of justice. This is important for a number of reasons, the most significant of which is the desirability of truth-seeking efforts, and indeed the victims' right to know and society's interest in uncovering the truth after mass violence in Muslim-majority societies. Islamic law promotes justice: shielding perpetrators of harm from accountability violates the high aims of justice of the *maqasid as-shariah* and the principle of *maslaha*. More pragmatically, citizens of Muslim-majority societies have a right to know the truth about past harm and hold those responsible to account. The following section considers three types of violations that could be investigated by invoking the right to truth through an Islamic lens.

A. Key Violations: Torture, Extrajudicial Killings and Forced Disappearance

Having ascertained the general compatibility of the right to truth as emerging in IHRL and Islamic law, the discussion turns to the three key violations that are often associated with the right to truth: torture, extrajudicial killings and forced disappearance.[151] As the analysis of the right to truth in Chapter 4 illustrated, the procedural limb of the prohibition of torture and the right to life (underpinning the prohibition of extrajudicial killings) has been invoked even in the more conservative ECHR system to invoke the right to truth (in addition to other enumerated rights), and the link between the right to truth and forced disappearances are contained in an international treaty (the International Convention for the Protection of All Persons from Enforced Disappearance). A further violation for which the right to truth could be invoked is rape and gender-based violence, on the basis of its established connection to torture in international law (also discussed in Chapter 4). The *shari'ah* provides a strong foundation for truth seeking in relation to violations against physical integrity, as indicated by one interviewee:

> There are several stories in Islamic law and Islamic heritage that aim at finding out the truth, especially with regards to crimes against physical integrity, including physical assault, manslaughter and murder. These stories support the ideas and principles on which transitional justice is based, which include encouraging perpetrators to confess their crimes as a form of purification from guilt – a concept reflected in many narratives contained in Islamic traditions about people whom, on their own initiative, acknowledged the crimes or sins they had committed, desiring the forgiveness and mercy of Allah.[152]

[151] As listed by Klinkner and Davis (n 3) 21.
[152] Secular jurist (Sunni tradition) interview.

The paragraphs that follow illustrate how this general principle in Islamic law relates to torture, extrajudicial killings and forced disappearance specifically.

i. Torture

At first glance, there is no apparent conflict between Islamic law and the prohibition of torture enshrined in Article 7 of the ICCPR and the Convention Against Torture and other Cruel, Inhuman or Degrading Treatment or Punishment (CAT).[153] The secular jurist (Sunni tradition) interviewed stated vehemently that torture is considered a major sin in Islam, and recalled the hadith: 'God tortures those who torture.'[154] Baderin reports numerous Qur'anic verses and *hadith* prohibiting torture, and juristic support. He cites Article 20 of the OIC Cairo Declaration on Human Rights in Islam, which prohibits 'physical or psychological torture or to any form of humiliation, cruelty or indignity' and medical experiments. Sadiq Reza offers a more nuanced account of torture in Islamic jurisprudence, referencing divergences of opinion as to its use as an investigative technique.[155] And despite ample historic and contemporary evidence of torture in Muslim-majority contexts, the *fiqh* seems to prohibit investigative torture.[156] As Reza posits, neither Islamic law nor international human rights standards have eradicated torture in Muslim societies; instead, only a democratic state with effective internal mechanisms to hold authorities to account for torture and other forms of abuse, a free press and other basic guarantees will be more likely to achieve that result.[157] Torture as an investigation technique, therefore, is a political choice of the authorities in power in Muslim-majority societies.

There is, however, an area of Islamic law that, prima facie, contravenes the prohibition of torture. The *hudud* punishments (discussed in Chapter 5) inflict physical pain, and therefore violate the definition of torture provided in Article 1(1) of CAT. These punishments include amputations, crucifixion, stoning, lashing and death.[158] Despite the general prohibition of torture, Article 1(1) contains the (paradoxic) exception for 'pain or suffering arising only from, inherent in or incidental to lawful sanctions', which in principle could allow for the corporal punishments of *hudud*.[159] Baderin, however, recalls that the standard of proof for *hudud* is 'beyond any atom of doubt' in line with the tradition of the Prophet favouring an error in clemency, making the infliction of these punishments extremely rare.[160] Through these 'procedural shields' he suggests

[153] Baderin (n 104) 76–77.
[154] Secular jurist (Sunni tradition) interview.
[155] S Reza, 'Torture and Islamic law' (2007) 8 *Chicago Journal of International Law* 21.
[156] ibid 21, 40.
[157] ibid.
[158] Baderin (n 104) 79.
[159] ibid 78. Baderin notes that HRC General Comment 20 extends the prohibition to corporal punishment. See also Reza (n 156) 22–23.
[160] ibid 80–81.

that the infliction of *hudud* punishments can be averted without contesting their divinity. While in principle tensions between the *hudud* and the prohibition of torture remain, the application of these punishments in Muslim societies is based on human decision-making, and can be averted in light of procedural guarantees and political choices.

Both investigative torture (and by analogy torture in custody) as well as barbaric punishments amounting to torture in light of IHRL are at odds with an oft-recited tradition of the Prophet: 'God will torture, in the hereafter, those who torture people in this life.'[161] Based on the overarching justice aims of the Islamic *shari'ah*, there is evidence to support the prohibition of torture as enshrined in IHRL through Islamic law, and pursue the quest for truth in cases of violations after mass violence to ensure accountability for perpetrators and justice for victims. Much like the prohibition of torture in international law, however, it is clear that the Islamic norm is only as effective in practice as much as there is political will to prevent and account for torture in any given context.

ii. Extrajudicial and Unlawful Killings

Extrajudicial and unlawful killings fall within the Islamic criminal law category of *qisas* (discussed in Chapter 5). The victim's family are entitled to justice (through *diyya* or other forms of compensation) regardless of the status of the perpetrator as an individual or an agent of the state. The principle of 'no wasted blood in Islam' guides the right to truth in relation to killings.[162] As such, the state and society owe victims (and their family) protection, which encourages authorities (and police) to conduct investigations, search for evidence and identify perpetrators.[163] This is supported by the *al-qasama* principle, which guarantees victims' rights, and in particular the need to know as much as possible about the facts of a killing.[164] In cases where the perpetrator cannot be identified, this principle provides for the payment of *diya* through public funds (*bayt al-mal*), consolidating the authorities' responsibility in establishing the truth about the killing and holding the perpetrator to account (even financially).[165] In practice, however, when a state-mandated or state-endorsed killing has occurred within a specific context, the barriers to justice and accountability are informed by the power dynamics and political climate, despite the Islamic law rules of *qisas* and *diyya*.

Much like the tensions between the prohibition of torture in IHRL and the *hudud* punishments, the treatment of the death penalty in international law and Islamic law merits closer scrutiny. The ICCPR provides the general international

[161] Reported in Baderin (n 104) 76.
[162] Maged, *Transitional Justice in Islamic Sharia* (n 6).
[163] ibid.
[164] ibid. Note that *Al-Qasama* stems from '*Qasam*' which means to swear. *Al-Qasama* is one of the ways to identify the perpetrator of a murder (translator's note).
[165] ibid, citing Ibin Abdeen.

law position on the death penalty, which is not abolished in toto but reduced 'only for the most serious crimes in accordance with the law' (Article 6(2)).[166] Broadly, the international law prohibition but for the most serious crimes is echoed in the Islamic law position limiting the death penalty to a handful of *hudud* crimes, where evidentiary standards are beyond an atom of doubt (see discussion above). Moreover, the sanctity and protection of human life in Islamic law are evidenced throughout the Qur'an, which includes 'take not life which God has made sacred, except by way of justice' and multiple reports of the Prophet's leniency.[167] Article 2 of the OIC Cairo Declaration on Human Rights in Islam prohibits killing 'except for a Shari'a prescribed reason', referring to *hudud* penalties.[168] Nonetheless, the application of the death penalty in Muslim-majority states is largely a policy choice more than an Islamic requirement.[169] Strictly speaking, the *shari'ah* does not mandate capital punishment for crimes falling outside the *hudud*, which enjoy higher standards of proof and due process guarantees. In addition, the punishments for residual *tazir* crimes are discretionary, and as such rulers can uphold IHRL standards without contravening Islamic law (discussed in Chapter 5). Thus, killings in custody or elsewhere by state agents or other actors with the complacency of the authorities that do not fall within the narrow category of *hudud* punishments and applied after stringent procedural guarantees are likely to be unlawful killings. The families of the victims are entitled to the truth about their loss and perpetrators should be accountable for their violent misconduct – even when the state authorities themselves are implicated. These findings echo the interviews with the Islamic scholars.

The Shia Seyyed's take on the right to truth for extrajudicial killings focuses on two aspects: firstly, the avoidance of unlawful killing by the ruler; and secondly, the importance of ensuring justice for the family of the victim:

> As we saw above, there are many ways in which the right to truth can be found in and applied to Islamic *shari'ah* and *fiqh*. Islamic law encourages seeking the truth for the protection of rights; this is the one of the requirements of justice that Islamic law is based on. *Imam Ali* advised some of his governors: 'Careful, do not kill without a legitimate reason. Killing without a legitimate reason is closer to a curse, has the worst consequences and takes your blessings and powerful position from you. The first judgement that God will make on the Day of Redemption is related to the killing that happened among people. Killing will not strengthen you as a ruler, it will weaken you and remove you from your chair. There is no excuse to God or to me for murder,

[166] On the death penalty in general, see inter alia WA Schabas, 'International Law and the Abolition of the Death Penalty' in CS Steiker and JM Steiker (eds), *Comparative Capital Punishment* (Cheltenham, Edward Elgar, 2019).

[167] Baderin (n 104) 71, and Qur'an 6:151 reported in Baderin (n 104) 67.

[168] Reported in Baderin (n 104) 68. Baderin, (n 104) 69–74, considers murder, adultery, apostasy and armed/highway robbery as falling within this category – although murder is dealt with through *tazir/diyya*.

[169] WA Schabas, 'Islam and the Death Penalty' (2000) 9 *William & Mary Bill of Rights Journal* 223.

> because you will be ending someone's life. And if you had a citizen who made many mistakes, be wary of punishments that lead to death. And remember that if someone was killed by another, you are not worthy of your position as a governor until you give the family of the victim their rights.'[170]

As can be seen, the victim satisfaction element is presented as a driver of the authorities' ideal response to unlawful killing, which contributes to building the argument that an actionable right to truth finds a basis in Islamic law.

iii. Forced Disappearances

The third (and possibly most important, given the treaty provisions in the International Convention for the Protection of All Persons from Enforced Disappearance) instance in which the right to truth has been invoked in TJ is forced disappearance. Forced disappearances have been a tragic feature of conflict and authoritarianism in the Middle East and other places where there are Muslim-majority societies[171] Islamic law does not seem to contain any direct references to the right to truth in relation to this violation, but as the provision is contained in an international treaty it would be possible for the legal system of a Muslim-majority society to subsume this norm as it does not contravene the *shari'ah*. Moreover, the justice aims of the *shari'ah* and the principle of *maslaha* (discussed in Chapter 5) suggest that there is scope to prohibit forced disappearances through the residuary criminal category of *tazir* and grant the families of the victims the right to know the whereabouts of their loved ones through ordinary state legislation. This would extend to the government investigating forced disappearances during its own mandate, but also those that occurred during previous regimes. Mohamed 'Arafa has argued that 'a consecutive régime would be in charge of paying the *diya* in forced disappearances settings committed by the former government, though they had no hand in the crime'.[172] While this is an area that still requires further study and conceptualisation in Islamic law, as well as implementation in Muslim-majority countries, it is clear that the *shari'ah* would support this position. Forced disappearances contravene one of the core aims of Islamic law (*maqasid as-shari'ah*), namely the protection of family.[173] On this basis, family members of a disappeared person would be

[170] Shia Seyyed interview.

[171] This is widely reported in the media and in human rights reports. For example 'Egypt: 2,723 enforced Disappearances in 5 Years' (*MEMO*, 7 September 2020) available at www.middleeastmonitor.com/20200907-egypt-2723-enforced-disappearances-in-5-years/, citing a report by the Egyptian Commission for Human Rights (in Arabic). For some background on non-transitional contexts in the region experiencing forced disappearances, see ÖS Göral, 'Any Hopes for Truth? A Comparative Analysis of Enforced Disappearances and the Missing in the Middle East, North Africa and Caucasus' (Truth Justice Memory Centre, 2019), available at enforceddisappearances.dealingwiththepast.org.

[172] MA Arafa, 'Transitional Justice, the Seeds of Change: Secular Law or Divine (Islamic) Law, Quo Vadis' (2017) 9 *Creighton International & Comparative Law Journal* 39.

[173] As discussed in ch 5, the *maqasid as-shari'ah* are understood as including, at a minimum, the protection of religion, life, intellect, offspring and property.

entitled to enquire as to the whereabouts of their loved one, and demand the authorities investigate appropriately. As such, even in the absence of an explicit principle in Islamic law and jurisprudence prohibiting forced disappearance and providing a right for family members to know the truth about their loved one, a purposive reading of the *maqasid as-shari'ah* would support this provision as new, state-made legislation. This is a good example of how the holistic justice aims of the *shari'ah* offer a truly flexible instrument to pursue its aims set out in the *maqasid*. Therefore, what might initially seem like a gap in the comparison between the international framework of TJ and Islamic law can be bridged: Islamic jurisprudence provides a way for Islamic law to evolve and respond to new challenges in a way that remains true to its aims and for the public benefit (*maslaha*). It would therefore be absurd to suggest that the *shari'ah* does not support the right to truth in relation to forced disappearances.

B. Individual and Collective Dimensions of the Right to Truth

In addition to the specific acts of violence that call for the right to truth as emerging in international law, the dual individual and social dimensions of the right to truth discussed in Chapter 4 find support in Islamic law. There is support in the Qur'an for victims' right to truth in relation to murder, reflected in the general principle that 'no blood goes in vain in Islam'.[174] According to the secular jurist of Sunni tradition interviewed for this project, this implies that authorities have a responsibility to seek the full and complete truth when human rights violations occur, and should be

> an incentive for judicial officers to seek the truth behind the crime of murder, as to the events that transpired, including knowing the circumstances in which the violations took place, as well as the reasons for them, and finally gathering the evidence of the crime and the perpetrator.[175]

The Islamic tradition, and in particular criminal justice, places emphasis on justice for victims understood broadly.[176] *Hudud* crimes 'disrupt social harmony' and violate the *maqasid as-shariah* (the core objectives of Islam), but are crimes against God and so do not require direct victims to instigate proceedings. Prosecution, therefore, can be initiated as a matter of public law, much like in some continental inquisitorial systems. On the other hand, *qisas* and *tazir* crimes are better suited to a victim-centred approach. This is because *qisas* 'empowers the (direct) victim or their family (indirect victims) to play a

[174] Secular jurist (Sunni tradition) interview, citing Qur'an Sura al-Takweer 81:8 and 9.

[175] The issue of 'circumstances' has also been discussed in the ECHR jurisprudence on the right to truth/right to know/duty to investigate (see ch 4). The precise meaning and scope (and temporality) of 'circumstances', however, remains a contested issue.

[176] HO Yousuf, 'Transitional Justice in the Middle East and North Africa – Taking Account of Islam' (2017) 14(1) *Muslim World Journal of Human Rights* 145, 164ff.

central role in determining the fate of the offender' – which includes the victim's prerogative to offer mercy or pardon, leaving 'ample room for forgiveness'.[177] The residual category of *tazir*, a discretionary penalty, allows judges to 'apply the "rule of lenity" rather than the prescribed punishment'.[178] It furthermore allows the political and judicial authorities to use flexibility 'and discretion to criminalise and punish offenders respectively' for all those violations not explicitly contained in Islamic law.[179] Criminal justice is not, however, the only element of Islamic law than can support a victim's right to truth.

A victim's individual right to the truth for abuse suffered at the hands of public officials or third parties (where the authorities failed to protect or investigate) could be brought jointly within the scope of Islamic criminal law and cross-cutting human rights legislation, specifically through *maslaha*. Given the centrality of criminal justice in Islamic law and jurisprudence, employing the category of *qisas* and the victim's right to compensation as a form of tangible justice may yield more fruitful results than attempts to use human rights language alone to promote the right to truth in Islamic law.[180] In particular, as discussed in the previous chapter, the victim's right to compensation under *qisas* empowers not only the direct victim (who in many cases would be deceased or disappeared), but also their family, in the determination and request of compensation. As recalled by one interviewee, blood relatives also have the right to forgive in this world by accepting *diyya* and pardoning the offender.[181] The discretionary nature of *qisas* allows for leniency and forgiveness (prized in Islamic law), avoiding corporal and capital punishments. This approach would enable victims and their families to request an account of the truth through a trial or an extrajudicial means permitted in the Islamic legal system which contribute to the aims of TJ (for instance, *sulh*, discussed earlier in this chapter), instead of the classic *diyya* retribution or blood money.

Demanding perpetrators' participation in truth-seeking activities (judicial and extrajudicial) could be requested through *diyya*. State authorities committed to truth seeking and human rights standards could provide an appropriate institutional and legislative framework for the implementation of the right to truth through trials, truth commissions and other means. In light of IHRL guarantees that states may adopt voluntarily and in line with Islamic law aims, this model may creatively allow for the victims and their next of kin to request trials, truth commissions and other forms of truth seeking to satisfy their individual

[177] ibid 167–68.
[178] ibid 168–69.
[179] ibid.
[180] There is ample literature on IHRL as foreign imports (at best) or neocolonial practices (at worst), which informs TJ research as well, as discussed earlier in this book. Notably for IHRL, M Mutua, 'Savages, Victims, and Saviors: The Metaphor of Human Rights' (2001) 42 *Harvard International Law Journal* 201, and in relation to TJ, AA An-Na'im, 'Editorial Note: From the Neocolonial "Transitional" to Indigenous Formations of Justice' (2013) 7 *International Journal of Transitional Justice* 197 (see also previous chapters).
[181] Secular jurist (Sunni tradition) interview.

right to truth (which may also contribute to uncovering the truth in the context of historical TJ). Therefore, the individual right to the truth can be constructed through criminal proceedings through *qisas* in cases of offences against the person. For crimes falling within the *tazir*, the discretion afforded to lawmakers can enable the right to truth if there is the political will to do so.

The collective and societal significance of the right to truth discussed in Chapter 4 expands the scope beyond direct victims. Given the centrality of collective benefit in Islamic law, as discussed in Chapter 5, the societal dimension of the right to truth is situated firmly within the scope of *maslaha*, given its importance for direct victims and their families as well as for society as a whole reckoning with legacies of widespread violence. Accordingly, the principle of *maslaha* has the potential to ground truth-seeking mechanisms, allowing victims to exercise their right to the truth and the rest of society to find out about past abuse, for example through truth commissions and public inquiries. Nonetheless, political considerations may limit the uses of *maslaha*, and moreover, there is no fixed understanding of what constitutes public benefit or common good in a society (as discussed in the previous chapter, this is a necessarily dynamic and responsive concept). In some contexts, authorities could impose their own vision of what is best without democratic consultation, reproducing old patterns of marginalisation and structural violence to decide whose suffering matters. For example, a post-transition elite may decide that silencing the previous regime and excluding it from accessing truth-seeking mechanisms falls within the scope of the common good for society – TJ processes will be designed accordingly, and the truths uncovered will be partial, contested or misleading. The dialogue between the international framework of TJ that underpins the pursuit of legal truths and equivalent principles and practices of Islamic law could help doctrinally, but the limitations of the political climate cannot be overlooked.

The Islamic scholars interviewed for this study expressed a favourable opinion of the right to truth in the *shari'ah*, and individual and collective dimensions emerge as an inextricable whole. The secular jurist (Sunni tradition) explained that:

> Islamic law does not only aim at revealing personal truth which is based on a person's narrative, but also seeks to establish objective facts that establish general rules, which in turn contribute to knowing the truth in a comprehensive and inclusive manner.[182]

The Shia Seyyed's understanding of the collective dimension of the right to truth in Islam specifically noted:

> Support for the collective right to truth can be found in the fact that Islam imposes an obligation upon the nation to protect the oppressed. If the nation does not protect the weak from the unjust person, then it will not deserve to be sanctified. As one *hadeeth* says: 'God will not sanctify a nation that does not protect the unjustly treated from the unjust person.'

[182] Secular jurist (Sunni tradition) interview.

> There are many *hadeeth* that call for the protection of the unjustly treated and warn against unfairness, especially unfairness against the vulnerable. As one *hadeeth* says: 'the grievous unfairness is that against the vulnerable.' And this is what spreads a culture based on an inclination to fight for the truth; as the *hadeeth* says: 'he who does not speak the truth is a muted evil.' And the inclination to stand beside the oppressed to protect them, as one *hadeeth* says: 'God said: I will avenge the unjust person sooner or later, and I will avenge anyone who was able to protect a weak person, but he did not.' And that is why God is responsive to the oppressed person's prayer: 'fear the prayer of a person who has been unjustly treated when he asks God for his rights, God will not prevent anyone from having their rights.'[183]

According to that interviewee, the role of international bodies and NGOs working towards these aims is complementary, and does not contradict the Islamic understanding of the individual right to truth:

> It is doubtless that the existence of international organisations and non-governmental organizations that protect rights contributes to people's ability to demand their rights when they are violated.[184]

The discussion indicates that there is ample scope to support both the individual and collective notions of the right to truth in Islamic law. The convergence of the international norm and its Islamic equivalent suggests that the dual nature of the right to truth is in effect supported twice: first, emanating organically from Islamic principles; and second, through the impact of international organisations and civil society, the 'truth entrepreneurs' (to borrow from Patricia Naftali's terminology discussed in Chapters 3 and 4[185]) that promote awareness of this right in Muslim-majority societies.

C. State (Authority) Duty to Investigate

The comparative analysis of the right to truth in Islamic law cannot be divorced from the corresponding state duty to investigate articulated in international law, and illustrated in greater detail in Chapter 4 with reference to the jurisprudence of the IACtHR and ECtHR. As discussed earlier, the justice aims of the Islamic *shari'ah* require the authorities to ensure justice for victims, even when alleged perpetrators are part of the government or other state actors. As such, it is quite straightforward to extrapolate the state duty to investigate past harm as a concrete means to deliver justice to victims and their families, in line with the *maqasid* of the *shari'ah*. Of course, the implementation of the state duty to investigate, in Muslim-majority contexts like anywhere else, is subject to the

[183] Shia Seyyed interview.
[184] ibid.
[185] See eg P Naftali, 'Crafting a "Right to Truth" in International Law: Convergence Mobilizations, Divergent Agendas' (2016) XIII *Champ Penal/Penal Field* 1.

political willingness of the governing elite, despite the high standards of justice set out in the *shari'ah*.

The scholars interviewed on this point stressed the importance of the authorities' duty to investigate harm inflicted. The secular jurist (Sunni tradition) explained that:

> In Islamic law, the ruler is obliged to find the perpetrators of crimes (such as physical assault, manslaughter and murder), and implement applicable punishment such as *qisas* on the perpetrators, or determine the *diyah* (blood money/compensation) for the victims, when accepted by his/her family. … [T]his will not be accomplished unless acts of violence and violations are investigated, whether these acts were done individually or collectively.[186]

If a (Muslim) state is negligent or reluctant to investigate and prosecute alleged perpetrators of human rights violations, this is incompatible with the aims and provisions of the *shari'ah*. From a spiritual perspective, a ruler is accountable before God (echoing the discussion of the *forum internum*, elsewhere in this chapter), and 'every Muslim aware of any violations committed by the ruler, should document it as proven facts until the judgment of the ruler on the Day of Resurrection'.[187] The secular jurist (Sunni tradition) also mentioned the historic example of the Diwan al Mazelem (the *mazalim*, discussed previously), describing it as an ombudsman's office to look into a number of grievances, including human rights violations. That mandate 'relied on principles of Islamic law which require the administration of justice and repealing injustice resulting from violations by rulers exercising authority over their subjects'.

The Shia Seyyed's position on this is based on the central notion of fairness in Islamic law, which incorporates the duty to respond appropriately when rights have been violated:

> The state in Islamic law should be a fair state. It should not ignore people's rights when they are violated, or when people are harmed or ill-treated. As it is said: 'the steadiness of states comes with fairness'. And 'fairness is the strongest essence' and the just ruler is one 'who takes from the strong to give to the vulnerable' and 'one hour of being fair is better than seventeen years of prayer' and 'an hour of being unfair in ruling is worse than committing sins for sixty years'.[188]

One comment by the Shia Seyyed on how the right to truth builds trust in the judicial system (and authorities more generally) was particularly fascinating because it mirrors the preoccupation expressed in the Separate Opinions in the *El Masri* case discussed in Chapter 4.

> The government's protection of individuals' freedom and its effort to make them trust the judicial system is one of the factors that enable them to demand their rights. One of these rights is to know the truth about the violence and the unfairness that

[186] Secular jurist (Sunni tradition) interview.
[187] ibid.
[188] Shia Seyyed interview.

> people experience. And a just ruler is one who encourages individuals to challenge wrongness and to demand justice.
>
> When *Imam Ali* was the ruler, he said to his subjects: 'do not feel that I will be dismissive of what you tell me that is true or just. A ruler who is dismissive of this will find it even more challenging to make just or right decisions. I am not perfect, so never stop telling me what is just or true.' And on another occasion, he said: 'the unjustly treated are precious to me until I get them a right they had, and the strong is weak for me until I take a right from them.' And: 'support the oppressed to demand their right from the unjust person.'
>
> A just ruler is he who elects for the judicial system qualified, educated and intelligent judges who are brave enough to speak the truth. *Imam Ali* advised one of the governors: 'when you judge amongst people, judge whilst being conscious of how vital your powerful position is to God; judging is the source of justice for God which exists to protect the weak from the unjust person, to take from the powerful and give to the vulnerable, to apply God's sanctions (*hudud Allah*) in the right manner, these sanctions that make this country and its people better, be careful and considerate when you judge amongst people.'[189]

The insights offered by the scholars interviewed for this project point unequivocally to the same direction: the Islamic position on accountability for harm inflicted requires the authorities to investigate alleged perpetrators and hold them to account in order to satisfy the right of victims and their families to know the truth about abuse suffered.

V. CONCLUSION

This chapter demonstrates that the broad understanding of justice within the Islamic legal tradition can contribute wide-ranging support to the aims of truth seeking and the right to truth as emerging in the current international framework of TJ. This understanding encompasses justice for victims (and their families), accountability for offenders and acknowledges the societal need to create a record about the past; these core themes in TJ are also amply reflected in Islamic law and jurisprudence. In particular, the aims (*maqasid*) of the *shari'ah* and the guiding principle of *maslaha* provide doctrinal arguments in favour of the right to truth in the legal systems of Muslim-majority societies. Historic practices and contemporary examples of Islamic law and jurisprudence, as well as applied experiences in the Arab region, illustrate the importance afforded to seeking and recording the truth in order to satisfy victims and hold perpetrators to account beyond the narrow confines of criminal retribution. Finding out the truth about harm suffered is a value held dear in Islamic law, and the preference for leniency that has emerged since the earliest days of Islam suggests that truth

[189] Shia Seyyed interview.

seeking can be uncoupled from traditional penal procedure and indeed operate as a vehicle for accountability and victim satisfaction through other more conciliatory means.

Islamic law principles and historic practice provide in fact for both judicial and extrajudicial routes to uncover the truth. This is evidenced in the value placed on achieving justice for the sake of victims and their families through trials (before a *qadi*) and appeals as reported in the *hadith*, as well as the importance given to legal record-keeping that could be consulted beyond the parties to the case (such as the Ottoman *sijillat*). Outside the courtroom, *sulh* may provide a unique tool for truth seeking and building collective memories, by adapting a traditional Islamic conflict-resolution process to contemporary requirements. Likewise, the *mazalim* model, an administrative court of sorts where citizens petition against injustices inflicted by the authorities, has the potential for development as a forum for grievances, incorporating aspects of contemporary secular truth commissions and public inquiries.

The limited truths emerging from the conventional protocols of trials and quasilegal practices in Muslim-majority contexts reflect the same constraints of legal truths as conceptualised in (secular) TJ. In both judicial and extrajudicial mechanisms for uncovering the truth about past harm set out in Islamic law and historic practice, the substantial accountability for harm inflicted before God takes precedence over legal procedures based on human efforts. In other words, Islamic law invests spiritual value in pursuing the truth about past abuse that goes beyond the narrow parameters of man-made processes. The more recent examples from Muslim-majority societies addressing contested truths and attempting to build collective memories through truth-seeking initiatives show that the meeting between transitional truth seeking and Islamic principles and actors has, to date, been tentative (if not absent). What emerges clearly, nevertheless, is that despite the overall positive potential implications for TJ, the invocation of religion cannot be untangled from the complexities of the political and social context and must be approached critically.

Support for the right to truth in Islamic law and jurisprudence can be deduced from Islam's holistic understanding of justice, based on the *maqasid as-shari'ah* and the principle of *maslaha*, as well as the historic practices of courts and other forms of judicial and extrajudicial mechanisms to pursue justice and thus provide an accurate account of the truth. The interviews with senior Islamic legal thinkers substantiate this. Islamic law accommodates the victims' and families' right to know the truth about harm suffered in relation to serious violations regularly associated with the right to truth (torture, unlawful killings and forced disappearances, as well as rape) as conceptualised in international law.

The individual dimension of the right to truth can be constructed through the centrality afforded to victims and their families in criminal proceedings through *qisas* in cases of offences against the person and discretionally through the *tazir* for residual offences. The collective dimension of the right to truth in Islamic law can be situated within the scope of *maslaha*, which has the potential to ground truth-seeking mechanisms allowing victims to exercise their right to truth and the rest of society to find out about past abuse, for example through truth commissions and public inquiries. What emerges from the materials reviewed and the interviews, however, is that the individual and collective dimensions of the right to truth are inextricably linked, which fits the holistic vision of justice within the Islamic tradition. As such, there seems to be ample scope to situate the right to truth as emerging in the international legal framework of TJ within the legal systems of Muslim-majority societies, and Islamic law and jurisprudence appear to support the essence of this right.

Conclusion

FOR INDIVIDUALS AND societies emerging from serious violence, whether in the context of war or under authoritarian regimes, the right to find out the truth about past harm, build shared – albeit contested – memories of the past and hold perpetrators to account is gaining momentum as a normative principle in international law.[1] This is evidenced in the development, invocations and uses of the notion of the right to truth across different forums, including the European, Inter-American and UN rights systems (discussed in Chapter 4). In order to enhance its global legitimacy as an emerging norm in international law, the right to truth must resonate in the legal cultures of different societies – including Muslim-majority settings informed directly or indirectly by Islamic law.[2] The broad convergence of the international legal framework underpinning transitional truth seeking and Islamic law principles and practices can support the conceptualisation and implementation of the right to truth in Muslim-majority contexts emerging from a period of serious violence.

This book offers answers to two interlinked questions: How can the truth-seeking element of the international legal framework for TJ be embedded in Muslim-majority societies? And to what extent does Islamic law and jurisprudence support the notion of the right to truth about past violence, as emerging in international law?

The study demonstrates, first, that there is broad support in the *shari'ah*, Islamic jurisprudence and legal practice to embed the truth-seeking elements of TJ and the related right to truth premised on the international law framework (evidenced in Chapter 6). As such, in contexts where Islamic law might be relevant, accountability – uncoupled from prosecutions (though not necessarily exclusive of them) – for serious violence can be pursued on the basis of a blend of international human rights law and *shari'ah*-based sources. The benefits of this approach are apparent: local legitimacy and cultural resonance of transitional truth-seeking initiatives can boost chances of success and buy-in during the process. This is notwithstanding possible tensions between certain interpretations of *shari'ah* and human rights standards, which can be addressed constructively and successfully as amply demonstrated in the growing literature on Islam and human rights (discussed in Chapter 5). Moreover, the invocation

[1] See eg M Klinkner and H Davis, *The Right to the Truth in International Law* (Abingdon, Routledge, 2020); P Naftali, *La Construction du 'Droit à la Vérité' en Droit International* (Bruxelles, Bruylant, 2017).

[2] HO Yusuf, 'Transitional Justice in the Middle East and North Africa – Taking Account of Islam' (2017) 14(1) *Muslim World Journal of Human Rights* 145.

of divinely inspired justice standards that converge substantively with international law standards can be used as an emancipatory tool for individuals and societies to demand action from unwilling political elites. How the right to truth may be actioned at local level remains a question to be answered within each context, and future research will be needed to evaluate some of the general points presented in this book with reference to specific countries, conflicts and authoritarianisms. Likewise, decisions around the most appropriate avenues through which to conduct truth-seeking initiatives depends on the specifics of each setting, as well as the balance between prosecutorial action and other forms of judicial and extrajudicial truth seeking: that will also require further study. Naturally, the translation into practice of the findings presented here is vulnerable to political contexts and power structures within each society (and beyond), but this does not detract from the usefulness of the right to truth as a valuable instrument to empower victims and societies at large to seek the truth about widespread harm arising from conflict or authoritarianism.

Second, this book shows that the inherently pluralistic nature of the international legal framework for TJ is capable of greater engagement with Islamic law ideas and practices, when relevant to some local settings. This is facilitated by the 'mess' of TJ norms,[3] blending different legal sources at international, regional, domestic and local level, as well as unofficial norms and normative impulses deriving from a range of customs and beliefs, including religion (discussed in Chapter 1). The tools of comparative law help identify and understand the role of formants, including cryptotypes and mute law,[4] which shape legal systems regardless of the formal enshrinement of certain principles in black-letter law (discussed in Chapter 2). This is true for the international legal framework of TJ, as it emerges through the contested – but ultimately constructive – dialogue between local and regional experiences and global rules championed (and constrained) by the UN.[5] Alongside the relative incoherence of the international legal norms in the framework of TJ, the formulation of the global benchmarks as identified by the UN (in particular through the work of the office of the Special Rapporteur on the promotion of truth, justice, reparations, and guarantees of non-recurrence) is clearly informed by a range of regional and local experiences. This has added depth, nuance and space for doctrinal (and applied) disagreement on the question of what constitutes the international law of TJ – including for truth-seeking aims – but it also elevates certain lived experiences and doctrinal positions to the detriment and exclusion of others.

[3] C Bell, 'The "New Law" of Transitional Justice' in K Ambos et al (eds), *Building a Future on Peace and Justice: Studies on Transitional Justice, Peace and Development* (Berlin, Springer-Verlag, 2009).

[4] See R Sacco, 'Legal Formants: A Dynamic Approach to Comparative Law' Instalments I and II (1991) 39 *American Journal of Comparative Law* 1 and 343.

[5] L Grover, 'Transitional Justice, International Law and the United Nations' (2019) 88 *Nordic Journal of International Law* 359.

As such, the international framework of TJ is more than the sum of the 'uncontested' norms enshrined in the sources of public international law and its relevant specialised regimes (specifically, international human rights law, international criminal law and international humanitarian law). Norms and normative practices emanating from different localities find a home in the soft law elements of TJ and over time can trickle upwards to shape the global legal paradigm. The discussion on the right to truth in Chapter 4 illustrates how the repeated uses of a concept might point to the existence of a norm in international law, despite falling short of the requirements for being a source of law set out in Article 38 of the ICJ Statute. The still-developing international legal framework for TJ is fertilised by a plethora of regional and local experiences, and by ways of thinking about the law and justice in relation to truth after mass violence.[6] For this reason, exploring the possibilities of Islamic norms and practices is important to ensure all regions and religious communities (in their diversity) are included in the evolution of international law standards pertaining to transitional truth seeking, as a normative space which cannot afford to express a single monolithic vision of justice.

There is a general caveat to these points. All law – regardless of its divine or secular foundations – exists and operates in this world as an expression of human agency.[7] The identification and consolidation of positive norms and natural law alike is the product of human efforts that exist in the unique social, political, cultural and economic structures of a certain context (where multiple legal systems or influences may overlap). The age-old debates in international law about the formulation of customary international law, or general principles of law,[8] attest to the fact that 'good' international law follows 'good' arguments by key human commentators, whose ideas travel and consolidate over time and space. Likewise, in Islamic law, debates around the most authentic understanding (and interpretation) of certain norms are an example of the human dimension of divinely inspired justice as well: the OIC, Al-Azhar and other prominent interpreters of Islamic law are likely to overshadow other voices by virtue of the cultural (and political) power they yield, but they need not be the only voices. It is clear that every legal system is shaped by its key actors, who function as gatekeepers, promoters or disruptors of the canon, shaping or hindering fresh interpretations and new directions of the law. Likewise, religious actors globally,

[6] See R Shaw and L Waldorf (eds), *Localising Transitional Justice: Interventions and Priorities After Mass Violence* (Stanford, CA, Stanford University Press, 2010); L Viaene and E Brems, 'Transitional Justice and Cultural Contexts: Learning From the Universality Debate' (2010) 28(2) *Netherlands Quarterly of Human Rights* 199.

[7] See eg L Nader (ed) *Law in Culture and Society* (Chicago, IL, Aldine, 1969); SE Merry, 'Human Rights Law and the Demonization of Culture (And Anthropology Along the Way)' (2003) 26(1) *Political and Legal Anthropology Review* 55; R Cotterrell, *Law, Culture and Society: Legal Ideas in the Mirror of Social Theory* (Burlington, VT, Ashgate, 2006).

[8] MC Bassiouni, 'A Functional Approach to "General Principles of International Law"' (1990) 11 *Michigan Journal of International Law* 768.

regionally and locally play a decisive role in how Islamic law evolves – and how it interacts with international law (including the TJ framework) as well as how it responds to local and global political realities. Accordingly, with regards to the promotion of the right to truth as a cornerstone of TJ, truth entrepreneurs have promoted the spread and reiterations of this emerging norm in different settings. The developments, applications and contestations of law are therefore in the hands of its human custodians.

HOW ISLAMIC LAW CAN EMBED AND DEVELOP TRANSITIONAL TRUTH SEEKING

The principles and practices of Islamic law, its rich heritage and ability to evolve and respond flexibly and dynamically over time to respond to new challenges, while maintaining the broad justice aims of the *shari'ah* intact, have a lot to contribute to the field of TJ, including truth seeking. Doctrinally, the objectives of the *shari'ah* (*maqasid as-shari'ah*) and the notion of *maslaha*,[9] public interest or common good, can offer a solid foundation for embedding the truth-seeking component of TJ in Islamic law, and supporting the right to truth as a tool to pursue knowledge and accountability for past harm. The expanding list of objectives of Islamic law includes the protection of religion, life, intellect, offspring and property, as well as justice, freedom and equality, and even social welfare, freedom, human dignity and fraternity. The values championed through these objectives seem to starkly oppose torture, extrajudicial killings and disappearances, most usually linked to the right to truth. In particular, the protection of life can support the right to truth in relation to extrajudicial killings, and to an extent to torture, alongside human dignity; the protection of offspring can be interpreted to converge with the principle that underpins the family's right to know the whereabouts of a disappeared person, or their remains. The more general concepts of social welfare, justice, freedom and equality suggest that the aims of the *shari'ah* are capable of promoting the broad aims of truth seeking that go beyond the single individual. The inclusion of collective rights alongside individualised rights illustrates the protection Islamic law affords both. This is an important aspect to consider when analysing the contribution of Islamic law to transitional truth seeking: it recognises that individuals and societies are intertwined, and as a whole have an interest in the implementation of the *maqasid as-shari'ah*. Alongside the aims of Islamic law, the normative principle of *maslaha* can also contribute to the development and implementation

[9] See eg F Opwis, 'New Trends in Islamic Legal Theory: *Maqāṣid al-Sharīʿa as a New Source of Law?*' (2017) 75 *Die Welt des Islams* 7; A Duderija, 'Contemporary Muslim Reformist Thought and Maqāṣid cum Maṣlaḥa Approaches to Islamic Law: An Introduction' in A Duderija (ed), *Maqasid al-Shari'a and Contemporary Reformist Muslim Thought: An Examination* (New York, Palgrave Macmillan, 2014).

of transitional truth seeking. *Maslaha* has been indicated as the *summa* of the *maqasid as-shari'ah*, and justice is one of its corollaries. Given the notion of *maslaha* is used to supplement gaps in the textual sources of Islamic law, it could be used to embed emerging rights – such as the right to truth – within the parameters of the *shari'ah*. What is striking about both the *maqasid* and *maslaha* is that despite their divine foundations in the *shari'ah*, they express universal values that in general terms coincide with the human rights project that has informed the TJ field.

The pursuit and preservation of truth in Islamic law finds broad support in the tradition of record-keeping evidenced the Ottoman *sijillat*[10] that maps directly onto the notion of (transitional) archives as a repository of accounts of past violence. In transitional contexts today, there is no Islamic law reason not to set up living archives, which can be made accessible to the public (even digitally, with due consideration to privacy issues), in order to compile a repository of court decisions and extrajudicial mechanisms, official documents and reports, and any other relevant material that contributes to piecing together mosaics of truth after serious violence.

Specific mechanisms in Islamic law offer practical solutions to truth seeking in light of the variety of judicial and extrajudicial pathways to justice, mediation and accountability for serious harm: in addition to ordinary trials, these are *mazalim*, *fatwas* and *sulh*. Like other legal systems, Islamic law can pursue the truth about past violence through ordinary justice mechanisms, including prosecutions, before ordinary judges. Moreover, in order to oversee the actions of state officials, Islamic law offers an option of extraordinary judicial reviews by the (administrative) *mazalim* courts.[11] The possibility in early Islamic practice to hold the authorities to account through the *mazalim* could be revived by successor regimes, but also by current regimes seeking to liberalise, to investigate abuses of power in violent dictatorships and responsibilities for specific episodes or patterns of violence. Furthermore, the *mazalim* could be developed as ad hoc forums for a range of grievances in the context of TJ, with the potential to incorporate aspects of contemporary truth commissions and public inquiries.

Extrajudicial truth-seeking mechanisms include *fatwas*, offering the possibility of obtaining independent legal opinions without binding force in regulating a dispute.[12] A *fatwa* is a text constructed by a jurist, which could be used to incorporate an account of the facts of an issue or dispute and thus contribute to

[10] G Burak 'Evidentiary Truth Claims, Imperial Registers, and the Ottoman Archive: Contending Legal Views of archival and Record-keeping Practices in Ottoman Greater Syria (Seventeenth–Nineteenth Centuries)' (2016) 79(2) *Bulletin of SOAS* 233.

[11] Tillier, 'The Mazalim in Historiography' in A Emon and R Ahmed (eds), *The Oxford Handbook of Islamic Law* (Oxford, Oxford University Press, 2019).

[12] WB Hallaq, 'From Fatwas to Furu': Growth and Change in Islamic Substantive Law' (1994) 1(1) *Islamic Law and Society* 29; A Zomeño, 'The Stories in the Fatwas and the Fatwas in History' in B Dupret, B Drieskens and A Moors (eds), *Narratives of Truth in Islamic Law* (London, IB Tauris 2008).

truth-seeking initiatives. Another important potential extrajudicial mechanism for truth seeking based on Islamic law is *sulh*, a unique mediation mechanism before an independent arbiter based on presenting competing narratives and reaching an agreed outline of the facts, even when they differ.[13] The merits of uncovering and reconciling contrasting accounts of the past through *sulh* for violence relating to conflict and authoritarianism includes its openness to including a range of voices beyond the direct parties to the dispute, whose claims can be summarised and synthetised by the final decision. Instead of obscuring or denying different accounts of the harm, *sulh* offers a versatile and pragmatic tool in Islamic law that could assist transitional truth seeking. As such, *sulh* deserves greater attention in transitional contexts, and further research in this area would be desirable.

A final, general point on how legal systems informed by Islamic law might embed transitional truth seeking rests on the centrality of victim satisfaction and the holistic aims of justice promoted in the *shari'ah*, both of which possess an individual and a collective dimension. These two principles cannot be easily diluted in light of the exigencies of transition; there are likely to be compromises, dissatisfaction and no clear collective memory of the past piecing together difficult and conflicting narratives (in addition to a range of other shortcomings). But despite the support offered in *shari'ah* to transitional truth seeking and the related right to truth, its operationalisation is not straightforward.

There is ample scope to experiment with different modalities of truth seeking in Muslim-majority societies, reviving traditional Islamic mechanisms for transitional contexts (such as those discussed above, ie *mazalim*, *fatwa*, *sulh*) or adopting TJ mechanisms used elsewhere, such as truth commissions and public inquiries, which do not contrast with the *shari'ah*. The shared goals and values of *shari'ah* and the international human rights norms that shape the global framework of TJ, taken together, offer a strong and convincing argument in support of the right to truth of victims and their families, as well as a society's right to know the facts of past harm. As illustrated in Chapter 3, no one mechanism will deliver full, definitive factual truth accepted by all concerned, and political contexts in which transitional truth seeking occurs are not necessarily ripe – or indeed fertile – for the right to truth to be actioned. The truth uncovered through any truth-seeking mechanism is the product of formalised mechanisms that operate contextually, and consequently the legal truth is itself a site of contestation and revisitation. In comparing the potential and limitations of these mechanisms, the stumbling blocks of truth seeking based on secular international law principles are likely to be similar in religiously inspired mechanisms drawing on Islamic law and practice: both are the product of human effort, based on higher-order values (one secular, one religious). The challenges,

[13] See eg R Diab, *Shades of Sulh: The Rhetorics of Arab–Islamic Reconciliation* (Pittsburgh, PA, University of Pittsburgh Press, 2016); A Othman, '"And Amicable Settlement is Best": Sulh and Dispute Resolution in Islamic Law' (2007) 21 *Arab Law Quarterly* 64.

however, are no excuse to avoid transitional truth-seeking initiatives and action the right to truth: episodes and patterns of serious violence in conflict or under authoritarian regimes are repugnant in both international law and *shari'ah*, and cannot simply be swept under the carpet and forgotten. When international law falls short of holding those responsible for harm to account, journalists, historians, artists and many more piece together complex histories of violence so that, over time, truths are gradually revealed in their complexity and cacophony. When religiously inspired justice in this world fails, the believers among victims and survivors, and societies at large, can still seek solace in the fact that one day perpetrators and their associates will meet their maker and receive judgment. Whichever way transitional truth seeking is framed, and even when secular and religious normative values are woven together, it should always be remembered that the truth produced will be relative to context and open to further future interpretations.

Index

www.ingramcontent.com/pod-product-compliance
Ingram Content Group UK Ltd.
Pitfield, Milton Keynes, MK11 3LW, UK
UKHW021909150926
475560UK00003B/265